International African Library 16
General Editors: J. D. Y. Peel and David Parkin

POETRY, PROSE AND POPULAR CULTURE IN HAUSA

International African Library

General Editors

J. D. Y. Peel *and* David Parkin

The *International African Library* is a major monograph series from the International African Institute and complements its quarterly periodical *Africa*, the premier journal in the field of African studies. Theoreticallv informed ethnographies, studies of social relations 'on the ground' which are sensitive to local cultural forms, have long been central to the Institute's publications programme. The *IAL* maintains this strength but extends it into new areas of contemporary concern, both practical and intellectual. It includes works focused on problems of development, especially on the linkages between the local and national levels of society; studies along the interface between the social and environmental sciences; and historical studies, especially those of a social, cultural or interdisciplinary character.

Titles in the series:

POETRY, PROSE AND POPULAR CULTURE IN HAUSA

GRAHAM FURNISS

EDINBURGH UNIVERSITY PRESS
for the International African Institute, London

For Wendy, Eleanor, Jack and Katie,
Dalhatu, Dauda, Omar and Dije

in memoriam
Ibrahim Yaro Yahaya

That's what we're looking for
the right words that people can make use of
Yazi Dogo

© Graham Furniss, 1996

Transferred to digital print 2009

Edinburgh University Press Ltd
22 George Square, Edinburgh

Reprinted 1997

Typeset in Linotronic Plantin
by Koinonia, Bury, and
Printed and bound in Great Britain by
CPI Antony Rowe, Chippenham and Eastbourne

A CIP record for this book is available
from the British Library

ISBN 0 7486 0786 2

CONTENTS

PREFACE

In writing this book in English I am conscious of the problems of cultural translation that beset my every move. One person's mental map of another culture is necessarily idiosyncratic and, since many readers of this book will not be familiar with the Hausa language, to a great extent I am clearly asking them to take my word for it. Nevertheless, while the emphases and preoccupations may be mine, I hope it will become clear, through extensive citation of the wide-ranging and substantial work by my Hausa-speaking colleagues, that the picture, even if not the shading, is one shared, to a greater or lesser extent, by a considerable body of scholars in Nigeria and abroad.

So why am I writing this book? Apart from the exigencies of my position on the treadmill of late twentieth-century industrial academe, I have three prime motivations. The first is to bring together disparate pieces of teaching, writing and understanding that I have deployed over some years in teaching Hausa literature. During that time I have tried to bring out the features of the various literary genres of Hausa and to describe and analyse the relationships between oral and written forms, the effects of the colonial and post-colonial experience, continuities and disjunctures as literary genres have developed over time, and the relationships between literary forms and the intellectual and political texture of Hausa society.

My second motivation arises from a sense that a debate is taking place about post-colonial literature and society in Africa in which writing in English about writing in English or French is pursued without any acknowledgement that a whole other world of debate has been going on vigorously and at length in African languages. Since it is not in English it cannot be listened to by critics, writers and commentators who do not themselves know those languages. Yet writing in African languages is a potent political totem in that first debate, whether it is Ngugi promoting writing in Gikuyu (Ngugi wa Thiongo 1986), or Chinweizu and Madubuike (1985) attacking what they see as obscurantism in Nigerian writers writing in English. In their seminal book *The Empire Writes Back* (1989), Ashcroft, Griffiths and Tiffin propose the term 'post-colonial literatures' because 'it points the way towards a possible study of the effects of colonialism in and between writing in English and writing in indigenous languages' (Ashcroft, Griffiths and

Tiffin 1989: 24) . Yet, when they consider such indigenous languages, it is in terms of arguments about such matters as whether it is better or worse to gloss non-English terms when writers are seeking to appropriate metropolitan English to their own purposes (1989: Ch. 2). It is as if all post-colonial discourse is focused in one way or another on what to do about English. There is a complete absence of any recognition that there is a long-standing debate to which English as a language and English as a variety of cultural traditions is pretty nearly irrelevant. Turning to African languages is seen as representing a false attempt to rediscover an unattainable pre-colonial purity that ignores the reality of the colonial experience (Ashcroft et al. 1989: 195) . Yet, in fact, the idea of an 'authentic' indigenous tradition and the nature of the colonial experience are small parts of a debate about society that has long been going on in a language such as Hausa, not as a peripheral satellite world struggling to find itself in relationship to English and European culture, but as a vigorous arena in its own right relating to its own cosmopolitan traditions of cultural thought. The adaptive, changing nature of culture in which orthodox and heterodox tendencies tend to stake out their claims to space does not necessarily mean, as is claimed by Ashcroft et al., that the focus is for or against metropolitan culture:

> Post-colonial culture is inevitably a hybridized phenomenon involving a dialectical relationship between the 'grafted' European cultural systems and an indigenous ontology, with its impulse to create or recreate an independent local identity. Such construction or reconstruction *only occurs as a dynamic interaction between European hegemonic systems and 'peripheral' subversions of them.* It is not possible to return to or to rediscover an absolute pre-colonial cultural purity, nor is it possible to create national or regional formations entirely independent of their historical implication in the European colonial enterprise. (1989: 195–6; emphasis added)

Aspects of recent post-colonial theory have been trenchantly and perceptively discussed in a recent article by Karin Barber (1995) to which the reader should refer. My intention here, then, is to provide the English-language reader with some idea of the debates and representations of society to be found in Hausa literature, some sense of the forms and traditions which people deploy, some feel for the cultural architecture, the 'dynamic interactions' and the 'hegemonic systems and "peripheral" subversions' that operate within the Hausa cultural world. The problems of cultural translation to which I referred at the beginning start with this intention. The most immediate and practical problem is rendering 'texts' in English. To what extent will you, the reader, expect or want explanation and background? How free or close should the translation be in relation to the original? Is it doing a disservice to the original only to provide extracts or summaries?

These are constant questions with no lasting right answers. In order to cover a wide range of material and issues and yet produce a manageable text, I have opted for a minimum of textual annotation, and a translation style which I hope will be readable – avoiding quaintness or stiltedness – while adhering reasonably closely to the original. I have used both extracts and complete texts depending upon whether the accent is primarily upon content or upon overall style in addition to content. I have been faced with a particularly knotty problem in relation to prose texts. It is not feasible to present whole translations and yet, in view of the fact that many of the stories are completely unknown to people who do not know Hausa, it has seemed to me to be important to provide the reader with some sense of what these stories are about. I have therefore provided summaries of some novels and novellas and illustrative extracts. Constraints upon space have precluded the addition of an appendix containing summaries of a broader range of prose texts.

An even more serious problem of cultural translation relates to the insertion of this material into the world of English-language cultural presuppositions. Time and again in teaching I have encountered, for example, expectations of what the terms 'poetry', 'song' and 'novel' *should* mean but which, even after redefinition on the basis of Hausa understandings of what the terms signify, provoke a bewilderment when faced with an event, a text, with which students are not familiar. The most recurrent of such impasses occurs when a student is faced with the didacticism so integral to modern poetry. Likes and dislikes are built upon a notion of poetry as directed towards aesthetic pleasure conveying 'heightened forms of perception, experience, meaning, or consciousness in heightened language' (Preminger and Brogan 1993: 938); didacticism (a much older end within the European tradition) is reacted to with discomfort. Poetry-writing in Hausa is going in many different directions currently and Hausa reactions differ according to the cultural conventions that are seen to be adhered to or contravened. I have tried in this book to explain how such cultural forms are grounded in a matrix of expectations in the hope that the reader will be able to understand something of the cultural context and thereby have something with which to fend off his or her own prejudiced reactions. Having made a plea for understanding these forms on their own terms, it is, however, clear that this book cannot but be a bundle of my own presuppositions, constructs and partial understandings. I can only hope that they will be reasonably obvious for the reader to unpick.

My third motivation is a more personal one. In Ziguinchor, in the Casamance region of Senegal, in late 1967, Xavier Badji and Justin Boissy first introduced me to the pleasure of Diola song, round the fire, with roasted oysters, under the stars. Three years later in Kano, Nigeria, Omar Hassan, Dije his wife, their friends and children showed me the hospitality that had me hooked on Hausa. Tilling the soil that year as the rains began, a group of friends were chanting under their breath as they worked. I asked what it was they were 'singing'. It was my first introduction to the poetry of Sa'adu Zungur, and the beginnings of the interest that has finally seen interim fruition in this volume. To them I offer back this book as my song.

Many individuals have been more than generous with their help, encouragement and support in the preparation of this book. For their criticism of draft chapters, I am grateful to Neil Skinner, Stanislaw Piłaszewicz, Sa'idu Ahmad, Jean Boyd, Umaru Balarabe Ahmed, Ziky Kofoworola, Murray Last, Abdulƙadir Dangambo and Russell Schuh. I am also indebted to Karin Barber and Tony Kirk-Greene. For their guidance and help in Nigeria in 1993, I owe an immense debt to Ibrahim Yaro Yahaya, Abba Rufa'i, Dalhatu Muhammad, Abdulƙadir Dangambo, Garba Magashi, Giɗaɗo Bello, Ziky Kofoworola, Kabir Galadanci, Bello Sa'id, Sambo Junaidu, Abdullahi Bayero Yahya, Omar Bello, Sa'adiya Omar, Haruna Birniwa, and many other ex-colleagues and students. In preparing the manuscript in London I have benefited from the suggestions of a number of colleagues and friends: Philip Jaggar, Malami Buba, Murray Last, Liz Gunner, Richard Fardon, Sulaiman Ibrahim Katsina, Edward Powe, Joe McIntyre. Claire Ivison was kind enough to prepare the maps. The long-standing friendship of the late John Lavers and his wife, Baba, was a source of encouragement throughout. *Allah ya jikansa, amin.*

I received the warmest academic hospitality from the Department of Nigerian Languages and the Centre for the Study of Nigerian Languages, both at Bayero University, Kano; from the Department of Nigerian and African Languages and the Centre for Nigerian Cultural Studies at Ahmadu Bello University, Zaria; from the Department of Nigerian Languages at the University of Sokoto, and from the Department of Languages and Linguistics at the University of Maiduguri. I am grateful to these institutions and their universities for their kind support.

For financial support in undertaking this project I also wish to thank the British Academy and the Research Committee of the School of Oriental and African Studies.

I am grateful to the following for citation permission: Tijjani Tukur, Aƙilu Aliyu, Na'ibi Sulaiman Wali, Mudi Sipikin, Alhajiya 'Yar Shehu, Ibrahim Yaro Muhammed, Sa'idu Baɓura Ahmad. For permission to reproduce extracts from my previously published papers, I am grateful to the editors of *Oral Tradition, Bulletin of the John Rylands University Library of Manchester, African Languages and Cultures* and *Harsunan Nijeriya.*

NOTE ON TRANSCRIPTION

Hausa texts are rendered in the standard Nigerian orthography, but allowing for dialect variation where appropriate. A small number of special characters and particular pronunciations occur in the Hausa: d / D and b / B
represent glottalized stops; *'y* represents a glottalized glide; k / K and ts are
ejectives; c and j represent alveopalatal affricates. Vowel length and tone
have been marked only when they form the topic of discussion; in standard
Nigerian orthography they are not marked.

NOTE ON TEXTS AND TRANSLATIONS

Depending upon available space, Hausa texts and English translations are
sometimes laid out side by side and at other times sequentially. The provenance of the Hausa is given at the bottom of the column of Hausa text.
Where both Hausa text and English translation are from a single source,
then the provenance is given below the English text alone. Occasionally the
English translation has been modified, and this is indicated by using the
phrase 'adapted from'. Where a translation has been made by Sulaiman
Ibrahim Katsina and myself working together, then the following attribution
has been given: (GF & SIK). Where no attribution is provided, the translation
is by myself alone.

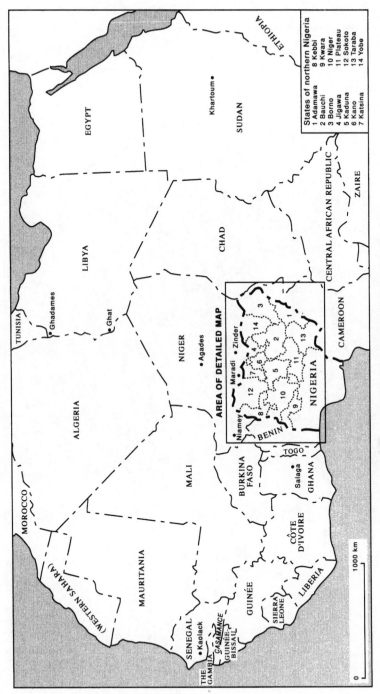

Map 1: West Africa: place names appearing in the text

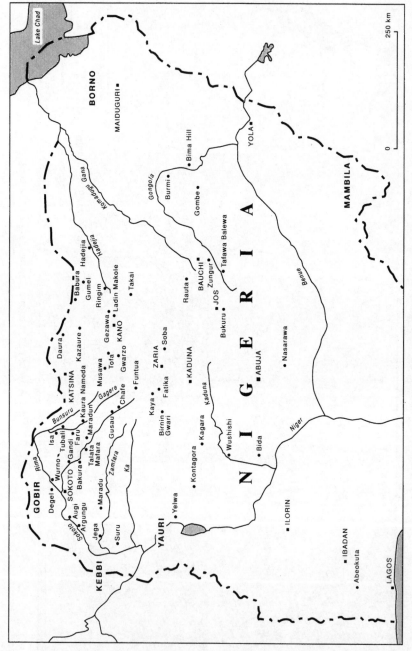

Map 2: Northern Nigeria: place names appearing in the text

INTRODUCTION

A history of Hausa literature would, no doubt, adopt conventional organising principles whereby 'early' forms would be seen as the bedrock upon
which 'modern' literature has developed. Such an evolutionist view,
pedagogically standard in Nigeria and elsewhere, is widespread in the
discussion of African literature more generally. Out of 'traditional', oral
indigenous genres developed 'modern', written, European-type genres.
With such a framework in mind, this book would have started with oral
narratives, and proceeded chapter by chapter until we had arrived at
superseding modern prose- and poetry-writing. However, this book is not
organised according to such principles and its approach is quite different.
Genres are historically embedded and as later chapters will demonstrate,
have their own history of change and development, but the view that informs
the overall organisation of the book is one that sees genres as parallel
domains of discourse, constrained arenas in which we observe the simultaneous production of multiple, mutually allusive genres, all of which draw
on existing repertoires and all of which also innovate. Rejecting an evolutionist perspective produces a concomitant shift of attitude towards one of
the major divides in the discussion of African literature. Rather than see
texts/performances as manifestly separated into two exclusive categories, the
'oral' and the 'written', by which the 'oral' is repeatedly raided for influences
upon the 'written', such a view entails an attentiveness to the migration and
overlap of textual materials between media of communication (speech,
writing, recited reading, written recension of oral improvisation and elec-
tronic media) in the process of working and reworking theme after theme.

A central focus of this book, then, is on the interaction of genres operating
within particular social and ideological contexts. Interaction goes beyond
'influence' to encompass circumstances where some genres are at least
partly composed out of other genres: a situation which single-genre scholarship has been incapable of addressing. Thus, *karin magana* 'proverbs,
proverbial speech', for example, can be cited in isolation as complete texts;
but they can also be viewed as the building blocks of numerous larger
genres, functioning as key points from which an entire oral or written narrative may be suspended. Allusion and parody, as well as incorporation, are
pervasive and can only be understood through an intergeneric perspective.

The operation of genres within specific contexts leads the discussion to concentrate not upon the classification of genres solely according to formal features but rather to consider the function, focus and intent of different kinds of utterance. This permits a more flexible and dynamic account of what writers and speakers are *doing* when they write and speak in particular forms and contexts. The focus upon individual communicative acts is complemented by an attentiveness to the social location of different genres. Going beyond a simplistic 'popular' versus 'aristocratic' dichotomy, the discussion illustrates, for example, the difference in ideological tone, in mode of address, and in degree of accessibility and incorporativeness between the Arabic-inspired written religious verse of clerics and the satirical songs of street entertainers. The discourse of cleric and entertainer is one in which they, along with many other voices, speak in contradistinction the one to the other while they, and millions of others, listen, agree, disagree, laugh and answer back.

HAUSA SOCIETY AND ASPECTS OF NIGERIAN HISTORY

The Hausa language is spoken by more than 50 million people in Nigeria, Niger, northern Ghana, and in communities from Kaolack in Senegal to Khartoum in the Sudan.[1] The Hausa-speaking 'heartlands' are in the areas of Kano, Katsina, Sokoto (generally north-central and north-western Nigeria) and the southern strip of the Republic of Niger, with Hausa communities and minority groups in northern Ghana and in many towns and cities from Senegal to the Sudan. Much of the discussion in this book relates to cultural forms from precisely that 'heartland': Kano, Katsina, Sokoto, as well as Zaria, and other parts of northern Nigeria. Little is said here about the literature and popular culture of Hausa communities of Niger (although there is discussion of a study by Janet Beik of theatre in Niger),[2] or of Ghana (see, for example, Schildkrout 1978), Chad (see Works 1976), or other parts of West Africa (see, for example, Cohen 1969). The language and culture of some communities in the Hausa diaspora are little known to outsiders: the Hausa-speaking communities in the ancient desert towns of Ghat and Ghadames are a prime example.

From before the sixteenth century, city states emerged in Hausaland with an urban aristocracy whose lifestyle depended upon the surpluses produced by a rural agricultural hinterland.[3] Administration depended upon complex structures involving royal families, district heads, village chiefs and ward heads. A wide variety of titles distinguished rank and function within the city state. Occupational guilds of metalworkers, leatherworkers, dyers and a wide variety of other crafts were also organised into hierarchical structures from chief down to youngest apprentice: cloth dyeing (see, for example, Shea 1975, 1983), tanning, leather-working, textile manufacture, blacksmithing (see, for example, Jaggar 1994), sewing and embroidery, to the

processing of agricultural produce.[4] Trading in such manufactured commodities, as well as in those such as livestock, slaves, salt (Lovejoy 1986) and
kola nuts (Lovejoy 1980), were specialised occupations. Long-distance
trade through the whole savanna region, across the Sahara and down to the
sea produced both a rich merchant class and a cosmopolitan heterogeneity
to Hausa cities. After the arrival of Islam in the fourteenth century, a class of
Islamic clerics emerged in the major northern cities whose activities had a
lasting influence upon the direction of state administration and upon popular adherence to Islam. The pre-existing indigenous religion involving spirit-
possession, *bori*, came under strong pressure from the new religion adopted
at the centre. Maguzawa, non-Muslim Hausa speakers, who adhered to the
earlier religious beliefs, became more and more isolated in remote rural areas.
Bori in the cities became relegated to the social margins. An Islamic religious
reform movement, led by the Fulani cleric Usman Dan Fodio at the beginning of the nineteenth century, began both a centralisation of Hausa states
into the Hausa/Fulani 'Sokoto Caliphate' and a more widespread popular
conversion to Islam. From 1804, fifty years before Bismarck united the
thirty-nine German principalities, the leaders of the Sokoto Caliphate were
beginning the process of uniting the Hausa states under one flag. The
descendants of the reform movement of 1804 were faced with the arrival of
the British and the French at the end of the century. Lord Lugard's forces
inflicted a measure of military defeat upon northern cities such that a complex pattern of some resistance, some withdrawal and more accommodation
emerged in the establishment of British rule in Northern Nigeria. The deal
struck between Lugard and the leaders of the Hausa states involved confirmation, and often reinforcement, of the position of the chief in exchange for
allegiance to the crown through acceptance of direction from a local British
political officer, the Resident. One important component in this original
deal was the agreed exclusion from the North of Christian missionaries.
This was in contrast with the situation in Southern Nigeria where Christian
missionaries and their schools had been operating for a considerable period.
By the time that Nigerian independence was on the agenda in the years after
the Second World War, it had become clear to the small number of leaders
of the North who had experience of both Western education and Islamic
education that there was a great imbalance between the North and the
South in terms of Western education. While Islamic education remained a
moral and religious imperative for the North, it was clear that the reins of
political and economic power in independent Nigeria would lie in the hands
of those with Western education. Fear of domination by the South was a
major political factor in the late 1940s and 1950s. The political leadership
of the North at that time lay in the hands of Ahmadu Bello, the Sardauna of
Sokoto, who saw clearly the need to raise his own political cohorts. Political
consolidation of the North, which contained many different ethnic and

interest groups, was a priority for him, along with organising a political élite for Nigeria as a whole. He had the overwhelming support of Northern traditional rulers, and Hausa-isation was one of the planks of his policy at the margins. In the main, regions of Nigeria in those years voted en bloc; the population of the North was assessed as being larger than the combined West, dominated by the Yoruba under Chief Awolowo, and East, under the leadership of Chief Nnamdi Azikiwe. Political control of Nigeria, after independence in 1960, was in the hands of Ahmadu Bello's Northern People's Congress (NPC). Some six years later, the Sardauna and the prime minister, Abubakar Tafawa Balewa, were killed in the first military coup and so began a series of military administrations of Nigeria until the re-emergence of a civilian administration, under Shehu Shagari, in 1979. The tensions between the regions boiled up into the secession of the East, as Biafra, in 1967. The ensuing civil war ended in defeat for Biafra and its reincorporation into Nigeria in 1970. In seeking to defuse the tensions between the three major regions, the federal government, under Yakubu Gowon, sought to split the regions into smaller states, a process which was repeated a number of times over the years, going from 12 original states to some 30 states at present.[5] The prospects for Biafran secession had been predicated to a large extent upon the presence of major oil reserves in the east.

With the major rise in world oil prices in 1973, Nigeria began a decade of unparalleled expansion. Huge amounts of hard currency oil revenues were accruing daily to the central government coffers. Bureaucracies at national, state and local level burgeoned and money was easily to be made through government contracts. Major expansion in infrastructure was accompanied by high salary increases, accelerated promotion for many and the bulk appearance of consumer goods such as radios, televisions, motor bikes and cars. Petrol was cheap and the urban well-to-do watched the meteoric rise of a class of super-rich. The boom was followed in the mid-1980s by a crash and the bleak austerity of a structural adjustment programme. The fall in the value of the naira produced expensive and scarce imported goods and spare parts, depreciating salaries, and rising unemployment. The civilian regime of Shehu Shagari was overthrown by the military in 1983 and a proposed return to civilian rule was thwarted by the military once more.

For the Hausa-speaking northern states, the years since independence have seen many changes. In politics, the hegemony in the North of the NPC and its direct successor in the 1979 elections, the National Party of Nigeria (NPN) was dented by the electoral strength of the northern opposition under its leader, Aminu Kano. Populist anti-establishment tendencies in the North had had little electoral success in the 1950s with the Northern Elements Progressive Union (NEPU); but its successor, the People's Redemption Party (PRP) still under Aminu Kano, took control of the governorship and state legislature of the most populous northern state, Kano, in 1979, as well as the governorship of Kaduna State. The very fact that in 1979 the NPN clearly no longer entirely controlled the North, although it put together a sufficiently widespread alliance of conservative forces across Nigeria to take control of the Federation, meant that radical political voices (see, for example, Furniss 1990) and a variety of factions and alliances could emerge within what had hitherto been a solid northern bloc.

The post-independence period also saw the erosion of the direct power of traditional rulers. Control of the police, the prisons, taxation and a variety of other dimensions of local power were transferred to central state authority. Military governors became the local controlling agents with their own state bureaucracies. Traditional rulers performed ceremonial functions while acting as occasional spokespersons for their communities; their information networks remained unrivalled until recently, and their patronage was still sought in a variety of social and political initiatives. In more recent years, the state, through employing bureaucrats to head local authorities, has made its presence felt down to village level through agricultural and other development programmes. The sidelining of traditional rulers has also been part of a process whereby a generational shift has transferred power and influence to much younger men. In the last twenty years, time and again a newly appointed local-government officer in his twenties or thirties has come to have control over groups of much older traditional officials. The rise of the young has been a direct consequence of the promotion in the 1970s of Universal Primary Education. The imbalance, referred to earlier, between the north and the south in terms of the number of people with Western education continues to bedevil the relationship between them. Nevertheless, the growth in the numbers of northern school leavers, college graduates, trained people of various kinds, has produced both a great demand for salaried employment and a pool of relatively young people who were able to move, particularly in the boom years, into positions of great power and influence. This has meant that alongside the more traditional patterns of status and rank there are now complex sets of interlocking criteria by which sometimes conflicting statuses can be ascribed and utilised; money, military rank, bureaucratic position, religious affiliation and status, educational attainment and 'classmate' status, all overlap with social class or genealogy. Twentieth-century northern Nigeria is now a society in which old social distinctions are overlaid with new social formations – an urban working class (Lubeck 1986), a large bureaucracy of salaried government employees, a commercial class, alliances between military, civilian and traditional élites, and a complex national economy where oil revenues have become the key driving force[6] – and it is a world in which the position of women is under continuing debate.[7]

The boom years also saw a move into the cities by young people seeking fame and fortune. Government initiatives have, from time to time, tried to return people to the villages. Long before the boom years, a common pattern in the cycle of rural activity was to move from work in the fields during the rains and harvest (May to October) to dry-season trading or other craft occupation in the remainder of the year, often involving temporary migration to town. A number of agricultural development projects sought to expand on irrigated farming to allow all-year production. In the 1970s, Operation Feed the Nation sought to expand local food production sufficiently to reduce food imports. While many young people may have been encouraged to remain on the land and, in the face of the recent recession, may have decided so to do, nevertheless, the cities of the northern states have grown dramatically in the last two decades. The 1991 census put the population figure of Nigeria at 88 million with some 40 million in northern states.

LANGUAGE, CULTURE AND IDENTITY

To a degree unusual in societies where one or two languages predominate, many ordinary citizens in Nigeria are multilingual and operate with a number of languages on a daily basis. With some 400 languages spoken in Nigeria, Hausa as a lingua franca, particularly in the north of Nigeria, brings together people from many different language backgrounds. Switching languages and cultural styles is a commonplace for many Nigerians. In such circumstances any individual may have a portfolio of fragments of identity that they may deploy according to the demands of the moment – Nigerian English, Fela and suit in the morning; Hausa, Shata and *babbar riga* 'long gown' in the afternoon; and Igala, drums and wrapper at night. Cosmopolitan culture is increasingly the order of the day in the cities and towns of Nigeria. In this environment 'being Hausa' is not necessarily a fixed attribute: identity is by no means convergent with language, for example. Simply to say that someone speaks the Hausa language is to say as little about identity as saying that someone speaks English or Serbo-Croat. Determining whether you are Serb or Croat depends not on the language you use, because it is the same language, but on what you say in Serbo-Croat and which heroic epics you subscribe to, and your life may depend upon it. Being Hausa is, in addition to a myriad other social factors, a question of what you hear, know and understand of parts of 'Hausa culture' and what you yourself contribute. In this book I try to indicate some of the parts of the cultural jigsaw map expressed through the Hausa language, upon which people orient themselves to differing degrees in making themselves more or less 'Hausa'.[8] It may be a jigsaw that does not fit together: some parts mesh with others, some do not; different people and groups see different parts, and certainly different people discern different pictures from the half-completed images. Nevertheless, it is manifestly the case that many different people are concerned to put such a jigsaw map together. An effect of the cultural nationalism of the 1970s, spearheaded by academics in northern Nigerian universities, was to rehabilitate some marginalised pieces, traditional tales, and pull them back into the cultural mainstream, represented by the curriculum of northern schools, as we shall see in Chapter 3. Many textbooks have been produced in English and in Hausa in Nigeria which spell out the components that go towards making up 'Hausa culture', everything from religious verse to traditional handicrafts (for example Dangambo 1984b; Madauci, Isa & Daura 1968; M. B. Umar 1978; I. Y. Yahaya et al. 1992).

Culture in this sense, then, is not a given entity, but a resource that is being constantly re-worked, both by jigsaw-makers and by jigsaw-doers. As tradition is reinvented so culture is also reconstructed.[9] An approach that takes as its focus the constant construction of both oral and written literature within culture necessarily considers the 'text' as a component within a variety of processes, one of which is the marking-off of particular pieces of communication as special, focused expressions that have a specific purpose. This process is fundamentally political and ideological: the agency of individual voices – regardless of whether the text is presumed to be original or a handed-down text of supposedly communal origin – relates to what is being said with what purpose by whom to whom and why. To consider these questions is not simply to describe the physical circumstances of performance. It is to examine the relationships between the content of the text, the exigencies of its form, the agency of its aesthetic and expressive dimensions and the politics of the debate in which it is situated. Each chapter approaches these issues somewhat differently depending upon the nature of the material under discussion.

1

THE ARCHITECTURE OF LITERATURE
AND THE INTERPLAY OF VOICES

The Introduction has placed an emphasis upon the relations between parallel domains of discourse and the communicative acts involved in the production of literature. At first sight, it would appear that the chapter that follows, on prose-writing, is perhaps furthest away from this immediate communicative-event focus. Nevertheless, as a literary form created *ab initio* in the 1930s, imaginative prose-writing was cast in a particular mould that held sway for some forty years: the structure of stories was repeated, and the characters and their interactions were of a particular kind. At the same time, the early novels work with the stuff of popular discourse, the stereotype characters, styles of language, and recurrent interactions that come from a wide variety of sources: 'traditional' narratives, historical and religious traditions, as well as recognised rhetorical forms. It was only in the late 1970s that the nature of the novel form and the thrust of character inter-action and description changed. But in the make-up of the original set of novels there were two very different voices represented: the laughing, whim-sical, satirical voice of popular humour; and the serious, didactic, moral representation of upright, honourable behaviour. These counterpoint voices recur again and again across many different genre boundaries and on a wide variety of subjects.

Later chapters, such as Chapter 7 on 'tied' singers, set individual singers and groups at the centre of the discussion, looking at the nature of the utter-ance in the communicative context. The cardinal characteristic of such sing-ers is that, in their capacity as 'tied' singers, they are acting within the con-straints of patron–client relationships. Their words are currency in an ex-change that involves recompense by the patron. But in looking at famous 'tied' singers it becomes clear that some of them have moved up-market from patron to patron, and some have worn different hats in different cir-cumstances, acting as established singer for a particular emir in one context and as singer for other temporary patrons in others. The negotiation of such relationships will carry with it the deployment of differing types of information and the adoption of differing styles of language. Yet, through-out, an underlying body of skills in the use of language is infinitely adaptable to the demands of particular circumstances. Moreover, a fundamental characteristic of such clientage relationships, is that the currency will be the two-sided coinage of praise and vilification. The power of speech, and the politics of speech, in such circumstances relate to the latent ability to move backwards and forwards across that boundary between praise and vilification. The creativity of the artist in such circumstances lies as much with manipulation of these two categories in context as in the 'text' itself of the language deployed.

POPULAR AND SPECIALISED CULTURE, INCORPORATIVE AND EXCLUSIVE TENDENCIES

It would be tempting to see, in the courtly praise-song of these famous praise-singers, a manifestation of a class-defined 'high art' as opposed to the 'popular art' of the *talakawa* 'ordinary people'. However, there are complex issues here, and such a bipartite division may not necessarily help us in capturing some of the key relationships between cultural forms. In terms of performance skills and artistic techniques there is little to separate the praise of emirs from the praise of farmers or of hunters. There is occasionally apparent, in the content of courtly praise, information relating to genealogies, and other esoterica, which may be less comprehensible to the ordinary listener; however, the content of hunters' or wrestlers' praise-song may be equally esoteric, if not more so. Clearly, the degree to which the content of a form is intended to be special, separate, esoteric and perhaps secret will reduce its potential to constitute an inclusive, incorporative form which is available to people of many different backgrounds and classes. This characteristic, its degree of esotericism, may be a 'defining' feature of a genre or indeed may constitute simply one pole on a continuum of styles within a genre. (Within written poetry, for example, one well-known poet, Mudi Sipikin, is acknowledged to be clear and straightforward in his use of language, while Aƙilu Aliyu is known for his use of unusual, specialised and older vocabulary; these characteristics are then part of the critical debate about the aesthetics of poetry that goes on in Hausa.) Courtly praise-song, then, may deploy esoterica that are fully understood only within the orbit of the local aristocracy and, furthermore, the values being promoted in such song may be institutional values primarily attached to the office rather than to the individual, such as power, authority, lineage, prosperity, tradition and influence (M. G. Smith 1957). Nevertheless such praise-song is not a private pastime simply to amuse the courtiers. It is directly intended to communicate such values to the population at large every time the emir makes a public appearance. It marks the patron off as being different, the communicative context is one in which an audience is being told how different *they* are from the emir. Not only are they being told about it, the very act of singing *makes* them publicly different from the emir.

The same internal tension within a genre between the expression of esoteric and technical/specialised knowledge and the desire to communicate with people who do not already have that knowledge is to be seen in the field of poetry-writing. On the one hand there are many poems written which discuss and present religious ideas of considerable complexity with which the average person is perhaps unfamiliar. These ideas are often the subject of long years of teaching within the Koranic system of education, and the producers of such poetry are members of the cleric class, the *malamai*, who can debate theological issues at length among themselves. Poetry about *tauhidi* 'theology', *fiqh* 'law', *nujum* 'astrology', may represent a form of debate within the nearest thing to a hermetically sealed social environment. Nevertheless, ever since the Jihad (lit.) 'struggle' of Shehu Usman ɗan Fodio at the beginning of the nineteenth century, one of the prime functions of religious poetry-writing has been to battle for the hearts and minds of ordinary Hausa people, as discussed in Chapter 8. From that time it was necessary to write in such a form of Hausa that the strong messages of reform and renewal were not drowned in a sea of incomprehension. As we shall see as this book progresses, that didactic thrust has formed a dominant characteristic of expressive culture across a number of literary genres. This purposive thrust may be more apparent in some genres than others. Nevertheless, it is clearly apparent that in poetry, as in song, theatre and much prose-writing, there is often a message to be put over; and that didacticism has been, in some senses, a stamp of 'public culture'. It is only in recent years that the private musings of individuals, the love poetry and the pulp novel have begun to make an appearance on the public stage.

If courtly praise-song and religious verse veer toward the specialised, exclusive end of the cultural spectrum (and they are, to some extent, voices that speak for the aristocracy and the cleric class respectively), then there are other forms which sit clearly at the other end, the popular, incorporative, eclectic end. Freelance song, market-place burlesque, other market-place entertainment by such as *'yan gambara* 'rap artists', operate as commentary upon the daily life of ordinary people, occasionally providing a satirical counter-voice to the discourse of the clerics or the court, but for the most part painting pictures of events, types of people, actions that typify everyday northern Nigerian life. Some performers define themselves in relation to the concerns of the didactic culture to which I have already referred. The singer Dan Maraya Jos, for example, a very popular solo performer who appears regularly on TV and radio, has a strongly didactic streak in his singing, but his concerns are distinctive: he sings of the lot of manual labourers, of the ordinary man, of the rich and the poor. Other performers, such as the burlesque artist, Malam Ashana, consciously satirise other singers and recognisable rhetorical styles of public discourse.

It would be an oversimplification to identify too closely non-esoteric, non-specialised culture with the culture of 'ordinary people'. The songs, litanies and music associated with the spirit-possession cult, *bori*, are very

much part of a widespread popular culture, yet deal with esoteric information which is fully comprehended only by initiates, although many people
will have some familiarity with the names and characteristics of some of the
major spirits. At the same time, *bori*, and all that is associated with it, is one
of the prime ideological targets of the didacticism of Islamic religious poetry.

Another factor which enters into this discussion of specialised versus
popular culture and which, to a great extent, determines the degree to which
a particular form, or a particular performer, gains wide currency, is the relationship between the cultural product and the media through which it is
transmitted.

COMMUNICATION MEDIA AND THE DEVELOPMENT
OF ARTISTIC FORMS

Long gone are the days when the only way of seeing and hearing a verbal art
performance was by being physically present as the story was told, the song
was sung, or the play enacted. It is commonly held among a number of
academics and commentators in Nigeria that performances of some 'traditional' literature (and part of the programme of some cultural commentators
is to identify and revalue *al'adun gargajïya* 'traditional customs') have all but
ceased under the deleterious effects of radio, television and 'modern
culture'. One effect of this view has been the establishment of state- and
federal-level bureaux/ministries of arts and cultures, which have seen it as
their function to protect and enhance 'culture'. To some extent the effect
has been to allow some security and freedom to particular artists who have
been able to write and perform poetry, sing their songs, or whatever, with
remuneration being provided by these organisations. In some cases, it has
had the effect of simply transferring the clientage relation from previous
'customers' to the state with all the consequent effects upon content and
performance occasion. State co-option of art forms is, however, nothing
new. It has a long and illustrious history going back at least to the early
nineteenth century. One consequence of the 'cultural revival' movement,
whether through state organisations or elsewhere, has been to 'fix' a notion
of 'tradition' and this is most evident in the formation of dance troupes,
often labelled as representing particular ethnic groups, that are bussed from
one state event to another to put on repeated disembodied performances.
Nevertheless, the very fact that there has been a movement to revalue whatever is seen to constitute 'traditional' culture has meant that opportunities
and sponsorship have been offered to artists of many different kinds. Three
generations of novels, in 1933, 1979 and 1982, were the product of organised creative-writing competitions. State festivals of arts and culture have
been fora in which a wide variety of artists have been able to perform before
large audiences. And most important of all, the radio and TV stations have
taken with alacrity to the broadcasting of performances by singers and poets

in addition to the sponsorship of their own TV drama shows. While TV has remained primarily an urban phenomenon until very recently, radio has been ubiquitous in city, town and village for at least thirty years. Regardless of whether we are concerned with oral song or written poetry, the dominant medium for their transmission is oral and visual – poetry is written to be recited (the key focus for a group of poets writing in the mid-1970s was their access to radio once a week for the recitation of their poems); some of the early prose texts from the 1930s have now resurfaced as frames for TV series and adaptations.

In similar fashion, the picture of what constitutes written poetry and imaginative prose-writing in Hausa is intimately bound up with the history of the development of written media. In the nineteenth century, poetry circulated within the cleric class, a 'restricted literacy' (Goody 1968), in the form of Arabic script (Hausa *ajami*)[1] manuscripts that were copied by hand and then passed on. Annotation and adaptation were part of that process. With the introduction of printing presses in the colonial period there was the possibility of setting poetry and producing editions by the hundred or thousand. However, the first presses functioned primarily in roman script to produce government publications of one kind or another. A printing press established in Kano was able to set the standard Arabic script, and the early *Northern Provinces Newssheet* was produced in roman and in Arabic script, but most *ajami* poetry was written in the Maghribi script, quite different from the standard typeset form. Nevertheless, handwritten manuscripts still circulated in the colonial period with the occasional printing undertaken privately in the Middle East or Egypt. As far as poetry was concerned, the key technological development came in the early 1960s with the introduction of offset printing both into government presses and into commercial presses in the Sabon Gari quarters 'new town/strangers' quarters' of northern cities. Offset printing meant that no special skills in setting type in Arabic script were required. Any original manuscript in any script style could be photographically copied and any number of copies reproduced, so long as the printer could read the order of the page numbers and knew which way up the pages were. This technological development produced a great increase in the availability of religious and other poetry which was privately printed with money provided by either the author or a patron. Networks for the distribution of such material existed through the book-traders in major markets and, in the case of sect literature, through the sect organisation itself. Established publishing houses have rarely realised the potential of such small-scale distribution activities, preferring in the main to deal with the very few Western-style bookshops that are familiar with the accounting and bureaucratic conventions operated by such publishers. Nevertheless, a glance at the books for sale in market stalls will always produce the odd second-hand copy of a 'published' work either of prose or poetry that has crossed the boundary between the two worlds. The problems of distribution for Western-style publishers are not new. Skinner (1970b) outlined the problems faced by NORLA (Northern Region Literature Agency) in the late 1950s, when a large staff with a fleet of landrovers was distributing material to all corners of the Region: material that was often priced below cost in order to encourage sales. As Skinner indicates in his review of the history of NORLA, the commercial potential of publishing for people literate in Arabic script was considerable, and NORLA started to take advantage of it before the scale of the losses being incurred brought its eventual closure in 1959. Reliable and creditworthy distribution networks were at that time particularly problematic.

The major publishing houses, among them Longman, HudaHuda, Evans, Oxford and most particularly the Northern Nigerian Publishing Company (NNPC), with their formal distribution networks through bookshops, have been hit by the recession in Nigeria and have consequently cut back drastically on publishing in Hausa at least. The NNPC has a unique position in northern Nigeria as the inheritor of the booklist of what was, for many years, the sole Hausa-language publisher in Nigeria. The first novels and roman-script poetry were published in the 1930s and 1940s by the government-owned Literature Bureau. The first Hausa language newspaper, *Gaskiya Ta Fi Kwabo* 'Truth is Worth More than a Penny' was founded under its auspices in 1939, and much poetry first saw the light of day in its columns under the editorship of Abubakar Imam. This agency later became the Gaskiya Corporation, which was intended by its founder, Rupert East, to be a literature-producing co-operative on a large site, practically a village, in Zaria. In the 1950s, the publishing side of the Gaskiya Corporation, by that time known as NORLA, produced a large amount of Hausa poetry and material in other northern Nigerian languages. Publishing, and the growing backlist of Hausa publications, reverted to the Gaskiya Corporation until after the closure of NORLA in the 1960s, publishing again devolved to another company (NNPC), a partnership between Nigeria and Macmillan. It was only in the 1970s and early 1980s, with the oil boom in Nigeria, that other publishers entered the field in earnest hoping to take advantage of the boom in literacy which would take place as a consequence of the federal government's introduction of Universal Primary Education in 1979. With the fall in the value of the naira during the recession since the mid-1980s, most of these publishers have pulled back drastically and many manuscripts, the product of the growth years, lie gathering dust on editors' shelves. So the enterprising have reverted to private publication if they can afford it. Down the years it has been the editorial policies, the sense of purpose, and the commercial circumstances of the Gaskiya Corporation that have had the major influence on the picture of what has come to constitute Hausa written literature. It was Rupert East's view, expressed in the terms of his day, that it was important to produce indigenous creative writing in Northern Nigeria, which saw the production of the first novels:

> there is a moderate, and rapidly growing number of literates in the vernacular, particularly Hausa, written in roman script. But until recently there has been no literature, and very little 'reading matter', for them to make use of their ability when they have got it. We have taught them to ride, but have given them no horses. (East 1936a: 351).

Abubakar Imam's view of the social usefulness of poetry influenced his selection of poems to publish in the newspaper (Furniss 1977: Ch. 2). Skinner describes the influence of the government-inspired adult-literacy campaign that lay behind the founding and direction of NORLA (Skinner 1970b). Husaini Hayatu sets out the commercial and political difficulties that have recently impacted on book production at the NNPC (Hayatu 1991: 184–90).

SPEAKING AND WRITING, PROPOSING AND ANSWERING

Oral and written literature have sometimes been seen to be two separate categories of material. In this book, the emphasis is not upon the oral and the written as categories but as communicative media having their own particularities and processes. Different genres may have a variety of different ways in which they are expressed and communicated. Written poetry, for example, has characteristics relating to the processes of composition, retention, reformulation and transmission which are directly related to the fact that such processes are carried out, or can be carried out, in writing.[2] At the same time, such poetry is often recited in particular circumstances to particular audiences with particular intentions. The rhetoric of the oral performance of such poetry may or may not be related to the apparent patterns inhering in the 'text'. In contrast, oral performances which do not relate to any pre-existing 'fixed' text will raise many further issues about the processes of composition, memory, creativity in performance, illocutionary force, and the aesthetic and other reactions of the audience.

While orality and writing raise their own sets of questions about process and product,[3] it is also clear that many Hausa performers and commentators consider that the difference between certain categories, for example, song and poetry, is predicated upon this division into oral and written. Poets describe what they do as being different from what singers do according to a number of criteria, and this distinction is one of them (Muhammad 1979). And in so doing they draw attention to the processes of borrowing, adaptation and reworking that go on across that particular divide at many levels, in content, in style and in form. (Schuh (1994), for example, has pursued the metrical borrowings that have taken place between song and poetry.) Nevertheless, even if I am not deploying the terms 'oral' and 'written' with any confidence as terms for categories of material, it is clear that genre definition in Hausa, by commentators, students and academics, more often than not starts with a primary classification into *adabin baka* 'oral literature' and *rubutaccen adabi* 'written literature'; a neat shorthand for a descriptive classification but which obscures issues of process.

One characteristic of orality pertinent to much of the Hausa literature discussed in this book is the fact that so often the event, the performance, is directly involved both in making propositions and in answering other people. Not only is there necessarily an audience present, whose external reactions can, to some extent, be described, but the very nature of the text, and the rhetoric that accompanies it, is clearly *directed*. Rarely is there a text which appears simply to be a narrative or a reflective expression seemingly unconscious of its listener. Time and again, the text and its performer are clearly involved in a purposive relationship of advocacy or ideological engagement. Religious didacticism, praise, vilification, social comment, propaganda, satire – all these are the stuff of Hausa literature and stake out a claim in an ongoing dialogue about society. Oral performance is the most apparent context in which to see this process in action, but it is also to be seen in written literature, and in all the media both oral and written. In this sense, then, creating a feeling of what is going on, and what should be going on, in Hausa society is an intensely political process in which singers, poets, writers and performers are creating an image for other people to recognise, relate to and adopt. Whichever way those other people react, it is the power of symbolic creativity in the words of the artist, be they poets or politicians, which stands at the core of social knowledge.

PERCEPTIONS OF GENRE

In the earlier part of this chapter I use the terms, 'song', 'poetry' and 'narrative' without any discussion of what it is I am referring to in Hausa and the distinctions that are recognised in the Hausa language. While this book is organised around these genre distinctions, the purpose behind the use of such genre distinctions perhaps needs some comment. First, genres constitute bundles of features relating to a wide variety of criteria, deployed differently according to the genre under discussion – aspects of form, immediate circumstances and style of performance, social context of creation and performance, status of performer, nature of content and illocutionary intent, among others. A prime concern of a number of commentators in Nigeria has been to define and group genres as they have sought to enumerate those things that go to make up 'traditional' culture (see above, p. 7). Genre theory has been a subject of discussion for many years, but the characteristic I wish to single out here is the idea of genres not as categories of cultural 'object' but as sets of 'appropriateness conditions' for certain kinds of messages. In other words, if you wish to say a certain kind of thing, there are certain ways in which you can say it more appropriately than others. To praise yourself in Hausa there are certain rhetorical techniques available to you in the form of epithetic speech (*kirari*) which has its own conventions about form and content. You can dip into that cultural pot, and borrow, or make your own, or even satirically subvert, but that resource has a name and set of circumstances in which it is usually and typically, and therefore recognisably, deployed. In the context of the ensuing discussion it is the fact that, for example, poetry has certain expectations attaching to it allowing didacticism as a dominant tone that assigns cultural legitimacy to any voice that teaches and preaches certain kinds of messages if that voice is using the genre known here as 'poetry'.

A simple list of the genres of Hausa literature, as I am admittedly about to provide, obscures an important characteristic of the dynamic relationships between such forms. Not only are genres defined by their practitioners in relation to one another ('we do this and they do that'), the practitioners operate complex networks of borrowing, countering and redefinition which means that the genre is never an entirely fixed set of features even if the label appears to stay the same. Furthermore, any listing obscures the fact that some genres constitute the building blocks of others and may appear as performed events in their own right in one context and then, in another context, appear as constitutive elements in another genre. Some are inclusive overall terms for a type of discourse, others are strictly specific and exclusive. Epithets may be strictly specific to the self-praise performances of wrestlers in one context, and be merely a passing device in a novel where a character nods in the direction of that 'other' language code external to the narrative.

Similarly, the relation between genres may involve the satirical subversion of a dominant form by another. Burlesque performers play with the recognised features of certain speech styles, undermining the seamless join between appropriate form and expected content, substituting inappropriate content and thereby highlighting the form which no longer has the gravity which it originally possessed when it was hidden away as the unnoticed vehicle of its usual content.

With these caveats I set out the Hausa terminology for the major genres of literature. A number of prose forms are usually distinguished – among prose narratives *labari* and *tatsuniya* contrast as 'presumed real' and 'fictive' respectively. While the term *tatsuniya* is predominantly therefore 'traditional tale', it is sometimes also used to denote a conundrum or riddle, more often referred to by *ka cinci ka cinci* 'pick-up-pick-up' which acts both as name conveying the interactive nature of the genre and as introductory formula. *Tatsuniyoyi* (pl.) 'tales' refers to animal/trickster tales, to narratives of 'human to human' interaction, and of 'human to supernatural being' interaction. Within short-form verbal art, *karin magana* distinguishes 'proverbs/sayings'. (The Hausa term implies 'folded speech' thereby 'allusive diction', which requires, on the part of the listener, interpretation of imagery or secondary reference.) A functional distinction among short-form expressions identifies *kirari* as 'epithet', often used in praise, and *habaici* as 'innuendo' depending upon the presumed intent of the speaker. Rhythmic or non-prose language is generally represented by the term *waka* which, in common parlance, is a single term covering both instrumentally accompanied, solo or 'lead and chorus', oral song and also another genre: written poetry intoned without accompaniment. Muhammad (1979) has set out the distinctions, terming them *waka* I and *waka* II respectively. In drawing the distinction in normal Hausa parlance they would be distinguished as *wakar baka* 'oral *waka*' and *rubutacciyar waka* 'written *waka*'.

There is a further range of labels for creators of such genres and for other performers. *Mai tatsuniya* simply implies 'story-teller', but the term *maroki* 'one who begs' for 'singer', implies specifically a praise-singer in search of reward for his services; *mawaki* 'one who sings' on the other hand could be applied to a singer or a poet. There are further terms for public entertainers of various kinds, *'yan kama* 'burlesque players', *'yan gambara* 'rap artists', and a wide variety of types of musician (see Ames 1973b), including those musicians and performers associated with the spirit-possession cult, *bori*. A forthcoming book in Hausa by Abdulkadir Dangambo (1996) will, I understand, examine a range of Hausa genres covering prose, poetry and drama.

LITERATURE AND THE NATURE OF HAUSA SOCIETY

In the Introduction, modern Nigeria is presented as a fast urbanising world of cosmopolitan cities and towns. Such cities are surrounded by a rural hinterland that is, in places like areas of Bauchi State, as cosmopolitan as any city, with a patchwork of different languages spoken in small areas in close proximity the one to the other. Even the relatively homogenous Hausa heartland rural areas are by no means undifferentiated. M. G. Smith (1978: 30–4), for example, writing about the Daura emirate in 1952, describes, in addition to Hausa and Fulani populations (some of the latter being nomadic cattle herders, others being settled town dwellers), villages that were predominantly Kanuri, descended from immigrants from Zinder which had been a vassal state under Borno; villages that were Buzaye, serfs of Tuaregs from Asben who had been settled on agricultural land by agreement between the Tuaregs and the Daura aristocracy; and villages, or rather scattered settlements, that were populated by Maguzawa, non-Muslim Hausa speakers pursuing their own way of life.[4] And among the general population some groups had emigrated to settle in Gumel and Kano, while other villages were populated by descendants of slaves who, in the nineteenth century, were involved in agricultural work for their absentee owners. (Lovejoy 1978).

Nigeria of the last thirty years has seen myriad local distinctions overlaid with a variety of national cultures, of which Hausa is only one. Nevertheless, the national media, through their local radio and TV stations, have created of people like Mamman Shata and Dan Maraya Jos, figures who have, at the least, a regional presence in the states of the old North, and, to some extent, a national presence. This creation of a 'cultura franca' has gone on, not in place of local cultures, but in addition, as an extra Hausa-based element of northern identity. As I have intimated above, this complex cultural world, cosmopolitan and eclectic, has within it people who are looking to reconstitute and define what was, at some supposedly earlier period, a 'traditional' Hausa culture and society. This is manifested in moves towards insistence on supposedly truly Hausa terms in place of borrowings, particularly from English and to 'strengthen traditional culture'. One small manifestation of this mood, commented upon by S. B. Ahmad (1986: 109–10) was to be seen in the way in which a radio presenter, who had solicited 'traditional tales' from his audience, would then edit out any reference to any marks of modernity, such as radios, schoolrooms, cars, and so on, thereby ensuring that the world of the traditional tale remained firmly grounded in a semi-mythical, pre-modern view of society where there were emirs, *malams*, villagers, pagans, country bumpkins, courts, markets and walled cities, but little of the twentieth century.

The pre-modern world, an image of which is being captured in the 'invention of tradition' to which I have referred, consisted of city states in which hierarchical principles of organisation underlay both an urban society and a rural world.[5] Hiskett summarised the nineteenth-century organisation of Hausa society as follows:

> Apart from the *ulama'* and the wealthy merchants (Hausa *attajirai*) there were four main classes in Hausaland c. 1214/1800 and no doubt they had been much the same for several centuries. They were: the *sarakuna*, 'chiefs', and *fadawa*, 'courtiers', who together made up the ruling class; the *'yan birni*, the town and city population, both slave and free; the people of the countryside comprising free peasants and both the slaves of the *rumada* (sing. *runji/rinji*), 'slave-villages', and the agricultural slaves who worked the *gandaye* (sing. *gandu*), 'farms', ranging from large holdings owned by the *sarakuna*, *fadawa* and rich merchants, to the small-holdings of individual freemen and freed slaves. Finally, there were the nomads, the people of the *rugage* (sing. *rugga*), the Fulani cattle-encampments. (Hiskett 1984a: 97).

The broad characterisation of earlier Hausa society into *sarakuna* 'an aristocracy' and *talakawa* 'commoners' itself encompasses great complexity in social status and position. The position of slaves, for example, varied greatly. There were trusted slaves of the emir, men of responsibility and power, who could themselves own slaves, and who could amass considerable wealth;

some were *cucanawa* 'persons born into slavery' rather than slaves acquired through purchase or raiding. *Bayin gida* were domestic slaves in well-to-do households. In addition to slaves living in urban environments with their owners, the rural world saw a variety of slave positions. We have already referred to *rumada* 'slave villages' producing agricultural goods for their absentee urban landlords; small-scale, free peasants would also often have a few slaves who worked their land alongside them.[6]

Within urban environments, and to some extent in rural areas, the craft organisations – metalworking, tanning, dyeing and many others – were, as we have seen, involved in the production and marketing of a wide variety of commodities. The picture of this pre-modern world being formed in the current notion of 'tradition' features such occupations, along with archetypal kin relations and classic aristocratic figures, and picks up on the cameos provided by, for example, the 'traditional tales' so favoured by our radio presenter. In these cameos, for example, in the stories recorded in Edgar's *Litafi na Tatsuniyoyi na Hausa*, moments of confrontation between stereotypes in this world are recorded and played out: 'The chief and the wife of his slave', 'The slippery trader and the boy', 'The *malam* [Islamic cleric] and the *bamaguje* [non-Muslim Hausa]', 'The head butcher and the leper', 'A city man and a country man', 'The poor man and the buzu [Tuareg serf]' (Skinner 1969). These stereotypes remain the currency of much contemporary social comment in a wide variety of oral and written genres, and although new directions are being taken in assessing and characterising the modern world, there remains a sense of security and groundedness in the knowledge that there once was a 'Hausa' world, and 'Hausa' values to rely on. Much of the discussion in the chapters that follow traces different voices and their contributions to the constitution of the expressive, literary, dimensions of this entity, 'Hausa culture'.

2

IMAGINATIVE PROSE-WRITING

THE FIRST HAUSA NOVELS: ABUBAKAR IMAM AND THE WRITING OF *RUWAN BAGAJA*

Between April and August 1934, Abubakar Imam, a 23-year-old teacher at Katsina Middle School, was engaged in revising his manuscript entitled *Ruwan Bagaja* 'The Water of Cure' for publication.[1] A year earlier, the first creative-writing competition had been organised by Rupert East, superintendent of the Translation Bureau in Zaria, through the Education Department of Northern Nigeria. The field was not huge. Most potential writers, now junior teachers, were the product of one training college in Katsina where East had taught history and geography. Revisions to Imam's manuscript had been suggested by Rupert East. On 30th April 1934, East wrote comments to Mr Allen, then in charge of Katsina Middle School, to be relayed to Abubakar Imam:

> Many thanks for your note, and for sending back Malam Abubakar's manuscript. I sympathise with the author, and quite understand if he feels a certain amount of resentment at having his book cut about so much. At the same time I don't see how we can publish it as it stands, as he has taken many of his stories almost word for word out of other books, and if we published these under his name it would set a bad precedent. I made a special point of the work being original, when I came round.
>
> Apart from this the book is very well written, quite one of the best that have been sent in, and it would be a great pity if the trouble he has taken were wasted for the lack of the small extra labour required. Actually all that is needed is for him to write five or six short stories out of his own head to replace those which have to be cut out, and adjust the connecting passages so that the narrative runs on continuously. (Mora 1989: 23)

By August, East was writing to Abubakar Imam as follows:

> Greetings and good wishes from Mr. East to Mallam Abubakar Kagara. I wish to inform you that we have nearly finished editing your

book. The stories you have sent have been included to replace those removed earlier. However though the ending of the book appears similar to stories from 'A Thousand and One Nights,' I have decided to leave it without any cutting.

There is only one thing which I hope you will try and do; that is to change page one which sounds like the beginning of 'Sindbad the Sailor!' This is in order to avoid reader's disinterest if they should feel they know the story already. What you should do is write a brief introduction about the story teller up to the point where you wrote, 'At that stage the host cleared his voice and said, "First of all my name is Alhaji Imam".'

R. M. East
Superintendent of Education
i/c Translation Bureau

(translated from Hausa in Mora 1989: 24)

Early editions of the book lacked the later divisions into chapters and employed section headings that broke the text up into sometimes as little as half-page pieces. The exchanges between Imam and East reinforce the view that the underlying framework for the book was a string of episodes with 'connecting passages'.

RUWAN BAGAJA

Ruwan Bagaja 'The Water of Cure' is a story within a story.[2] The narrator, the central character Alhaji Imam, tells his own life story to an audience that has assembled to hear a visiting story-teller. From East's letter it is clear that the 'story within a story' frame was added to what previously had been simply an autobiographical narrative. Yet that later addition sets the tone for features of the internal story. A competitive relationship between characters is set up by Alhaji Imam's claim that the story-teller hardly lives up to his name, having asked for a break after talking for only one day, whereas Alhaji insists that his own story, heavily abridged, might *just* squeeze into ten days. Exaggeration, bluster and banter, so typical of much humour in Hausa, is captured both in this response by Alhaji Imam and in an earlier moment when the story-teller, having made a simple enquiry as to who lives in Alhaji Imam's house, is addressed by one of the household servants: 'Is there anyone in the whole wide world who does *not* know Alhaji Imam?' While East never, as far as I am aware, set out what it was about Imam's writing that so impressed him,[3] it must surely have been Imam's ability to capture the wit and humour of everyday banter in his writing that set him apart, to some extent, from other writers, as well as his strong comic sense and ability to characterise through action and dialogue.

The episodic pattern of the story develops through a quest narrative[4] in which our hero goes in search of *ruwan bagaja* 'the water of cure', moving from youth to adulthood, and from home in Kwantagora to India and a fantastical world of jinn and then back home again. That main section of the book is encased in a double frame. First, at the beginning of the story Alhaji Imam's real father is murdered by a stepson, Saƙimu, and towards the end of the story Alhaji Imam avenges the murder by killing Saƙimu. Second, and following upon that frame, Alhaji vows to vindicate his adoptive father, the *imam*, who has been humiliated at court by the king. This entails his departure into the big wide world in search of the 'water of cure'; then the acquisition of *ruwan bagaja* provides the means to conclude the narrative. The travels of Alhaji Imam form the core of the book, and it is in this section that we see features that have since been echoed time and again in Hausa prose-writing. A mix of realism and fantasy permeates the book (Skinner 1971a). On the one hand, the book begins in Kwantagora not far from Abubakar Imam's birthplace, Kagara, in present-day Niger State. The characters are recognisably stock figures in representations of Hausa society, the *imam*, the *sarki* 'chief', *malamai* 'Islamic clerics', as well as our hero and his mother. But by the end of the book our hero is encountering monsters, being assisted by jinn and flying through the air. The text is also full of implausibilities and coincidental encounters (Pweddon 1977) which add to the unrealistic, whimsical tone of much of the text.

The implausible coincidences often involve the repeated meeting and parting of Alhaji Imam and his partner/competitor Zurƙe ɗan Muhamman. As Don Quixote had his Sancho Panza, so Alhaji Imam has his Malam Zurƙe, sometimes a travelling companion, sometimes a disguised adversary.[5] Pweddon (1977) sees the adversarial relationship between these two characters as part of a broader pattern of conflict in the book between appearance and reality, man and the physical world, Islam and 'unconventional beliefs' (Pweddon 1977: 44) as well as internal conflict within characters. The characters' first encounter is typical: Alhaji has told us of his complete inability as a child to master even the basics of Koranic education. But on his travels he arrives in a town, Saburi, inhabited by the uneducated. (Pweddon (1977: 5) situates this encounter between Islam and non-Islamic communities in Abubakar Imam's experience of the relationship between Islam and the Kamuku pagans of the Kagara/ Kontagora region. Abubakar Imam's own father had been a respected *malam* from Sokoto who settled among the Kamuku.) Welcomed by the townspeople he makes himself out to be a learned scholar from 'the lands of the Arabs', although the phrase from the Koran *muduhammatani* 'with dark green foliage' (Pweddon 1977: 48 and fn. 41) is all that he knows. Having spent six months teaching the inhabitants a variety of ways of intoning the phrase, a new *malam* arrives in town who quickly recognises him for a charlatan and a rogue. Determined to best him, the new *malam*,

Zurƙe ɗan Muhamman, challenges Alhaji Imam to a public demonstration of learning. The contest takes the form of mutual questioning upon points of Islamic learning and law. Dismissing Zurƙe's baskets of tomes, Alhaji draws a crescent shape on the sand and demands an interpretation. Each attempt to relate the sign to letters of the Arabic alphabet are met with derision by Alhaji who, finally, when Zurƙe admits defeat, reveals the sign to be the shape of the new moon. The assembled multitude of the ignorant immediately recognise this answer as the 'truth' and acclaim our hero while driving the ignominious Zurƙe out of town. Following each such encounter, Alhaji Imam accumulates goods and cash which he leaves with a local patron for safe keeping and then moves on. Frequently, he gets the better of Malam Zurƙe in one way or another, but confrontations occur with a Lebanese merchant, an emir's chief bodyguard, a woman in a market, a Fulani traveller, a European. In repeated encounters Alhaji is involved with the manipulation of appearance and reality (Pweddon 1977). Seemingly honest, he gains the trust of the Lebanese merchant only to cheat him; feigning madness before an emir he escapes punishment; by deceit he performs wonders, thereby convincing another duped community that he must be a saint. His duplicity does not always work to his advantage: having been blinded, temporarily, he claims confidently to be able to see, cantankerously upbraiding any who try to help him, with the result that he steps off a boat into the middle of a lake when told by Malam Zurƙe that they have arrived at the bank. Interspersed among these conceits and deceits there are the briefest of funny stories: chased up a tree by a crazy camel he shouts abuse at passing Fulani who, approaching in fury, distract the camel into chasing them; feigning aggressive madness he dupes Malam Zurƙe and his wife into conscientiously waving away flies from one of his recently deposited turds.

These brief episodes, strung together to create one of the earliest examples of imaginative prose-writing, resonate with and pick up on other forms of oral humour.[6] When Alhaji Imam is released from the madhouse, the text makes reference to his being appointed the 'king's fool', a courtly position of entertainer, wit, licensed critic and go-between particularly associated with the Zaria emirate (Kofoworola 1982). Within the repeated sequences of pretence where Alhaji and Zurƙe insinuate themselves into serious social occasions – the Friday prayers, the *alkali*'s 'judge's' court, the emir's court – there are strong echoes of the behaviour of the *'yan kama*, the traditional burlesque entertainers (Furniss 1991b; Gidley 1967). It is the interactive nature of the trickery between Alhaji and Zurƙe and others which most directly evokes such performers. Pweddon indicates that the character Malam Zurƙe was in fact based upon a market entertainer whom Abubakar Imam knew from Katsina market:

But Zurke was a certain funny man in Katsina market. We were young (but) we would often like to see him wear rags going round the market playing music, dancing. Well, he was the one called Zurke. He was not referred to as Malam. It is I who called him Malam Zurke to make the story balanced and interesting. In other words, I just took Harith and Abu Zayd who were in *Maqamat* (*The Assemblies* translated by Thomas Chenery; London 1867 and republished in 1969), two people each trying to trick the other. (Pweddon 1977: 86–7)

Abubakar Imam, in his discussion with Pweddon, furnishes a neat example of the way in which Imam drew both from his familiarity with Hausa oral tradition and from literary sources such as the many books of Middle Eastern and European tales and stories that were available to him through Katsina College and through Rupert East.[7]

Resonances of the performances of popular entertainers are supplemented by echoes of recognised oral genres: the 'funny story/joke', such as the one about the camel and the Fulani youths, is termed *labarin raha* 'amusing story' (Katsina 1984). Katsina (1984) juxtaposes *labarun raha* , which can be told at any time, with *tatsuniyoyi* 'tales' which he claims are traditionally more restricted in performance. In his discussion, *Ruwan Bagaja* and the later three volumes of *Magana Jari Ce* are termed *labarun raha*.

Within *Ruwan Bagaja*, our hero moves effortlessly from a 'real' world in which people ride in boats across water to one in which our hero, on sinking to the bottom of a lake, encounters water spirits with huge heads who cure him of his blindness, shower him with gifts, and take him back to dry land. Later, on seeing jinn open up the earth with secret words, he copies them, to reveal an entrance into which he goes, discovering his arch-enemy Sakimu who begs for mercy. Finding a convenient sword he dispatches Sakimu, only to find, on rubbing the sword, a jinn to obey his every command. With the aid of the king of the jinn, our hero finally finds the object of the quest, the water of cure, and returns home miraculously by taking a water-borne journey which brings him up in a well in Kano city. While in *Ruwan Bagaja* there are clearly references to motifs from *The Thousand and One Nights* and other works (although the parallels are more precise in *Magana Jari Ce* where, for example, the Pied Piper of Hamelin story is rendered in a particularly successful episode), the interaction between people and jinn or spirits is particularly reminiscent of the tale tradition in Hausa where the logic of character and motivation takes precedence over any pretence of verisimilitude. *Tatsuniyoyi* deploy stock human characters, animals and supernatural beings in abundance, as we will see later in this chapter.

Finally, in October 1934, the book was ready and East wrote again:

We have finished your book at last, and sent it off to the printers. It should be ready in about three months' time. I am sorry that you have had such a lot of work to do on it, but I am sure it was worth the trouble. Now that parts of it have been re-written it is quite one of the best which have been sent in.

I have sent a voucher for £1 (One pound sterling) to the Provincial Superintendent of Education by this mail, which is your share of the prize. You will get some more money as a percentage on the sale as soon as the book starts to be sold.

I hope you will write another book. If it is as good as the last I will certainly get it published for you. I think you have got the gift of writing, and there is no reason why it should not be a very profitable hobby for you. As soon as people get the idea of reading and buying books we shall be able to publish larger editions, and give a bigger percentage to the authors.

If you do think of writing another book you needn't make it as long as the last, 15 to 20 thousand words is enough. But you must make up your own stories, or if you take other people's, disguise them so that they look like your own! You might write a sequel – 'Further Travels of Alhaji Imam' – if you like, or else something quite new. I hope you will try to do this sometime. (Mora 1989: 24–5)

Rupert East clearly meant what he said when he expressed admiration of Imam's writing style for he went on to encourage Imam to continue writing:[8]

These books (the five produced for the competition) proved to be quite useful reading material in schools. Having realised the potential of my writing skill, Mr. East decided to request my temporary transfer to the Literature Bureau, Zaria. He collected several types of books on European fables and Arabian nights stories for me to use as background material. I spent about six months in Zaria in 1936 during which time I wrote the three volume *Magana Jari Ce*.

I was given an house at Kofar Tukur Tukur near the offices of the Literature Bureau. I would spend most of the mornings reading stories and discussing various writing approaches with Mr. East. In the evenings I would go down to the Native Authority orchard near the General Hospital at Tudun Wada. There I would sit under a tree or go to the footbridge over Kamaca stream to watch the running water. There I did all my writing. The following morning Mr. East would go over what I had written and suggest changes or other stories to be read. In this way all the stories were completed within the six months and I was happy to be back at my teaching post in Katsina. (Mora 1989: 26)

A more elementary general-science reader was required for schools and so East spent a period in September and October of 1938 in Katsina working with Imam on the two volumes of *Karamin Sani Kukumi Ni* 'A Little

Knowledge is a Dangerous Thing' (Mora 1989: 27; Pweddon 1977: 10). East tried to arrange for a more permanent secondment to the Literature Bureau in Zaria. After some resistance from Imam, which entailed East getting the governor to write to the Emir of Katsina, Alhaji Muhammadu Dikko, the Emir directed Imam, in November 1938, to go to Zaria to take up a position with Rupert East as the Hausa editor of the fledgling Hausa newspaper, *Gaskiya Ta Fi Kwabo* 'Truth is Worth More Than a Penny' (East 1943; Mora 1989; I. Y. Yahaya 1988/9). The first issue of the newspaper appeared in January 1939. Abubakar Imam put the purpose behind the publication of the newspaper as follows, 'Dr. East ... told me that they were planning to publish a Hausa language newspaper in order to counter the German propaganda on Hitler's activities and plans for Africa' (Mora 1989: 31).

GANDOKI, SHAIHU UMAR AND THE OTHER EARLY NOVELS

As a result of the Literature Bureau competition of 1933, four manuscripts, including *Ruwan Bagaja*, were submitted to East[9] and, along with a fifth text co-written by East and John Tafida, were published as the first pieces of creative prose writing in Roman-script Hausa (Cosentino 1978). Abubakar Imam's elder brother, Bello Kagara, wrote a 45-page work carrying the name of its hero, *Gandoki*, combining historical description of the arrival of the British with fantastical exploits of stirring deeds and great victories.[10] Abubakar Tafawa Balewa,[11] a graduate of Katsina College who had returned to his adopted home town of Bauchi in 1934 to begin teaching at Bauchi Middle School (Clark 1991: 23), wrote a novel of some 50 pages, *Shaihu Umar*, in which the hero of the title, and his mother, endure hardship having been taken as slaves across the desert.[12] The fourth text, 47 pages,[13] entitled *Idon Matambayi* 'The Eye of the Enquirer'[14] was by Muhammadu Gwarzo (1911–91) and related the escapades of a trio of robbers and villains, Idon Matambayi and his two sidekicks, Dauke and Kwace. The fifth book, *Jiki Magayi*, is a story of thwarted love transformed into an overwhelming desire for vengeance. Retribution, in the end, brings destruction on the wronged and the wrongdoer.[15]

Gandoki by Bello Kagara

Gandoki, the name of the central character being the title of the book (the name implies 'avid spectator/excitable person'), is accompanied in the first part of his adventures by a contrasting pair of sidekicks, his valiant son, Garba Gagare, and his feckless servant, Inda Gana. As with *Ruwan Bagaja*, the story is framed as an autobiographical narrative told at the request of some children, and the thread leading through the story is the bravery and prowess of our heroes during many travels and exploits.[16] Where Alhaji Imam's path intertwines with Zurke in *Ruwan Bagaja*, in *Gandoki* the equivalent of Zurke is split into two contrasting characters, more companions than opponents. Again, like *Ruwan Bagaja*, the story moves from a 'real' world to a fantastical world of jinn, to the island of Ceylon, and to magical exploits, and then at the end of the book back to a new reality in Nigeria. In contrast to *Ruwan Bagaja*, the first 'reality' is not of a timeless, 'typical' Kontagora world but is historically grounded in the period of the arrival of British military forces in northern Nigeria. In an unpublished interview with the author, Bello Kagara, conducted by Bala Abdullahi Funtuwa working with A. Neil Skinner,[17] it is clear that the author is drawing on his experience, as a young man, of moving, in the company of people opposed to the British, from Kontagora to Birnin Gwari, then to Fatika in Zaria emirate, and on to Kaya where, he says, the British finally captured the Sarkin Sudan, Nagwamatse. In the story, Gandoki fights with the forces opposed to the British and when the Sarkin Sudan indicates that, to avoid further bloodshed, they should lay down their arms, Gandoki will have none of it. At this point his servant Inda Gana leaves him to go off and join the British forces; his son, on the other hand, remains stalwart at his side. He joins the forces of the Sultan of Sokoto and fights at the battle at Bima Hill, one of the final battles between Sultan Attahiru and the British. After foraging for food, Gandoki returns to find his son asleep, having fought off a horde of heavily armed strangers. The transition from a world marked by reference to the real battle of Bima Hill and the eastward flight of the Sultan Attahiru to a fictional world of flight through the air and jinn is attained through the device of going to sleep in one world to awake in another. In this new world, the second part of the story, our two heroes are repeatedly victorious over one enemy after another and leave behind them an ever-growing list of successful conversions to Islam. Finally, determined to return home and drive out the infidel Europeans, Gandoki and Garba Gagare arrive to find a peaceful and happy society. Accommodation with this new way of life is finally reached, and Gandoki determines to turn to study and prepares to go on pilgrimage, putting Garba Gagare into school. They encounter marvels of modern life such as aeroplanes, telephones and artillery. Being a military man, Gandoki is stirred to see soldiers on parade, reminding him of old times. At the barracks in Zaria, Gandoki comes across Inda Gana, now gunner sergeant and, on being asked how his wars had gone, he replies that 'ignorance was the cause of their opposition to the British'.[18] This last note of accommodation may have been an afterthought, in response to the circumstances of 1930s Northern Nigeria. However, it is clear from both the text and the interview by Bala Abdullahi Funtuwa that the central theme of the story is the notion of combat, whether in the real or the fantastical world, and the need to deal with being driven out and defeated.[19]

Gandoki is implacably opposed to the British forces. When the *alkali* of Wushishi (a place on the route taken by the British from Bida to Kontagora) sends the British gifts against the wishes of senior people in the town, then

Gandoki dispatches him and takes his head back to Kontagora. Repeatedly Gandoki dispatches traitors of one kind or another as well as the forces of the enemy. When finally the Sarkin Sudan considers conceding defeat, Gandoki's response is 'Never!' Defeated physically, the Sarkin Sudan is taken by the British to Yola before being returned to Kontagora. Kagara compensates for this setback by describing magical and wondrous powers that the Sarkin Sudan was able to deploy, such as miraculously appearing outside a room into which he had been locked, or appearing on the further bank of a river without having crossed. These powers astonish the British. Physical defeat is matched by magical success. Similarly, a contradiction appears between a notion of success in combat that relies upon an impressive appearance, physical prowess and skilled horsemanship as the keys to victory on the one hand, and the technological, mechanical superiority of the gatling gun and artillery on the other. Gandoki and his son Garba Gagare embody the cultural stereotype of the combatant. In the story, the characteristics of this stereotype are conveyed in the actions of the hero but most particularly and pervasively by the way he speaks. Impressive effect, in the warrior, is conveyed to a large extent by the aggressive and stylised manner of his speaking. In this respect *Gandoki* draws heavily upon a dimension of Hausa oral literature which Powe (1984) has termed 'combat literature'. Powe's discussion centres on the cultural forms associated with boxing, wrestling, hunting and other such activities that he investigated in the 1980s. In the current context it is the act of identification, and specifically self-identification, combined with a competitive, aggressive, laudatory intent relating to the role of the warrior which concerns us. At the beginning of the story Gandoki identifies himself as *Na-Garba katsalandan ba da ruwanka ba* 'Father of Garba, there is nothing that is not my business!' This appellation is after the manner of *kirari*, often rendered in English as 'praise-epithet'.[20] Shortly thereafter Kagara writes:

> Ya tashi tsaye ya yi kirari, ya ce, 'Sai ni gyauro mai ganin badi! A gaya wa yara Gandoki, yaya halaka za ta same ni bayan an tsare ni daga gare ta? Ga ni kuma tare da layar kaka-ka-yi-ka-fita. Ni da ni ke shirin fada da aljannu balle mutane? Maridin aljanin da ke cikin duniyan nan duka ni ne kansu ni ne karfe ci karafa na Garba! Ni ne dodo, ko da na goye na tsoronka!' (Kagara 1934: 1–2)
>
> 'He stood up to his full height and proclaimed his *kirari*, "It is no one but myself – the self-sown groundnut crop which survives to see the next year. Tell the boys it is I, Gandoki, how can destruction overtake me when I have been protected against it? Here am I with my charm that lets me escape from any peril. I who am preparing to do battle with jinn – what should I care about human beings? All the worst jinn in the world are no match for me. I am the blade that breaks all blades – the

father of Garba, I am the ogre which even the baby on its mother's back is afraid of!'"

Dialogue in the narrative is permeated with the style and manner of Hausa oral combat literature as Gandoki praises himself or, as the story develops, his son Garba Gagare. From Gandoki's perspective, defeat is not an option, it is not part of his vocabulary. As with the combat literature studied by Powe, defeat is spoken of only when it relates to the rival or the opponent, not to the self. From this position there is only one place to go when faced with the reality of defeat, and that is into the world of imagination where great victories remain possible.

In Kagara's interview with Bala Funtuwa, he indicates that *Alfu Laila* 'The Thousand and One Nights' was an important influence upon his writing of Gandoki (see also Skinner 1971a: 173) and it can be seen in our heroes' flights through the air, battles with jinn, marriages to princesses and sojourns in India and Ceylon. The transition back to the 'real' world is effected in stages. From a world peopled by jinn, Gandoki moves to a world of people, still in India, who cannot see the jinn who accompany and assist him. In that world he defeats, admittedly with difficulty, a mighty chief, Goringo, and his son. The son he manages to convert to Islam; the intransigent father he kills. The final move is back to Hausaland without any of the trappings of the previous world.

Within the first section of the story, in Nigeria during the early years of the British conquest, a moral contrast is drawn between Gandoki's son and his servant, Inda Gana. Inda Gana, the servant acquired by Gandoki in Bida, assists Gandoki in murdering the *alkali* of Wushishi by night, and subsequently shows himself to be untrustworthy and ungrateful. While travelling with Gandoki's wife and small child, Inda Gana hogs the water they are carrying with them; he becomes a liability when he is bitten by a snake and has to ride; when responsible for looking after the wife and child, he and they fall off the horse in a steep gorge and are unable to get out. His uselessness is compounded by his disloyal decision to go and join the British forces. In contrast, Garba Gagare, a true son, goes out to find food and water for the family on that same journey, cares for his mother, and remains utterly loyal to his father. During the latter part of the story he elects twice to go with his father 'so that we may die together', and in battle comes to his father's aid. Gandoki tends Garba after a battle, they both have protective charms and they pray together. Gandoki heaps *kirari* upon his son: *Duka wanda ya goye ka bai yi aikin banza ba. Da haihuwar yuyuyu, gara da daya kwakkwara. Karo da goma kalacin safe!* 'Whoever carried you on her back was not wasting her time. Better one strong child than a myriad births. Defeat ten strong men for breakfast!' (1972 edition: 17). Yet at the same time there is a latent rivalry between them. At one point Garba, disguised, takes on Gandoki in combat and, when he reveals himself, Gandoki, attributing his actions to high jinks, is told by Garba that he fought to show him that Gandoki's son is not a nobody, and to give him a taste of what it is like to be on the other side in battle. Within the terms of the warrior stereotype, Garba Gagare is represented by Gandoki as the model of the 'good man'.

Shaihu Umar by Abubakar Tafawa Balewa

The third book in our list, *Shaihu Umar*, presents a very different model of the 'good man'. Again, the title of the book is the name of the hero, and again, in response to a questioner, the hero narrates his own history.[21] The most striking parallel between all three books is, however, the journey which structures the story to produce separation, trial and reunion/return (Cosentino 1978: 24). In the case of Shaihu Umar, separation is more than departure into the big, wide world. Captured by slave-raiders he is separated as a child from his mother. The relationship between him and his mother provides one of the central points of the whole story. Shaihu Umar is finally briefly reunited with his mother while in exile, but her death, soon after, means that his return to Nigeria is not accompanied by a rounding off of all outstanding issues. He does return to Nigeria to become a scholar/teacher, but only after years of struggle and hardship as a slave in Libya, followed by a period of success and liberty through the support of a benevolent patron, Abdulkarim. Commentators have focused upon the way in which the person of Shaihu Umar represents an ideal of the exemplary Muslim: patient, good tempered, resilient, conscientious and moral (Cosentino 1978: 22; Skinner 1971a: 173–4; Piłaszewicz 1985: 219–20). Abdulraheem (1979), discussing the novel and the play adaptation by Ladan and Lyndersay,[22] situates Shaihu Umar in the context of the religious leadership role of a *shaikh* in Islam. In similar vein, Nasr (1984) sees the major themes of Shaihu Umar in the elevation of the role of the *malam* (the Islamic scholar/cleric), the propagation of Islamic values and the condemnation of slavery. In an important essay, Kirk-Greene sets the character of Shaihu Umar within a broad moral framework summarised in the notion of *mutumin kirki* 'the good man':

> The threads of his immaculate character are woven, page after page, into this final composite pattern of Umar in his old age, back in Hausaland as a venerable *malam*:
>> None who had studied under Shaihu Umar had ever known him impatient, nor had they ever known a day when they had come to his study and he had said that he was tired, except perhaps if he were unwell ... This Shaihu Umar was a man beyond all others, the like of whom is not likely to be found again. Whatever evil thing befell him, he would say, 'It is God who relieves all our troubles.' He never became angry, his face was always gentle, he never interfered in what did not concern him, and he never wrangled with anyone,

let alone did he ever show the slightest cantankerousness. Because of his *hali*, this character of his, it came about that in the whole country no one ever criticised him. And many people began to say, 'Surely this is no mere man, he is a saint'.

It is my contention that in Shaihu Umar we may see the very apotheosis of *mutumin kirki*, of the good man in Hausa. (Kirk-Greene 1974: 17–18)

Shaihu Umar contrasts with the other books discussed above in eschewing the fantastical flight and the miraculous world of jinn. Where, on the one hand, *Ruwan Bagaja* draws from, and is, in some senses, directed at the familiar world of earthy jokes, a bantering style and tales of the fantastic, and *Gandoki* addresses both tales and the 'combat literature' referred to earlier, deploying the rhetorical style of the Hausa *kirari*, *Shaihu Umar* taps into a different set of references. As Cosentino (1978: 22) remarks, 'Balewa has attempted to work out in prose the kind of homiletic themes which are the hallmark of nineteenth century Hausa poetry'.[23] *Shaihu Umar* is a serious work with a strong didactic streak. We will examine later in Chapters 6 and 8 the ideological gulf created and reinforced by the poets of the nineteenth-century Jihad between serious literature, typified by homiletic poetry, and frivolous *hululu* 'idle chatter', typified by tales and scurrilous song. Cultural evaluation and revaluation has been adjusting the boundaries and arguing the toss about such distinctions ever since. But clearly, in the moment when this new form, imaginative prose-writing, was being forged, to some extent *Shaihu Umar* looked one way and *Ruwan Bagaja* looked the other.

Idon Matambayi by Muhammadu Gwarzo

Idon Matambayi is a much less well-known work and is, like *Shaihu Umar*, without the fantastical elements of *Ruwan Bagaja* and *Gandoki*.[24] But the story-line stands in contrast with *Shaihu Umar* in taking as its central characters a group of thieves. Rather than the good man faced with adversity and tribulations which are overcome, here we see the 'bad men' and their decline into punishment for their misdeeds. The central character, Idon Matambayi, falls in with two, and eventually three, other thieves who then proceed to move from highway robbery to mounting a raid on the well-defended house of a rich merchant. Their plans to raid the house involve them in making preparatory sorties into the strongly policed town during which they compete to see which of them is best at outwitting the town's renowned police chief. Through pretence, they gain access to the house and the confidence of the house owner. Three of them carry out the robbery leaving the fourth to take the blame. Finally, the thief who took the blame gains his revenge by deceit on two of the others, and the eponymous hero, who has returned to his home town to settle down, has all his money and property destroyed in a fire. In Skinner's (1980: 50) classification of the tales in Edgar's (1911–13) *Litafi na Tatsuniyoyi na Hausa*, undertaken in conjunction with Skinner's translation that appeared as three volumes of *Hausa Tales and Traditions* (1969), he proposed a distinct category for stories about thieves. Such reworked stories are also to be found in chapters, such as 'Banza ta Kori Wofi' and 'Jarrabawar da aka yi wa Sarkin Barayi Nomau', of Abubakar Imam's classic-three volume *Magana Jari Ce*. While *Idon Matambayi* appears not to be widely known, it clearly drew upon a well-worked theme of Hausa stories, and a number of later novels in the late 1970s and early 1980s were of a similar type. The text is also noteworthy in that it deploys direct speech to a very considerable extent; nearly a playscript, it relies upon the dialogue between characters for much of its characterisation and for the plot development. In that respect *Idon Matambayi* is reminiscent of the graphic forms of television drama which appeared some thirty years later.

Jiki Magayi by John Tafida and Rupert East

The final work in this original group of five, *Jiki Magayi*, is nowadays credited to John Tafida, although originally it went under the joint names of Tafida and East.[25] Again involving a quest for a magic potion, but intended for destruction not cure, the story is 'of a great and tragic love, of hatred and the growth of a thirst for revenge' (Piłaszewicz 1985: 220). Zainabu is betrothed to Abubakar but, before they can marry, an older man, Shehu, uses a charm to alienate her affections from Abubakar. Abubakar swears revenge and goes off in search of an equally potent charm with which to avenge himself. His search takes him into a fantastical forest where he finally acquires the potion he is looking for. Meanwhile Shehu and Zainabu have had a child, Kyauta, to whom Abubakar administers the potion on his return. Kyauta turns from a well-behaved child into a thief and a liar. In order to get away from the shame of their son's behaviour, Shehu and Zainabu go to another town to settle. Kyauta, having come by chance to this same town, breaks into Shehu and Zainabu's house not knowing who lives there. Being surprised by Shehu in the dark, Kyauta kills him. On hearing from his mother that he has killed his father Kyauta vows to find Abubakar and kill him. When finally he does find him, Abubakar dies moments before Kyauta can dispatch him.

Both Skinner and Cosentino, in commenting upon this book, emphasise the expiation of original crime through implacable revenge producing, thereby, the restoration of order. The fantastical element of the quest into the forest becomes secondary to the working-out of the relationships between the characters, 'On the whole, this is a tale of satisfying realism in its description of human weakness and passion, with the fantastic element used to color and deepen the tale of single-minded search for revenge' (Skinner 1971: 175). Nevertheless, the progression from original crime through to retribution is a well-established sequence in the tale tradition, as we shall see later, and while Cosentino points out the differences between *Jiki Magayi* and tales, he also acknowledges the underlying continuities between them (Cosentino 1978: 26).

DESCENDANTS OF THE 1934 VINTAGE

Prior to these five books published in 1934 there had been a number of publications of translated material as well as anthologies of tales and other narratives, the most notable being Edgar's (1911–13) *Litafi na Tatsuniyoyi na Hausa*. Translations of the *Thousand and One Nights* had started to appear as early as 1924 (Edgar 1924; Kano 1924). In 1931, an anthology of stories, tales and proverbs, entitled *Labaru Na Da Da Na Yanzu* 'Stories of the Past and of the Present', had been published for the Translation Bureau in Zaria by the Education Department of Nigeria (Hadeja and Whitting 1931),[26] The three-volume *Magana Jari Ce* by Abubakar Imam published in 1938 and 1939 was, in many ways, a continuation of the writing he had started with *Ruwan Bagaja*. His role in the Literature Bureau and his involvement with the newspaper *Gaskiya Ta Fi Kwabo* and the successors to the Literature Bureau are discussed in the next section.

After 1934, imaginative prose-writing can be divided into a number of periods. Little was published in the 1940s;[27] a number of books appeared in the early 1950s to be followed, in the late 1960s and early 1970s, by a new generation of writers. The most recent flowering of prose-writing is to be seen in the products of the Nigerian boom of the late 1970s and early 1980s, which departed radically from the earlier styles of writing. These 'boomtown novels' were also stimulated by writing competitions, the first organised by the successor to the Literature Bureau, the Northern Nigerian Publishing Company (NNPC), and the second by the Nigerian Federal Ministry of Culture.

Magana Jari Ce

Sitting by the Kamaca stream in the Native Authority orchard near the Tudun Wada General Hospital in Zaria, Abubakar Imam put together the stories which became *Magana Jari Ce*. He reports that it took him about six months during 1936 (Mora 1989: 26). The three volumes contain a little over eighty stories some of which are clearly derived from the books which Rupert East lent him. Pilaszewicz (1985: 222) credits Grimms' fairy tales, *The Decameron*, Arab and Hindu tales, and legends about the Jihad leader, Shehu Usman dan Fodio, as being among the sources. Imam himself says: 'He [Rupert East] collected several types of books on European fables and Arabian nights stories for me to use as background material' (Mora 1989: 26). Westley (n.d.) has examined the stories in some detail and comes to the conclusion that none of the *Magana Jari Ce* stories can be directly attributed to the *Thousand and One Nights*, postulating that most of the stories are extensively reworked, although some can be more directly attributed, such as the judgement of Solomon being from the Old Testament, and stories of Usman dan Fodio being taken from written versions in Edgar (1911–13).[28] In any case, many commentators over the years have echoed East's comment on Abubakar Imam's facility as a writer expressed in a discussion about the Hausa newspaper *Gaskiya Ta Fi Kwabo*: 'It is without question that the new colloquial and vivid style of writing Hausa, invented by the editor, Malam Abubakar, but now increasingly imitated by writers all over Northern Nigeria, is the main cause of the paper's popularity' (East 1943: 73). *Magana Jari Ce* has been held to be one of the best examples of Hausa writing style to date.[29]

The book is constructed after the manner of the *Thousand and One Nights*, in that a narrator relates story after story, not in this case to delay execution but to delay the imminent departure of a headstrong prince. The narrator is a parrot who, being charged with the care of the youth who wishes to join his friend in going to war, tells him stories and keeps him from leaving. On returning from battle, the king appoints the parrot to the viziership in place of his treacherous human vizier. In the second volume the parrot becomes involved in a story-telling competition with the parrot of another king. And in the third volume the parrot is teaching his son the art of story-telling.

The stories told by the parrot cover a variety of topics and styles. There is a retelling of the Pied Piper story, funny stories of confrontations between a variety of classic Hausa stereotypes, the country bumpkin and the city slickers, the three thieves, the Fulani man and the butcher, and many more. Most of the stories have a moral, but nearly all are amusing in one way or another. Westley (n.d.) sees in *Magana Jari Ce* a lively re-telling of fables,[30] as compared with the lifeless 'collection of bits and pieces' represented by *Labaru Na Da Da Na Yanzu*. Like so many of the anthologies of Hausa tales, the latter is a collection of plot summaries that do not, and cannot, do justice to the oral performances that they purport to represent. Imam, on the other hand, was able, in Westley's view, to create successfully a new way of telling:

> It was his ability to adapt his materials not only to the characteristics of the Hausa language and the circumstances of Hausa culture but to the context of literacy itself that made *Magana Jari Ce* a success. The transition from the oral to the written clearly involves more than the preservation of oral features in a literary matrix. Literacy itself demands a transformation of the process through which meaning is achieved. The relationship of the composer both to audience and to tradition is ineluctably altered by literacy. *Ruwan Bagaja* is a reflex of the oral tradition preserved by writing but not enhanced by it. The leisure of writing with its potential for the development of language creates new opportunities that span the distance between writer and reader which literacy itself creates. Abubakar Imam realized many of these potentials in *Magana Jari Ce*. (Westley n.d.)

THE EARLY 1950S

As indicated in Chapter 1, the development of creative writing in Hausa is intimately bound up with the history of the institution which was in turn, the Translation Bureau (1930–4),[31] the Literature Bureau (1934–45), and the Gaskiya Corporation (1945 to date) but whose publishing side was at one time NORLA (Northern Region Literature Agency, 1954–9) and then later the NNPC (1966 to date).[32] This institution dominated publishing in Hausa until the late 1970s when a number of other publishers entered the field.

From the late 1930s, East had been pressing the colonial government to expand the activities of the Literature Bureau. East's dream was the foundation of a community of Nigerians and Britons living and working together, working side by side on the various crafts and skills of the publishing business: writers of school books, journalists, editors, illustrators, managers, printers, binders, distributors and sellers. This was the idea behind the Gaskiya Corporation which he finally managed to sell to the then governor of Nigeria, Sir Arthur Richards, as the Second World War came to an end. Fine buildings were put up at a site near Tudun Wada in Zaria – with printing presses, offices and surrounding houses for both European and African staff (Skinner 1970b). The ideals behind the Corporation, framed in the colonial views of the time, were set out by East in 1946, focusing upon the development of the Corporation's newspaper, *Gaskiya Ta Fi Kwabo* (East 1946). In time the 'pairing' of European and Nigerian individuals, such as L. C. Giles, European Editor, with Abubakar Imam, Hausa Editor, of the newspaper, which gave rise to questions as to status, salary and control, was succeeded by other arrangements. Abubakar Imam was made Editor in 1948 after a dispute involving a large proportion of the Nigerian staff of the Corporation over 'conditions of service' (Mora 1989: 113–51). The Corporation did bring together a number of Nigerians who went on to become significant figures in the North, Nuhu Bamalli, Abubakar Tunau and Abdulkadir Makama among others, in addition to Abubakar Imam.

The early 1950s saw the production of a number of prose works in addition to a wide variety of other types of material.[33] The Corporation published three novellas, *Iliya Dan Maikarfi* by Ahmadu Ingawa in 1951,[34] *Gogan Naka* by Garba Funtuwa and *Sihirtaccen Gari* by Amadu Katsina in 1952.

Iliya Dan Maikarfi is the story of a disabled and weak child visited by angels who transform him into a great warrior. He goes on to perform stupendous feats of arms in defence of Kib and its ruler, Waldima, before finally praying to God to be turned to stone. Piłaszewicz (1985: 224) points out the apparent similarities, noted by Sceglov, to a Russian epic poem involving Kiev and Prince Vladimir. Like *Iliya Dan Maikarfi* (J. Mohammed 1989), *Gogan Naka* 'Your Hero' follows the pattern of *Gandoki* (Mustapha 1992) in that the central character, Dangana (later discovered to be called Abdul Bakara) and his son Indo, accomplish wondrous feats, in Bokhara and other far-off lands, defeating armies of elephants. Finally, Indo finishes up as a great king in Egypt. *Sihirtaccen Gari* 'The Enchanted Town' is another story of magical places and fantastical events. Gaskiya Corporation was producing other materials at this time including tracts on health, education, hygiene and many other 'public enlightenment' themes. A book that reformulated many of these didactic themes in the form of a story of two people, Bala and his wife, Babiya, by Nuhu Bamalli was first published in 1950 and reprinted frequently thereafter.

These three stories were followed by a series of others that came out under the imprint of NORLA, and they too followed the tone and style that had been set by the early novels. NORLA, whose Vernacular Literature division was headed by A. Neil Skinner, supported the publishing both of original writing, and translations into Hausa of foreign books.[35] Thus in addition to *Da'u Fataken Dare* 'Da'u, Traders of the Night' by Tanko Zango in 1952 and *Bayan Wuya Sai Dadi* 'After Pain Comes Pleasure' by Abdulmalik Mani in 1954, translations were published of Robin Hood, Baron Münchausen, and the adventures of Hajji Baba of Isfahan.[36]

Da'u Fataken Dare tells the story of a band of thieves whose hideout in the bush is the base from which they raid the town. A fight with a powerful adversary produces a result in which the leader of the gang, Musa, is destroyed by jinn inhabiting a lake into which he has fallen. The theme of the story is reminiscent of *Idon Matambayi* from 1934, and the amalgam of human and fantastical forces is a feature shared with both *Gandoki* and *Ruwan Bagaja*. *Bayan Wuya Sai Dadi*! is another novella that deploys the quest theme. In this case the pot of gold at the end of the rainbow is a well in the desert that is full of treasure finally discovered by another pair of characters, this time Tuareg men.

CIRCA 1970: 1934 REVISITED

The late 1960s and early 1970s saw a new crop of novellas published by the Gaskiya Corporation and its successor, the NNPC. The first, *Tauraruwar Hamada* 'The Sahara Star' by Sa'idu Ahmed, appeared in 1965 to be followed by *Nagari Na Kowa* 'Good to Everyone' by Jabiru Abdullahi in 1968, *Tauraruwa Mai Wutsiya* 'The Comet' by Umaru Dembo in 1969 and *Dare Daya* 'One Night' in 1973.[37] These echo the earlier novels of 1934.

Tauraruwar Hamada tells of a thief's quest to kidnap a girl at the behest of a king who has been refused the girl in marriage. The bulk of the narrative involves repeated episodic adventures in which the 'hero', Danye and his sidekick, Dabo, inveigle their way into other people's confidence and trick them, or are entrapped only to escape, sometimes by magical means. With a talking snake the mixture of realism and fantasy is again apparent, and a final scenario in which our hero settles down rich and famous brings the parallel with *Ruwan Bagaja* even more to the fore.

Nagari Na Kowa tells the story of Salihi, another epitome of the resilient, tolerant, pious, good man, and his struggle to bear misfortune when, following the death of his parents and his patron, his patron's money is found to have disappeared and Salihi is unjustly blamed. He eventually rises from the position of abused prisoner to become just ruler through a number of miraculous events in which he is able to solve problems that had confounded all others. There are close parallels between the picture of the good man in Hausa presented here and that in *Shaihu Umar*.[38] Dangambo (1974) comments upon the social realism of the novel and its discussion of virtue, seeing Salihi's father as the central model of virtue. Dangambo's discussion focuses upon the moral dimensions of the main characters in the story.

Tauraruwa Mai Wutsiya tells the story of a boy named Kilba who, with the aid of a visitor from outer space, Kolin Koliyo, makes a journey through space where he encounters extra-terrestrial beings before finally returning home. Commentators (for example Piłaszewicz 1985: 225) have remarked that this constitutes the beginnings of a new type of novel in Hausa. Clearly, the story displays the influence of news of spaceflights and the training and activities of astronauts, but whether this marks a new departure in the novel is debatable. A. G. D. Abdullahi (1984) has drawn attention to the mixture of cultural influences in the story, from Indian cinema to Western science to Islamic religious beliefs. In many ways, the journey is a familiar theme; the transition from reality to fantasy, with jinn replaced by extra-terrestrial beings, is also familiar; and the hero's survival through tests and dangers is a standard feature of novels that had gone before. On the other hand, Piłaszewicz draws attention to the fact that many previous texts (with the exception, perhaps, of the first section of *Gandoki* set in Nigeria of the British conquest) are set in a 'pre-modern' Hausa world, a reconstructed vision of an ahistorical Hausa society without planes, trains or telephones. This ideological construct is perhaps more significant for the world of the 'traditional' tale, but it is noticeable also in the constitution of these early Hausa novels.

Finally, *Dare Daya* tells an involved tale of rivalry between branches of a ruling family, in which a beloved baby son is snatched away by the rival faction and, as with Moses, is found later in a basket on a river by a poor fisherman. As the boy matures, not knowing his true origins, he goes through close encounters with his real family who are searching for him until finally, as warrior champion for an enemy king, he is recognised in battle by his opposite number, his real sister. All is revealed, peace ensues and the original wrongdoers commit suicide. The movement from original wrongdoing to eventual restitution involving the growth to maturity of a central character and his discovery of a hidden truth, is very reminiscent of *Jiki Magayi* although lacking the tragic element in *Jiki Magayi* whereby the hero killed his own father in error.

This period of the late 1960s and early 1970s, coinciding with the civil war in Nigeria, saw the publication of novellas which, in many ways, were closely similar to their forerunners from the 1930s. Framed by a quest, or the movement from wrongdoing to restitution, they displayed many of the typical earlier features: the episodic adventures of a hero and his sidekick, the mixture of reality and fantasy, and the characterisation of a stereotype of moral uprightness and fortitude. As in the earlier period, where one book presented the exploits of a cheating, reprehensible counter-hero, a 'trickster', another presented the ideal of the moral man. These two dimensions of representation, the 'praiseworthy' and the potentially 'reprehensible', are recurrent aspects of much of Hausa literature.

THE 1980S AND THE BOOMTOWN NOVELS

In the early 1930s it was a creative-writing competition that sparked the original batch of stories. In the late 1970s and early 1980s, at the height of the Nigerian oil boom, two further competitions produced a new crop of novels, different in many ways from that which had gone before. The successor to the publishing side of the Gaskiya Corporation, the Northern Nigerian Publishing Company, based in the same buildings in Zaria as the Gaskiya Corporation, instituted a competition in 1979 for which they had twenty-two entries. Four of the entries were translations, eleven manuscripts were turned down, three were declared winners and therefore went forward for immediate publication, and four were kept for later publication (Kudan 1987). The overall winner was *Mallakin Zuciyata* 'Power over My Heart' by Sulaiman Ibrahim Katsina, and the other two were *So Aljannar Duniya* 'Love is Heaven on Earth' by the woman writer, Hafsatu Abdulwahid, and *Amadi Na Malam Amah* 'Malam Amah's Amadi' by Magaji Dambatta. All three appeared together in 1980.[39] Two years previously the NNPC had published a novel entitled *Kitsen Rogo* 'Illusion' by Abdulkadir Dangambo.[40]

The earlier novel, *Kitsen Rogo*, has little of the previous mixture of fantasy and reality and has taken a contemporary social and political issue as its central theme. The story is about a village boy, Ibrahim, who comes to the city in search of his fortune.[41] Changing his name to Musa, he swiftly becomes involved in dealing in stolen property, and the low life of bars and hotels while living in a slum. Eventually arrested, he is finally released, after serving a prison term, into the arms of his father who takes him back to his village. Back home he is a reformed character, and ends up married and with a job in a local ministry. Strongly didactic, the story presents the problems of rural–urban migration in graphic detail. Didacticism on contemporary social, political and religious issues is a familiar feature of the poetry tradition in Hausa. *Kitsen Rogo* represented one of the most direct transpositions of that style into imaginative prose-writing.

Mallakin Zuciyata is a similarly didactic piece, tracing the life of a family in a small town community. Mallam Kalla, a trader, lives with his family in fictional Ginin Gwani. They suffer the depradations of thieves. They find it difficult to obtain fertilisers for their farm when they need them. They have a son, Usman, who is fostered by a couple, Sa'idu and Kilima when Kalla dies. Usman meets a girl, Sakina, at school. A rich man sees Sakina and wants to marry her. Sakina's father holds out against her mother who wants Sakina to marry the rich man. On graduating from university, Sakina becomes a teacher and Usman, an agricultural officer. With the support of Sakina's father they succeed in getting married.

The story touches upon a number of common themes of recent novels: the corrupt official who comes to grief (the fertiliser trader); the rich entrepreneur and his use of wealth to gain a wife against the wishes of the girl and her true love; the importance of education; monogamous marriage; and the central concept of the good citizen (Piłaszewicz 1991/2). While these themes are intertwined in this novel in equal measure, one of them, the conflict between the wishes of the girl and boy in their pursuit of true love and the pressures put upon the girl to obey her parents and to accept an arranged marriage, is a theme which has produced a major growth industry in recent years as love stories have sprung up through private printing, particularly in Kano – a subject we will return to at the end of this chapter.

So Aljannar Duniya focuses upon this latter theme of love and conflicting obligation, but in this case the love between two Fulani youths, Boɗaɗo and Yasir, is thwarted by the intervention of a female jinn.[42] Even when they are married, the jinn proceeds to bring calamity upon them. Yasir has to go through numerous tests and magical procedures before they are finally rid of the jinn's presence and are able to recover from the illnesses that have afflicted them. This novel, while concentrating upon the more modern love theme, harks back to the early novels in the degree to which fantasy and fantastical trials and tribulations are an integral part of the movement towards a resolution of the problem set by the intervention of the jinn.

Amadi Na Malam Amah follows the pattern of *Ruwan Bagaja* and others, involving the hero in a journey during which he experiences magical happenings and encounters fantastical creatures whom he manages to defeat. Within this group of stories, features characteristic of earlier novels are combined with strands that move more to realism in the description of contemporary Nigerian society. These strands combine didacticism with the acting-out of modern-day contradictions as, for example, between the expectations of arranged marriage and the perceived countervailing force of personal freedom, or of monogamy as against polygamy.

In 1980 the Nigerian Federal Department of Culture organised a competition for creative writing in Nigerian languages and undertook the publication of a number of Hausa-language works through *Nigeria Magazine* using the Gaskiya Corporation as printers. In addition to a play and a collection of love poetry, four novels were published; the winner of the competition being, as in 1979, Sulaiman Ibrahim Katsina with his novel *Turmin Danya* 'The Strong Man'.[43] The other three novels were *Tsumangiyar Kan Hanya* 'The Driving Whip' by Musa Mohammed Bello, *Karshen Alewa Kasa* 'The Discarded Left-over' by Bature Gagare, and *Zabi Naka* 'Choose Yours' by Munir Muhammed Katsina, all published in 1982.

The runners-up included the most substantial novel to date, the 342-page thriller, *Karshen Alewa Kasa* which addresses one of the pressing issues of post-civil-war Nigeria: the fate of thousands of demobbed soldiers. Written in a racy, conversational style, the story traces the central character, Mailoma, alias Kazunzum, alias Maguzi, as he brings together a cut-throat band of ex-soldiers and forms a marauding force that indulges in murder, robbery and mayhem, seeking to control the drugs trade and eventually to take over the country. The scale of the intended enterprise can be judged from the fact that Mailoma asks his associate, Markus, to supply him with 100 automatic weapons, 150 hand guns, grenades and tear gas. Eventually, with blackmail, treachery and gruesome death at every turn, fit for the plot of a bloodthirsty western, the main characters die of snake bite or in a hail of bullets. Marking a major departure from previous writing, the story is brim full of features of modern Nigeria: fast cars, booze, gambling, sex, violence; and people representing various components of Nigerian society: girl friends who speak their minds in no uncertain terms, Igbo ex-soldiers, *Maguzawa* (non-Muslim Hausa) villagers in Mailoma's home village, white Christian missionaries, Christian converts, and a wide variety of stock characters from northern Nigerian society. With little of the overt didacticism of *Tura Ta Kai Bango* (a novel by S. I. Katsina, discussed later in this chapter) or *Mallakin Zuciyata*, this novel owes more to James Hadley Chase (a commonly available author in the English-language market in Nigeria), Frederick Forsyth and the cinema of *The Good, the Bad and the Ugly* than to earlier Hausa writing.

Tsumangiyar Kan Hanya represents the strand of writing, both in plays and narrative, which sets out social and domestic issues and addresses the conflicts that arise as 'Western influence' is seen to undermine the assumptions and patterns of Hausa social life. Framed as a 'rise and fall' story, the central character, Sambo, is initially happily married to one wife, Hafsi, and earning a living as a driver. As time goes by he becomes more affluent and takes a second wife, Zinaru. With more money he goes on pilgrimage. Corrupted by money, he begins to spend much of it on girlfriends and a succession of wives on whom he lavishes great wealth. When finally he ends up deserted by these women and reduced to straitened circumstances, he realises the error of his ways and goes to ask Hafsi to come back to him from her parents' house where she has gone. Returned to his original state, moral equilibrium is restored. The message is not, however, monogamy – right at the end he marries a second wife, Fati – but rather that it is better to avoid the profligacy and corruption that can be the by-products of wealth.

Zabi Naka, like *Ruwan Bagaja*, *Shaihu Umar* and others since, is set as an autobiographical narrative, and like *Karshen Alewa Kasa* addresses the issue of post-civil-war society and the fate of ex-soldiers. The central character, Namuduka, joins the army after a childhood in which his parents, evicted, in debt and with his father unemployed, are killed in a road accident. He becomes a delinquent in spite of the care and attention of a foster parent and spends a period in jail learning from thieves and rogues. He distinguishes himself in the army, but after the war he, along with many others, is demobbed and finds himself unemployed and on hard times. Forming a band, Robin-Hood-like, he proceeds to rob the rich and protect the poor. At the end of the story he has become rich and returns to his home town. Punishment for his misdeeds is commuted following the demonstration of support by many ordinary people. Piłaszewicz provides a translated extract illustrating the philosophy behind Namuduka's actions:

> Although I encouraged you to give yourself up to the robbery, still we are not going to harm anyone, but those who deserve it. Our robbery will not damage the country, but rather will improve it. We are going to harm only those people who do not wish the citizens any good, who grab the money out of the country and make a profit out of its natural resources which are intended for everyone. (Piłaszewicz 1991/2: 33)

This vision of a Nigeria at the mercy of plundering, powerful men – a vision no longer bounded by northern Hausa village, town or city life, but encompassing a nation state, with its ordinary citizens having rights and obligations to each other and to the state – is a new construct represented in this 1982 generation of novels.

Turmin Danya

Such a view of Nigerian society in which rapacious entrepreneurs along with corrupt bureaucrats and their allies have taken control of every aspect of social and economic life, is most graphically represented in the novel which was awarded the first prize in the competition run by the Federal Department of Culture, *Turmin Danya*. The oil boom of the 1970s in Nigeria produced rapid changes in the social fabric of Nigerian society. The particular nature of wealth accumulation during that period produced anomalous and contrasting perceptions of opportunity and social status. On the one hand, there were those whose wealth-creating activities were clearly based upon their investment in manufacturing, assembling and trade. Often these were families and organisations who expanded upon a pre-boom base. On the other hand, there were those who profited by their political control over the distribution of the oil revenues from abroad down through federal, state and local organisations. These latter patrons established their clienteles through the provision of government-funded contracts to undertake a wide variety of projects – setting up schools, building roads, culverts and houses – and the clients who undertook these contracts became rich on the profits. While the pre-boom merchant class was also fully involved in the contract business, there arose, certainly in northern Nigeria, a popular image of the incompetent shyster, a jack-of-all-trades contractor, the *dan kwangila*, who fails to build the culvert, or whose school falls down in the first rainy season, and who becomes a ubiquitous figure on the northern social scene.

In *Turmin Danya* this rapacious entrepreneurial class is represented in the personage of Alhaji Gabatari. Alhaji is portrayed in the early part of the book as a man of great personal wealth who, in addition to his three wives, employs a go-between to procure girls whom he then keeps in a number of establishments around town. He pays Mista Samai, the chief customs officer, to turn a blind eye to the smuggling of cigarettes and other contraband from over the border into the fictional town of Karaini, either in his own vehicles or those of his associates. Anyone wishing to do any such deals has to go through Alhaji Gabatari since he controls the customs and the local police. Those who attempt to circumvent him or try to put the police on to him are themselves caught in the act. In between his dalliance with his lady friends he suborns the local authorities who have put various construction contracts out to tender; squeezes those in his debt for every penny; quarrels with his mother about money she has spent; arranges for a major cross-border shipment; and fixes it so that the electricity is off when the shipment passes through Karaini and the police are well out of the way. The arranged marriage of his daughter to a big man in the transport business is the occasion for a major bout of conspicuous consumption, and he plants bribery money on an officer who has double-crossed him. Through all of this, the occasional individual stands out against his web of corruption. Muktari, the only uncorrupt, lowly customs officer, refuses to take a kick-back from Alhaji. In the final stages of the story, an incorruptible building inspector refuses to accept Alhaji's money and declares the construction undertaken by Alhaji to be unsound and fraudulent; one of the *malamai* 'Islamic clerics' who are being paid to produce success for Alhaji's ventures declares the process of getting spiritual forces on board to be un-Islamic; Alhaji's girlfriend, having been given the ownership of the house built for her by Alhaji, declares her love for the go-between and proposes that she and he set up in business together; and when Alhaji falls ill from too much drug consumption, no one wants him better. At the very end, a new national leader orders the replacement of customs officials and a clamp-down on smuggling. As a result of a letter from Muktari, the honest customs officer, police from out of town are mobilised to stake out the border when Alhaji and associates are due to bring in a large consignment. The trap is sprung and Alhaji's network of collaborators is picked up; in the arrest of the smugglers, Alhaji pulls out a gun and during the ensuing exchange of fire kills a policeman. At the trial, collaborators are given prison sentences and Alhaji is sentenced to death for the killing of a policeman. Girlfriend and go-between walk off into the sunset!

In constructing the image of the entrepreneur in this highly moralistic book the author is at pains to capture not only typical characteristics which the reader can identify in people around him or her, but also to summarise and establish the stereotype. The typification presented here in this book is assuredly not the only way the type is portrayed in the north of Nigeria: these things are always the subject of debate and counter-characterisation. Nevertheless, this particular position represents a commonly held view among the educated as well as many ordinary people, as far as I am able to tell. The selection of translated extracts that follows picks out not key moments of the action or plot but descriptions and verbal exchanges that summarise key identifiers in terms of appearance and observable behaviour – Alhaji Gabatari's physical surroundings, his personal appearance, his ownership of property, his treatment of neighbours, his control over commercial relations, his control over public officials, his method of obtaining contracts and his involvement in smuggling.

In contrast to many previous prose narratives in Hausa, and like its 1982 contemporaries discussed above, *Turmin Danya* uses detailed description of the immediate physical environment. The book opens with the office in which Gabatari operates; status and the nature of social interactions between Gabatari and visitors are determined by these surroundings. The notion of an office as group workplace, with the pursuit of various business-related activities and a division of functions, is consciously ruled out through the image of the single desk, and the rolling-up of all functions in the one man:

> In the shade of the porch stood beautiful flowers in large earthenware pots. The house was large, a concrete construction with shops on each side. In the centre of the building was an office with a large glass door. Fixed above, a signboard read, 'Gabatari's Trading, Transport and General Contracting Company'. On the linoleum that covered the floor lay a thick brown carpet that gave as you walked on it as if walking on pillows stuffed with silk-cotton bolls. Lined up to one side were a three-seater sofa and a number of matching easy chairs. Their colour toned with the carpet.
>
> Facing the chairs was a large desk of polished mahogany sporting a shine in which you could see yourself reflected. It was embellished with red leather tacked down with embossed gold-coloured pins. A set of wire trays held a series of files intended for receipts and important

letters. Some papers lay on the desk and to one side sat a telephone. A swivel chair stood behind the desk.

Alhaji Gabatari sat at the desk and this was the office in which he received guests, he was clerk, secretary, manager and director of this company of his which, apart from contract work, conducted its trade entirely on the black market. (trans. from Katsina 1982: 1)

Unusually again for Hausa narratives, there is a picture of the physical appearance of the man himself, marking him out as a physical type, a 'fat cat' careful of his appearance, but, most significantly, not an outsider: not the fair skin of someone of Fulani descent, nor Syrian trader, nor southerner. Clearly, 'one of us', but, as the book goes on to show, no longer really 'one of us':

Alhaji Gabatari was a man of medium build, so dark-skinned that his skin seemed to glisten; his eyes and nose were of considerable size as was his mouth. Although a smoker he took great care of his teeth and they shone as a result. He was a young man of 37 but his opulence had brought him the beginnings of a substantial paunch. (trans. from Katsina 1982: 2)

Within a description of the town and its people, Alhaji Gabatari is such that he is seen as representing the new affluent class: buying up property close to the main roads thereby relegating the ordinary people more and more to the overcrowded back streets or into dormitory suburbs:

Then he got into his car and headed for home. The house was at some distance in the old part of the town within the old walls of Karaini. And it was not at all like his office in the new part of the town. Although the town had long since filled to overflowing, people were reluctant to move outside because they seldom wanted to move to where they had no relatives who could help in time of need. The town was surrounded by a wall which had started to crumble and in fact in some places buildings had been put up on top of it. But in other places the wall was still high. There were places where the wall had been made into part of a building. The town had nine gates, some new and some that had been there for a very long time. But not one of them still had the original doors. Through each gate went a major road that led into the town and these roads nearly all joined up inside. They had all been made after the arrival in the country of the Europeans. Apart from these there were very few other large roads inside the town. Like in the old Hausa cities the original streets of this town were narrow. Often they were covered with refuse and thick with mud. Some were clean, where people had directed the drainage out at the back of the house. The majority of the houses were made of earth, and the spouts of the roof drains kept the streets looking good. Some houses were single storey, here and there was a two-storey house. Some had been finished off with a coat of cement on top of the earth construction. Others had seen no cement at all. Modern times had seen the beginnings of building with breeze blocks. Dotted around were such houses belonging to the well-to-do, the 'nice clothes *and* a pillow for the head' people. As you walk along the streets of the town you constantly come across people in cars, on motorbikes, on bicycles, and on foot, and you see people selling things on the side of the road like groundnuts and boiled cassava. And there are shops and stalls everywhere.

At one spot students are learning to read the Koran; at another there are mechanics. And there are hotels where you can eat and places selling food. Alhaji Gabatari was lucky that his house stood on a wide street. His car could get right up to the door of his house so he did not need to go asking other people for a place to leave his car. Although there were streets in the town they generally had no names, only the quarters of the town had names, though just recently names of streets had started to be written up. The quarter where Alhaji lived was called Fanyawa. It was a quarter filled with ordinary people; however, because of the major road that ran through it the more affluent had started to take over. They were for ever buying the best places from the ordinary people thereby relegating them to the overcrowded lanes and congested quarters. Money talks.

The road on which Alhaji's house was situated ran from north to south. It faced east. It was a large house with two storeys. There was a patio outside the main door with flowers planted around and two papaya trees with an open space beyond. To the left was a door leading through to his wives' rooms and beyond that the garage doors. (trans. from Katsina 1982: 9–10)

While his appearance and his cars mark him out visually, it is his behaviour that confirms his estrangement from the expected norms of social interaction. The contravention of norms of social interaction is most pointed when Alhaji is involved in dealings, not with underlings, but with people to whom normal politeness would be appropriate in circumstances where they have nothing to gain from Alhaji nor he from them, such as neighbours:

Alhaji entered through the glass doors into his main reception room. A number of well-built men sat around the front door. They did nothing but eat and cause trouble for people who came to the house, particularly those who had incurred Alhaji's displeasure. It was difficult for someone to come to Alhaji's house without being in some way belittled; unless he came with his own army. Whenever Alhaji travelled in his car he wound up the windows and turned on the air-conditioner.

He payed no attention to the people on the street and wouldn't dream of lifting a hand in greeting. As far as he was concerned since he needed nothing from anybody why should he waste his time with greetings? (trans. from Katsina 1982: 10–11)

The key to the story of *Turmin Danya* is of course Alhaji Gabatari's control over commercial activity in the town. As a fixer he is unparalleled and wealth flows from the control of contraband, Karaini being a town close to the border. In the following passage it is clear that a distinction is to be drawn between wealth in cash that typifies the *nouveau riche*, the entrepreneurs, and wealth in property and land that marks out the old élite. That old élite, undifferentiated in terms of aristocracy or old merchant class, is followed by specific reference to the aristocracy where Gabatari's money now gives him an entrée. To complete the picture, his influence based upon money extends to the judiciary as well. But, and here we return to the authorial position, in the end he is a bitter pill to swallow in the new social firmament:

> When it came to this kind of dealing Alhaji Gabatari was way ahead of everyone in Karaini, and in fact ahead of everyone in Tambuki and all the towns that used Karaini as a route for their imports and exports. Alhaji was the ladder on which you stepped to gain access to the customs men and reach an arrangement with them so that the goods passed without hindrance. Any plan in which he was not included was as good as ruined. The goods might be lost and sometimes even people caught. The people of Tambuki had often tried to get round him but their plans had always come to naught. He was like the rope that held a parcel together, without it it would all fall apart. For this reason he had become enormously wealthy and if measured in cash terms rather than land and property then he had already overtaken everyone in Karaini. The aristocracy had become his friends, a gathering was not complete without him and if the law caught up with someone then it was through him that the matter could be forgotten. When he stirred the bowl everyone drank however unpleasant the taste. (trans. from Katsina 1982: 7)

Corruption is the name of the game for both Alhaji and all those he deals with and the author spells out for the reader precisely how it works in its charming simplicity:

> Alhaji's tea arrived and he drank his fill. He began to feel sleepy but he had things to do. Tenders had been invited on a new contract so he had no time for a nap. Out of his bag he took a bottle of ICD [codeine] pills and swallowed two to give himself a lift. That was how he always was, he always took two, sometimes even four. He called them 'chalk' so people would not call him a drug-taker. That was what others called

them too. If he said, 'Bansuwai go and fetch me some chalk', then he knew what he meant. After swallowing the pills he made for the office taking tenders for the contract to build four office blocks. The contractors had to submit estimates of cost and whoever came nearest to the amount allocated or was the lowest offer got the job. He went straight to the chairman of the committee as soon as he arrived.

'I hear you are inviting tenders.'

'That's right. Are you wanting the job?'

'Of course.'

'Ah well, we do like to see your sort applying, who can do the job. We are not too keen on the small men who are always looking for more money.'

'We are aware of the help you do give us. Had it been anyone else I would not have bothered to come.'

'Have you written in?'

'I will do so.'

'You must.'

Alhaji put his hand in his pocket and took out a thousand naira for the chairman.

'Something to buy the kids chocolate with.'

'It is no trouble. Don't worry yourself please.'

'No, honestly, it's nothing. We trust each other, that's what brings us together, and that is why I give you this, for no other reason.'

The chairman took it.

'Thank you. Stop by the secretary and he will show you the estimate we made for the contract.'

'Thank you!'

According to the rules of tender, the ministry makes an estimate of costs and under no circumstances are any of the contractors to see it before the tenders are in ... Alhaji pulled his chair close up to the secretary's desk and said,

'Long time no see.'

'You are the one doing the boycotting. Unless there is a tender out we never see you. We are very cross with you.'

'Don't be cross.'

'Alright. Did you see the chairman?'

'I've come straight from his office. We were talking about the contract on offer.'

'Do you want to know how much we estimated for the job?'

'That would be good. If you don't see the estimate then you are wasting your time.'

The secretary said he had put a copy aside for Alhaji in any case. (trans. from Katsina 1982: 35–8)

In this novel the author addresses the reader directly with comments upon the morality of the story as it develops. Such direct didactic comment is very typical of the tradition of poetry-writing in Hausa. The author, familiar with English-language novels, has expressed the view that he would like to expunge such direct comment from the text, feeling that it is not appropriate for the novel form (S. I. Katsina personal communication). In *Turmin Danya*, an example of such comment is seen where the author remarks that the crooked entrepreneur is equivalent to the smuggler and they are equally criminal and corrupting, with the proviso, however, that not every entrepreneur is a crook:

> Apart from smugglers there's no one who cares less than contractors. Some of them, like Alhaji Gabatari, do both. Money by any means. They try any possible way to make money. The only thing they do with money is to carry on their evil ways, trying to corrupt those who have not yet succumbed to their style of doing things. Not every contractor is a crook but every smuggler does damage to his country and to his people. How can you say which does more damage to his country, the smuggler or the contractor? (trans. from Katsina 1982: 65)

Turmin Danya establishes the salient characteristics of the new entrepreneurial class through the picture drawn of Alhaji Gabatari, a new 'reality' for modern Nigerians far removed from the jinn-fighting joker or the epitome of moral uprightness of earlier novels. And again, Alhaji Gabatari's domination of society is not an inevitability to which people have to resign themselves. Isolated and ineffective at first are pockets of resistance to the web of control spun by Alhaji, but in the end those who hold out form part of the larger force unleashed by central government that sweeps away Alhaji and his ilk. The symbolic importance of the few figures in the story who stand against Alhaji cannot be underestimated. It is there that Sulaiman Ibrahim Katsina reveals his agenda for the renewal of Hausa society, but even there he comes up against the reality of individual powerlessness in the face of concerted corruption. It might be suggested that the author's fantasy lies in the notion that central government will be the agent of reform. Listen to one of the few voices in the story that resist:

> Alhaji travelled on until he reached the border. He got out, greeted the customs officers who were standing around and went in to see the senior officers. The more junior officers were overjoyed because they knew Alhaji would slip them money, so none of them wanted to go far in case they missed him when he reappeared. All except one – Muktari Mamman. One of them said, 'Things have really dried up recently. Nobody has been trying to bring stuff through. And I've got extra mouths to feed at the moment.' Another said, 'Yes, it's the same for me. Muktari won't take anything out of fear of Allah. Any old gristle is

good enough for me.'

... Muktari said, 'What you don't understand is that if Allah has determined that you will be rich you will be rich without taking bribes. So there is no reason to take money.'

Muktari Mamman was angry and upset. Crimes were being committed, goods were passing through without customs duty being paid, and there was nowhere he could take his complaint. The criminals enjoyed a lot more respect than he did. Thinking about it he decided to hold on and consider a way to counteract it all. Or he might just have to wait until Allah provided some remedy. Too much haste would be a mistake. It was possible that he might be got rid of before he had a chance to change things. (trans. from Katsina 1982: 58–9)

In the end Alhaji Gabatari is defeated through the *deus ex machina* of central government acting on information provided by the local resistance in the form of Muktari. Within the framework of the story, however, he has built up enemies among rivals and among disaffected clients such that his world has begun to come apart even before his arrest and execution. One of the more intriguing aspects of this novel, that has not been addressed here, is the relationship between Alhaji, his go-between, Bawale, and his favoured girlfriend, Bebi, who eventually takes him for a lot of money; control in the personal world of sex and clientage also slips from his grasp. The determination by the girlfriend and go-between to go it alone and dump Alhaji never reaches testing-point because Alhaji is removed by others from the scene, leaving them to enjoy the spoils of a different kind of war.

This novel sees the presentation to a Hausa-reading audience of a new phenomenon in Nigerian society: the rapacious entrepreneur of the boom years of the 1970s and 1980s. As *Karshen Alewa Kasa* and *Zabi Naka* present the social phenomenon of ex-soldiers and their post-war activities in Nigeria, admittedly from differing perspectives, so *Turmin Danya* draws a graphic representation of another new social phenomenon of the 1980s. The social realism and the ideological commitment evident in the didactic authorial tone of *Turmin Danya* make it very different from the style of writing that had traditionally been so typical of Hausa imaginative prose.

Tura Ta Kai Bango

Perhaps the most radical departure of recent years is represented by the third book by Sulaiman Ibrahim Katsina, published by the NNPC in 1983, *Tura Ta Kai Bango* 'Pushed to the Limit'. This story is a thinly disguised picture of a village near a northern Nigerian town, such as Katsina, during the lead-up to the 1979 election in Nigeria. Two young local men, Hassan Wurjanjan and his friend, Dawai, determine to set up a branch of the party opposed to the dominant conservative party in their area. Local business men, in alliance with the traditional ruler and his people, have the place seemingly under their control. When they discover that an opposition group is forming they bring all sorts of pressure to bear on friends, relatives and associates of the 'traitors'. Blackmail and beating are all part of the process. Nevertheless, popular support begins to grow and when it comes to the election, the story describes in detail a series of ingenious fiddles and electoral malpractices, from spoiling votes to switching ballot boxes to kidnapping scrutineers. The victorious conservatives proceed to hound and persecute the remnants of the opposition mercilessly. When finally the next election comes, however, the opposition are prepared for all eventualities. The people rise up and, through vigilance and force of numbers, prevent malpractice. The conservatives are swept from power and Hassan and Dawai, now in positions of power, dedicate themselves to helping their fellow Nigerians. While the National Party of Nigeria (NPN) are clearly the conservatives, the opposition remains unspecific as between the various parties, People's Redemption Party (PRP) or Greater Nigerian People's Party (GNPP) which had inherited, to varying extents in different places, the mantle of the old northern opposition, the Northern Elements Progressive Union (NEPU) of the 1950s and 1960s. Where the business man, Gabatari, had represented corrupt, oppressive forces in *Turmin Danya,* in this story Alhaji Kaukai performs the same function:

> Alhaji was nearly 47 years old. He was tall and fat with pale skin, a big stomach and several chins. He was the type of man who wanted everyone to think he was a kind man. He therefore went overboard in order to give the appearance of kindness. This was the manner in which he welcomed Hassan, and invited him to be seated on the mat; he motioned to a plaited palm leaf of many colours. Cushions were put out in case visitors wished to recline on their elbows. He said to Hassan, 'Now, Hassan, you are in town every day and yet I never see you. Have I done something to offend you?'
>
> 'No, nothing. You know how school can take up all my time in the mornings. And then there is looking after the farm and clearing the land.'
>
> 'Since you do so much work on the farm perhaps I can give you 100 naira or so to help a little.'
>
> 'I would be very grateful.'
>
> 'The Conservative Party had a meeting recently. Were you there?'
>
> 'Yes, I was there right to the end.'
>
> 'I've been hearing rumours that maybe you and certain others are planning to introduce that other wretched party to Koramu, here where we live. When I heard this I said no, it couldn't be you. How could you, a Koranic student, an important man, do such an immoral thing?'

Alhaji listened attentively for Hassan's response.

'What you heard is true. The Conservatives have no policies aimed at helping the common people. They only speak of protecting the aristocracy and the rich, the commoners are simply abandoned.'

'You don't understand the aims of our party. The rich and the aristocracy are the eyes of the common people. Where would you be without us?'

'No, Alhaji, the commoners are the mainstay of the rich and the aristocracy. Without them who would the rulers rule? And who would produce their wealth?'

'Now we won't argue, Hassan. You are like a brother to me, so I won't try to make you do something you refuse to do, but what I want you to do is join our party so that we can together push for progress in this town.'

'Progress for this town or progress for some people in this town? Our support will go to the party that represents the common people. I only wish you would come and join us, so we could go forward together.'

'I advise you to go and listen to your conscience and abandon this evil. I don't want to see you with the weight of such evil actions hanging over you.'

'Alhaji, if you have finished with me, I must be going.'

'Listen to us, Hassan. Look, here is the 100 naria I promised you.'

'You hold on to your 100 naira. If you think I am going to sell my freedom and dignity, you are mistaken. I was born a free man, and I shall die as a free man, not a slave, God willing.'

With that he departed, leaving Alhaji biting his nails and plotting his next step. (trans. from Katsina 1983: 38–9)[44]

In contrast with the early Hausa novels, the women portrayed in *Tura Ta Kai Bango* and *Turmin Danya* have some independence of mind, and constitute important characters within the story. In *Tura Ta Kai Bango*, it is Alhaji Kaukai's wives who are organising support among the women of Koramu, inviting them to lavish parties and social gatherings. Hassan's wife Hadiza, in consequence has considerable difficulty in countering the 'propaganda' put about among women by these conservative women:

When Hadiza went to Malam Garba's house to show his wife, Gala, where to put her mark on polling day, Gala said, 'But will your party hand out money if it is elected?'

'No party has said it will hand out money if it is elected.'

'What about this money sign here in this man's hand [on the Conservative Party logo]. Is that, or is that not, money?'

'It's money alright. But they aren't really saying they'll hand out money if they are elected; where would they find the money to give some to everyone in this country? They say it is their intention to make everyone rich as soon as they are elected. But how? That's something they don't say. They print pictures with money on them because they don't give a damn about us. They know that as soon as we see the prospect of money then we are hooked. At the end of the day they will give us nothing.'

'Are you sure? You mean there will be no handouts at all?'

'Who to? These capitalists simply fill their own pockets.'

'Who are these capitalists?'

'Those who exploit us, for them money is all that is of value. People mean nothing to them. Look at the wealthy people in this town, forever enjoying themselves. Any ordinary person who stands up to them always ends up in trouble.'

'You mean like when Alhaji Kaukai had the Sumaye boy imprisoned when he claimed his inheritance of farmland on his father's death, and Alhaji claimed he had rights over it?'

'Yes, precisely those kinds of evil tricks; the damage they do knows no bounds. That is why our party must win the forthcoming election. We all know that Allah created both the emir and the rat in the emir's house. One person's footstep is good enough for any other. When our party is elected we intend to break the chains of misery and slavery that have bound the common people.' (trans. from Katsina 1983: 69–70)

The moral didacticism of earlier work is here translated into direct political radicalism in a way which was entirely new to imaginative prose-writing. Nevertheless, radical writing in Hausa was burgeoning with the rise of the PRP and other political movements. Emanating, to some extent, from northern higher-education institutions, political tracts and radical journalism circulated widely during the early 1980s when this story was being written.[45]

PUBLISHING IN HAUSA AND RECENT DEVELOPMENTS: LOVE STORIES

Chapter 1 indicated that the oil boom of the 1980s saw spectacular growth in publishing in Hausa. The government introduction of Universal Primary Education in 1979 combined with cash both in the pockets of ordinary people as well as in the hands of Education Ministry officials charged with purchasing school books in bulk meant that international publishers saw opportunities in Nigeria, taking them sometimes into partnership with local publishers and sometimes going on their own. Thus Thomas Nelson, Evans Brothers and Longman, joined the longer established Oxford University Press and Macmillan. For Hausa this meant a burgeoning list of titles, many intended specifically for the school market, expanding on the long-established list belonging to NNPC in its partnership with Macmillan. Equally swiftly, when the value of the naira dropped and the economy faltered, these multi-national companies retrenched and cut back on their programmes or handed them on to their Nigerian partners. Other Nigerian companies – Triumph Publishers, Hudahuda Press (linked with Hodder and Stough-ton), and University Press (previously OUP) – continued to publish in Hausa but more sporadically. By 1989, the successor to the Gaskiya Corporation, the NNPC, had practically ceased publishing, beset by internal political wrangles and a harsh economic climate.[46]

The fact that such publishers have cut back drastically does not necessar-ily mean that publishing in Hausa has thereby ceased. The production of writing in Hausa has taken place over the years in a number of more or less discrete spheres and in different ways. Technological and social factors have affected the production of both prose and poetry so that the formal proc-esses of Western-style publishing are not the only channels that have been exploited.

During the nineteenth and early twentieth centuries, as was intimated in Chapter 1, writers were predominantly of the *malam* class, the literati versed in Arabic, studying the Koran and many of the branches of the Islamic sciences. Nineteenth-century writing typically was verse and Hausa verse formed one of the cardinal channels for the propagation of the faith among the peoples of the towns and cities of Hausaland. Intrinsic to the system of Islamic learning was a system whereby scholars with their pupils, *gardi*, lived a peripatetic existence on the fringes of small rural settlements, and at the same time, disabled mendicants, often blind, would travel from community to community reciting many of the more famous of the religious poems of the Jihad in return for alms (Hiskett 1975b). In this way religious literature made its way from urban to rural environments; from the literati to the ordinary people; and from script to voice.

In the traditional world of the Islamic literati, however, commercial con-siderations were, of course, secondary to the need to spread the word through the community. Where previously this had meant the copying and recopying by hand of manuscripts that were subsequently passed from hand to hand, the advent of photo-offset printing of *ajami* manuscripts, to which I referred in Chapter 1, meant that an 8-page manuscript could be produced in quantities of 2,000, for example, for a cost of approximately 10–15 kobo a copy (10–20 pence a copy in 1974). This entailed no typesetting, merely the production of a legible handwritten manuscript. In this way an author could take his manuscript to a printer and, either bearing the cost himself or with the financial aid of a patron, have a batch of copies printed. Although the same process could have applied to prose texts, it was the religious or-ders, the Tijaniyya and the Qadiriyya, who took most immediate advantage of the new technology in the 1970s to produce poetry and religious literature for distribution within the brotherhood networks and for sale through the established book trade in the markets. Stall-holders in the markets operate networks of agents who travel from quarter to quarter in the towns and through the villages carrying a selection of popular works, the great majority of them religious, for sale to the public at large.[47]

With the retrenchment of more formal publishing in the late 1980s, prose-writers began to turn back to the more informal private printing methods familiar from the world of *ajami* poetry. In so doing they made use not only of entrepreneurial patrons who saw some potential in the sale of popular books, but of organisational support structures which were also operating in the field of poetry-writing, and the distribution networks outside the formal sector.

A large number of clubs, societies, recreational organisations and informal organisations abound in Nigeria with elaborate constitutions and extensive lists of office holders. Within the area of poetry-writing two of the best known groups have been *Hausa Fasaha* 'Hausa Skill' and the *Hikima Kulob* 'Wisdom Club', which are discussed in Chapter 9. In the last twenty years a number of organisations in the cultural field have brought together writers, academics, teachers and others (*Kungiyar Nazarin Hausa* 'Association for the Study of Hausa'; *Kungiyar Marubuta da Manazarta Wakokin Hausa* 'The Association of Writers and Students of Hausa Song and Poetry'; *Kungiyar Mawallafa Hausa* 'The Association of Hausa Writers').[48] In the last few years, a number of clubs have been established which have provided their members with a way to get into print without the intermediary of a formal publisher, very much like the origins of Onitsha market literature. One of the most successful of these in the field of prose-writing has been the group in Kano known as *Raina Kama* 'Deceptive Appearances'. Their books are privately printed, mostly by a printer called Bamas in Kano, and often contain, in addition to the story, a group photograph of the members; photocopies of the covers of previous titles; lists of traders and bookshops from whom their books can be obtained; and, interestingly, an example of some writing in an invented script which they wish to promote as an entirely original Hausa invention.[49] Other groups, such as one called *Kukan Kurciya* 'The Cry of the Dove', also promote their previous titles and advertise their membership in their books. And in addition there have been a number of individuals producing titles, often with the endorsement of a notable academic or other figure, printed by a variety of Kano and other printers.

Clearly, there is a ready market for the novels these groups and individuals are producing.[50] Overwhelmingly, these books share the same themes: love, marriage, women's roles, domestic power relations, education, morality and the intergenerational struggle. A number of the writers are women and they are, possibly without exception, relatively young. The novels appear to owe more to English-language publishing of the Mills and Boon, and

James Hadley Chase variety than to any Hausa precedent. As far as I am able to gauge, their audience, buying books as never before, is also predominantly young, the product of the policy of Universal Primary Education instituted during the 1980s. In 1993 a typical novel of 100 pages by a member of *Raina Kama* was retailing at 15 or 20 naira, compared with 5 Naira for a Coke or 30 for a bowl of rice and stew.

Love, passion, and the power relations between men and women have not featured strongly in prose-writing heretofore. The appearance of a collection of love poetry, *Dausayin Soyayya* 'The Well-watered Pastures of Love' in the products of the Federal Department of Culture's competition was one of the first occasions when love had moved into the public world of written culture. Clearly, recent developments have put the subject squarely into the world of popular culture, bringing writing into a domain which has, until recently, been primarily oral: the domain of youth culture.

3

ORAL NARRATIVES: *TATSUNIYA* 'THE TALE', AND OTHER PROSE FORMS

HAUSA TERMINOLOGY IN RELATION TO NARRATIVE

Oral narratives have been among the earliest items, apart from vocabulary, to have been written down in roman-script Hausa. Nineteenth-century publications such as those of Schön (1876; 1885) and Robinson (1896) contained transcriptions of oral narratives along with biographical and other texts.[1] While *ajami*-script Hausa had been written since the Jihad period at the beginning of the nineteenth century, and perhaps earlier,[2] this material was predominantly poetry. With the advent of British colonial rule in the first years of the twentieth century, a major collection of narratives was assembled in print by the administrative officer, Frank Edgar. Edgar, working for the first resident of the then Sokoto province of Northern Nigeria, Major John Alder Burdon, assembled existing manuscripts and invited or instructed local Hausa *malamai* 'scholars' to put down in *ajami* any narratives they might know.[3] Edgar's collection was published in three volumes between 1911 and 1913 (Edgar 1911–13) and reorganised and translated by Skinner (1969).[4] Edgar's collection drew a primary distinction between *tatsuniyoyi* (pl.) 'tales' which were presumed fictional and *labaru/labarai* (pl.) 'traditions' which were stories that were presumed true. In Skinner's translation this primary distinction was further refined by grouping the *tatsuniya* (sing.) stories into animal stories, 'caricatures – ethnic and other stereotypes', moralising stories, 'men and women, young men and maidens', 'dilemma tales', and other content-based categories. Among the *labaru* were traditions of chiefly history: stories of the origins of states and kingdoms, stories of the deeds of Jihadist leaders, stories of wars and battles, great rulers and wise viziers.[5] Alongside these secular subjects there were the traditions of the Prophet, his Companions and Descendants which circulated throughout the Western Sudan.

In more recent discussion of the world of oral narratives rather different distinctions have been drawn. The word *labari* has tended to be used as a very general term implying any kind of narrative whether overt or hidden behind a proverb or other referential device. Thus Dangambo (1984b: 15–16), in pointing to the two different implications of the word *tatsuniya*: 'tale' and 'riddle', distinguishes between them by calling the one *tatsuniya mai labari* 'tatsuniya with a narrative', and the other *tatsuniya ta kacici-kacici* '*tatsuniya* with (lit.) "take-up-take-up"(a common term for riddle that conveys the interactive feature of the genre)'. Riddles are discussed in Chapter 4. Dangambo deploys further terminology to cover other aspects of what Edgar covered in his two-term system. *Almara* (sometimes *wasa kwakwalwa* 'sharpen the brain') he uses both for 'amusing stories'[6] and, more specifically for 'dilemma tales' which pose a question for the listener at the end, either a moral dilemma or a puzzle which might take some ingenuity to work out.[7] Two further terms are deployed. *Kissa* refers to 'true stories' of the Prophets and other Islamic religious narratives. *Hikaya* carries a functional connotation, referring to stories that have a didactic purpose, illustrated in Dangambo (1984b: 23). These terms are not exclusive in concentrating, for example, upon intentionality: to amuse, to teach; or upon content: the subject being a religious figure; or upon form: asking a question. These terminological distinctions are becoming increasingly the norm in academic writing in Nigeria as a result of Dangambo's position as a senior scholar of Hausa literature at Bayero University.[8]

TATSUNIYA: NARRATIVE CONTENT AND THE PATTERNS OF STORIES

Usually people refer to particular stories by the name of the central character(s). Heroes and villains, larger-than-life stereotypes, inhabit the centre of each story, predictable in their heroism or their villainy. Conflict or contest between protagonists is an important characteristic as the tale acts out the encounters and interactions between characters. Discussion of personal emotion or psychological state is unusual: such dimensions are conveyed primarily through the acting-out of the dialogue and action of the characters. The story-teller's art of 'acting-out' is focused on the use of voice and face. While the character stereotypes may allow the audience to grasp very quickly the potentials of any particular situation established by the story-teller, the direction of the interactions of two stereotypes is less predictable. Outcomes are more in the gift of the teller. The stereotyped characters of tales are both human (the ill-treated but faithful daughter, the corrupt judge, the pious *malam*,[9] the venal *malam*; the country bumpkin, the city slicker, the disobedient child, the arrogant prince, the Gwari man, the barber) and animal (hare, jackal, lion, hyena)[10] as well as liminal characters such as Dodo 'evil spirit/monster' and Gizo 'trickster'.[11] Each one among this cast of characters has an accompanying package of features ranging from aspects of personality, such as cunning, to manner of speech, such as a lisp in the case of the character Gizo, or incorrect pronunciation of Hausa in the case of the Fulani man:

> The spider (gizo) ... is the embodiment of cunning, dexterity and resourcefulness ... In some fables a small ground squirrel (kurege) replaces the spider. The lion (zaki) is the king of animals, a symbol of

power and dignity. The jackal has a special praise name, Malamin daji, (The Learned One of the bush), and he gives wise, though not always just verdicts. The goat (akwiya) and sheep (tunkiya) are by no means regarded as foolish animals, and the goat can outwit even the lion or the hyena ... (Piłaszewicz 1985: 193)

Using these standard characters, the narrator is able to assign roles, most typically the hero, the hero's assistant, the villain, the trickster and the dupes. The classic human characters are often paired as contrasts (partners in Hausa joking relationships): the city slicker against the country bumpkin; the non-Muslim Hausa, the *bamaguje*, against the Islamic teacher, the *malam*; the Kano man and the Katsina man; the Hausa man against the Gwari man. Westley (1986a) points to the significance of such dualities such that they are not simply the necessary representation of protagonist and antagonist in a story which relies upon contest or conflict, but rather they are the splitting apart of components within an idea, representing the embodiment of separate strands of thought:

One feature which clearly demonstrates the artifice of characters in oral narrative is their tendency to split into two or more identities to express an idea. In the three variants of 'Dan Kutungayya' the hero's brothers embody impetuousness while the hero himself continually behaves more cautiously. In order to express a theme of caution over ill-advised action the story develops this character split. (Westley 1986a: 142)

Following Westley then, it is possible to view the interactions of opposed characters as the working-out of ideas that contain within them internal contradictions. Filial piety, for example, as a theme explored through tales will frequently involve the representation in stereotyped characters of obedience and disobedience, dependence and independence. The playing-out of these dialectics in narrative becomes another way of outlining the themes of tales. Moreover, within the context of any particular narrative there may be an overarching morality proposed by the narrator such that approbation and disapprobation are distributed between characters: for example, the obedient child who suffers is ultimately rewarded and the spoilt child is punished. In this way, then, S. B. Ahmad (1986) groups tales into the following thematic categories: wicked treatment of children, forced marriage, disobedience to parents, reprehensible behaviour of the ruling class, oppression, and gratitude and humility, among others. Westley (1986a: 178–9) points out that the closing moral so typical of Aesop's fables is rare in Hausa tales. In his collection of tales there were none and he attributes those that occur in another published collection to the fact that the tales had been written down by *malamai* and not recorded from story-tellers themselves. Nevertheless, the moral frameworks of so many stories lead both S. B. Ahmad (1986) and

I. Y. Yahaya (1979a; 1979b) among others, to point to this educational function. M. G. Smith points to this broadly didactic function in his introduction to Skinner's *Hausa Tales and Traditions*:

> In a traditional preliterate society, folk education consists mainly in the transmission and reinforcement of stereotyped folk attitudes, values and conceptions, rather than in the transfer of technical 'knowledge' data or moral maxims ... There are tales of wells, or fishermen and of hunters, of hereditary thieves and other craft specialists, tales of madness and personal misfortune and social stereotypes of various ethnic groups – Maguzawa, or pagan Hausa, the Bugaje (s. Buzu) or Tuareg serfs, Fulani pastoralists and Nupe craftsmen, Gwari pagans, Arab merchants from Ghat or Ghadames, the Kanuri and the country bumpkins ill at ease in town ... These summary descriptions always refer to concrete social situations and to local types. (M. G. Smith 1969: xv–xix)

As we shall see, however, in a later section of this chapter, there are certain kinds of stories, namely trickster stories, where morality may appear ambiguous or contradictory. Any particular story may also be open to moral reinterpretation to provide an alternative gloss, as is also discussed later.

PATTERNS AND MODELS

In Chapter 2 we saw how the novel *Ruwan Bagaja* was constructed as a series of episodes framed within a quest story, the quest involving the righting of a wrong. The framework could be adjusted to include more or fewer episodes. Within many Hausa tales a similar frame encases a wide variety of repetitive elements. Perhaps the most common pattern is a transition from a situation of poverty, or some other form of lack, to one of riches or a situation where the lack has been liquidated.[12] This simple pattern can be extended to include a further reversal of fortunes, a further lack to be liquidated, or a parallel 'opposite', such as a second character who goes from riches to rags as the first character moves from rags to riches (S. B. Ahmad 1986: Ch. 4).

A common component within the performance of tales is song: song that is repeated, song that marks transitions, song that expresses the feelings of the characters, and song that draws the audience into participation in the performance. In S. B. Ahmad's study (1986) of stability and variation in oral narratives he points to the particularities of individual performers and their concentration in one case upon the didactic elements in stories, in another upon the extensive use of song, and in another upon a particular use of language. Features such as the occurrence of song vary from one performer to the next and are not an invariable feature of any particular story. Nevertheless, to be recognised as 'the same story' there has to be a shared core that is repeated from one rendering to another. In the case of tales the primary components of such a core are the outline plot and the relations between the central characters. The form of the story of the trapped lion rescued by the mouse that bites through the binding ropes requires a more powerful figure to be trapped with the weaker character able to find a way of release; this regardless of whether it is a lion or a buffalo, elephant or king helped by a dove, mouse, or lowly human being.

The variation that occurs between performances is not only in the strictly performative characteristics of voice and action. Two versions of the same story may present quite different moral viewpoints of the same people and events, or may reflect apparent differences in the background of the performers. Before looking at versions of two stories discussed by S. B. Ahmad (1986) and the differences between them, the context of the performance of the genre as a whole needs some clarification.

ATTITUDES TO *TATSUNIYOYI*

Prose-writing in roman-script Hausa can be traced to a particular historical moment in recent Nigerian history. The *tatsuniya* tradition is presumed to be of great antiquity and intriguing similarities between stories across diverse cultures have led scholars to examine such continuities in a variety of ways.[13] While colonial officials in the first years of the twentieth century collected tales in order to try to understand better the society in which they were working, the attitude of parts of Hausa society to tales and their performance needs to be understood if we are to appreciate the context within which they operate.

In tracing attitudes, particularly among men, to oral narratives in Hausa we can see a progressive marginalisation of the whole genre followed by a more recent move to rehabilitate it. S. B. Ahmad (1986) reports a view among the Islamic cleric class since the Jihad, and perhaps before, that oral narratives, *tatsuniyoyi*, while not specifically to be condemned, are *hululu* 'idle chatter' and to be avoided by all good Muslims. This position he credits for the fact that urban, male, public culture frowns upon the telling of such tales. Male heads of household would not consider it seemly to be present at, or to participate in, any such story-telling sessions.[14] Typically their attitude is that such activities are only for women and children in the privacy of the compound at the end of the day.[15] In Ahmad's collection, women narrators predominate. It is by no means clear that, in earlier times, story-telling was more generally current in male, public culture. What is clear, however, is that there has been a move to bring *tatsuniyoyi* more directly into public culture in recent years. S. B. Ahmad (1986: Ch. 2) reports that, since the 1970s, a cultural revival movement, which has been manifest in a variety of ways, sought to counter the 'idle chatter' tag attached to tales and to provide an educational justification for bringing tales more directly into formal

education and into the celebration of Hausa 'traditional' culture. State
ministries of arts and culture in Nigeria have been busily patronising dance
troupes, poets, singers and, to a lesser extent, story-tellers through the
organisation of festivals and other performance occasions. The drive to
incorporate tales into the formal educational process has been spearheaded
by university academics. Ibrahim Yaro Yahaya (1979a) put the case for
'Hausa folklore as an educational tool' concentrating upon the ability of
tales to inculcate moral values. This assessment of tales as fulfilling a
valuable educational social role within 'traditional' society constitutes the
counter to their being condemned as 'idle chatter'. Yahaya himself is the
author of a substantial series of primary-school books published by Oxford
University Press (Nigeria) in which he retells a large number of such tales.
Such books are intended for use both as reading materials and as models for
children in a classroom situation for telling and writing their own versions. A
broad revaluation of other types of narrative including the stories of origin,
of oral history generally, and their importance to the construction of Hausa
culture and identity, is found in Abdulkadir (1984).

The reassessment of the value of tales is part of a wider cultural movement to revive and strengthen the Hausa language and to rediscover the
value of cultural 'roots' in opposition to the advance of English and Western
culture, whether imported directly through textbooks and television or in
the form of an English-based Nigerian culture. Many of the protagonists of
this movement are themselves bilingual and 'bicultural', working within, or
being products of, the formal-education sector. Their aim is to secure the
long-term future of Hausa and of *al'adun gargajiya* 'customs inherited from
the past'.[16] In this sense, then, the move to bring in a particular genre from
the 'cultural cold' is part of a broader move to prevent the cultural
marginalisation of the language and culture as a whole in relation to competing languages and cultural forms within Nigeria. Within the panorama of
Hausa literature/orature, however, this recent history demonstrates the way
in which positions within a cultural 'pecking order' are renegotiable – a
dominant group, the clerics, marginalised tale-telling, or so it would appear,
only for a later dominant group, the modern-day intellectuals to rehabilitate
it. Manifestly, any pecking order is the projection of one particular group in
society. Other groups, other audiences, will look at their culture from other
angles.

TALES AS AN ARENA OF CONTESTATION

S. B. Ahmad (1986: 109–10) reports a tale-telling programme on Kano
State radio, presented by a man, in which the presenter recites tales sent in
to him by his listeners. Interestingly, Ahmad indicates that the presenter has
clear ideas on the constitution of the 'world of the tale'; he edits out any
reference to cars, telephones, radios or Europeans. The tales live in a

reconstructed vision of a mid-nineteenth-century Hausa world with aristocracy and peasants, *malamai* 'Islamic clerics' and other ethnic groups, but with nothing of modern Nigeria. This moulding of a vision, to which we referred in Chapter 2, represents a model to which the audience are supposed to adhere. Remodelling takes place all the time as different individuals take command of the space afforded them by such narratives. Tales constitute a mode of discourse within which women's voices can be heard. Men are now speaking through tales but this appears to be something of a relatively recent development. In the following discussion we look at Stephens' representation of one such woman's voice and Ahmad's presentation of competing voices as between a woman's and a man's version of the same story.

In discussing Hausa tales from Niger relating to marriage, Stephens writes:

> The first two major conflicts in another popular Hausa tale specifically pose the question of whether sons or daughters are more valuable (Stephens 1981: 531–43). The King of the East, father of several sons, is indebted to the King of the West, whose children are all daughters. The debtor refuses to make good his loan until his friend has a son come collect the debt. Sons, as opposed to daughters, thus represent superior wealth: without them the debt cannot be claimed.
>
> However the King of the West has a daughter, 'Yal Baturiya, a bold girl who declares that she is just as suited as a brother would be to collect her father's due. So she disguises herself as a boy and queries her father's stallion, 'Kili, horse of my father, if you take me, will you bring me back?' Receiving an affirmative reply, 'Yal Baturiya mounts her steed and sets off.
>
> Along the way she politely greets an ant who joins her quest. Once at her destination she announces her mission, and the men at court give her a series of tasks to do to prove that she is indeed a son, not a daughter. Each trial involves a choice, and each time alternatives are presented, the stallion Kili reveals the appropriate response for a boy. First she chooses correctly between two staple foods. Next, she sorts, rather than mixes, a collection of grain; her new friend, the ant, gives invaluable help. Finally she must go swimming to expose her private parts. Kili distracts her audience by charging after the king's horse … This final test passed, the debtor's nobles conclude they must pay off the disguised princess. As she departs, she taunts them with her proven equality, 'I'm 'Yal Baturiya and I came to fetch my father's money. I'm a girl, not a boy.' …
>
> This tale argues forthrightly that girls are equal to and as independent as boys. By disguising herself as a son, the heroine effectively portrays both genders simultaneously; her challengers are unable to tell the difference. She matches any brother she might have had in

defending her family's fortune, and her deception makes her superior to a large group of male adversaries. (Stephens 1991: 224–5)

While such representations of women and their relation to men clearly present a particular view, there has been little discussion, as far as I am aware, of the degree to which there is a dialogue between such views and other more male-oriented positions, either in the form of statement and riposte within story-telling events (Ahmad, Westley and Stephens all indicate a broad division of the sexes, at least as far as adults are concerned, in participation in such events), or in terms of views of male and female roles as between one genre and another. S. B. Ahmad (1986: 100–5, reproduced in S. B. Ahmad 1989) discusses the way in which a man narrator and a woman narrator, at separate times and without knowledge of each other's version, produce interestingly different interpretations of the same story. Ahmad summarises the shared core of the two versions of a story, entitled, in the one case, 'The Man Picked up by a Dove', and in the other, 'The Man who had a Gown of Dum-palm Fronds'. The summary core is:

> There was a very poor man, who was so poor that he could not clothe or house himself properly. One day a dove took pity on him and offered to make him rich if he promised to reply 'yes' whenever she called to him, saying 'poor man'. He readily agreed. The dove miraculously made him rich. Whenever she came and called 'poor man' he answered 'yes'. He then married a wife whom he loved very much. She objected to his answering the dove and he listened to her. So when the dove came and called, he refused to answer as he had done before. The dove therefore suddenly changed him back to his former state. (S. B. Ahmad 1986: 100)

Ahmad goes on to discuss two versions of the story, one by Kubura Magaji, in 1986 a 22-year-old housewife from Babura, married with two small children, the other by Sani Abdullahi, a 34-year-old married man known for his work as a teller of tales on Radio Kano:

> Version 82 was narrated by Kubura Magaji. She is a housewife and at the time she narrated this story had no co-wife. Her version would seem to reflect her anxiety at the prospect of a co-wife and expresses what she feels about polygamy. In her version she made the man marry twice and puts the blame for the man's tragedy squarely on the second wife. The first wife is portrayed as polite and understanding:
> ... He then married a wife. When the wife heard the exchange between him and the dove, she asked him 'Who is this?' He then said 'It is a small dove I picked up.' Then the first wife (satisfied) did not say anything.

When Kubura articulated her words she clearly adopted a respectful voice to convey this politeness. This contrasts sharply with the way she portrayed the second wife:

> ... Then the new wife said 'I am fed up with this noise (the exchange between the man and the dove). Why should you worry us with *zumun-zumun* (a mockery of the exchange) ... She dare not come to this house again.'

Not only are the words rude (*na gaji, surutu*) but also Kubura delivered them as such. In fact the second wife went further and intimidated the husband into not answering the dove. Clearly then the marriage to the second wife is a mistake since it leads him to break his solemn promise to the dove. Had he not married for a second time he would have continued to enjoy his riches. The moral then, from this point of view, is: never marry a second wife when the first is polite and understanding. And it was taken as such by members of the audience.

Version 33 on the other hand was by Sani Abdullahi ... who at the time of narration was married and head of his own family. He does not interpret the story from the same point of view as Kubura. In his version it does not really matter whether the man has one or more wives. The mistake, according to his version, is listening to any woman at all. Women, as portrayed by the wife, lack understanding and tolerance. The wife objects to the man's continuing to answer the dove's call on the following grounds:

> ... The girl remembered that her husband was an emir. She herself was the daughter of a rich man, her father was important in the town. Therefore she said to her husband 'Look, I am fed up with this stupidity. You are an emir, there is nothing you do not have. How can you allow a common bird to call you a poor man everyday and you answer her? As for me, my father is rich and an important man who has everything. Let me tell you, if ever that bird comes back and calls you a poor man again, and you again answer her, that would be the end of our marriage. You would then have to divorce me and marry a poor girl like you to live with.'

The wife is portrayed above as rude, intolerant and snobbish. She cannot see beyond the material possessions and seemingly unchangeable social world around her. The reason for this according to this version is that she is a woman. This misogynist view is reinforced when the man is returned to his former poverty-stricken state, on failing to answer the dove, by the statement that:

> ... he promised never again to take advice from a woman.

While Kubura Magaji's version concerns the problem of marrying a second wife, this version presents a view to men concerning women in general. Variations in the versions of the same story can represent a difference of moral or ideological viewpoints, in this case as between men and women. (S. B. Ahmad 1986: 101–4 reproduced in S. B. Ahmad 1989: 125–6)

Tales, then, can be an arena of contestation in addition to the didactic and entertainment functions which have been widely commented upon. While contest and conflict, whether serious or frivolous, are the stuff of tale content they can also function as an arena of debate between people over gender roles and relations, superior/inferior relations, intergenerational relations, and general behaviour and attitudes, regardless of whether they are fantastical stories of monsters and jinn or plain encounters between humans going about their daily business.[17] Using a variety of stereotypes, tellers of tales explore the infinite possibilities of encounter and attitude, attitudes both on the part of the characters as they rub shoulders with each other and attitudes of the narrators to the activities and words of their subjects. In this sense tales share with written prose and with drama, as we shall see in Chapter 5, a fascination with the interactions of people in a wide variety of power relationships, in the domestic sphere and in public life.

Rufa'i (1982) explores this issue of power relations specifically between *talakawa* 'ordinary people' and *sarakuna* 'the ruling class' by looking at four tales in which representatives of these two classes interact. His first example is the story of 'Ta Kitse' 'The Suet Maid'.[18] Rufa'i sees the ability of ordinary people to thwart the arbitrary and oppressive actions of an aristocrat within the story as particularly significant: the king is not able to dispose of the bull that has been forcibly seized without the agreement of the old woman who owns it; the king has to abide by the usual procedures of obtaining a wife when he wishes to marry the Suet Girl, he cannot simply take her by force. The derogatory view presented of the king is interpreted by Rufa'i in terms of the historical relationship between a Fulani upper class and a Hausa lower class:

> History shows that the Hausa and the Fulani have lived together for many years. Living side by side has produced familiarity and joking relationships. Perhaps it is this joking relationship which has produced the presence of Fulani in Hausa tales. If that is not the case, then it must be that Hausa people are venting their frustration at the fact that the Fulani have come to rule over them. Their frustration appears in tales where they can say what they like to indicate to the Fulani that it is not intrinsic cleverness that has brought them to power. Put another way, how could it be that wandering nomads have the wit to hold down city people? In short then, tales are an arena, a space in which to vent anger and frustration at the humiliation of the ordinary people at the hands of the ruling class ...
>
> This space for the expression of anger is perhaps what prevents the

ordinary people from rising up in revolt that could damage both themselves and others. In my view, this space, this arena is rather like Speaker's Corner in London's Hyde Park where people can come and say whatever they like in their attacks upon those in power and then go back home to their beds to sleep in peace. (trans. from Rufa'i 1982: 88–9)

Rufa'i's argument that tales function rather in the manner of rituals of rebellion, as safety valves in the maintainance of the status quo, is an interesting one that requires further case studies of situations in which political tensions, be they in the micro-environment of domestic tensions or in the macro-environment of broad political movements, are resolved through processes involving the articulation of symbolic representations such as are to be found in tales. Tales as a genre may not be the form deployed, but Rufa'i's point concerns the communicative function rather than the specific form. In many tales the power relations between superior and inferior are mediated by the archetypal go-between, the most complex figure in the panorama of stereotypes to be found in tales: the trickster.

TRICKSTER

One class of tale has come to exemplify the intrinsic ambiguity, and therefore contestability, of interpretation. The trickster tale is one of the most widespread types and, in many ways, has come to represent the whole category of *tatsuniya* in popular perception. For many people the first examples that spring to mind at the mention of *tatsuniya* are the tales of Gizo and his mate, Ƙoƙi. Gizo occurs in stories of animals and of humans. Straddling both worlds, he is the epitome of greed, laziness, cowardice and licentiousness while at the same time being cunning, clever and a successful deceiver. Gizo's world is one in which deceit, disguise and trick are being continuously perpetrated, either against him or by him. Each story in which he appears plays up one or other of his characteristics: overwhelmingly greedy here, villainous there, stupid in one instance, clever in another. Many different and sometimes contradictory characteristics come together in Gizo making him one of the more complicated personalities by comparison with the more one-dimensional figures that people other tales.[19] 'Gizo' is often rendered in English as 'spider' but a number of scholars have pointed out that Gizo is essentially human in his representation in tales:[20] he stands upright, has two arms and two legs and is small of stature. However, in illustrations in recent publications, Gizo has been represented physically as a spider and it may well be that a generation of Nigerian Hausa school children will indeed begin to cast Gizo as a spider in their mind's eye (Yahaya 1971/2). It is true that the word for a spider in Hausa, *gizo-gizo*, conveys a connection with Gizo, 'Gizo-like thing', and the word for one of the praying mantises is *ƙoƙi-ƙoƙi* 'Ƙoƙi-like thing', implying therefore a pairing of spider and mantis in their association with Gizo and Koki.

Many of the tales discussed by S. B. Ahmad (1986) carry an overall condemnation of oppressive behaviour by the powerful. There are narratives in which the more usual condemnation of certain kinds of behaviour is mitigated by their being seen as part of the only strategy available to the socially powerless. And this is where the trickster tales are of particular interest. Gizo tales can be viewed as one part of a dialogue about the exercise of power. Some tales in Ahmad's collection condemn oppressive behaviour by the prince, the emir, the judge, the man of substance, the husband. In so doing the tales accept the legitimacy of the power of these people if such power is exercised justly and with discretion. Gizo tales approach this issue from a different angle, to some extent, by presenting reprehensible behaviour, trickery, deceit, as potentially successful, even if not entirely acceptable, strategies for the survival of the weak and insignificant faced with the overwhelming power of other social actors. Gizo is not always punished for theft, for manslaughter or for causing mayhem. Gizo tales are often an ironically humorous, amoral demonstration of the only weapons available to the weak and powerless in society.

The potential for alternative attitudes to Gizo and his activities is very great and in the following extract from S. B. Ahmad (1986, reproduced in S. B. Ahmad 1989) we see radically different glosses placed upon Gizo's role in two versions of the same story, the one entitled 'Gizo and the Birds' narrated by a young man, Dan Liman, and the other 'Gizo and the Cranes' by Sani Abdullahi, the same narrator as discussed above. The summary core of the two stories is:

> Gizo asked some birds to take him to the tree top which was in the middle of a river to eat fruit. The birds agreed and lent him some feathers to enable him to fly. On reaching the tree top, Gizo prevented the birds from eating any. So when he was asleep they took away their feathers and left him stranded. When he woke up he fell down to the bottom of the river. There he claimed to be the relative of the 'yan ruwa 'water spirits' he found there. He was given shelter and then he was taken up to the shore. On land, an animal ate the fish Gizo had got from the river. Annoyed, Gizo tricked him, tied him up and branded him with an iron bar. The animal on being released later looked for Gizo in order to punish him. When they met, Gizo managed to escape by trickery. (S. B. Ahmad 1986: 93)

Ahmad traces the sequence of three episodes that makes up both versions of the story: (a) hunger, friendship, betrayal of friendship, punishment; (b) need to escape, friendship, betrayal of friendship and escape; and (c) lack of fair treatment, punishment (for the other animal), escape.[21] These recursive sequences are overlaid with interpretative differences as follows:

In 'Gizo and the birds' the story is set in the bush where harsh reality is the survival of the fittest. This setting and the details given about Gizo's actions justify his trickery and attract the audience's sympathy to him. This way of portraying Gizo starts right from the opening sentences:

> ... It was during famine. No food anywhere except in the middle of the river. Nobody could reach the food except, of course, the birds. *Well, Gizo was caught by hunger.* (emphasis added)

These opening sentences give the background of general famine and availability of food only to those who could fly. Thus Gizo's tricking of the birds is put into perspective and this background explains Gizo's gluttony when he was taken to the tree top. Further, the performer reiterates that *To shi Gizo ya riga ya sha yunwa* 'Well, Gizo had already suffered from hunger' to justify Gizo's greed.

Other sympathetic words for Gizo occur when the birds take away their feathers. He is described as *Af! anka bar Gizo huntu nai tsakar ruwa* 'Oh! Gizo was left helpless in the middle of the river' – a predicament provoking sympathy.

Later in the story the lion eats up Gizo's fish. The situation is again described in favour of Gizo:

> ... The lion ate up (the fish). Gizo did not even taste it. Poor Gizo, he was annoyed. He went and got his fish from the water spirits and it was eaten up before he could even taste it.

This description sympathizes with Gizo, and reflects badly upon the lion. And this indicates that the physical punishment inflicted on the lion by Gizo was justified.

This favourable treatment by the performer runs right through the whole narrative. In fact the tone of the story seems to be geared towards making Gizo a hero, a person who uses his wonderful talent not only to survive, but also to punish bullying animals like the lion. Even the very last sentence reinforces this bias: *To ka ji inda Gizo ya kubuta da zaki ya yi mai wulakanci* 'This is how Gizo managed to escape when he would have been disgraced by the lion'.

Clearly from the portions quoted and the general tone of the story, the performer is sympathetic in his portrayal of Gizo. This is not the case with the performer in Gizo and the Cranes. The performer of Gizo and the Cranes portrays Gizo as a cheat and a double-dealer.

In Gizo and the Cranes, Gizo cheats his wife by eating three of the four dates given to him by the cranes. His motivation for wanting to go to the tree top is not that he was hungry but because the dates were sweet. He burns other people's houses to convince the cranes it is morning simply because he is eager to go to the tree. He prevents the crane and his wife, who were kind to him, from eating the ripe fruits because he wants them all himself. The general tone of this version, unlike Gizo and the birds, is to make Gizo someone who causes trouble for others without the slightest justification.

The different portrayal of Gizo in the two versions demonstrates that performers can take opposite points of view, sustain them with the details they provide and at the same time maintain the same basic underlying structure of the *tatsuniya*. (adapted from S. B. Ahmad 1986: 93–100; see also S. B. Ahmad 1989: 121–4)

The trickster style of interaction between characters in a tale is not limited to Gizo. Deceit, trick and counter-trick are the stuff of other tales where, for example, the Kano and the Katsina man lock horns, or the pagan Hausa man outwits the *malam*. And as we have seen, this type of narrative had a strong influence upon early prose-writing in Hausa, most particularly upon Abubakar Imam's *Ruwan Bagaja*, where Alhaji Imam and Malam Zurke took turn and turn about in their attempts to trick each other.

4

SHORT-FORM VERBAL ART

In similar manner to the functional distinctions within terminology relating to narrative, so also within the field of 'short-form verbal art' there are a variety of terms, *karin magana, habaici, zambo, kirari, take*, which differentiate, to some extent, on the basis of communicative function.

KARIN MAGANA

Karin magana 'folded/broken speech' refers to one of the characteristic features of proverbial utterances: to contain hidden meaning that requires of the listener an interpretative leap.[1] It was this characteristic which Gidley's informants insisted upon as the central characteristic of *karin magana* as opposed to a variety of other types of saying (Gidley 1974). Other sayings could be accepted as standard, recognised phrases – catch-phrases, slogans and the like – but would not be deemed to display the necessary levels of hidden meaning appropriate to *karin magana*. In the case of Gidley's discussion, and in the teaching manuals of Yahaya et al. (1992: vol. 3, 30–1), the deployment in speech of *karin magana*, or any of the other types of phrase, were viewed as marks of *azanci*, implying skill, wit, and rhetorical ability, the opposite of the halting literalness of the child or the learner. This latter catch-all term relates to the aesthetics of language, whether it concerns the product of the poet, singer, writer or politician. The discriminations made by Gidley between sayings and *karin magana* proper reflect a honed aesthetic sensibility rather than an easily applicable set of commonly recognised categories. For many people, the phrase *karin magana* is the general term for a fixed phrase, often (but by no means always) with metaphorical significance and which conveys, at a level of generality, an axiomatic idea. The recognition of fixity (even if the phrase has variants) means that they stand apart from surrounding speech, not a novel metaphor deployed by a creative speaker, but the reiteration by one speaker of the speech of others. This reference to the speech of others can provide authority for the phrase, or place the speaker in a context in which responsibility for the words is devolved on to others in addition to the speaker. As precedent, as an appeal to ideas which are deemed to be generally held, as indirect speech with all its advantages of avoiding immediate confrontation or responsibility, *karin magana* then, constitute one of the building blocks of daily discourse.[2] H. S. Koko (1989) discusses proverbial usage among women in Sokoto, suggesting that women make greater use of the potential for veiled speech in *karin magana* than do men, and that they place great store by the ability to impress and be combative in speech. She goes further to indicate that, beyond differences in usage between men and women, there are specific *karin magana* that are the preserve of women, listing some 120 that are typically used by women.

In the literary genres, whether oral or written, discussed in this book, such sayings are ubiquitous. Bagaye (1992) points to the fact that many sayings have particular narratives attached to them, tales to which the sayings are the summation or the mnemonic. *Karin magana* are as much building blocks in song, poetry and narrative as they are in daily conversation and they display internal characteristics of pattern that make them part of the range of fashioned and honed language so typical of poetry and song. Indeed, when the structural patterns and imagery of poetry and rhetoric are examined, there is clearly little qualitative difference between the language characteristics of short-form verbal art and those of poetry.

A variety of characteristics of *karin magana* have drawn the attention of commentators, such as ellipsis (C. A. Hill 1972), lexical incompatibility (Skinner 1988) and internal balance and bipartite structure (Jang 1994), The 'textuality' of *karin magana* lies in the sense of their having been fashioned, and this fashioning is seen in their semantics, sound and structure. A full analysis of the manifestations of this fashioning is too large a subject for this discussion, but some of the more generally typical characteristics can be summarised. Jang (1994) points to a framework that operates on many levels. He sees a regularly repeated bipartite structure in *karin magana* where there is created a sense of balance between the two parts. The fulcrum upon which the 'see-saw' sits may be a pause, a gap, or may be a phrase, such as '... is better than ...', or '... is the answer to ...' or some other notion in which inheres a relationship between two entities.[3] Time and again Jang sees a quantitative balance between the two related parts: the number of syllables will be the same on each side of the fulcrum, and this will be reinforced by additional parallel features between them. But sometimes there may not be equality between the two sides, or there may be differences between the quantitative 'fulcrum' and the position of a break between grammatical phrases that make up the saying. In the following examples from Jang (1994) there is exact quantitative balance between the two parts:

Kome nisan daji / da gari gabansa.
Ana kukan ƙarya / ga mutuwa ta zo.
Ina ganin kura da rana / yaya zan yarda ta cije ni?
Na shiga ban ɗauka ba / ba ta fid da ɓarawo.
Mushen tinkiya / ya fi / yankakken biri.
Haƙuri / maganin / duniya.

No matter how extensive the forest, there is a town at the end of it.
You are shedding false tears, and here comes death.
I see the hyena by daylight, how could I let it bite me?
'I entered but took nothing' will not save the thief.
A sheep that has died is better than a slaughtered monkey.
Patience is the answer to the ways of the world.

The study by C. A. Hill (1972) is aware of the importance of such symmetry but concentrates on a particular characteristic that allows the achievement of symmetry while reinforcing the condensed, concentrated nature of such sayings. His work on ellipsis points out the many subtle ways in which ellipsis and symmetry complement one another: through the omission of the *ne/ce/ne* stabiliser, the person/aspect pronouns, negation markers; through nominalisation of verbal sentences, genitivisation, and many other processes. Hill also sees these same processes at work in the construction of identificatory praise-epithets which are discussed later in this chapter. The process of imposing symmetry and of concentrating meaning into more succinct expression is one of the central characteristics of the fashioning of the language of proverbs, and such fashioning is precisely the process of 'fixing' the 'fixed phrase'. Skinner (1988) draws attention to a further dimension of such fixed phrases at the level of meaning: the propensity for sayings to juxtapose, often between the two parts, two incompatible or opposed concepts, thereby requiring of the listener a leap of interpretation to find some way to synthesise the antithesis, to make 'sense' of the 'nonsense'. There is a *karin magana* which starts *gobara daga kogi* 'fire coming from the river' in which the juxtaposition of fire and water, with the implication that fire can come from water, is provocative. The listener, in making sense of it, is guided by the clues provided in the second half of the phrase *magani nata Allah* 'God alone could handle such a thing' (i.e. this situation is far too difficult to handle). Skinner provides other examples where incompatibilities demand interpretation:

Wanka da gari ba ya maganin yunwa.
Wankan wuta sau guda kan yafa.
Kasa ta gudu ta je ina?

Bathing in flour does not solve the problem of hunger.
    (i.e. having the equipment is no good if you don't use it properly)

Bathing in fire, one showers once.
   (i.e. once bitten, twice shy)
The earth runs off and goes where?
   (i.e. a total impossibility)

(Skinner 1988: 237, 238, 239)

Habaici and *zambo* are functional distinctions describing the illocutionary force of the piece of language in question. The first term implies 'innuendo' and the second 'ridicule'. They lie on a continuum that reaches to *zagi* 'abuse'. While *zagi* may employ particular and very colourful vocabulary, *habaici*, in particular, refers not to the vocabulary being used but the purpose behind the speaker's words. In this sense then, *habaici* can be applied equally as well to song, poetry and narrative (perhaps), as to proverb. However, typically it is to short-form fixed phrases that the word is most often applied, since innuendo relies upon hidden meanings such as are implicit in *karin magana*.[4] Differences in illocutionary force picked up by the Hausa terms can be illustrated by looking at the different purposes behind one single phrase, such as the *karin magana*:

Hadirin ƙasa, maganin mai kabido.   The dust storm is the answer to the person wearing a raincoat.

This phrase, as *karin magana*, refers to the lack of protection from an 'attack from below' provided by a shield oriented upwards. The phrase could be so deployed in a wide variety of contexts. Its use would be *habaici* if the implication were sardonic or critical implying that someone who thought they were invincible, for example, had come a cropper. In this sense, then, the *karin magana*, typically deployed by a speaker towards the listener, is being used as *habaici*, where the speaker's remarks refer to a third person, who may or may not be listening, rather than to the person addressed. In fact this phrase can be used in at least one further way. The following part of this chapter discusses epithets, and this phrase can be deployed epithetically as self-praise when, for example, a boxer shouts out *Sai ni hadirin ƙasa, maganin mai kabido* 'I am the dust storm, the answer to he who thinks he is protected'. The phrase can then operate as *karin magana*, *habaici* or as *kirari* (see below), depending upon the context.

KIRARI AND TAKE

Kirari and *take* have generally been represented as 'praise-epithets' and 'drummed equivalents of verbal epithets' respectively, although there is a confusing variety of usage in the literature as between these terms and a further term, *waka* 'song'.[5] In this discussion *take* is used to refer to short phrases, whether drummed or vocalised, that are then combined into *kirari* texts of some greater length. To varying degrees commentators have concentrated upon the purposive nature of the terms, foregrounding the intent to praise and exhort, whether it be in short phrase, extended sequence of phrases or in more elaborate song (Abubakar Ahmed 1980; I. Bello 1985; Dangambo 1979; Gidley 1975; A. U. Kafin-Hausa 1982, 1985; Mahmoud 1972; B. Yakubu 1972; Zarruḳ and Alhasan 1982).

Kirari, like the sayings discussed above, contain fixed phrases displaying all the characteristics of ellipsis, metaphor and internal patterning that are typical of such phrases. Powe (1984) provides an extensive inventory of short phrases (*take* in his terms) that are invoked by and for wrestlers, boxers and other combatants. For example:

Dan Bazamfara mai dambe!
Dan taguwa da saurin girma!
Dawan da kututturai; dawan da mala'iku!
Dawo Audu ci bayi; mai horo da masaba!
Duna na Sakkwato; mai raba gardama!

Man from Zamfara, a boxer!
Young he-camel of rapid growth!
A jungle filled with dangerous stumps; a jungle filled with death's angels!
Return to us Audu, capturer of slaves who punishes with a blacksmith's
    hammer!
Fearsome man from Sokoto; settler of disputes!

(Powe 1984: 373–4)

Each of these is deployed to identify one particular individual combatant, either shouted by the combatant himself or by someone else about him. Ames, Gregersen and Neugebauer (1971) demonstrate how such phrases can be recalled and relayed by drum, with or without the simultaneous vocalisation of the phrase. A number of drums, notably the variable-pitch hour-glass drum, *kalangu*, can render the high-low contours of a Hausa phrase.[6] This is done by matching the pattern of high and low tones with the high pitch produced by squeezing the tensioning thongs or the low pitch of released thonging on the drum, combined with a match between the heavy and light syllables inherent in any Hausa phrase and a pattern of short and long intervals in the drumming.[7] Ames, Gregersen and Neugebauer provide an example of the relationship between drum and voice (the example below has been adapted for ease of understanding):

dà ar–zì–kii dà has–sa–dàa   tàa–re su kèe kwaa-naa tàa-re su kèe taa–shìi
wealth   and   jealousy   together they lie   together they rise

(● short, O long, ✔ rising, ` low tone)

(adapted from Ames, Gregersen and Neugebauer 1971: 29)

The drum phrase evokes the words in circumstances where the words are already known. In the case of *take* that are attached to particular offices of state many local people will recognise the reference regardless of who the temporary occupant of that office may be. S. Ahmed (1984: 41) gives examples of *take* that are attached to the office of the emir of Zaria:

Sadauki ga saraki	Warrior among emirs
Adali ga sarki	Upholder of justice among emirs
Kyauren gabas ya taho	The door to the East is here/The white metal is here
Amalen gabas ya taho	The large male camel of the East is here

On the other hand, the drum/word phrase may be exclusively the property of an individual, be they boxer, young tearaway, or hunter, and recognised only among the immediate circle of that individual. In certain cases, particular celebrities and their identificatory catch-phrases can have very widespread currency.[8]

King (1967: 2), in discussing *kirari* for spirits in the possession cult, *bori*, termed them 'identifying praise epithet' that had to contain the essence of the thing or person identified. Ames, Gregersen and Neugebauer (1971) commented upon the identificatory function underlying *take* in these terms:

> *Taakee* [identificatory catch-phrase] of the youth are a kind of personal badge and socially approved way in which a young person can state publicly something he wishes to say about himself or others ... [*T*]*aakee* are not restricted to praise. They are commonly taunts and ridicule, ranging from mild humorous ones to bitter, scornful ones. The name of the person is never mentioned; rather he is obliquely referred to often with an ingenious use of metaphor. (Ames, Gregersen and Neugebauer 1971: 18–19)

In his detailed and provocative study of Hausa 'combat literature' (by which he means the oral literature associated with boxing, wrestling, hunting and other combative pastimes), Powe takes issue with the primacy of praise in defining *take* and *kirari*, opting instead, on the basis of his study, for the role of *take* (in word or sound) as 'identifiers', and *kirari* as 'poetic declamations consisting of adventures, lists, demands, openers and closers' (Powe 1984: 340). Such phrases display imagery and patterns of rhythmic language to great illocutionary effect in the invocation and identification of self, others, spirits, places or ideas.

The deployment of *take* and *kirari* may be intended to produce a wide variety of effects. In Hausa terms the most commonly ascribed purposes are *yabo* 'praise' but also *tumasanci* 'flattery', a broad concept that covers both directed flattery and the production of amusing, pleasing speech or conversation so as to put the target in good humour. In either case the term draws attention to the personally directed nature of this use of language. Even more direct and directed is the notion of *zuga* 'incitement/encouragement' where there is an openly conative intent, trying to make the target do something, particularly something requiring an effort or involving danger, which is why *zuga* is a primary characteristic of the deployment of *take* and *kirari* in wrestling, boxing and other combative activities, including, in times past, hand-to-hand combat on the battlefield. These purposive terms, such as *zuga*, apply not only to the forms under discussion here. G. Bello (1976) has discussed similar intentions behind much praise-song within the court tradition, the subject of Chapter 6. The traditional chiefly courts of northern Nigeria have been the locus of much *kirari* performance in the context of the praise-singing tradition.[9] A distinction has been drawn among performers between the praise-singing group and the individual praise-crier, the *dan ma'abba*,[10] whose shouted phrases are very often interpolated into the performance of a singing group. In addition to shouting out during the performances of singers, the praise-crier will shout out during public gatherings where the patron is present, be they traditional title-holder or military governor (see Gidley 1975).

Powe provides a detailed analysis of the many patterns to be discerned in lengthy *kirari* performances, but to provide something of the flavour of one such performance in which a *dan tauri* 'performer with knife blades' praises himself, I quote from Powe:

Ni na Ramlatu maye
Ramlatu na ga kin fi mata kyau
Mata halin ƙwarai suk fi ki
Ni baƙar wuta maci littafi
Ni kahirin kare, sai sarƙa
Ni babbaken ruwa na Yazidu
Kowa ya sha ni, ba shi ke labari
Aljana gafara, wuta sallamu alaikum
Arna ga babbanku, wanda bashi nan ya dawo
Sarƙa ba ta yi ɗin, sai bawa
In bawa ya ƙiya
Ku sa min yagwai
In yagwai ya ƙiya
Ku sa kistani
In kistani ya ƙiya
Ku kawo abawa
In wannan ya ƙiya
Ku kama gabanku
Shi kwana ƙiyama
Don ku watsaya
Ayihu, ayihu
Yaro, jaye! jaye!

I am of the sorceress Ramlatu!
Ramlatu, you are prettier than other women!
The character of women is better than yours!
I am the black fire that consumes books!
I am an unbelieving dog, only a chain!
I am the gathering water of Yazidu!
Whoever drinks me vanishes!
Excuse me, O djinns, greetings O fire!
Pagans here is your lord, he who was not here has returned!
If the chain doesn't work, try bark!
If bark fails
Try rope!
If rope fails
Try cord!
If cord fails
Try coarse thread!
If this fails
Grab your leader!
He will awaken in the afterlife!
So that you disperse!
Hey! Hey!
Boy, move back! move back!

(Powe 1984: 524–5)

Chain rhymes and concatenated sequences are not uncommon in the construction of *kirari* texts. In longer texts, particular performances represent particular combinations of epithets and catch-phrases, and each performance sees differing components, in differing orders.

Following Powe's terminology, we can see *take* as the basic building blocks with which a performer constructs a *kirari* – a text. Having created a text, in the sense of a body of material (which is essentially unfixed), the *take* becomes for performer and audience a mnemonic, a key to a world of known references and presuppositions. The 'basic building blocks' are available to build other kinds of constructs, and Powe illustrates the way in which popular singers have deployed the same kinds of forms in their songs. As we will see in Chapter 6, there are popular singers whose reputation has been based, in whole or in part, on their repertoire of songs for boxers, wrestlers and others. Song is usually instrumentally accompanied and performed by lead singer(s) and chorus. In the following extract from a well-known song by Hamisu Mai Ganga, *Sabo Wakilin Tauri* 'Sabo the Embodiment of True Grit', we see the combination of chorus and lead vocal deploying these same building blocks in song:

Assalatu Kanzilla
Zan soma sana'ata
Sai dai bisimillahi za na yi!

AMSHI

Tun da fari da farin farko
Na roƙi Rasululla
Ya mai sama Alla
Horo mana 'ya'yan arziki!

AMSHI

Amma Kano mun gode!
Sai mu gode Rasululla!
Mai sama Alla!
Alla yai mana Sarki adali!

AMSHI

Zamani sarkinmu
An tsara masallatai
An kuma girka masallatai
Sai lazami da wazifa za'a yi!

AMSHI

Malikiddayyanu
Alla ya yi wa bawa arziki!

AMSHI

An yi min izini mai daɓa
An sani za na yi zancen jarumi!

AMSHI

Ayya Sabo Wakili Tauri
Dominka suke cin tauri!
Sabo da kai suke nan saɓani!
Kuma suke nan kaskaifi
Da ba-duhu layar zana
Dominka maza ke cin sagau!

AMSHI

Amma Sabo Wakilin Tauri
Shinanmu da kai wacan!
Ni ban san ka kana tsoro ba!
Ban san ka da fasawa ba!
Ran da duk ka ji ɗan tsoro
Ko da ran da ka fasa
Da ni da kabilata mun bar
Mu ƙara gaya ma jarumi!

AMSHI

Amma Sabo Wakilin Tauri
Sabo ko Ibilishi ne kai?
Sabo ko Sheɗani ne kai?
Kan ba Ibilishi ne ba!
Kan ba Sheɗani ne ba!
Kana da baƙin aljan ko baƙin rauhani!
Da shi kake gama wannan magani!

AMSHI

Amma Sabo Wakilin Tauri
Yana da baƙin kambu!
Da zuciyarsa ta ɓaci
Sabo ya murɗa baƙin kambu
Gwauron Dutse ta narke
Ya shuri Dala ya kai Fanshekara!

AMSHI

Prayer is the bounty of God
I will begin my craft
But first I say 'In the name of God'!

CHORUS

From the first, from the very first
I implore God's messenger
O Lord on High, God,
Teach the wealthy a lesson for us!

CHORUS

But as for the situation in Kano, we thank you!
Let us give thanks to the Prophet of God!
Lord on High, God!
God has given us a just ruler!

CHORUS

In the time of our current ruler
Mosques have been restored
New mosques have been built
So that obligations and prayers can be performed!

CHORUS

King of recompense
May God bestow wealth upon his slave!

CHORUS

I have been given permission to speak
They know I'm going to sing of a brave man!

CHORUS

The amazing Sabo Wakilin Tauri
Because of you they take medicine to protect against iron!
Because of you they make charms to avoid damage!
They try to make their skins cut-resistant
And look for charms to make themselves vanish!
Because of you men make charms to strengthen their arms!

CHORUS

But Sabo Wakilin Tauri
We know you are superior to all that!
I have never known you to show fear!
I have never known you to delay!
The day you show the slightest fear
On the day that you delay
I and my group will desert you
And seek another for a patron!
But Sabo Wakilin Tauri
Are you Sabo or a devil?
Are you Sabo or are you Satan?
You are not a devil!
You are not Satan!
You have a black djinn or a black spirit
And with him you prepare your charms and medicines!

CHORUS

But Sabo Wakilin Tauri
He has a black bangle-charm!
When he becomes angry
Sabo rubs the black bangle-charm
And Goron Dutse hill melts
He kicks Dala hill so hard it reaches Fanshekara!

CHORUS

(adapted from Powe 1984: 603–12)

Where *take*, as headlines or catch-phrases, stand as introducers or metonymic representations of lengthier *kirari* declamations and songs (for King (1967) and Besmer (1973), the equivalent terms are *kirari* and *waka*), so also proverbs, *karin magana*, stand as summations or entry terms into longer narratives, *hikaya*, *labaru* or *tatsuniyoyi*. Where such phrases are deployed within other genres such as narrative or song they themselves stand as mnemonics for other longer texts, thereby providing levels of embeddedness enriching the referential density of the surface text.

Whether the emphasis is placed upon praise or identification in *take* and *kirari*, communicative function remains dominant in the everyday usages of the terms *karin magana, habaici, zambo, kirari* and *take*, overlaying the semantic and formal characteristics analysed, for example, by C. A. Hill (1972), Powe (1984) and Jang (1994). In themselves they display features of textuality – fixedness, metaphor, ellipsis and internal patterning – which mark them out as recognisably different from everyday speech. At the same time, they do not stand apart from everyday speech in terms of being confined only to special occasions or available only to certain people. Certain forms will tend to be deployed more often in certain circumstances – the performance of certain *kirari* will constitute part of the build-up to or aftermath of particular boxing or wrestling bouts – but they are the stuff of regular daily discourse in which people characterise each other and the events they observe and participate in.

INTERACTIVE GENRES: *TATSUNIYA* AS RIDDLE AND THE BRAIN TEASER

The alternative term to *tatsuniya* for a riddle, *kacici-kacici* 'take-up-take-up', referred to earlier, foregrounds the interactive features of the genre. The same introductory formula that is employed for tales occurs in marking the agreement by the two parties, caller and responder, to suspend everyday discourse for a moment and make the transition into the special speech of riddles: the caller says *Ga ta ga ta nan* 'Here it is, here it is' and the responder says *Ta zo mu ji ta* 'Let it come so we may hear it'. Since this formula is also used for introducing tales,[11] a subsequent, or alternative phrase is sometimes deployed, unmistakably marking the transition into riddle: *kullin kulifita* – itself a riddle, but a 'meaningless' phrase which implies, through an association with words conveying 'spherical object', that the answer to the riddle must have those qualities. The standard response to that phrase is *gauta* 'bitter solanum fruit' which is spherical. Furnishing the answer is an agreement to participate in the interactive process. Kraft (1976b) points to the fact that the riddle and the answer are conventionally linked. Riddles are not presented as direct questions. They are usually statements, and may contain an apparent contradiction that requires some resolution. Generally, people are not making them up, nor are they searching for a right answer when they reply. There is a standard riddle to which there is a standard correct reply. You either know the answer or you don't. Nevertheless, the participants recognise the appropriateness of the response on the basis of an understanding of the features of the first image which are abstracted and reinvested in the answer: when 'cotton' is proffered as the answer to the riddle 'I went to the bush and the bush laughed at me' it is the line of white on the newly split cotton boll which is seen to resemble the shining white teeth visible in a smiling face. I. Y. Yahaya (1988b) illustrates a number of riddle types including one in which the riddle is in the form of meaningless words which mimic the tones and vowel lengths of the appropriate answer. Bichi (1983/5) provides examples of some of the more well-known riddles, which include:

shanuna dubu maɗaurinsu ɗaya	tsintsiya
a thousand cows tied with a single rope	a broom
baba na ɗaka gemunsa na waje:	hayaƙi da wuta
father is in the room his beard is outside	fire in the hearth and its smoke
rigata guda ɗaya, aljihunta ɗari	gidan tururuwa
my gown has a hundred pockets	an anthill
tsumangiyar kan hanya, fyaɗe yaro fyaɗe babba	yunwa
a whip on the road which flogs young and old alike	hunger

I. Y. Yahaya (1988b: 251) provides examples of the sound mimic riddles, amongst which is the following, where the parallel low tones are marked by a grave accent:

Kùrkucif kùcif:	kwànciyar kàre
(meaningless representation ●f the sound of the answer)	the lying down of a dog

Part of the education/acculturation process whereby Hausa culture is transferred to the child or to the stranger is the marking of moments of 'cultural competence', and knowing the answer to riddles is one small marker of belonging. Measuring incompetence, not only in the child but also, more significantly in the outsider, the non-native speaker, is part of the function of the interactive genres which include both riddles and tongue-twisters, known often as *gagara Gwari* 'be beyond the Gwari person'. Tongue-twisters, as part of interactive wordplay, involve an agreement on the part of one person to be tested by another through the repetition of the particular phrase, such as:

> Da kwaɗo da ƙato suka tafi yawon ƙoto. Kato yai ƙoto, kwaɗo yai ƙoto, ƙato ne zai ƙwace ma kwaɗo ɗoto, ko kuwa kwaɗo ne zai ƙwace ma ƙato ƙoto?

> The frog and the giant went out to feed. The giant fed, the frog fed. Will the giant take the food from the frog or will the frog take the food from the giant?

Attempts to pronounce such phrases at speed produce peals of laughter among children and adults. Nevertheless, the premium put upon both cultural knowledge inherent in riddles and dilemma stories and the linguistic skill in alliterative patterning of this kind is, of course, not limited to these particular genres of wordplay. The aesthetics of other genres can place a similar premium upon these same skills. In Chapter 9 we will see how one of the best of modern Hausa poets, builds part of his reputation upon these and other features.

5

THEATRE AND MIMESIS

This chapter presents an overview of theatrical forms in Hausa and two case studies of more unconventional theatrical performances within popular culture. In Hausa the regularly used term for theatre/drama is *wasan kwaikwayo* which means literally, 'game of imitation'. Mimesis is the central concept behind *wasan kwaikwayo*. Mimesis is a more restricted concept than the broader phrase 'performing arts'. Performing arts covers most of the content of this book since songs, tales, and much poetry are performed in one way or another.[1] Theatricality is also a feature of festivals and court life, as well as a wide variety of cultural events both state sponsored and locally organised.[2] There are also theatrical aspects of the *bori* spirit-possession cult (Horn 1981), but this discussion will be limited to brief comment upon the mimetic features of that cult.[3] Mimetic performance encompasses both formal theatre – on TV or radio, or in live performances in which the acting space is inhabited by actors acting out rehearsed story-lines – and a broader range of entertainment in which improvised mimesis forms part of the process. Discussion here focuses upon the relationship between more formal theatre and other forms of popular entertainment.

TV AND RADIO DRAMA

Kallamu reports that in 1992 practically all local radio and TV stations in the northern states of Nigeria had Hausa drama shows of great popularity.[4] Radio drama dates from the 1950s when FRCN (Federal Radio Corporation of Nigeria) Kaduna put on *Dagurasa* produced by Adamu Gumel and a series aimed at farmers, *Basafce*, produced by Bashir Isma'ila Ahmed, (M. W. Yahaya 1985), while a series called *Sarkin Karfi* was aimed at children (Nafada, Sadauki and Kabir 1987: 5). Among the most long-running series that date from the 1960s was *Zaman Duniya Iyawa Ne*, written and produced by Yusufu Ladan,[5] in which one of the most famous Hausa actor/comedians, Usman Baba Fategi, made his debut. Fategi went on, in 1973, to star in his own show *Samanja Mazan Fama* on radio and TV with NTA Kaduna, and to write and direct other series including *Duniya Budurwar Wawa*, which is still going. *Samanja* 'sergeant-major' is built around the character played by Fategi and illustrates, in a variety of domestic and local circumstances around a barracks, the antics and escapades of an irascible soldier with clipped speech and direct manner. His verbal style is 'soldier speak' and draws upon the experience of ordinary Nigerians of the mixed English and Hausa of the Nigerian army (a style which is also drawn upon by one of the burlesque artists considered later in this chapter). Fategi himself, originally a Nupe from Kwara State, had experience of soldiering during the civil war in a signals unit, and drew upon that experience in forming the character of Samanja (Kallamu 1992). Two further popular shows are built around well-known actors. Kasimu Yero acts in a number of shows, but his most regular appearances have been in *Karambana* 'The Busy-body'[6] described by Kofoworola as follows:

> Karambana could be likened to the court jester in the traditional social setting transported to the modern social setting. He behaves in all sorts of ways, satirising men of various statuses in the society in order to purge them of their moral laxity, anti-social practices, misuse and abuse of office or privilege. (Kofoworola and Lateef 1987: 172)

This combination of humour with local and domestic political comment is ubiquitous in TV drama. I. Y. Yahaya (1991) makes the comment more generally in relation to Hausa drama:

> As a form of art, the main function of any drama performance is entertainment. However, the entertainment cannot be achieved in isolation from the focus of the content of the plays. Each performance is usually targetted to achieve a specific objective ... social criticism: exposing the follies of stereotype individuals, life-styles, malpractices among public officials, injustice, violation of social norms. (I. Y. Yahaya 1991: 24)

Humour as the crucial ingredient also arises later when we consider the forms of formal Hausa theatre that have grown up in the Republic of Niger.

Kasagi is another popular show, in which the actor Umaru Danjuma Katsina takes the central role (Kofoworola and Lateef 1987: 171). Again written and directed by a central actor, *Kasagi* contains a further ingredient that has been typical of much theatre – the exposition of particular social policy issues being promulgated by one arm or other of government. Kofoworola states that '*Kasagi* was meant to propagate the policy of the state government on prevention of migration of rural folks to urban areas' (Kofoworola and Lateef 1987: 172). Radio and television plays have generally had a didactic purpose covering such issues as the importance of education, the dangers of sending children out hawking on the streets, intergenerational conflict, and Westernisation, among many others, while often illustrating customs such as weddings, namings and festivals.[7] The choice of theme by directors differs little from the social policy priorities of the government. In the late 1960s, commercial sponsorship of drama by tobacco companies produced the radio shows *Noma Yanke Talauci* 'Farming is an Antidote to Poverty' and *Taba Sa Farin Cikin Aljihu* 'Cigarettes Make For Happy Pockets' (Nafaɗa, Sadauki and Kabir 1987)! Less directly manipulative, the Bank of the North has more recently sponsored the dramatisation by NTA Kaduna of the *Magana Jari Ce* stories by Abubakar Imam.

In many of these radio and TV series the actors and producers have previously or contemporaneously worked with Ahmadu Bello University (ABU) either through the Department of Drama or through the Centre for Nigerian Cultural Studies (CNCS) in which dance and theatre troupes have been operating for some years.[8] The growth of theatre during the 1970s and 1980s owes much to the work, emanating from ABU and the CNCS, in formal, scripted theatre – such as the adaptation for the stage, by Umaru Ladan and Dexter Lyndersay, of *Shaihu Umar*, the historical pageant 'Mai Idris Alooma' directed by Dexter Lyndersay, and the play *Queen Amina*[9] by Umaru Balarabe Ahmed; in community theatre – such as that documented by Crow and Etherton (1979), and in radio and TV – a recent development is the transition to film of the play *Kulba Na Barna* by Umaru Ɗanjuma Katsina, and the production of the original Hausa-language film *Kasarmu Ce*.[10] These initiatives were underpinned by the radio and TV stations and the state ministries of arts and culture, as well as commercial sponsors such as those mentioned above.[11] The cultural nationalism which revalued the role of tales in the constitution of Hausa culture promoted theatre in much the same way.

A typical TV series is described by N. M. Zagga (1985). At the time Zagga was writing, Sokoto TV were putting out a series entitled *Idon Matambayi*, produced by Bello Abubakar and Muhammed Ɗan'iya, which took as its theme 'traditional customs' and the confrontation between the old and the new. The episodes are set in a village peopled by stock characters: Hakimi 'village head', and his wives, Magarya, Yar mai alewa and Mai taru;[12] the imam; the up-to-no-good Ɗan wanzam 'barber', his wife, Ya mai albasa, and his sidekick Boka 'medicine-pedlar'; the villain, Mai gero; the non-Hausa, BaHausa; the headmaster, Hedimasta; the policeman, Saja; and the village head's servants, Dunfama and Agure. The typification of the characters, creating the stereotypes, is achieved through additional marking by clothing and by style of house: Hakimi is dressed in aristocratic robes and lives in a house that has a palace-like frontage (most shots take place in the area in front of houses or in the entrance rooms rather than in the interior of houses); Imam's house has a Koranic class taking place out in front; the barber's house is poor and dilapidated; BaHausa is dressed in a loincloth and carries a flywhisk while his house has a trader's stall outside; the headmaster wears modern shoes and carries a watch while his house is of modern block construction. In this environment Hakimi tries to regulate society while unable to regulate his domestic domain; the medicine pedlar sells potions to wives who are looking to do down their co-wives or to gain their husband's affections; BaHausa makes a hilarious mess of the Hausa language while illustrating a wide variety of non-Hausa ways and customs; and the villain carries on his skulduggery, usually coming out unscathed. In addition to these 'internal' characters, the village sees the arrival and departure of representatives of modernity from the city such as soldiers and census officials, as well as travelling embodiments of 'traditional' culture: the singers, boxers, wrestlers and entertainers of the rural and the urban Hausa worlds. In this peopling of a Hausa world, it is the interactions between these stock characters which gives force to the episodes as they are acted out. The graphic wit and comic action that sustains these plays are the same ingredients that made the *Magana Jari Ce* stories so popular. Not only do these radio and TV series take their titles from *karin magana* 'proverbs', such as those that captioned the early novels, but parts of those early novels, with their reliance on dialogue and comic interaction, are well suited to TV stage adaptation.[13]

DRAMA SOCIETIES AND SCRIPTED PLAYS

In Nigeria during the 1980s, there was a flowering of drama societies putting on plays in schools and universities, and in the occasional public arena such as the open-air theatre near Goron Dutse in Kano. Kallamu (1992) reports that a number of modern theatre groups have been able to sustain themselves through local sponsorship and ticket revenues.[14] Drama societies originated in the 1940s in schools where the first published book[15] of Hausa plays, *Six Hausa Plays* by Rupert East (East 1936b), had been studied as part of the curriculum. Yahaya (1991) reports that students in those schools, particularly Aminu Kano, Yusuf Maitama Sule, Alhaji Dogondaji, Shu'aibu Makarfi and Abubakar Tunau Marafa, went on to sketch out their own plays and directed their fellow students in putting on their own productions. While Aminu Kano's politically radical plays (*Kai Wanene a Kasuwar Kano?* 'Who are you in Kano Market?', and *Gudumar Dukan En-En Kano* 'A Hammer With Which to Beat the Kano Native Administration') were never published, Alhaji Dogondaji's *Malam Inkuntum*, which depicts conflict arising from the custom of giving a daughter away in marriage as *sadaka* 'alms gift' to a *malam* (in this case a particularly venal character), and Abubakar Tunau's *Wasan Marafa* (first produced in Sokoto Middle School in 1943), which preaches hygiene and sanitation and pokes fun at a conservative older generation, were published in 1955 and 1949 respectively. Plays which arise out of improvisation around a story outline have often been written down later, thus creating a fixed form from that which has earlier been adaptable and fluid. In the 1990s, the weekly magazine *Rana* has devoted a section to the printing of playscripts, and in the 1950s, according to Yahaya (1991) the published plays by Shu'aibu Maƙarfi, *Zamanin Nan Namu* (1959) and *Jatau Na Kyallu* (1960) arose out of adapted radio programmes.[16] *Zamanin Nan Namu* consists of two plays that address the conflict between conservatism and modernity, *Malam Maidala'ilu* and *'Yar Masu Gida*.[17] In the first, a daughter is sent to school by her father only to to be taken out by her mother who needs her to hawk her wares. When the father discovers this, he throws his wife out and entrusts his daughter to the care of another wife. The daughter, having finished school, makes effective use of her education in later life. The second play depicts the courtship and marriage of a girl in which grasping relatives reduce the girl to the status of a fought-over commodity. *Jatau Na Kyallu* tells the story of a man ruined by falling in love with, and marrying, Kyallu, a prostitute, but who then puts his life back together again with the help of his loving and supportive first wife. While some printed plays have come from the later writing down of an orally formulated drama, other plays have arisen out of the efforts of writers. In addition to the original scripts of, for example, *Uwar Gulma* (1968) by Mohammed Sada,[18] *Tabarmar Kunya* (1969) by Adamu Dan Goggo and David Hofstad (Dauda Kano), and the four plays by Umaru Balarabe Ahmed *Bora da Mowa* (1972),[19] there have been both translations, such as Ibrahim Yaro Yahaya's *Daren Sha Biyu* (Shakespeare's *Twelfth Night*) (1971), Ahmed Sabir's *Mutanen Kogo* (Tawfiq al-Hakim's *People of the Cave*) (1976), and Dahiru Idris's *Matsolon Attajiri* (Shakespeare's *Merchant of Venice* (1981), and original plays and translations by university students done as part of their dissertation work.[20]

COMMUNITY THEATRE AND DEVELOPMENT THEATRE

The didactic purpose behind some theatre, referred to above, has given rise to a number of developments, notably 'community theatre' emanating from Ahmadu Bello University, Zaria, and 'development theatre' as described by Beik (1984a; 1984b; 1986; 1987) for Niger. Crow and Etherton (1979) describe an experiment in taking theatre to the people instigated by the Drama Department of Ahmadu Bello University in 1977. Operation Feed The Nation (OFN) was the federal government's major policy thrust of that year, and the experiment was to see if communication with farmers could be effective using theatre in exploring the issues surrounding OFN. In Soba District, the visiting drama students were told to find out from farmers what issues they would like to see discussed in plays which the students would improvise with their co-operation. It became immediately apparent that the farmers were most exasperated by the fact that they had been promised fertiliser which never materialised. The method of approach adopted by the students meant that rather than having a script dictated by the Ministry of Agriculture, they were moving very rapidly into the representation of farmers' complaints about the non-operation of Operation Feed the Nation. As Crow and Etherton glossed the situation:

The *Wasan Manoma* ['Farmer's Play'] project leads us to conclude that live theatre can help objectify social relations and conflicts, and can thereby enable the audience to achieve self-awareness. This process may encourage discussion and subsequent action for the long-term benefit of the participating community as a whole. (Crow and Etherton 1979: 11)

A flavour of the representations created in such 'community theatre' can be gained from the summary of one of the plays performed during that experiment:

The final play was developed around the character of a serious-minded farmers' representative who consistently fails to put his case across on behalf of his fellow-farmers against the traders before the headman. The traders always manage to outwit him in the discussions, and continue to make their excessive profits, despite the pious words of the headman urging them to observe moderation in their trading. This farmer's son returns, now a graduate in agriculture, determined to work in his father's village so that he can understand the social application of the theory which he has learned. He is committed to forming a farmers' organization. He and his father start a small co-operative with the headman's blessing. The traders are not worried; but the initial success of the co-operative leads to its rapid expansion, and soon the traders find their lucrative fertilizer operation threatened. They are unable to cope with the new-found ability of the farmers to organize themselves. Eventually, in desperation, they decide to burn down the farmers' store which has just been stacked full of the season's fertilizer. Fortunately, the farmer's son is conscious of how much they stand to lose if anything should happen to the fertilizer and so he persuades the organization's members to agree to act in turn as guards. The traders are caught red-handed; but this is not the end, for they accuse the farmer-guard, in front of the headman, of being the culprit. The headman is disposed out of habit to believe the traders, until the farmer and his son arrive on the scene and confirm the traders' treachery. The headman's fury is now unleashed on the traders whom he had trusted. (Crow & Etherton 1979: 10)

The radicalism of the plays arose out of the farmers' own views of the problems they faced. As an experiment in which theatre moved out of the conventional environment of imagination and of the university into the daily life of farmers, it is also interesting that the boundary between the imaginary and the real became fluid as the farmers asked 'for the students to help them directly by supplying them with fertilizer from the University. The answer was always that the students could only offer advice, not tangible assistance' (1979: 11). Crow and Etherton also report that a headman objected to their

presence in his village 'if we planned to include drumming, dancing or singing in our plays' (1979: 6), and so the students eliminated all such components from their plays, although it appears that mimesis itself was not objected to. Since that time the Drama Department at ABU and the CNCS have
continued with their efforts in 'theatre for development' in a variety of directions (Kofoworola and Lateef 1987).

Beik describes a flowering of formal theatre in the Republic of Niger in
the 1980s arising from state support of drama societies within youth organisations, *samariya*. These societies gained access to their audiences through
live performances on stage in their localities and in national competition in
the capital, Niamey, and through radio and TV. Writing in 1986, Beik says,
'Almost overnight, television has added a national dimension to local theatre
production and given impetus to its growth' (Beik 1986: 23). The *samariya*
were designated by the military government as the 'local cadres for national
development' and in April each year, the state sponsored a week-long National Youth Festival at which troupes from each of the seven *départements* of
the country performed in competition. While the Niger government suggested that plays should address 'national development', the choice of topic
and the nature of its treatment were left up to the troupes themselves.[21] In
Beik's fascinating account it is clear that a process of oral improvisation in
rehearsal combined with intense discussion among the group of actors, similar to that described by Crow and Etherton, produced the final scene sequence and action/speech outline – final only in the sense that it marked the
transition from rehearsal to performance, not that the play underwent no
further change. Between troupes and between plays there was considerable
variation in the degree to which improvisation occurred within performances themselves. In most troupes that Beik describes there were one or two
central actor/directors who had the greatest say in who acted, which ideas
were appropriate, and which lines and bits of business were most effective.
The process of research and discussion in choosing a theme for a play and its
manner of presentation are graphically described in Beik's translation of a
comment by Yazi Dogo, director of the Zinder troupe which presented a
play about education, *Ba Ga Irinta Ba* 'No Wonder!' that was awarded first
prize in the 1980 festival:[22]

> At the time when we were beginning to prepare the play that we gave
> the name *Ba Ga Irinta Ba*, a lot of us sat down and we asked each one
> to bring themes in order to prepare our work for the Festival. We met,
> everyone brought his ideas, we examined them and said, 'This one is
> okay, this one won't do.'
>
> Well! We thought about them and said, 'Hey! There's one thing
> which concerns all of us, even the elders, even the government, and that
> is the problems of the students, the teachers and the children's par-
> ents.' So we said, 'Yes this is really appropriate, this is a good theme.'

So we began to research it, to seek it out. Now there are a lot of teachers in our troupe. They helped in the research, everyone brought his ideas; we collected them all, we arranged them, we took what was bothering the teachers, what was bothering the parents and also what was bothering the kids themselves. Yes. Then we agreed, 'Truly, it is necessary to prepare something about this because of its usefulness to all of us – for the parents to understand, for the elders also, to understand the problems at school.' That's how it was. (Beik 1986: 25)

This 'community creation' of oral theatre draws upon the same fund of stereotyped characters so evident in tales, and that also informs TV and radio drama in Nigeria: 'Characters, who are often stock types – the ignorant rich man, the traditional ruler, the gossiping wife, etc. – evolve with the process of transforming the framework of scenes into action on the stage' (Beik 1986: 27). While the characters may be easily recognisable, their interactions have to be carefully crafted:

Actors develop their roles during rehearsals, often a process of trial and error. The director or the group of leaders may name actors to certain parts for the early rehearsals. If the roles suit the actors, if they perform them adequately in the eyes of the group, they will stay with those roles throughout the play. If the actors feel uncomfortable with the characters they are to play, or if the director or others in the troupe feel there is something wrong with their portrayal, they will try someone else in the role. Everyone offers critiques of everyone else in the discussions after these trial scenes in rehearsal. (Beik 1986: 27)

The combination of humour with social and political comment, a mixture of entertainment with didactic intent which was so typical of Nigerian TV drama, is also the hallmark of this theatre in Niger. Again Beik quotes Yazi Dogo on this issue:

In recent years, the troupe more consciously concerns itself with conveying a didactic message, but their talent for humor is still very much a part of their plays. Yazi expressed the character of their theatre in this way:

At the time when we didn't understand the usefulness of the theatre, we put on plays and everybody laughed and left. That was how it was then. We would arrange things with no meaning, we'd work things up just so people would laugh. But now, people's consciousness has begun to understand the theatre, what it is becoming. That's what we're looking for, the right words that people can make use of. Just as they instruct people on the radio, or what they write in the journals, the advice – that's what we're doing in the theatre.

Now, whenever we're about to begin a new play, we examine

what its purpose is to be. Shall we do it just for laughs? Or so that people can work with what we say? We've seen that the usefulness in it is greater when people will work with what they've seen us do. It's like a lesson we're drawing in the play. That's what we've learned.

But then, given that, if a person sits for an hour or an hour and a half, watching, not moving his body, not laughing – that's no good. So in our arrangement, we mix it up a little, we put a few funny things in so that people enjoy it. Yes that's it

... In other troupes throughout the country, directors and actors continually mentioned the importance of both comedy and serious messages in their plays. The tension between message and comedy reflects the dual purpose inherent in their work: to educate and to entertain. (Beik 1986: 29)

Finding 'the right words that people can make use of' constitutes the serious didactic intent (whether radical or conservative), recognised by audience and actors alike, that is shared with a wide variety of the literary forms examined in this book. In the same way that the rehabilitation of traditional tales during the cultural revivalism of the 1970s and 1980s in Nigeria made great play with their educative function in 'traditional' society, so also the perceived educative function of this kind of theatre marks it off from simple frivolity for people who keep in mind the Islamic strictures against *hululu* 'idle chatter' that were propagated by the Jihadist leaders of the nineteenth century and remain a feature of attitudes towards a variety of genres and performers.

THEATRICALITY IN *BORI*

Similarly censorious attitudes are apparent in the views taken of the *bori* spirit-possession cult. As an un-Islamic practice the cult is roundly condemned. On the other hand Islam recognises the existence of spirits, jinn, which in Hausa are identified with the *iskoki*, spirits, of the pre-Islamic *bori*. As a cult of affliction, people come to it to resolve physical and psychological problems. Cure involves initiation through participation in sessions where people, in trance, are 'mounted' by a particular spirit. They then speak as mediums for the spirit riding upon the adept's shoulders. The calling of the spirit involves the use of drums, shouted epithets, dance and a typical fall upon the buttocks by the adept as trance approaches.[23] While most *bori* practitioners are women, their musicians, and the cult leadership, are mainly men.[24] The spirits inhabit a parallel world in a town called Jangare, with family groupings and hierarchies, and each has particular characteristics of speech, movement and appearance. King (1966; 1967) lists the epithets of 69 spirits recorded in Katsina, Besmer (1983) lists 253 spirits in his major work on the *bori* cult. Broadly-speaking the spirits are often distinguished as malevolent black spirits or beneficent white spirits.[25] R. Adamu (1991) describes a cult leader, a man called Sarkin bori Sule from Zaria, who started 'seeings spirits' from the age of 14. He was a *dan hoto* 'a dancer/hoe juggler', then a *dan tauri* 'a knife conjuror' and then a woodcutter before becoming a full-time *bori* specialist. Currently (in 1995) practising as a restrainer and treater of the mentally disturbed he was originally initiated by a woman called Jaware who had also initiated his mother and had treated him as a child for hearing voices.

Bori will recur in the context of this discussion because it is intimately bound up with certain kinds of song, musical instruments and musicians, discussed in Chapter 6, and because there are strongly mimetic elements in *bori* performances that are linked to the forms of drama considered in this chapter.

Increasingly, there have been two sides to *bori*. On the one hand there are the curative cult activities in which adepts enter trance, as discussed by Besmer (1973; 1975; 1983), Horn (1981), Monfouga-Nicolas (1972; J. Nicolas (1967) and others. On the other, there are the entertainment performances in which drumming and dancing are provided for weddings, local festivities and, increasingly, state-sponsored arts and culture events of one kind or another. These latter will often not involve trance.[26] Both types of occasion will involve the mimetic representation of one of the spirits by a medium. (On the theatricality of *bori* see particularly Horn (1981) and Chaibou (1979).) Whether trance is present or not, an actor takes on the appearance, personality and behaviour of the spirit. Besmer (1983: Ch. 4) outlines in detail the nature of the afflictions that particular spirits cause, their associated epithets and musical phrases, the sacrifices and medicines that are prescribed for the associated afflictions, and the dress and behaviour of the medium. The dress and behaviour of certain mediums are the significant, identifying characteristics.

In the discussion of tales and their relationship with early prose-writing we saw how certain stereotype characters, the chief, the profligate prince, the learned *malam*, the ill-treated but faithful daughter, the trickster, the non-Hausa Gwari man, the barber, the country bumpkin, in addition to the animals, lion, hyena, jackal, and others, are deployed repeatedly in encounter after encounter that explores morality, behaviour and identities within the construction of a Hausa cultural world. In the field of drama, both on radio and TV as well as in playscripts, we see a similar process at work. In the example of a TV play discussed above, we saw variations on these same stereotypes, the non-Hausa BaHausa, the up-to-no-good barber, the imam, the good wife, the villain, along with representations of modernity, also stereotyped, but which are generally excluded from the perceived world of tales: the headmaster and the policeman. In Beik's description of the Zinder play *Ba Ga Irinta Ba*, we also saw the presence of inspectors of education and the *nouveaux riches* in the form of Mamman Arrivé. In Chapter 2, the fixing of a new stereotype was traced in detail in the discussion of the rapacious entrepreneur in the novel *Turmin Danya*. These stereotypes, and the notion of stereotype itself summed up metonymically in a few features of behaviour and appearance, have resonances in the representations of characters in the *bori* pantheon. One of the most important *bori* spirits is Malam Alhaji, a classic representation of the learned malam, described by Besmer as follows:

> As the medium sits in trance he writes verses from the Quran with a native pen on a slate, reads and prays, and 'pulls' the beads of his rosary ... During a possession-trance ceremony his medium should be dressed in a white cape, gown, turban, jumper, trousers and wrapper, a red fez and native shoes and sit on a ram-skin mat. (Besmer 1983: 83)

As an interesting representation of linked opposites, *bori* gives Malam Alhaji two wives, the second of whom is Bagwariya 'the Gwari woman':

> Malam Alhaji's concubine or second wife is thought not to be the kind of woman a Quranic scholar might ordinarily choose as a wife, and most informants are anxious to explain how it may happen that such a marriage could exist ... Cult-adepts, themselves Hausa, view the Gwari woman in the stereotyped way in which they regard Gwari people in general. They are described as pagans, and for the Muslim Hausa this conception generates elaborate ideas about what they eat. Bagwariya is classified as a black spirit, not because of the illnesses she is said to cause, but because of the belief that as a pagan she neither prays to Allah nor observes Muslim dietary restrictions. She eats constantly, but dislikes food containing peppers. More importantly, she eats dogs and bush animals and is not particular about how they are slaughtered ... (Besmer 1983: 83-4)

The Gwari representation here echoes the image of the pagan outsider seen time after time in tales and in prose writing. Other types of outsider, common to tales, drama and prose, include the Fulani, represented, among others, by the character Barhaza, described by Besmer thus:

> During possession-trance this Fulani woman's medium imitates milking and churning gestures to the accompaniment of her music ... She acts shyly in the presence of crowds – behaviour expected by the Hausa of a pastoral Fulani woman – and must be restrained from running away if startled. She does not speak unless spoken to and when she replies it is in a strongly Fulfulde-influenced Hausa speech ... Unlike her black sister (Inna) Barhaza is believed to be a 'white' spirit, but this is a statement about the colour of her clothing. She wears a white wrapper, a white head-tie ring with strings of cowrie shells dangling from it, and thin silver bracelets. (Besmer 1983: 101)

There are of course many powerfully drawn spirits who are not directly, as far as I am aware, represented in the other cultural arenas to which I have referred. The important spirit Kuturu 'the leper' is one such:

> A medium ridden by Kuturu acts as a leper and compulsively begs for alms. As his trance state begins his fingers close on his palms; it is important that an attendant removes any rings the medium may be wearing before the fingers become 'frozen' as the spirit might harm his mount when he rides if anything is under or on his fingers.[27] The medium's nose runs, his distorted mouth opens far to one side of his face. He cannot walk but crawls with his feet bent under him, his toes curl downwards and joints below the ankle are immovable.
>
> Fully in charge of his horse, Kuturu dominates the trance area unless his superior, the Chief of the Spirits, is also present. He vigorously rubs the ground with his elbows and slaps it and parts of his body and head with his deformed hands. This action, along with vain attempts to wipe his running nose, gives the impression of one suffering spells of intolerable itching. This, however, is not the case; the flailing of arms is interpreted as a sign of Kuturu's considerable power. (Besmer 1983: 86)

Not only human representations are present in the *bori* pantheon. In addition to Zaki 'the lion' and Danko 'the snake' there is Kure 'the hyena'. As in tales, the hyena figures strongly. Married with three daughters, Kure is irascible and dangerous: 'He prefers to rage around in front of the musicians, snapping at anyone who comes close to his horse's drooling, snarling mouth. During such a demonstration the role of the attendant becomes unusually important, since if he was to loose the leash tied to the Hyena the audience might panic' (Besmer 1983: 93–4)

This discussion has touched upon the continuities in representation of characters as between the tale, drama and prose-writing traditions and the ritual world of *bori*. *Bori* as a belief system and as a cult of affliction is beyond the scope of this discussion. The interested reader is directed to the works of Besmer and others given in the references.

POPULAR ENTERTAINERS

The typification of outsiders represented by Barhaza or Bagwariya is part of the broad process of representing the nature of society within Hausa culture. In Chapters 6 to 9 we will see the way in which poetry and song represent and participate in that construction. The next part of this chapter is devoted to the role of popular entertainers in typifying society 'from the bottom up', sometimes presenting a satirical pastiche on other aspects of Hausa culture, and sometimes picturing the concerns and interests of ordinary people.

In Hausa there is a great variety of terms that describe popular entertainers in addition to the singers/musicians that are discussed in Chapters 6 and 7.

Many of the types of entertainers discussed here are at the same time musicians and singers or work with musicians. Overviews of such entertainers are given by U. B. Ahmed (1985), Ames and King (1971: Ch. 2), Kofoworola (1981; 1982; 1985b), Kofoworola and Lateef (1987) and I. Y. Yahaya (1991), among others. A brief description of some of these types is followed by discussion of those forms which involve dramatic interaction between performers.

'Yan kama 'burlesque artists'[28] are perhaps the most overtly mimetic of such performers and are discussed in more detail shortly. 'Yan gambara 'rap artists' like the 'yan kama deploy two or three people interacting with each other as they move through markets and other public places.[29] Wawan sarki 'king's jester' is a performer most extensively described in the context of the Zaria traditional court.[30] 'Yan hoto are dancer-jugglers, associated with farmers, who throw heavy hoes high in the air and then catch them during dance routines to the accompaniment of drumming (Kofoworola and Lateef 1987: 98–103). 'Yan tauri 'tough men' perform endurance tricks with 'sharp' blades; 'yan dabo are magicians specialising in sleight of hand; 'yan wasan wuta perform feats with red-hot metal; gardawa work with dangerous animals, particularly snakes, hyenas and scorpions,[31] and 'yan wasan kaho throw themselves between the horns of enraged bulls and hang on for grim death (Joe 1984)! This array of popular entertainers, and others, in the past and, apparently, to a lesser extent today, have worked the markets and public spaces of towns and villages throughout the Hausa-speaking areas of Nigeria and its neighbours. The following discussion considers three of these categories in some detail, 'yan kama, 'yan gambara and wawan sarki.

In the performances of one particular dan kama, Malam Ashana ('Mister Matches'), it is the satiric/culturally subversive relationship of his material to other genres and other 'performance styles' within Hausa that is the focus of attention, while the performance of 'yan gambara, illustrating a register of racy popular language, is discussed as an example of the same typification process that we have seen, and will see more of, in other genres. The discussion of wawan sarki, drawn from Kofoworola's writings, points to the role of sanctioned verbal licence within the environment of a traditional court.

'YAN KAMA

The bulk of the following discussion draws upon conversations with, and observation of Malam Ashana ('Mister Matches') and his co-performers in September 1989, as well as records he made in the mid-1970s.

'Yan kama, 'the catchers', the practitioners of the art of kamanci (according to Malam Ashana the name derives from their habit of 'stealing' food in the market), perform in groups of two or three for money in markets and at social gatherings. Gidley (1967: 76–7) describes typically distinctive dress involving a wooden sword, a drum, a small cap, a chest bare to the waist and other mock accoutrements. While such an appearance immediately marks out the *dan kama* from the crowd, as an entertainer working from within his audience he also makes use of the elements of surprise and disguise to confuse the boundary between the real and the feigned. Gidley quotes from a narrative by the late Emir of Abuja, Sulaimanu Barau, in which he, the Emir, relates how a *dan kama* dressed/disguised in correct formal attire for attendance at the serious theatre of an emir's court shocked the assembled company by entirely inappropriate behaviour before revealing himself as a *dan kama* to the great amusement of all present. As a satirist and imitator, the *dan kama* subverts the business of other people's serious performances by disrupting them and drawing attention to the conventions surrounding them.

Gidley provides illustrative examples of the material used by these entertainers in performance. Imitations of *wa'azi* 'admonition', *addu'a* 'prayer', serious religious songs, famous praise-songs and religious traditions, all form part of the typical repertoire. In each case, and again typical of *'yan kamanci*, the 'comical pastiche' involves the substitution of the topic of food for the serious subject of the original. (From Malam Ashana's point of view there is nothing more serious than food!).

From Malam Ashana's recorded performances that are sold on disc in Nigeria, it is clear that his repertoire corresponds closely with the groupings set out by Gidley. There are imitations of *wa'azi* 'preaching' and parodies of serious songs by others, *Tuwon Masara* 'Maize Meal' is a take-off of Shata's *Ku Tashi Ku Farka 'Yan Arewa* 'Arise You Men of the North'; *Sojojinmu Tuwo Ya Kare* 'Our Soldiers, the Food is Finished' a take-off of a civil-war song in praise of soldiers; *Don Allah mata ai koko* 'For God's Sake, Women, Prepare the Porridge' is a parody of Shata's *Don Allah Mata ku yi Aure* 'For God's Sake, Women, Get Married'. However, Ashana also sings perfectly serious praise-songs, such as *Kanar Dada* 'Colonel Dada' and *Ado Bayero* 'Ado Bayero'. T. A. Gaya (1972) provides transcriptions of a number of Ashana's songs and routines including a number that gain their humour from *batsa* 'ribaldry' of their language. Perhaps his best known parody is of the song by Sarkin Tabshi in praise of independence which begins:

> An ba mu mulkinmu mun gode Allah murna muke duniya ta yi dadi.
> We have been given our independence, thank God, we rejoice and the world is a sweeter place.

Ashana sang:

> Duniya ta yi kyau arziki ya yi tun da mun karɓi girki ga matanmu.
> The world is good, blessings abound, now that we have wrested the cooking away from our wives.

M. S. Bello (1986) gives a further example of Ashana parodying a song by the well-known popular singer Alhaji Mamman Shata. Where Shata sang:

Tun daga Lawali har ga Risala
Har Attaura har Linjila
Hak Kur'ani babban kundi
Ina ayar da ta ƙanƙare aure?

In the book Lawali or the Risala
Or the Old or the New Testament
Or in the Holy Koran, the great source
Where is the verse that criticises (lit. scrapes out) marriage?

Ashana's mocking take-off said:

Don na ce mata su yi koko
Masu kunu suka tozarta ni
Tun daga Lawali har ga Risala
Har Attaura har Linjila
Har Kur'ani babban kundi
Ina ayar da ta ƙanƙare koko?

Because I said women should prepare the koko porridge
The kunu-drink makers have attacked me
In the book Lawali or the Risala
Or the Old or the New Testament
Or in the Holy Koran, the great source
Where is the verse that criticises/scrapes out the last of the koko?

(M. S. Bello 1986: 56)

For Gidley, 'yan kama live on the legitimate side of a classificatory line demarcating 'traditional' Hausa orature in which there is a series of discrete genres each with its own separate legitimate status, tatsuniya 'tales', waka 'song/poetry', kirari 'praise-song/epithet', karin magana 'saying/proverb/riddle', kamanci, and others. 'Yan gambara and others live on the illegitimate side of the tracks purveying abuse, scandal, obscenity.

A view which compartmentalises such genres as discrete and separate and legitimate/illegitimate, ignores the possibility that the one may be a parody, a subversion of the other, part of a subculture that is essentially in contradiction to dominant cultural forces. Manifestly it may be an entertainment, an amusement, but equally it may, by its parody, be drawing attention to the pomposities, the rhetoric and the verbal or performance features of its target.

Gidley makes much of the harmlessness of the humour of the ɗan kama. While acknowledging that 'yan kamanci is situated in a cultural milieu that embraces both the man in the street and 'broad-minded rulers', and that the man in the street was in need of relief (from what we are not told) it is clear that, for Gidley, the avoidance of abuse in language links closely with respect for the ruling élites and the maintenance of authority unharmed, 'The nonsense is not generally hurtful when performed according to the tradition, ...

nor is it detrimental to authority' (Gidley 1967: 71).

Gidley's notion of a lack of 'detriment to authority' in performances by *'yan kama* would appear to relate first, to a style of language: non-abusive; and second, to the fact that the content of the material does not constitute a substantive attack upon the holders of authority. Yet it may well be more useful to consider not what the performances do *not* do, but what they *do* do in their use of language in performance. Here I would submit that the selection for the purposes of parody of registers of language appropriate to 'serious' stylised public utterances is in itself significant. The content of the parody does not constitute a counter-argument to the content of the original, but the very fact that inappropriate content is forced upon the imitated style highlights the features of that style such that they themselves become a part of the comedy and thus are perhaps never to be seen in quite the same light again. Indeed, the rhetoric of the original may have been well nigh invisible in its familiarity to the listener. The sudden spotlight on style is not necessarily subversive of the content of the original but of the sanctity of its form. And verbal authority can rest as much on an acceptance of style as of content. As in the cases quoted in Gidley where a *dan kama* in disguise infiltrates the world of court ceremonial, his trade hinges upon the substitution of levity for gravity.

A performance by *'yan kama* relies upon repartee between two or three people, and the crux of the humour lies in the imitation of recognisably distinctive styles of speech. There are a number of levels to a discourse established by the performance. First, there is the level of repartee of call and response between lead and sidekick(s), interspersed with dialogue between lead and members of the audience. Second, there is a relationship established between the serious content of an original and the topic of food as subject-matter of the parody. This relationship is not of similarity or contrast but of incongruity/absurdity created by the enforced linking, through imitation, of the essentially unrelated. Third, there is a dialogue between languages. As discussed below, the Hausa parody plays with the *gravitas* associated with Arabic, or the oddities of parade-ground English. And fourth, there is the central defining relationship, based upon exactness of similarity, between the stylistic characteristics of an original and the representation in the parody. Bakhtin expresses this relation most clearly:

> It is the nature of every parody to transpose the values of the parodied style, to highlight certain elements while leaving others in the shade: parody is always biased in some direction, and this bias is dictated by the distinctive features of the parodying language, its accentual system, its structure – we feel its presence in the parody and we can recognize that presence, just as we, at other times recognize clearly the accentual system, syntactic construction, tempi and rhythm or a specific vulgar language within purely Latin parody (that is, we recognize a French-

man or German as the author of the parody). Theoretically it is possible to sense and recognize in any parody that 'normal' language, that 'normal' style, in light of which the given parody was created. But in practice it is far from easy and not always possible.

Thus it is that in parody two languages are crossed with each other, as well as two styles, two linguistic points of view, and in the final analysis two speaking subjects. It is true that only one of these languages (the one that is parodied) is present in its own right; the other is present invisibly, as an actualizing background for creating and perceiving. Parody is an intentional hybrid, but usually it is an intra-linguistic one, one that nourishes itself on the stratification of the literary language into generic languages and languages of various specific tendencies. (Bakhtin 1981: 75–6)

The following discussion of the performance context of certain 'set texts' in Malam Ashana's repertoire, his 'texts in action', is based on a performance on Sunday, 3 September 1989, in Ladin Makole market not far from Kano. In discussion with Malam Ashana at an earlier date I talked of the records that he had made for sale during the 1960s and 1970s and of his more recent appearances on Kano television, where he had appeared with members of his troupe in a studio setting. Malam Ashana insisted that these were inappropriate circumstances in which to really see a *dan kama* in action, rather I would need to go with him to a market. A fee was negotiated with me whereby Malam Ashana would travel to Kaduna, fetch two of his troupe, and I would then accompany them to Ladin Makole market where I would film them in action. The discussion that follows is based upon observation of Malam Ashana performing for reward in the market. However, this would not constitute an accurate representation of his current means of livelihood. Fees from radio, television and occasional patrons are of much greater significance to him.

Text recitation

The first 'set text' is a 'routine' that was sold as a 45 r.p.m. record some years ago and which formed a component in his trajectory through the market at Ladin Makole. As a result of the recording it is a well-known routine and receives a mixed reception. The ambiguity of response comes from an uncomfortable ambiguity of perceived intent. A number of commentators with whom I discussed the performance indicated that the piece could be taken either to be making fun of *malamai* 'Islamic clerics' which is legitimate if risky, or could be seen to be mocking the recitation of the religious texts themselves which is not to be tolerated.

Malam Ashana takes for his model one of the important and serious religious occasions involving public performance in front of, on occasion, as many as a thousand people – the public exegesis of verses of the Koran and other religious texts during the evenings of the month of Ramadan, the fast. This process, *tafsir*, involves a Koranic student, normally of some maturity, a pupil of the *malam* 'learned man', reciting lines and half-lines from the religious texts interspersed with explanations in Hausa by the *malam* of the meaning and implications of the Arabic. The Arabic is intoned rather than simply spoken and the explanations tend to be rapid-fire and forcefully articulated. Malam Ashana, in his parody, picks up the intonation and affixal morphology of the Arabic, the rapid verbal exchanges between his models, and the brevity of explanation. The substitution of alternative subject matter, food, with mock Arabic built around Hausa words (see Gidley (1967: 60–1) for further examples) makes comic the manipulation of a language, control of which normally endows prestige. The imitation of *tafsir* is acute in its observation and remarkable in its co-ordination between Malam Ashana and his colleague. The performance lasts not more than a few minutes, yet a great deal of accurate and incisive observation is mixed with incongruous humour in that very short space of time. In collaboration with Yusufu Kankiya I set out below a Hausa transcription of an extract from the text with the nearest thing to a translation we have been able to make.

'Exegesis'
Hausa text of *'Fassara da Karatu'* [32]

Hausa words contained within the mock Arabic are marked in bold; figures in the margin refer to line numbers corresponding to the translation below.

A: Ashana
F: 'Friend'
A: Ya bismillahi kuramani mu ci.
F: To malam da ka ce 'ya bismillahi kuramani mu ci' domin ci da sha a gare mu ne kadan rana ta yi.
A: To.
F: Sai mun ci mun sha muke amfanin wani, wani ma yake amfaninmu.
5 A: Wa **saya**kum,
F: Ko da sayen tsire zalla malam.
A: Mm.
F: **Wasaye**ntakuna – idan ka sayi tsire, w**azuga**kum – a zuge maka a takarda ko a faranti.
A: Na'am!
10 F: Wa**yas**ta'aluna – yas, yar da,
A: Na'am!
F: A ya da tsinken. A jikin tsire ba wani haramun sai tsinken nan.
A: To,
F: I, shi ne haramun.
15 A: Watau a jikin tsire,

F: Ba haram!

A: Sai tsinke,

F: Sai tsinken nan kawai;

A: Shi ne wayastaluna?

20   F: Shi ne wayastaluun.

A: Too!

F: I.

A: Allah shi gafarta malam!

F: Datsright.

25   A: Wasayakum,

F: To, ka ji sayen nama danye wajibi ne ga maigida.

A: To, watsokakun,

F: Tsoka zalla malam.

A: Wawajiyakum,

30   F: Da wajiya.

A: Yawatantakwashin tumaturrruwantakuuwam,

F: To, gafarta malam, da ka ce 'ya watantakwashin tumaturuwan-
takuuwam', shi tantakwashi ba a samunsa koina a majalisar dinkin
duniya kasuwa.

A: Allah shi gafarta malam.

Translation

In the following translation mock Arabic has been retained around English
translations of the words highlighted above in bold.

A: In the name of Allah let's eat.

F: Well, malam, in saying 'In the name of Allah let's eat' we mean we
must eat and drink when the day is full.

A: I see.

F: Only when we have eaten and drunk are we useful to others and
them to us.

5   A: Wabuykum,

F: Even if its only kebabs, malam.

A: Mm.

F: Wabuyingtakuna – if you buy kebabs, waplonkum – they'll be
taken off the skewer and plonked on to paper or plate.

A: Indeed!

10   F: Wachuckta'aluna – chuck, discard,

A: Indeed!

F: And the skewer chucked away. There's nothing forbidden on the
skewer only the skewer itself.

A: I see.

F: Yes, that's forbidden.

15   A: You mean, on the skewer.

F: Nothing's forbidden!

A: Only the skewer,

F: Only the skewer alone;

A: That is wa**chuck**taluna?

20   F: That is wa**chuck**taluun.

A: I get it!

F: Yes.

A: How very knowledgeable the *malam* is!

F: Dat's right. (Eng.)

25   A: Wa**buy**kum,

F: So you see it is incumbent upon the head of the household to buy raw meat.

A: I see, wa**boneless**kun

F: Nothing but solid meat,

A: Wa**fatty**kum,

30   F: With plenty of fat.

A: Yawa**marrowbone**n **tomato**wantakuuwam,

F: Well, sir, when you said 'Yawa**marrowbone**n **tomato**wantakuu-wam', the marrowbone is nowhere available in the market of the United Nations.

A: How very knowledgeable the malam is!

Patterns

The full text of 'Fassara da Karatu' (see Furniss 1991b) has an accelerative quality to it entirely separate from any question of performance speed or style. Like swinging a sling three times round the head before letting fly, a recursive pattern in the interplay between the two actors debouches into a sequence of closely parallel and closely packed exchanges tracing the series of actions building up to the climactic act, in the world of the *dan kama,* of actually eating; whereupon the 'routine' abruptly tails away.

In all parts of the routine one actor offers items of mock Arabic and the other provides an authoritative but spurious gloss. The exegesist is then supported by the first actor who interpolates words of agreement, or repeats back the statement or offers the statement back as a question seeking confirmation, or may ask an incidental question, ending finally with agreement between them. Where a *malam* will take as his text a religious verse, Malam Ashana takes food as his text, creating humour out of his seriousness about food, touching incidentally upon one of his recurrent themes, the necessity for men to take up arms to wrest control of the kitchen away from women.

'Parade'

A further 'set text' that occurs in the filmed performance is also to be found on a record made by Malam Ashana entitled 'Parade' where the object of his attention is a very different kind of public performance again involving the comic manipulation of a foreign language – an army parade. In this case the imitation particularly picks up the use of English and the absurdity of soldier-speak.

As in the case of the previous example, the pastiche draws its bite from the substitution of food-related references for the highly conventionalised content of parade ground interchanges. Incongruity is the basis of the humour but it is also the key to the stock-in-trade of the *dan kama* which is the foregrounding of the medium rather than the message. Where the conventional format – complete with its overtones of seriousness and importance – of religious-text exegesis is usually transparent, implicit and goes largely unnoticed by the listener, the pastiche abruptly drags the format centre-stage and highlights the potential divisibility of form from content. Subversive is the act that ruptures the seemingly seamless whole that is the serious social performance. In the case of 'Parade', the 'other' text against which this pastiche operates is one in which little of great moment would normally be conveyed but is full of highly stylised interchanges making it ripe for imitation. Where the religious-text exegesis played with the admixture of Hausa and Arabic, in 'Parade' the play is between Hausa and English where the English is an approximation of military speech styles. Under military government, the pastiche is perhaps slightly more *risqué* than it might otherwise be, but a military man would be hard put to find anything objectionable in its content, more that it simply holds up for notice and amusement his particular verbal style:

> CO   (Commanding Officer) (Ashana): Ai su waitan! A duba hanka-linka da kyau. Sajan tuwo wanda ya ke aiki a kicin, shi ne malam Muhammadu Kano. Yanzun nan za mu kirawo ka, ka yi attenshun in ba ka riyt wan, in ba ka dama da hagun, ka duba sa'annan ka yi begila, sa'annan mu taimaka maka domin mu karɓi girki a hannun mata. Mu ne waɗanda za mu shiga cikin kicin Malam Muhammadu Kano!
>
> MK: Yessa!
>
> CO: Kamfanin ku!
>
> MK: Fast bataliya.
>
> 5   CO: Lamba nawa?
>
> MK: Lamba two.
>
> CO: Lamban tabarmanka?
>
> MK: Lamba three.
>
> CO: Lambar kicin da kake shiga?
>
> 10   MK: Lamba four eight.
>
> CO: Sabo da haka yanzu ina begilanka?
>
> MK: Hup din.
>
> [*Bugle imitation with drums beating a tattoo*]

CO: Paraaaa shan! Sulemanu Kano.

SK: Alright.

15　CO: Kamfaninku?

SK: Fast bataliya.

CO: Lamba nawa?

SK: Lamba four.

CO: Lamban tabarmanka?

20　SK: Five.

CO: Lambar kicin da kake shiga?

SK: Seven.

CO: Kwaɗayi gidan mutane.

SK: Ten.

25　CO: Good! Skola Yako.

SY: Yes siiir!

CO: Kamfaninku?

SY: Fast bataliya.

CO: Lamba nawa?

30　SY: 3892.

CO: Kai!

SY: Ya!

CO: Lamban tabarmanka?

SY: Lamba 679.

35　CO: Lamban cokalinka?

SY: 3895.

Translation

CO (Ashana): Ai su waitan! Look sharp there. Sergeant Pap who works in the kitchen, that is Malam Muhammadu Kano. You are going to be called out, you will come to attention and right turn, you will turn right then left, you will have a good look and then blow on your bugle, then we will help and we'll wrest the cooking away from the women. We are the ones who will go into the kitchen, Malam Muhammadu Kano!

MK: Yessa!

CO: Your company?

MK: First battalion.

5　CO: What number?

MK: Number two.

CO: The number of your mat?

MK: Number three.

CO: Number of the kitchen you frequent?

10　MK: Number four eight.

CO: So now where is your bugle?

MK: Hup din.

[*Bugle imitation + drums beating a tattoo*]

CO: Paraaaa shan! Sulemanu Kano.

SK: Alright.

15 CO: Your company?

SK: First battalion.

CO: What number?

SK: Number four.

CO: Number of your mat?

20 SK: Five.

CO: Number of the kitchen you frequent?

SK: Seven.

CO: Greed at another's table.

SK: Ten [code for muscling into someone else's mess room and eating for free]

25 CO: Good! Skola Yako.

SY: Yes siiir!

CO: Your company?

SY: First battalion.

CO: What number?

30 SY: 3892.

CO: You!

SY: Ya!

CO: Number of your mat?

SY: Number 679.

35 CO: Number of your spoon?

SY: 3895.

As in the case of the religious-text exegesis, the routine deploys recursive patterns in which the 'commanding officer' asks each soldier in turn for a series of numbers. The 'underlying text' is the simple, formal request on parade for a soldier's number. In this case, the humour is based upon the extension of that question not only to the soldier's battalion but, true to the classic *dan kama* substitution, the number of his spoon, his mat and his kitchen!

Evident in these two routines, 'Exegesis' and 'Parade', is the characteristic so typical of orature: a recursive pattern, sometimes dismissed as mere 'repetition', which establishes both a salience for the internal structure of each segment and an overall form to the routine. The inherent tension between repetition and progression, as in country dancing or certain types of games, produces key moments where the leader makes a decision whether to 'go round again' or to move on to the next stage (see Furniss 1991b).

Malam Ashana 'Mister Matches'

Malam Ashana lives in Mandawari ward in the old city of Kano with his (allegedly) 110-year-old mother, Hajiya Innatu, and his only daughter. He is now in his late fifties or early sixties and rarely performs in markets these days. Television appearances are somewhat more lucrative, as is the occasional commissioned performance. Twenty years ago he worked with a sizeable troupe: his main men, Inuwa and Sule Yaro, then some six others also, Musa, Yakubu, Uba, Sani, Ibrahim and Alhaji Adamu. Today, a number of them still work in Kaduna, where there is considered to be a larger concentration of generous patrons, and in Zaria.

His mother, Hajiya Innatu, is an indomitable old woman, from a family of drummers and singers. It was she who taught Malam Ashana and his brothers to sing and drum and perform as *'yan kama*. His father's line were clerics, *malamai*. Ashana's father, Malam Tarumi, died when the children were young and the old lady brought the children up on her own. By Ashana's own calculation he has been performing as a *dan kama* for some 46 years. In the years of the Emir Sanusi (1953–63), Hajiya Innatu and her sons were patronised by royalty; Sanusi giving them a house in Gwagwarwa and another in Mandawari ward where they still live. In recent years however they have fallen on hard times.

In commenting further upon his texts in action, I would like to concentrate upon four things: the creation and manipulation of performance space; the control and manipulation by Ashana of the people around him; sanctioned transgression; and the relationship between 'set text' and improvised 'business'.

Performance space

Manifestly the market is a theatre with well-established, commonplace, performance conventions. The business of buying and selling is conducted within the sight and hearing of many passers-by, yet any one transaction takes place in a conventionally private place: others stand and wait their turn, discreetly they 'do not watch' or 'do not listen'. The routinised exchanges are entirely audible but go 'unnoticed' – until an altercation changes all of that; an altercation breaches normal practice and private place becomes arena; just as quickly the crowd is gone and a conventional privacy returns. But 'arena' is not the right word – the crowd forms not as if in ordered ranks but as a pressing throng in which there is but one recognised boundary or point of separation – the line which separates spectator from participant. It is, of course, not a physical line but a line of perception which may or may not coincide with a physical divide.

Malam Ashana, as he works the market, is constantly attending to that line. It is a line that presses in on him and with which he plays. In physical terms, Ashana moves from place to place within the market. Moving on entails a repeated lapse into confusion as he walks followed by his men, Inuwa and Sule Yaro. He is surrounded by jostling people as he picks his way along the narrow paths through the market. These are paths which are occupied by others, paths to which others have rights of access and on which the theatre of buying and selling is also being conducted. The throng going with him overwhelms the 'legitimate users'.

Suddenly, Ashana drops anchor. His first action is to re-establish contact with his men, turning and gesturing them to come to a little distance from him. Typically he establishes a geometry, a triangle between himself, his men and the object of his attentions – a stall-holder, a vendor, a passer-by. Immediately their priority is to clear a physical space, to create order from the confusion of excited onlookers. At all times, Ashana maintains the initiative, verbally, physically, with his drumming, with his appearance. The crowd draws back to form a circle around the group and their free-standing protagonist, or forms a semi-circle in which the stall is the linear backdrop with the stall-holder centre stage. To provoke the withdrawal of the 'front' of the crowd Ashana uses a series of sudden actions to invoke a frisson of fear, not of injury but of being singled out for transformation from onlooker to participant. He darts into the crowd, grabs a child, spins it round, pushes it back into the crowd, he reaches out and grabs a hat and throws it off into the air, he makes to strike, he runs at the wall and they break and turn. But the semi-circle is never stable, people are pushing forward, others try to get a better view. Ashana launches into his piece of action or text; however, with his men, he guards the integrity of the performance space by occasionally and unexpectedly breaking off to force back the crowd until finally a rush out of the arena by Ashana marks the dissolution of the frame and provides the signal for the circus to move on. The stall-holder, who, up till the arrival of Ashana, had been conducting his own private theatre, has had his stage usurped, and has been made a more-or-less willing participant in a public play for which he knew little of the script.

Watching Ashana at work it is clear that certain well-established routines, such as 'Parade' and 'Exegesis' require the prior establishment of discreet space and a physical delimitation of the place of the audience and of the actors, a place at which the actors act and the audience observes. In other situations Ashana controls physical space while at the same time manipulating the people around him so that they are switched by him from observer status to participant and back again.

Control

Essential to Ashana's technique is his control of people for the brief period in which he interacts with them in his role as a *dan kama*. His theme is always food. As he moves through the market, he chances upon hawkers of beancakes, of cooked meat, of vegetables, fruit, sweet drinks; he ignores cloth-sellers, metalworkers or any other purveyors of non-comestibles. Passers-by he may pick on briefly. As he moves at the head of the crowd he picks on a vendor. First, he makes contact, a gesture, a word, an engagement with that person; then he waits for the crowd to gather round and his drummers to catch up to form the physical arrangement referred to above. As they form up, his 'protagonist' realises what is coming and is usually caught with no way out. Ashana will either engage him or her directly in dialogue, act out a bit of business with one of his men in front of the stall; or simply mime a routine – in each case the stall-holder finds that some item from his wares has been appropriated into Ashana's act, is being consumed or taken away, in mock theft or in seeming payment for Ashana's attentions. The stall-holder sometimes also 'pays' for Ashana's services with cash thereby marking closure in the routine. It is difficult for the stall-holder to regain control of his environment by attempting to tell Ashana to go away – any such attempt is immediately turned to his advantage by Ashana who mocks him further. In one case observed, an old lady tried to shoo him away, only to end up incorporated into a humorous routine herself.

The performance requires the expenditure of great energy and it is the high level of energy combined with the suddenness of decisions – to move on, to stop, to switch attention from one person to another – which retains for Ashana control over proceedings. No one stops him, no one prescribes for him and, gently manipulated, people pay.

Transgression

Some of Ashana's routines are subversive in that they are pastiches, as I have described, that point up the characteristics of certain types of texts from the 'serious' world. The very act of pointing them up by substituting incongruous subject matter is the basis of the bite and the humour. In his performance there is another form of subversion that provides the 'shock', even if only mild, that underlies his humour. In his actions and behaviour he repeatedly breaches conventions. Not only does he exaggeratedly make as if to steal, with one of his men as accomplice, from a stall-holder, he does actually take and eat that for which he does not pay. He takes and gives to his men. He uses and spoils saleable goods in the course of a mime. Admittedly, he does, also, sometimes look for the stall-holder's tacit permission, but not always. Real theft in the market would be a serious matter.

To upbraid a stranger on his or her appearance or language would normally provoke a serious altercation; to attack a child would provoke adult outrage; to physically manhandle an adolescent girl so that she bursts into tears would be a serious breach of etiquette; to flirt outrageously in public with young women would be considered shameless. All these Ashana does, before a transient and itinerant audience, and always with humour. It is significant that these episodes are brief, Ashana does not push his luck, he

drops into a piece of business and quickly drops out again. For the participants and the audience they have hardly grasped what has happened before
he has moved on.

Text and business

In Ashana's progress through the market there is a constant tension between
continuity and rupture, between repetition and progression. His drumming,
and that of his men, fills the interstices between routines and moments of
interaction with people in the market. The continuity provided by the drumming runs on underneath dialogues and monologues and has a crucial role
in maintaining the sense of energy and excitement essential for Ashana's
control of events. At the same time that continuity is the background for
sudden excursions, changes of venue and changes of topic.

In the pattern of the texts presented above it is possible to see the way in
which set routines, set 'texts', deploy recursive routes along with points of
rupture at which a new direction can be taken. A parallel recursiveness is to
be seen in the way in which each new venue involves repeated setting-up,
repeated patterns of interaction with both audience and stall-holder/pro-
tagonist and repeated methods of exit in order to move on. At least as far as
set routines such as those given here are concerned, patterns of the text
operate in parallel with patterns in action.

'YAN GAMBARA

'Yan gambara (named after the gambara drum they play) are termed 'stroll-
ing minstrels' by Kofoworola (Kofoworola and Lateef 1987: 94). From the
rhythmic style of speech in performance S. B. Ahmad and Furniss (1994)
have termed them 'rap artists'.[33] Much of the ensuing discussion is adapted
from Ahmad and Furniss (1994). Kofoworola (Kofoworola and Lateef
1987) discusses the performers led by Lawai Gambara from Kofar Kaura in
Katsina. Yusufu (1972) bases his discussion on the groups led by Sale
Maigambara, Ado Maigambara of Jos, Duna Maigambara of Zaria (who
may be the same as the Muhammed Duna discussed below) and one Shehu
Maigambara. Their performances are built around a variety of verbal routines, extravagant self-praise, banter and insult between themselves, and
funny anecdotes. Yusufu transcribes a piece of self-praise from Sale
Maigambara:

> Kai, bara damisa, bana zaki, in ko ta shekara kutunkun ɓauna, kai, aiki
> ba ka son a fara a bari, kiri? Ni ke maganin gujajjen bawa, ni zarto
> maganin kara mai tsutsa, a kai mu a dosa in dai waƙa ce.

> You were a leopard last year but this year a lion and next year a big
> bull-buffalo; oh, work hates to be started and left unfinished; I am an
> ox-hide rope the answer to a run-away slave, I am a saw the remedy for

a worm-eaten staff. Let us be matched anywhere if it is a question of song. (adapted from Yusufu 1972: 5)

One of the most typical characteristics of *'yan gambara* is insulting banter, and Yusufu again provides an example of a piece of dialogue between Shehu Maigambara and his sidekick, Abdu:

s: Abdu kake zare idanduna kamar rago na karo, ga ƙaton ciki kamar sacen sha bakwai!
a: Ni ka yi wa haka, cikin ritsitsi kamar ɗan maraƙin dala
s: Mutum ba ya yin haka, da 'yar maran nan kamar biri ya hau keke,
a: Af, ni ka yi wa haka, da ɗan dantsen nan kamar na tsohuwa ta shekara ba lafiya.
s: Kai ma ka iya, fuska ƙiris kamar romo ya ɓare, ga ƙashin hancin nan kamar itacen shanyar rini.

s: What Abdu, why do you look like that, your eyes like those of a charging ram! With a stomach as big as a 17-shilling gown!
a: You dare say that of me! Your stomach so big and fat like it's full of two shillings worth of heifer!
s: You don't say that to a friend! Look at your lower half, the stomach's like a monkey riding a bicycle!
a: What are you saying to me! Your arm is like an old woman's who has been lying ill for a year!
s: You really master the art! You who have such a small face like a drop of broth, and the bridge of your nose is small and bent like the wooden pegs used for drying dyed cloths! (adapted from Yusufu 1972: 9)

It is the characteristic banter between two or more *'yan gambara* which provides the sense of dramatic performance that is the theme of this chapter.

In early September 1989, a colleague, Sa'idu Ahmad, and I encountered a group of *'yan gambara* entertaining passers-by on market-day at Ladin Makole market near Kano, Nigeria. They were the lead performer, Muhammed Duna, his main partner in performance, Idi ɗan Gyatuma, and a younger member of the troupe, Dan Bado, who occasionally interpolated responses.

The discussion that follows comes from a paper co-authored with Sa'idu Ahmad and presents extracts from a filmed performance by these *'yan gambara*, with the text transcribed and translated from the spoken Hausa. The focus of the commentary below is upon the typification process and the 'chains' of association that are to be seen in the discussion of 'drivers' and the standard of driving on Nigerian roads. With the daily slaughter that occurs on Nigerian roads this is a subject of perpetual comment among ordinary people whose journeys to and from home villages and markets put them at the mercy of local bus and lorry drivers. This is one section in a longer performance that talked of a variety of issues – people from Tofa town, prostitutes, and many other subjects.

D: Muhammed Duna
G: Idi Ɗan Gyatuma

(Direbobi)

D: Ɗan Gyatuma!
G: Iye
D: Na gaya wa direbobi
     Ka ga wannan ma ɗan Fulanin tuƙi ne
     Ibrahim direba kenan
     To Ibrahim direba ya burge mu!
     Ɗan Barebari mai tuƙin fa?
     Bayan ya ban kuɗi
G: Iye
D: Ya kuma ban tufar da zan sanyawa
G: Ya ba ka
D: Kuma na tambaye shi na ji batun gaskiya
G: Kwarai
D: To ni dai ban hana a hau bisa mota ba!
G: Haka aka yi
D: Ɗan Gyatuma waɗansu da tuƙi ake
G: Kwarai
D: 'Yan burar uba waɗansu da hauka suke!
G: Ba shakka
D: Wai ashe tuƙi ya yi kyau ido ke nunawa?
G: Kwarai da gaske
D: 'Yan burar uba waɗansu da hauka!
G: Ba shakka
D: A shekara tuƙi ake amma ba riga
G: Allah ya kiyaye
D: Wai ka ga direba sai haukan wofi
G: Iye
D: Sai ka ga kafiri da riga ba hannuwa
G: Allah ya kiyaye
D: Kamar ungulu kan bene!
G: Ɗan burar uba!
D: Sai ka ga ɗan hawa a nan ba fa wucewa,
G: Ai ƙanƙane
D: Mota ta mace yana zare idanu,
G: Ɗan burar uba!
D: 'Ku zo ku tura ni!'

G: Subhanalillahi

D: Ana 'wannan ɗan hawan ba za ta wuce ba?!'
Ji kafiri baƙin goshin sai ka ce zabirar wanzamai!

G: Allah ya kiyaye!

D: Ɗan Gyatuma!

G: Na'am

D: Allah ya jiƙan maza

G: Allah amin

D: Sani direba Tofa na tuna shi
Allah ya jiƙansa

G: Allah amin

D: Wai shi Ɗan Wali?
Ubangiji ya yi kiransa

G: Allah amin

D: Allah ya sa kiyamarsa da sauƙi

G: Allah amin

D: Ya biya kiɗana ba bashi ba
Yanzu sai Muhamman Mutari
Mutari ɗan mutanen Kabo
Mai tuƙi mala'iku na tura mai.
Amma ka gano direba sai haukan wofi
Ɗan burar uba baƙar mara sai ka ce Barau ya hau keke!

G: Allah ya kiyaye

D: Sai riga ba hannuwa kamar ungulu kan bene!

G: Allah ya kare!

D: Wannan Ubangiji Allah ya kare

(Drivers)

D: Ɗan Gyatuma!

G: Yes

D: I told the drivers
You see this Fulani man is a driver
He is Ibrahim the driver
Yes, Ibrahim the driver amazed us!
What about the Kanuri driver?
After he gave me money

G: Yes

D: He also gave me clothes to wear

G: He did indeed

D: I asked him and I heard the truth

G: Absolutely

D: I am not opposed to people being drivers!

G: That's right

D: Dan Gyatuma, some people do drive

G: Absolutely

D: And some sons of bitches are crazy!

G: Without a doubt

D: When driving is done well isn't it clear for all to see?

G: Quite right

D: Some of these sons of bitches are crazy!

G: Without a doubt

D: They'll drive for a year and yet have no decent clothes

G: Lord preserve us

D: You'll see a driver going crazy and all for nothing

G: Yes

D: You'll see a rogue in a gown with no sleeves

G: Lord preserve us

D: Like a vulture on a tall building!

G: The bastard!

D: You'll see a slight rise in the road and he can't make it past it,

G: Just a small one

D: The engine's dead and his eyes are bulging,

G: The bastard!

D: 'Come and give me a push!'

G: Lord protect us

D: Someone says, 'Can't the car manage this slight slope?!'
   See the rogue with a dark forehead like a barber's bag!

G: Lord preserve us!

D: Dan Gyatuma!

G: Yes

D: May God be merciful to people

G: Allah amen

D: Sani the driver from Tofa I remember
   Lord have mercy upon him

G: Allah amen

D: What about Dan Wali?
   The Lord has called him

G: Allah amen

D: Lord make his stay in the hereafter peaceful

G: Allah amen

D: He paid for my music and no debt was incurred
   And now Muhamman Mutari
   Mutari the son of the people of Kabo
   He who drives with the guidance of angels.
   But you'll see another driver who's utterly crazy
   A black-arsed son of a bitch like a monkey on a bicycle!

G: Lord preserve us
D: With a sleeveless gown like a vulture on a tall building!
G: Lord protect us!
D: Lord preserve us from all this.

The section 'Drivers' begins with the establishment of two parties to a discourse, 'me' and the general category 'drivers'; drivers as a category are then modulated to a particular driver, the Fulani man, Ibrahim, and the notion of a relationship between 'us' and Ibrahim is taken forward by 'the driver amazed us' which is ambiguous: is it amazement at his skill/excellence/ goodness which immediately sets a laudatory tone slotting into the 'genre language' of praise, implying potentially a patron–client relationship between 'me' and Ibrahim? Or is it amazement at his awfulness which would imply the other side of the praise coin – a potential vilification? The ambiguity is not resolved in relation to Ibrahim because the topic of one particular driver produces an associational leap to another, 'the Kanuri driver'. But in this case the question posed by the original ambiguity is resolved in a clear affirmation of a patron-client relationship in 'he gave me money [and] ... clothes to wear'. The next link picks up the original notion of a dialogue between 'me' and 'a driver' but inserts a new factor, the notion of truth, and leads into a 'moral' framework of 'good' and 'bad'. Truths are moral truths. These contrastive categories then provide an alternating sequence of statements about 'good' and 'bad' drivers prefaced by an authorial disclaimer of bias against the 'driver' category as a whole, 'I am not opposed to people being drivers'. This alternation is followed by an expanded discussion of bad drivers.

Immediately after this lengthy expansion, which contains the imitation and the epithetic flourish as the rhetorical high point of the discussion, there comes a junction/section marker, 'Dan Gyatuma! Yes', at which the performer can make and mark a transition to another topic. Here, however, he opts to go round the subject again, making a loop through the sequence of components referred to above. First, the naming of a driver, Sani, then 'Dan Wali, with whom he was in a patron–client relationship 'He paid for my music', and a third, Mutari, whom he again praises, 'He who drives with the guidance of angels.' In contrast with the first time around, the later two drivers have died and the performer and respondent invoke God's mercy upon them. The possible implication is that they died in road accidents, although that is not stated, thus reinforcing, in that ambiguity, the overall point about death on the roads. The rhetorical punch of the second circuit of the topic lies again in the final invective against bad drivers and the invocation 'Lord preserve us from all this.'

Manifestly, there are repetitive patterns apparent here in the ideational structure which indicate the necessary components in a certain sequence:

'me' and 'drivers', a clientage relationship (praise), an evaluative framework of 'good' and 'bad', rhetorical invective, and a junction point.

Rhetorical questions and epithetic speech

In addition to the ideational structure of the piece, there is a dimension of language use which overlays the patterning apparent in the section: changes in language style corresponding to commonly recognised registers. These referential overtones reverberate through the piece. The interaction between performer and respondent(s) is discussed in more detail below, but there is a mode of rhetorical question to which the respondent's comments do not constitute an answer. It is the performer who answers himself: 'What about the Kanuri driver? After he … gave me money he gave me clothes to wear'; 'When driving is done well isn't it clear for all to see? Some of these sons of bitches are crazy!'; 'What about Dan Wali? The Lord has called him'. The extract makes use of epithetic (*kirari*) speech which, as discussed in Chapter 4, is typical of praise and invective. Redolent with attitudinal rather than propositional characteristics, such speech styles make extensive use of imagery. This performer uses the evaluative density of epithetic speech with its striking imagery to carry the 'punchlines' of the piece. But epithetic speech, rather than simply 'epithets', comes in a variety of recognised forms. There is the simple use of name plus juxtaposed occupation/place of origin as in *Ibrahim : direba* 'Ibrahim : the driver', *Dan Barebari : mai tuki* 'the Kanuri man : the driver', but there is also the more extensive vilificatory epithet consisting of topic plus comment (sometimes extended with simile) as in the following, *direba : sai haukan wofi* 'driver : going crazy and all for nothing'; *kafiri : da riga ba hannuwa kamar ungulu kan bene* 'rogue : in a gown with no sleeves like a vulture on a tall building'; *kafiri : bakin goshin sai ka ce zabirar wanzami* 'rogue : with a dark forehead like a barber's bag'. The penultimate epithet of this section is picked up and repeated later in the second half along with an even stronger piece of epithetic invective: *dan burar uba bakar mara : sai ka ce Barau ya hau keke* 'a black-arsed son of a bitch : like a monkey on a bicycle'. The 'punchline' of the first part of this extract finishes on a vilificatory epithet, but an important, and amusing immediately preceding piece is in a contrastive mode: it is not authorial commentary as with epithet but an anecdotal imitation acting out the crazy driver and his useless vehicle:

> You'll see a slight rise in the road and he can't make it past it, the engine's dead and his eyes are bulging, 'Come and give me a push!' Someone says, 'Can't it manage this slight slope?'

In the extract discussed above there is an ideational pattern through which one topic is linked to the next, and a moral framework for the piece is established. This pattern is repeated and is overlaid by a series of switches of register, one of which, epithetic speech, is deployed to provide the punchline of the piece. The epithetic-speech genre is most intensely evaluative providing the strongest vilification of the performer's target: the bad driver.

These components go towards establishing that which makes this performer's production distinctive. The next section discusses other aspects of the performance of the text which also contribute to the establishment of distinctiveness before turning to the significance, for its persuasiveness and ideological 'force', of one particular feature: the seemingly interactive, dialogic form of the performance.

Immediately apparent from the video recording is the striking combination of verbal style with drum accompaniment. The drum accompaniment provides a constant rhythmic pattern against which the words operate. We have not investigated in detail the relationship between words and drum, but it appears that each verbal phrase is accompanied by four measures in the drum pattern; this is immediately followed by a pause in the recitation by the main performer during which the respondent interpolates responses of various kinds. This pattern of main line, pause with accompanying insertion timed according to the lights of the drum rhythm, provides a general frame within which the performer operates. This is visually represented in the extract by each line of text.

Perceptually more striking and salient, however, is the style of verbal performance of the words themselves. The performer shouts his words over the top of the loud noise of the drum, great volume is accompanied by speed, since the drum rhythm sets up a considerable tempo. These prime performance characteristics establish immediate perceptual distinctions between this genre and other named genres of Hausa entertainment and oral performance. The shouted spoken word of *'yan gambara* is differentiated from the sung *waka* of popular singers or the chanted recitation of the *waka* of poets. This shouted spoken style is apparently typical of *'yan gambara* and is perhaps most reminiscent of the 'rap' style of some modern popular music.

Interaction and the non-dialogic

A striking characteristic of the performance by these *'yan gambara* is the speed of the interchanges between the lead performer, Muhammed Duna, and his main respondent, Dan Gyatuma. Nearly every line by Muhammed is immediately responded to by Dan Gyatuma giving the strong impression that not only is the performance dialogically structured but that a dialogue is actually taking place. The issue we discuss now is the nature of the relationship between the two performers 'in dialogue', and between the performers and the audience as witnesses to this performance.

In looking at how people argue or how they interact there are many features to explore: propositions, contradictions, counter-propositions, ironic restatements, repetitions, questions, answers, qualifications, additions, silence interpretable as confirmation and silence interpretable as disagreement.

Generally however, dialogue takes place where there is at least some independent input from more than one party; 'independent' in the sense that the
second party does more than simply repeat or affirm propositions from the
first. In another part of the performance discussed here, the overwhelming
incidence is of confirmation, in one way or another, by Dan Gyatuma (G) of
what is being said by Muhammed Duna (D). Call and response, question
and answer typify the performance. Even where Duna asks a question it is a
yes/no question and he is answered by an affirmation:

> D: Any old woman is a mother to you?
> G: Any old woman is a mother to me.

or,

> D: You hear me tell the truth, don't you?
> G: I hear the very perfection of truth.

or,

> D: Do they really mint money?
> G: They do indeed, Duna.

Again and again, Dan Gyatuma intervenes to confirm in a wide variety of
ways what Duna has been saying. The text given above provides the interpo-
lations as well as Duna's propositions. Only on one occasion in another part
of this performance did Dan Gyatuma intervene independently against a
proposition by Duna and then it is a qualification of an apparent self-criti-
cism by Duna:

> D: In all my family I am the only good-for-nothing.
> G: It's not true! You're no good-for-nothing, you're just earning your
>   daily bread.

While the performance involves a continuous flow of verbal interaction
between performers, it is a flow which, in the terms outlined above, is predominantly non-dialogic; it is a monologue in dialogic form (in contrast
with other performances where a single actor articulates both parties to a
dialogue, be it client and oracle in divination, or griot representing characters in a drama). However this flow of interaction has considerable rhetorical effect upon the persuasiveness of the performance in terms of getting
across to the audience both the typification of the subject matter and the
ideational evaluations that go with it. While members of the audience exercise, no doubt on reflection, their own independent judgements as to
whether they accept and endorse Duna's typifications of prostitutes, of Tofa
people, of drivers, or of 'yan gambara (the full text is to be found in S. B.
Ahmad and Furniss (1994)), the presence at the very same split second of a
voice which is saying 'it's true, it's true' tends to incorporate into the
moment of understanding a truth-value overtone to the proposition. It is in
the dynamics of the relationship between proposer, confirmer and listener

that the confirmation tends to exclude or pre-empt the possibility of counter-perception in the listener.

In discussing the way these performers typify 'drivers', we saw that the pattern in the presentation of the subject matter and characteristics of the performance event, from drum accompaniment to call-and-response form provided the elements of 'textuality' contributing to a distinctive, recurrent set of 'special language' features – a 'genre'. As the audience smiled with recognition and we smiled with them, we participated in the transfer of a particular view – of drivers, or of the people of Tofa town. The major components of that view were a particular typification and an evaluative overlay upon it.

WAWAN SARKI: THE EMIR'S FOOL

The existence of an emir's fool is reported by Kofoworola (1982, Kofoworola and Lateef 1987) in his discussion of the performing arts linked to the emir's court in Zaria and in M. Yahaya (1991). It is unclear whether court jesters have existed, or indeed still exist, attached to other courts, although M. Yahaya (1991: 30) claims they exist under a different name in the courts of Kano and Katsina. In addition to courtiers, messengers, musicians, praise-singers, bodyguards, and a wide variety of other functionaries, traditional courts are, and were, bound up in complex ceremonial surrounding the person of the emir.[34] Yahaya talks of a special relationship between the fool and the emir, providing for private communication and an independent voice in palace intrigues, 'the emir's fool is the one courtier who has the power to say anything to the emir, no matter how bitter' (trans. from M. Yahaya 1991: 10); he was a conduit used by other courtiers in their communication with the emir. Kofoworola goes further to suggest:

> He bridges the communication gap between the ruler and the ruled. He is informed of any serious breach of administration by the ruling class and, in his characteristically humorous manner, 'pulls the ears' of authority to what might develop into a serious conflict between the rulers and the ruled. (adapted from Kofoworola and Lateef 1987: 87)

This position of sanctioned licence is a hereditary one in the Zaria court. Yahaya lists the names of those who have held the position since the beginning of the nineteenth century (M. Yahaya 1991: 15). Kofoworola provides a graphic description of the appearance and behaviour of the emir's fool:

> He appears like a monstrous figure having clad himself in the skins of beasts. His head is clean shaven and on the bald head (and face) is rubbed blue and black powder. Two narrow pieces of leather are attached to a he-goat beard fixed on his chin, the leather pieces holding it on by coming down from the two sides of his head. (adapted from Kofoworola 1982: 137)

Wawan sarki will jump into action, and make a loud shrill noise through his nostrils. As he lands he will look the emir right in the face as if they are equals. Moving his face in all sorts of ways to evoke laughter, he will dash towards the emir with his big curved stick as if he intends to hit him with it. As the audience is taken aback he stops suddenly a few yards in front of the emir. Raising his big stick he will look at the emir again with a very firm countenance. Then he frowns just as one would at a stubborn child about to be punished. He shakes all over like someone in a fit of anger. Then gently he lowers his stick and lapses into loud laughter, looking around at the audience as if to inform them that he is just playing ... Tradition has it that an emir is supposed to be a firm, tough and bold person ... He must be serious and stern looking. A device to achieve some of these qualities is the use of *amawali* – the lower edge of the turban covering the mouth. This leaves only the mouth and the nose exposed, thus masking off any sign of emotional expression such as laughter ... He appears motionless and emotionless ... This is the idea behind the emir talking through an intermediary. When he sits on the throne to receive homage and obeisance from his citizens, he does not talk, there is no response to the stream of persons passing through to pay their tribute or homage. He does not even nod his head. But he has a large number of courtiers ... that will shout in chorus the emir's greetings and response to the homage-paying citizens: *sarki ya gaishe ku!* 'the emir acknowledges your greetings!' (adapted from Kofoworola and Lateef 1987: 86–7).

In discussion with Kofoworola the Wawan Sarkin Zazzau said:

> Who owns the town?
> Yes, I am the wawan sarki, the king's fool
> Sarki is the owner of the town
> As for me, I am his court jester
> As for me, I am his servant
> And throughout the landscape of Northern Nigeria
> I am the greatest king's fool
> No other king's fool has ever been taken on Hajj by Sarki
> Except me and my wife together.
>
> (Kofoworola and Lateef 1987: 88–9)

In the same way that we saw a genre of acting, in the case of *'yan kama*, able to transgress the boundaries of normal social behaviour in the market, so also we see here, in the context of a traditional court, the licensed transgression in behaviour and speech of the king's fool. The boundary between the real and the pretend is manipulated by these theatrical forms. Pretence is most clearly marked by the anecdotes told of the *'yan kama* who appear dressed as learned scholars at a court in session and then, having begun to infringe the boundaries of acceptable behaviour by arguing or using inappropriate language, suddenly reveal themselves as burlesque artists, to the relief, shock or amusement of all present. These breaches of the rules of 'real-life' theatre, be it the ordinary drama of market transactions or of formalised etiquette in the court, point up the existence of conventions and norms in daily life. Following Bakhtin, we see here, in the performances of *'yan kama*, the racy language of *'yan gambara* and the sanctioned transgression of the king's fool, a 'fully articulated superstructure of laughter, erected over all serious straightforward genres' (Bakhtin 1981: 17).

MIMETIC PERFORMANCE OCCASIONS IN THE HAUSA CALENDAR

The humorous sketches that go to make up TV plays, the stock characters and the domestic and village scenes that are reproduced time and again in scripted and improvised plays draw upon the fund of 'traditional' oral tales and the performance styles of the popular entertainers such as are discussed above. A further strand in the background, a familiar 'acting' tradition, is the mimetic entertainment that is performed at particular times of the year as part of the cycle of public celebrations and events.

In the discussion that follows, I am working on the basis of descriptions provided by others who have not generally indicated the degree to which they are describing actual events that take place regularly now in the 1990s, or are describing, or reconstructing, another element in 'tradition' – a composite view of what the past is supposed to have been like. Nevertheless, it is clear from the texts written in Nigeria for the general public (often drawing on the early text by Madauci, Isa and Daura (1968)) and for schools (Dangambo 1984b; Yahaya et al. 1992) that many scholars perceive these performance occasions, along with 'traditional' trades, medicines, kinship organisation, precepts of moral training, and marriage customs, as well as the genres of oral and written literature discussed here, as an integral part of Hausa 'traditional culture' to be propagated and preserved.

WASAN GAUTA AND *KALANKUWA*

As the king's fool is an integral part of court life in Zaria so there is a form of drama, *wasan gauta* which, according to Kofoworola (1980/2: 283–7; 1981b: 170–3; Kofoworola and Lateef 1987: 82–3), is also a part of court life, at least in Kano. Once a year the women of the royal household put on a dramatic entertainment under the patronage of the emir, performed within the palace to people of the palace. The play imitates contemporary personalities and events in the court.

In fact one of my informants said that the satiric imitation of the important personalities of the royal court is aimed at drawing their attention to issues that concern public opinion about them. As it has been suggested, the performance is meant to expose certain characters of the courtiers which are otherwise hidden from the emir. He (the emir) is made to recognise certain temperamental traits or character in his personality which he does not know or realise. (Kofoworola 1980/82: 284–5).

According to Kofoworola (Kofoworola and Lateef 1987: 83), during the colonial period this form of drama underwent adaptation and, as *wasan Gwamna*, became a vehicle for satirical comment upon the role of resident, district officers, doctors, nurses, education officers and others. No longer exclusively by women and far less private than previously, performances were enacted before colonial officials and traditional authorities as a comment upon their roles and relationships.

A similar form of entertainment which is created by and for ordinary people but which imitates court life and the personalities and stock characters of the courts is termed *kalankuwa*. With alternative names (U. B. Ahmed (1985: 43) cites *magi* for the Daura, Kazaure, Gumel and Haɗeja areas, and *assabano* for the Gobir area), *kalankuwa* is part of the series of sports and festivities that traditionally take place in the period immediately after the harvest (see I. Y. Yahaya 1991). Extending over two or three days, young people led by a *sarkin samari* 'youth leader' organise amongst themselves a dramatic entertainment, to take place in the evening in an open space in the town or village, during which one of them acts the part of the emir while others play vizier, judge, policeman and others. A variety of scenarios are improvised; disputes are brought before the emir, who refers them for consideration by his judge; cases are considered; judgements are made. U. B. Ahmed (1985: 43) indicates that *kalankuwa* can sometimes involve reciprocal performance visits from one town or village to another. The stereotypes that are acted out in *kalankuwa* can also occur in another form of mimetic performance termed *tashe*.

TASHE

Tashe is the name not for one event but for a whole series of mini performances that go on through the month of Ramadan, the month of the Fast, normally after dark when the fast is broken. Again performed mostly by young people, *tashe* involves moving from house to house enacting a particular scene and very often being rewarded by being given *sadaka* 'alms' by the householders so entertained. M. B. Umar (1981) derives the name from the necessity to rouse people (*tashi* 'to arise') before dawn so that food can be taken before the fast begins each day. There are a large number of recognised routines/acts that are performed as *tashe*. While they have traditionally been oral routines passed on from older to younger as a combination of character, dress and 'call and response' song/verbal routine, they have in recent years been transferred to print thereby beginning to fix them 'for posterity'. Z. I. Bello (1991) provides descriptions and song/verbal texts for 126 such *tashe* routines.[35] One of the most often cited is entitled, *Ka yi rawa malam!* 'But you danced, *malam!*' in which the stereotype of the learned *malam* is portrayed, doing what he should not, that is, dance. The routine is described by Bello as follows:

> This *tashe* is done by children and young people and it is done to amuse. First one of the young people dresses up as a learned and venerable *malam*. He puts on a cotton beard and sideburns, and carries a leather book satchel, an ink pot, a sheepskin to sit on, a writing board and all the other things a *malam* uses. When they are all ready then they go out from place to place and perform. The *malam* dances round and round while the others say:
>
> CHILDREN: You danced, *malam*, you definitely danced!
> MALAM: I didn't, I didn't!
> CHILDREN: Go home and tell them the *malam* danced!
> MALAM: I didn't, I didn't!
> CHILDREN: You danced, *malam*, you definitely danced!
> MALAM: But look at my beard!
> CHILDREN: You danced, *malam*, you definitely danced!
> MALAM: Look at my sideburns!
> CHILDREN You danced, *malam*, you definitely danced!
> MALAM: And my writing-board!
> CHILDREN: You danced, *malam*, you definitely danced!
> MALAM: I didn't, I didn't!
> CHILDREN: You danced, *malam*, you definitely danced!
> MALAM: All right then, let me have a go!
>
> (translated from Z. I. Bello 1991: 22–3)

In another routine known as *Jatau mai Magani* ('Jatau with the Medicines') the stereotype of the *boka* 'medicine-pedlar' is brought to life. According to Alhamdu's observations (1973), the young man playing Jatau is imitatively garlanded with potions, charms, medicinal plants and the like. On entering the routine, Jatau declaims the efficacy of his medicines against every conceivable illness, borrowing from the *dan kama* his opening joke that food is the medicine for hunger, and then going on to produce bits of the *giyarya* tree 'Mitragyna inermis' as medicine for diarrhoea, chilli pepper as the medicine for soup, palm fronds as medicine for mats, and a whole series of objects with incongruous associations provided for them, all within the framework, 'here is X, the best medicine for Y'.

Another of our stereotypes that goes back to the earlier discussion of TV drama and beyond is the non-Hausa Gwari man. In the *tashe* routine *macukule* a young actor is dressed up as a Gwari man, equipped with a donkey skull, and march around declaring how delicious food is when it is made from dogs, or cockroaches, etc. (G. Abdu 1981).

A number of commentators indicate that there are routines specifically for girls and others specifically for boys. Alhamdu (1973) illustrates with the following texts of two call and response routines for girls (rendered below as C and R), the first entitled 'Sharu's Marriage has Ended!'

C: Sharu's marriage has ended!
R: How can I be patient!
C: Always 'be patient', always 'be patient'!
R: How can I be patient!
C: I am sleeping here no longer!
R: How can I be patient!
C: Always beaten, always abused!
R: How can I be patient!
C: Always patient, and at night he abuses my father!
R: How can I be patient!
C: I am sleeping here no longer!
R: How can I be patient!
C: Sharu has eaten everything!
R: How can I be patient!
C: Look how high the plate was piled!
R: How can I be patient!

In the second example the main girl stuffs a pillow up her shirt to look pregnant:

C: Who's the father?
R: She's pregnant!
C: Honestly I don't like that name!
R: She's pregnant!
C: I am going to fall out with that man!
R: She's pregnant!
C: This is going to go before the judge!
R: She's pregnant!
C: I am going to have a fight with that man!

In addition to these forms of what U. B. Ahmed (1985) calls 'community drama' there are other forms of apparently mimetic performance, for example, *giwa shan laka* 'elephant in the mud' in Zamfara, *bikin bude daji* 'Opening-the-bush Festival' in the north of Sokoto State, which Ahmed relates to customs within the non-Islamic *Maguzawa* cultural worlds.

In this chapter we have seen both formal theatre and a variety of popular mimetic genres. Formal theatre draws from the stock of stereotyped characters so ubiquitous in tales and elsewhere. The most typical technique of composition involves improvisation of script and business within a prearranged story-line and overall framework. A strongly didactic element is evident under the comic surface of most plays. Within the world of popular dramatic performances in burlesque and other forms, pastiche and racy humour provide an alternative voice, articulating the concerns of ordinary people, or, as in the final examples cited above, providing a momentary glimpse of people answering back.

6

SONG AND FREELANCE POPULAR SINGERS

In June 1973 one of the most popular of Hausa singers, Alhaji Mamman Shata, was in conversation with Dandatti Abdulƙadir, talking about himself and his art:

> ... Yes I think there are more than one thousand discs. The length of the discs vary, some of them are fifteen minutes others are thirty minutes and the longest ones are forty-five minute discs. In the 1950's these discs were made in London and now the discs of my songs are made in Lagos by 'Tabansi Company'. According to my memory, I would now have one thousand nine hundred and ninety-eight discs. And last week I made some when the manager of 'Tabansi' records visited me. (trans. in Abdulƙadir 1975: 258)

Every individual has his part to play in a society like ours. Let me start from the top. The kings and judges keep the peace, they also collect taxes with which the country is developed. The teacher teaches the children in order to produce manpower. The police keep watch in order to stop thieves and other dishonest people from stealing. These are all important roles played by people of different status.

Now let us turn to oral singers in general. I know this society has very little regard for oral singers; they are not considered as an important part of the society. Sometimes they are dismissed as beggars. Well to me the singers also play important roles in this society. Some of them are chroniclers that keep the traditional history of our society alive. They pass the information from one generation to the other. Particularly those who are attached to royal families. These singers keep the genealogical trees intact and also record any important event that takes place in the society. So they are the custodians not only of oral songs but also of oral history. In the olden days, they played an important role in the tribal wars. They used to give encouragement to the soldiers as well as entertain them ... It is difficult to say exactly what I do but I will try to tell you what I think my role is as an individual. First, I was at one time or another instrumental to the fame of certain individuals in my society. I composed songs in their praise and their names; as a result they became known in the society. I do not restrict myself to the names but I also mention their profession whether a doctor, teacher, lawyer or customs officer. As a result people know the different kinds of jobs that exist in their society and students will aspire to such positions.

Another thing I do for my society is keeping track of all the important events that happen in the society. I try to sing a song to commemorate such events. I have songs concerning education, war, health, Independence Day, changing our driving from left hand to right hand side. I also composed a song against corruption in the society. I am particularly happy with my song concerning our recent (civil) war. I called on both sides to stop killing each other and asked them to settle their differences on the table rather than on the battlefield. The other song which I think enlightened the society is the census song that I made before the count took place. As a result people became aware of the importance of the count. Previously people connected the count with taxation, so they tried to hide their true numbers. Both the radio and Ministry of Information have made intensive use of oral singers in educating the people on important things. (trans. in Abdulḳadir 1975: 266–8)

Alhaji Shata may perhaps have been a little out on his number of records but there is no doubting the great ubiquity and volume of his recordings and performances. The catalogue of the Oral Documentation Unit of Ahmadu Bello University lists numerous recordings of variants of some 130 major songs by him. Local radio and TV stations carry his music repeatedly and at length and he remains perhaps the greatest of popular singers. But he is by no means alone. There are many other Hausa performers whose songs circulate through live performance and through the thriving trade in cassette tapes (discs having been somewhat superseded and compact discs being still on the way) in Nigeria and more widely in West Africa.

FREELANCE AND 'TIED' SINGERS

In the extract from Shata's discussion with Dandatti Abdulḳadir[1] we see him making a number of points that are of general significance in relation to the role of song and singers in Nigerian society over the last fifty years and more. He draws a picture of a status-conscious society in which each person has his place determined by birth and by occupation, whether hereditary or acquired. But it is clear that the traditional class structure of society, based upon a differentiated aristocracy, a merchant class, a cleric class, a peasantry, craft guilds and agricultural slave populations has long since been overlayed with a pattern of integration into occupations and statuses derived, through Western education, from participation in the modern society of the nation state, with its middle classes of professionals, civil servants, and military and business élites. Within the 'traditional' framework, singers were of low social status as a socially dependent category of person along with a wide variety of other clients whose non-material products were offered to their patrons in return for material reward. In the world of modern Nigeria where wealth, fame and thereby achievement are much more determinant factors in the ascription of social status, someone like Shata, whose performances have brought celebrity as well as real wealth for reinvestment in his hotel and other businesses, is in an ambivalent position in which he is, at one and the same time, appreciated and famous in modern Nigeria but of low status in 'traditional' Nigeria.

Shata also points to the similarity in function between himself as being 'instrumental to the fame of certain individuals in my society' and those singers who are 'attached to royal families'. The implication that there is a distinction between himself as a freelance and them as tied singers is an important one. While both types of singer are involved in praise and commemoration Shata represents the freelance singer who both performs in praise of patrons and is free to sing on whatever subject pleases him, while the others perform for one single patron and are the custodians of genealogies and oral history. I. Y. Yahaya (1981) makes a primary distinction between these two categories as do Abdulkadir (1975: 49–50), Daba (1981) and others. As we will see later, these are *categories* of singer between which individual singers may move. Certain famous royal singers, such as Sa'idu Faru (S. M. Gusau 1988), are said to have never performed anything other than royal praises while others have switched patron, or moved from freelance to 'tied to royalty' status. Other categorisations of singers are also made. The 'targets' of performance, sometimes the same thing as patrons, constitute the basis for a distinction between, for example, *makaɗan sarauta* 'musicians to the aristocracy', *makaɗan jama'a* 'musicians to the people', *makaɗan maza* 'musicians to tough men (boxers, wrestlers, etc.)', *makaɗan bori* '*bori* musicians' and *makaɗan sana'a* 'musicians to occupations/craft guilds'. Such distinctions are drawn by Ames (1973b), Dangambo (1984b: 2), and Piłaszewicz (1984), among others.

Ames comments upon the degree to which music-making and singing are viewed as a craft. He therefore foregrounds a distinction between amateur and professional musicians. An example of amateur musicians are those who perform for *'yan tauri* 'tough men'; these musicians he considers, on the basis of his survey of music in Zaria in the early 1960s, to be men who rely mainly upon their trade as butchers and hunters for income. He also classes the music-making of women and girls as being non-professional in the same sense. His discussion is focused upon those musicians who 'count music as their basic craft' (Ames 1973b: 134): professionals whom he groups primarily on the basis of the targets of their performances. Increasingly over the years it has become difficult to maintain the amateur–professional distinction among musicians/singers. Many individuals gain income from other sources than performance, and some are more successful than others. At the same time, however, the idea of a distinction between 'we who write and recite for the good of the nation and our fellow man' as opposed to 'they who fawn and ingratiate themselves for cash' is an important one in the self-identification of poets as against singers, as we will see later.

THE FUNCTIONS OF SONG

The latter part of Shata's discussion relates to the function of song and the singer in contemporary Hausa society. Later on in this chapter we discuss the distinctions that are drawn between song and poetry in Hausa, but in the context of what Shata is saying here there is a close similarity between them. They both contain a strongly purposive element, a desire to instruct, to inform and, ultimately, to convince. They both do other things in addition, but Shata's emphasis on this aspect of singing is significant. He points to two types of discourse: that which 'keeps track' of important events in society, and he mentions the change from driving on the left to driving on the right as an example; at the same time he refers to songs about education and health, and against corruption. He reiterates and reconfirms to his listener aspects of a moral vision, sets of values, in such of his songs that are so intended. This purposiveness, perceived as a legitimate part of his social role, has meant that the singer, and the poet, have regularly participated directly in a wide variety of religious, social and political movements. The most widely discussed of such movements has been the religious reform movement, the Jihad of the early nineteenth century, in which poetry was one of the cardinal weapons in the battle for the 'hearts and minds' of the people.[2] But Shata points to precisely the same conditions wherein agencies in the modern Nigerian state have utilised the power of the singer and the poet in their multifarious battles for the hearts and minds of the descendants of those same people. International development agencies (working on the sensible principle that externally imposed projects are more likely to produce costly failures than those which are internalised by local people as being 'their own'), their earlier equivalents in colonial ministries of agriculture and education, political parties, modern state ministries, and companies looking to advertise their products, have turned to singers and poets to get their messages across, be they bits of 'serious' propaganda or light-hearted advertising jingles.[3]

I. Y. Yahaya (1981) illustrates the function of praise-song in terms of the values of traditional leadership. In the first part of his discussion, following

G. Bello (1976), he shows how singers foreground five primary attributes in a ruler:

descent

religiousness/piety

military achievement

administrative expertise

generosity.

As Smith (1957) points out, the assessment of such characteristics is carried out in relation to the expectations of the office rather than of the individual who fills it. It is the difference between the expectations articulated by the praise-singer of the office and the actual performance of the current office-holder which provides the singer with his leverage. The converse of praise is vilification and the singer is able to deploy both in pursuit of reward. Within the world of royal praise-singing, both are deployed: praise of the royal patron and vilification of his rivals both within his extended family and beyond. In the world of the more lowly itinerant praise-singer, praise can be heaped upon the generous temporary patron and vilification upon the stingy. As Smith puts it:

> Among the Hausa *roko* is an informal regulative institution through which praise or shame are distributed. As an informal regulative institution, it simultaneously imposes social control and reflects honour on the formal agencies of social control. (M. G. Smith 1957)

The public performance of the praise-singer not only articulates the identity and attributes of the ruler, it also marks out the distance between *masu sarauta* 'aristocracy' and the *talakawa* 'ordinary people' (Mashi 1986: 32). As praise-singing has moved into the arena of modern politics so these same attributes are re-articulated and adapted for modern politicians.[4] In this and the following chapter we look more closely at these and other functions and relations, but first we need to see the range of kinds of song, the nature of performance and the kinds of performer that are commonly encountered in Hausa society. Most attention has been paid to the tradition of court praise-singing in Hausa. In this discussion we will approach that topic after having looked at more popular kinds of song with which it contrasts in style and subject matter. Threaded through the discussion is the issue of the relationship between oral song and written poetry and between popular, incorporative culture and more specialised, exclusive cultures, as discussed in the Introduction.

DISTINGUISHING BETWEEN SONG AND POETRY

In Hausa, there is a single term to mark consistently rhythmically patterned language as distinct from ordinary speech (poetry as against prose, using the terms in the title of this book). The word *waka* refers to this kind of language. As indicated in the first chapter, a further distinction is commonly drawn between *wakar baka* 'waka of the mouth' and *rubutacciyar waka* 'written *waka*'. In this book the terms 'song' and 'poetry' refer to these two forms.[5] Muhammad (1979) has provided one of the most succinct summaries of the distinctions between these two forms. Inevitably, the distinctions drawn by people rely upon perceptions of tendencies rather than absolutes; people define themselves and their art in terms of contradistinctions, as doing what other people do not do or vice versa. This sense of distinctiveness between singers and poets belies the extensive interaction between the two genres in terms of mutual, reciprocal influence.[6]

In terms of form, D. Muhammad (1979) indicates that where poetry has regular stanzas, line-end rhyme schemes, and generally operates with Arabic-derived metres, song operates with variable length verses with refrains and uses rhythmic patterns that appear not to be derived from Arabic metres.[7] M. B. Umar (1984) highlights the summative function of the refrain: 'The refrain is usually a couplet that summarises the essential features of the song, especially its thematic and structural qualities.' The following (from a song by Sa'idu Faru) is characteristic:

Gwauron giwa na Shamaki, Baba uban gandu
Abu gogarman Magaji mai kansakalin daga.

The fearless champion of Shamaki, Baba the father to Gandu
Abu the dauntless (favourite) of Magaji, the owner of the war sword.
(Umar 1984b: 38–9)

In public performance, song is usually instrumentally accompanied, often sung by a group with lead singer and chorus, and is performed without reference to anything written down; poetry can be chanted publicly without accompaniment but is often simply read in silence. The process of composition also tends to differ; where poetry is written and reworked by the individual poet, song is often composed within a group and re-performed from memory. In the case of Mamman Shata, he claims to compose in performance; others may rehearse before performance. Modern poetry has developed out of the religious-verse tradition of the nineteenth century, modern song draws from the courtly praise-singing tradition and a variety of other forms of popular song of unknown antiquity. Finally, poets have tended to be scholars or students from the cleric class, singers have often inherited a family profession in which they are bound in strong patron–client relationships with a socially superior patron:

W1 [song] is often a family profession, is heavily patronised, and the artist is liked for his artistic composition/performance but not otherwise respected, while W2 [poetry] is non-professional and is not as clearly patronized, and the artist is respected for his message rather than for his performance. (D. Muhammad 1979: 87)

REFRAINS AND CHORUSES

In talking to a group of poets in 1973 (Furniss 1977: Ch. 2) I found that for them the most salient characteristic of the form of poetry, as distinct from song, was the existence of rhyme schemes. The equivalent in song was the pattern of verse and refrain. The salient characteristics of song, from which they wished to distance themselves, were the presence of musical accompaniment, and a 'professionalism' meant, not as a compliment to their skill, but as a slight upon their determination to 'do it for money'. In the following discussion I outline the main features of the forms of song and indicate some of the varied styles and combinations of voice plus instrument to be encountered among professional singers.

Mamman Shata is a dominant figure, not only in the general music scene but also within the group in which he performs. Generally, he makes up the *amshi* 'chorus refrains', feeds them to the *'yan amshi* 'members of the chorus' and in addition to being the solo creator of his verse lines, his initial verbal phrases provide his lead drummer with the cue upon which to build in making the drum phrases that will accompany his songs.[8] Operating with as many as six or seven men in his chorus and another five or six drummers using, among others, the variable pitch hourglass drum, the *kalangu*, Mamman Shata will sing his verses of variable length before his *'yan amshi* mark time with, usually, a two-line refrain, as in the following example from a song entitled *Yawon Duniya* 'Wandering the World':

SHATA: Ahab! jama'a duka wanda yai yawo
          Zai hirgita zai ga ban tsoro.
CHORUS: Jama'a duka wanda yai yawo
          Zai firgita zai ga ban tsoro.
SHATA: Ku tuna duw wanda yai dandi
          Zai hirgita zai ga ban tsoro.
CHORUS: Jama'a duka wanda yai yawo
          Zai firgita zai ga ban tsoro.
SHATA: Ni nan san zai ga abin tausai
          Wani gun ya zame abin tausayi.
CHORUS: Jama'a duka wanda yai yawo
          Zai firgita zai ga ban tsoro.
SHATA: Saukammu Yammai

Watammu biyu a Yammai
Watammu biyu daidai zaɓe.
[a further 42 phrases before the refrain is repeated][9]

SHATA: Alas, countrymen, whoever roams abroad
           Will be terrified and will find cause for fear;
CHORUS: O countrymen, whoever roams abroad
              Will be terrified and will find cause for fear.
SHATA: Remember that whoever seeks the bright lights
           Will be terrified and will find cause for fear;
CHORUS: O countrymen, whoever roams abroad
              Will be terrified and will find cause for fear.
SHATA: I myself know he'll find things to pity
           While he himself will become a thing of pity
CHORUS: O countrymen, whoever roams abroad
              Will be terrified and will find cause for fear.
SHATA: After our stay at Niamey
           Our two months at Niamey
           Our two months there, precisely so.

(King 1981: 131–2)

   The relationship between lead and chorus and thus between verse and refrain can be more complicated than the simple repetition of a couple of refrain lines. King (1981) outlines two techniques, *karɓi* 'receiving' and *karɓebeniya* 'swopping', that can additionally function between the parties to the song.[10] *Karɓi* is a technique whereby, in addition to the refrain, the chorus come in to varying degrees to participate in or take over the singing of verses. Clearly this is a technique that can only be employed where the lead is not extemporising and the chorus know what the lead singer is going to sing. Mamman Shata is well known for his extemporising and this is undoubtedly the reason why the bulk of his songs have simple repetitive refrains (I. Zurmi 1981: 100). In the following example from a well-known song, 'Bakanda-miya',[11] by the famous 'tied' praise-singer, Narambaɗa, in praise of the emir of Gobir na Isa, Ahmadu, the *karɓi* is briefly interrupted by a return to the lead singer singing solo before going on to the main *karɓi* and refrain:

LEAD: Ai ga giwa tana abin da takai,
KARɓI: Ga 'yan namu na kallon ta babu damar cewa komai;
LEAD: Ai ba tun yau ba tun shina can Sardauna nai,
KARɓI: Har ya kai wurin da anka naɗa mai Sarki,
              Bai ci amana ba, bai yi shawagin banza ba,
              Don ya san uban da yaz zana mai suna.
REFRAIN: Gwarzon Shamaki na Malam toron giwa,
              Baban Dodo ba a kam ma da batun banza.

LEAD: Yes, see the elephant about its business,
KARBI: Observe the lesser beasts who can but look and make no comment;
LEAD: Indeed it's some time since he held office here as Sardauna,
KARBI: Until he was elevated and turbanned as Sarki,
He betrayed no trust, he wasted no time,
For he was fully aware of the father whose name he bore.
REFRAIN: Fearless one of Shamaki, of Malam, bull-elephant,
Father of Dodo, not to be approached with triviality.

(King 1981: 123–4)

Karbebeniya involves close interlacing of the parts by the lead and chorus, reminiscent of the tight repartee of the *'yan gambara* we considered in the previous chapter. From the same song by Narambaɗa, King illustrates this interlacing:

LEAD: Amadu Sarkin Gabas da Sarkin Raba
KARBI: sun ji daɗi
ran nan gamon da mun kai bakin gulbi
LEAD: Sarkin Baura na Dange, Sarkin Sudan na Wurno,
KARBI: su ko can
ba abin da sunka sani sai girma;
LEAD: Yau kuma halin Hasan
KARBEBENIYA: ga Garba na yau yak komo;
LEAD: Dum musuluncin Hasan
KARBEBENIYA: ga Garba na yau yak komo;
LEAD: dut tauhidin Hasan
KARBEBENIYA: ga Garba na yau yak komo;
LEAD: duk alherin Hasan
KARBEBENIYA: ga Garba na yau yak komo;
LEAD: duk imanin Hasan
KARBEBENIYA: ga Garba na yau yak komo;
KARBI: duk da ƙulla zumuncin Hasan
KARBEBENIYA: ga Garba na yau yak komo;
KARBI: kowa kas sani Batoranke ya dar mai,
baga na yau ba, can ga Bello mazaizan farko,
REFRAIN: Gwarzon Shamaki na Malam toron giwa,
Baban Dodo ba a kam ma da batun banza.

LEAD: *Sarkin Gabas* Amadu and *Sarkin Raba*
KARBI: rejoiced
on that day as we reached the bank of the stream
LEAD: *Sarkin Baura* of Dange, *Sarkin Sudan* of Wurno,
KARBI: were there

	aware of naught else but their power;
LEAD:	Today again the character of Hasan
KARBEBENIYA:	has returned in the present person of Garba;
LEAD:	All the dignity that was Hasan's
KARBEBENIYA:	has returned in the present person of Garba;
LEAD:	All the acknowledgement of God that was Hasan's
KARBEBENIYA:	has returned in the present person of Garba;
LEAD:	All the kindness that was Hasan's
KARBEBENIYA:	has returned in the present person of Garba;
LEAD:	All the faith in Islam that was Hasan's
KARBEBENIYA:	has returned in the present person of Garba;
KARBI:	All that forged the brotherhood of Hasan
	has returned in the present person of Garba;
KARBI:	Everyone one knows is outranked by the aristocrat,
	But not just by this one, but since Bello the first hero.
REFRAIN:	Fearless one of Shamaki, of Malam, bull-elephant,
	Father of Dodo, not to be approached with triviality.

(King 1981: 128–9)

Complex techniques of interlacing in the performance of song are characteristic of groups where a number of performers are involved in the process of composition and rehearsal. In the case of the group led by Musa Dankwairo, Musa himself increasingly shared the lead part in the singing with his sons, Daudun Kida, Sani Zakin Murya and Marafa, who swopped and interlaced their interventions in performance (Sada, 1979; and personal communication). It is not clear whether these styles represent different categories of groups or whether the natural 'life-cycle' of a group involves a transition from dominant single author to group composition and performance as the lead grows old and his chorus members take up and take over. In the case of Dankwairo's group, the members of the chorus were also the drummers and this pattern is repeated in other groups such as those led by Sarkin Tabshi of Katsina (where the *tabshi* drum is used)[12] and another 'tied to royalty' group that was led by Sa'idu Faru, using *kotso* drums.[13] The pattern adopted by Mamman Shata with separate drummers and chorus also holds for a group formed by one of his trainees, Mammalo Shata, and for the group led by Shehu Ajilo (Dan-Musa 1990). A number of the most famous tied singers of the last fifty years, Jankidi, Dankwairo, Narambada, Sa'idu Faru, Sarkin Tabshi and Aliyu dan Dawo, have now died, and I am unaware of any research into whether their groups have split, stopped playing, reformed, or have been usurped in their clientage roles by other groups.

In performance a group may find itself accompanied, sometimes both without its consent and against its will, by at least one *dan ma'abba* 'praise-crier'[14] an individual who shouts over the top of the singers, occasionally correcting them, calling out praise-epithets and providing additional, often specialised, information both directly to the audience and to the singers for incorporation in the song as it goes along. Particularly where the praise-singer is not local, these local 'yan ma'abba, who may well know the details of genealogies and history, will be an invaluable source of information for the singer as they look for background and detail to incorporate in their songs but, in the view of the singers, they can also constitute an unwelcome distraction.

PERFORMANCE STYLES AMONG FREELANCE SINGERS

Group performance is not the only kind of professional singing in Hausa. While it is typical of tied singing, a variety of different performance techniques are to be found among freelance singers. We look at freelance, popular singers in more detail below, so here I provide simply a brief introduction to some of the other styles of performance. One of the most famous freelance singers, Dan Maraya Jos, sings solo, accompanying himself on the kuntigi, a small single-stringed lute. Singing solo, his songs do not deploy the verse and chorus form to any great extent. Haruna Oji, another popular solo singer uses the gurmi, a two-stringed lute (Kofoworola and Lateef 1987: 239) in accompanying himself. Kassu Zurmi, a singer well known for his songs about boxers, hunters and thieves, sings solo but with the accompaniment of drums (A. Magaji 1980). Conversely, Ahmadu Dan Matawalle, whose songs are unusually about the natural world and not sung in praise of any patron, uses a chorus but no accompanying instruments (M. S. Aliyu 1980). Binta Zabiya, a popular woman singer whose reputation is based upon her songs for bori spirits, sings generally solo but to the accompaniment, in her early years, of a drum (Yar'adua 1983: 8), and later of a garaya 'two-stringed lute' in addition to rattles. Other popular women singers such as Uwaliya Mai Amada and Maimuna Barmani Choge perform often with an accompanying chorus of women and the playing of kwarya the 'upturned calabash floating on water', a distinctive style about which we say more later. Garba Supa (Dan-Musa 1990) combines drums, a chorus and his own playing of goge, a single-stringed bowed form of fiddle, an instrument particularly associated with bori. The combination of goge and drums is a popular style with singers such as Amadu Doka (playing the smaller bowed fiddle, the kukuma, also played by Ibrahim na Habu and Hajiya Faji (M. S. Ibrahim 1976)), while Garba Liyo's reputation is based to a considerable extent not upon singing but upon his instrumental recordings on the goge with accompanying drums and dancers.[15] With the exception of this last form of music, there appears to be a concentration, in the aesthetic appreciation of many people, upon the words and the language, upon the singing rather than the instrumental accompaniment. Though this seems to reflect a more traditional view of music and song, it is a perspective that is being altered by the influence of many other forms of West African and Western music as well as the long-standing effect of popular Indian films.

THE RELATION BETWEEN WORDS AND MUSIC: LINGUISTIC TONE AND MELODY

We saw with *take* in Chapter 4 that certain drums are able to render pitch variation and rhythmic sequences that correspond with the tone pattern and syllabic pattern of a Hausa verbal phrase. The complexities of the relationship between tone pattern and song melody have been the subject of a number of studies and it would appear there is a lot yet to be said on the subject. Interestingly, field recordings by A. V. King from 1964 of a song, on this occasion entitled *Wakar Indefenda*, by Sarkin Tabshi of Katsina, were the basis of a study by Richards (1972), and it appears that similar, if not the same, recordings by D. W. Ames from September 1964 formed the basis of a study by Besmer (1970), though the song was given the title *Nijeriya ta tsare gaskiya*. At the risk of oversimplification it is generally agreed that the melody does correspond to the tone pattern of the text of the song, as Besmer puts it:

> a comparison of types of musical (melodic) phrases with the tonal patterns of linguistic phrases indicates a close correlation between the choice of a specific musical phrase for phrases in the text with identical tonal patterns. Yet, it was not possible to formulate an internally consistent set of principles capable of describing those instances in the song where phonemic tone and vowel length seemed to be set aside. It appeared that variation was most frequent at phrase endings where cadential formulae took precedence over linguistic formulae. (Besmer 1970: 423)

The reservations expressed by Besmer relate to sections of song where correspondence is minimal. Richards, in saying that 'the parallelism between text-tone and melody ... is greater than would occur by chance' (1972: 153), acknowledges, however, that the parallel is visible/audible in only 53.4 per cent of the syllables of the song. Leben, considering the paper by Richards, says that if the patterns of downdrift that occur in Hausa intonation are taken into account then the case is much stronger (Leben 1983). In a study which examines the level of correspondence between tone and melody on the one hand, and linguistic and performance rhythm on the other, McHugh and Schuh (1984) look at recorded performances of a number of written poems and demonstrate that in some cases there is remarkably close correspondence, but in others much less, although some poems demonstrate close rhythmic correspondence while melody moves more away from tone pattern. The following illustration of the relation be-tween tone and melody is adapted from Besmer (1970: 422):[16]

| bàb-bár ká-sár Shée-hù | Dán Hóo- di- yòo | Nii-jée- rí- yàa   táa tsá | rèe gàs ki   yáa |

'The great land of Shehu Dan Fodio, Nigeria upholds the truth'

The other dimension of correspondence, this time between voice and instrumentation relates to the rhythmic structure of song. Inherent in all Hausa words are sequences of 'heavy' and 'light' syllables which provide a basis for rhythmic pattern regardless of stress or other features imposed upon any particular utterance. This distinction between heavy and light syllables provides the basis for the metrical patterning we see in connection with poetry in the next chapter. It is also significant in providing rhythmic sequences in song, against which, and with which, drummers or other instrumentalists can play.

THE RELATION BETWEEN WORDS AND MUSIC: RHYTHM AND SYLLABLES

As indicated in Chapter 4 (n. 7), the Hausa language allows only three kinds of syllables in the construction of words. These syllables consist of a consonant followed by a short vowel (cv), a consonant followed by a long vowel or a diphthong (cvv), or a consonant followed by a short vowel followed by a consonant (cvc). No other kinds of syllables are found in Hausa or fully Hausa-ised words. The fact that cv and cvv are open syllables and cvc is closed is not material either to the metres of poetry or to the rhythms of song. The crucial distinction is between cv as a light syllable and cvv/cvc as heavy syllables (sometimes termed short and long syllables). Time and again in poetic metres two light syllables equal a heavy syllable. As two crotchets make a minim, however fast or slow the music is played, so two lights equal a heavy in the sequence of any Hausa sentence. In the sentence given above from the song by Sarkin Tabshi there is clearly evident a particular sequence of such syllables (separated inside words by hyphens in Besmer's example):

bab- bar ƙa- sar Shee- hu Dan Foo- di- yoo, Nii- jee- ri- yaa taa tsa- ree gas- ki- yaa
CVC CVC CV CVC CVV CV CVC CVV CV CVV CVV CVV CV CVV CVV CV CVV CVC CV CVV

Represented as a rhythmic sequence, then, by a dash for a heavy syllable and a 'v' for a light syllable we see the following pattern:

$$- - v - - v - - v -, - - v - - v - - v -$$

This regular pattern is evident from the intrinsic structure of the Hausa words and is not necessarily the same thing as the intervals and actual performed durations that could be observed from a particular rendition. Performed rhythms, often with drum accompaniment, take account of the beats that occur in line-end pauses and allow for the singing of heavy syllables as light or vice versa (Schuh 1988: 220–1). The system for accounting for rhythmic pattern in song and poetry outlined by Schuh derives from the work of A. V. King and differs from the classical Arabic metrical system which has been extensively applied to Hausa by Arnott (1975), Galadanci (1975), Hiskett (1975b) and M. S. Zaria (1978), among others. This 'beat and measure' system groups rhythms according to the number of half-beats (a light syllable = a half-beat) in a measure (Schuh 1988: 224). There is thus a 'five metre' in which there are five half-beats in a measure, a 'six metre' with six, and so on. Schuh presents the same example from Sarkin Tabshi given above as being in a five metre in which, after an initial take-up beat in each half-line, there are three measures of five half-beats (– v –). As we see in Chapter 7, Schuh indicates that the beat-and-measure system can account for patterns occuring in written Hausa poetry which are not strictly allowable within the Xalilian system of Arabic metrical scansion.

The Arabic system of scansion accounts for rhythmical regularity with names for particular feet and metres. For example, the sequence of heavy and light syllables (v v – v –) to be seen, for example, in the words *a samaaniyaa* 'in the sky' is captured by the Arabic term *mutafaa'ilun* which embodies that pattern. A number of 'words' constructed around the consonants, m, t, f, ', l, embody other such patterns (*faa'ilaatun* = – v – –; *fa'uulun* = v – –). A sequence of two, three or sometimes four feet will constitute a metre and have a name. Lines made up of repetitions of *mutafaa'ilun*, for example, are in the metre *kaamil*.[17] D. Muhammad (1977) has drawn attention to the existence in Hausa of an indigenous way of representing rhythmic regularity in song. This system, like the Arabic variations on certain consonants, uses certain variations on special words to render in sound particular sequences of heavy and light syllables. Those commentators who consider the use of Arabic-based descriptive terms to represent an overemphasis on foreign cultural influence, rather than a useful method of representing quantity-based metre, point to the existence of this system and to the fact that the overwhelming majority of Hausa poets and singers are unfamiliar with Arabic metres.[18] I am unaware of any systematic study of this representational system. Aminu (1993) has presented a listing of some of the representational words (e.g. *aiyaarayee* = – – v –; *yaarayee* = – v –; *dariyee* = v v –) grouped into *gimshikai* 'pillars' and *mataimaka* 'helpers' and a number of named sequences rather like metres.[19]

While there is clearly more to be said on the question both of the Hausa way of representing rhythms and on the issue of the most appropriate way of accounting for the crossing over of rhythms between the song and the poetry traditions, it is clear that embedded in the first few lines of many songs lie melodic patterns that are linked to the tonal patterns of the words and rhythmic patterns that are associated with the natural beats provided by the syllabic structure of those same words. The sense of chant that comes from listening to much Hausa song is surely derived from these two dimensions of the interplay between the words themselves and the performed patterns of melody, accompaniment and rhythm.

FREELANCE POPULAR SINGERS

Some of the most popular Hausa singers are women. Three of the best known are Binta Zabiya,[20] Uwaliya Mai Amada and Maimuna Barmani Choge.

Binta Zabiya, the subject of a study by Yar'adua (1983) was born in Mani, near Katsina in about 1913, from a Tuareg serf family which had moved from Maraɗi in Niger. The family Hausa-ised itself: 'after they had settled they gave up their *buzu* customs and picked up Hausa ones' (Yar'adua 1983: 7). From the age of 25 she was initiated into *bori* and many of her songs are for spirits: Barahaza, Sarkin Rafi, 'Dan Galadima, Maye, Wanzami and others. She sang other songs, some of the best known are about men she had been involved with: one of her earlier husbands was called Bala Mila, a professional driver from Kano, and it was after her divorce from him that she established herself as an independent woman,[21] working professionally with a drummer called 'Dan Zakara, and moving with a man called Gwanda from town to town and from bar to bar. Mack (1983: 33) quotes a song by Binta Katsina performed on the occasion of an academic conference at Bayero University when she sang about all the things women can do if they put their minds to them – working in government ministries, running schools, flying planes, or running the government. Perhaps her most famous song was about her man Gwanda in which she tells of his tangles with the European authorities over the theft of some money which resulted in his being hauled up before a court, first in Maraɗi in Niger, then in Katsina, then in Kano, and finally in Nasarawa where he was sentenced to seven years in prison. On his release he is determined to go home to Agades. Her relationship with him is a turbulent one as the following extract suggests:

Yanzu yanzu Gwanina	Now, now my hero,
Abin yai mani bibiyu	Things have come in pairs,
Ga ciki ga goyo	I'm pregnant and I've a child on my back.
Farka na mani kuka	My boyfriend is calling to me
Kuma ga miji a gaban gado	But I have my husband beside me on the bed.
Farka bar mani kuka	Boyfriend, stop calling to me,
Bari sai mijina yai barci	Wait till my husband is asleep,

In aje mishi ɗa nai	And I can dump his son on him
In zo gare ka mu kwana	And come to you for the night.
Ina tare da Gwandan Karsigi	With Gwandan Karsigi
Na ji daɗi	I am so happy,
Na yi guɗa nai tsalle	I shout and jump for joy,
Na yaba maka Gwanda	I sing your praises Gwanda.
Ina tare da Gwanda wata rana	When one day I was with Gwanda,
Na sha wuya nai kuka	I suffered and cried,
Ni dai kâi ni gida	'Please take me home,
Gwandan Karsigi na tuba	Gwandan Karsigi I am sorry.'
Ki daina mana kuka	'Stop crying' he said,
Wuya ba ta kishin maza	'Suffering does not kill,
Amma ba ta da daɗi.	It's just not pleasant.'
(Yar'adua 1983: 147-8)	(GF & SIK)

This directness of personal statement contrasts with the impersonality of much praise and purposive song. It is a style of popular song also encountered with Maimuna Barmani Choge.[22]

Barmani Choge was born in about 1945 in Funtua and participated from an early age in the performance of Sufi religious litany singing, known as *kidan Amada*, also known as *kidan ruwa/kidan kwarya* 'drumming on an upturned calabash in water' (Mashi 1982). Performed often by groups of women in purdah, this repetitive style of litany singing involves an act of devotion through the mentioning of saints, particularly of the Tijaniyya or Qadiriyya sect:

Ina manzo ina manzo	Call on the Messenger, Call on the Messenger!
Ku kira mai fada	Call on God's favoured one!
Amshi: Ga mu tsaye	Here we are standing!
Ɗan Marina waliyyin Allah	Ɗan Marina, God's saint!
Ɗan Masani waliyyin Allah	Ɗan Masani, God's saint!
Mai kalgo waliyyin Allah.	Mai kalgo, God's saint!
(Mashi 1982: 1)	(GF & SIK)

This became a recognised style separated from the strictly religious *zikr* context. Having started by accompanying older women performing the religious singing, Barmani Choge branched out into composing her own songs of a secular kind using a chorus of women, Rakiya, Zulai, Hajara and A'ishatu, who played the calabashes with their hands. Her songs are many and various, some are praise or purposive like the songs cited by Mack (1983), some are more personal like the following extracts from a well-known song, *Dare Allah Magani*, about how it feels to have your husband announce the forthcoming arrival of a second wife:

Yan'uwana dangin Fatsima
Wa yake so ai mai kishiya
    Amshi: Dare Allah magani
Dakata ka ji sanƙira kaɗan
Muna zamanmu da Malam Malami
Ba fushi ba tashin hankali
Tun ina yarinyata da ni
Sai na ce masa yai mini kishiya
Sai ya ce mani ke ɗaya kin isa
To da dai ya ga tsufa ya gabato
Tsufa ya riƙa tar da ni
Sai ya ce mani aure za ya yi
To ni ban taɓa ko zaginsa ba
Ran nan na ce mashi ka ji munafiki
    Amshi: Dare Allah magani
Wanda yai maka hanyar kishiya
Kai wata tara ba ka gai da shi
Dare da rana Allah ya isa
    Amshi: Dare Allah magani.

(Mashi 1982: 9–10)

Ku tsaya ku ji sunan kishiya
Baƙar kunama mai harbin tsiya
Baƙin maciji mai cizon tsiya
Karya matsettseku mai baki ɗari
mai haƙorin cizo shegiya
In ta kama sai ta girgiza
    Amshi: Dare Allah magani.

(Mashi 1982: 39)

    Amshi: Dare Allah magani
Ina zaman gidan miji
Zama irin mai ban sha'awa
Na jin daɗi babu hayaniya
    Amshi: Dare Allah magani
Wata rana miji ya ce mani
Yana son zai mini kishiya
Na ce, Malam, ai haka ya yi kyau
Ashe zan sami abokiyar zama
    Amshi: Dare Allah magani
Bai sani ba, akwai nawa a zuciya
In dai ni ce a wannan gida
Ba na barin har wata shegiya
Ta shigo min wai ita kishiya

Amshi: Dare Allah magani
Dare na yi
Na ce wa mijin 'Zan tafi unguwa'
Na zarce sai gidan wani malami
Malamina yai min marhaban
     Amshi: Dare Allah magani
Na ce malam, ina son ka taimaka
Mijina zai mini kishiya
     Amshi: Dare Allah magani
Malam ya ce, 'Ai da ma na sani
Amma ina son in sanar da ke
Wannan aure, dole, za a yi
Babu mai sa ya wargaje
Akwai taimako ɗan ƙanƙane
Da zan ba ki shi, in za ki so,
Bayan wannan aure ya tabbata
Za ki yi ƙoƙarin ki wargaza'
     Amshi: Dare Allah magani
Malam ya ba ni ƙunshin magani
Malamina ya ce da ni:
'Ki barbaɗa wannan magani
A cikin butar sallah tasa'.

(Maikafi 1977: 39–40)

My sisters, women, relations of Fatima,
Who wants to have a co-wife?
     Allah is the light in the darkness.
Wait a little, *sankira*, I will tell you.
I was living happily with *malam*,
Without rancour or falling out.
When I was a very young girl
I asked him to take a second wife,
And he said, 'You are enough for me!'
But when he saw old age approaching,
Bearing down upon me fast,
That's when he said he wanted a second wife.
I had never so much as insulted him,
But on that day I said, 'Look at this hypocrite!'
     Allah is the light in the darkness.
Whoever causes a second wife to be brought to your house,
Don't even greet them for a full nine months!
May God deal with them in his own way, day and night.
     Allah is the light in the darkness.

Wait and hear the names of a co-wife,
Black scorpion with the terrible sting!
Black snake with the terrible bite!
The bitch, the leech with a hundred mouths,
And what biting teeth, the bastard!
With teeth embedded she shakes her head to and fro.
  Allah is the light in the darkness.

  Allah is the light in the darkness.
I was living with my husband
A really pleasant existence,
An enjoyable life with no quarrelling
Allah is the light in the darkness.
One day my husband said to me
He wanted to take a second wife.
I said, 'Malam, that's alright,
I will have someone to live alongside me.'
  Allah is the light in the darkness.
He did not know I had my own plans,
If I am the one in charge of this house
There is no way I will allow some bitch
To come in as my co-wife.
  Allah is the light in the darkness.
As night fell,
I told my husband, 'I am going out somewhere.'
And I went straight to a *malam*
Who welcomed me.
  Allah is the light in the darkness.
I said, '*Malam* I want your help,
My husband is bringing in a second wife.'
  Allah is the light in the darkness.
The *malam* said, 'I already knew,
And I want to tell you that
This marriage will definitely go ahead,
Nothing can stop it,
But there is one small thing I can do
To help you if you want.
After this marriage has taken place
You can try to destroy it.'
  Allah is the light in the darkness.
The *malam* gave me a potion
And said to me,

'Sprinkle this potion
Into his religious ablution kettle!'

(GF & SIK)

In addition to songs which reflect the tensions of co-wifehood, there are love
songs by Barmani Choge of considerable force, for example as presented in
Maikafi (1977):

To bismillah Rabbana zan fara
Ka ba ni bishara, ka daɗan imani
Ayya ra naye iraye nana ye
Arauye iye dide ayyara na ye
Wata ran da damina ga hadiri
Ga iska kamar ta tumɓuke bukka
Ga tsananin sanyi ga duhuwa
Da dare baƙi ƙirin irin na damina
Kowa ya yi barci sai minshari
Wasu ko har sun yi zango saba'in
Ni kuwa daidai da rintsawa ban yi ba
Don na yi na yi in yi na ko kasa
Sai hawaye kurum ke ta zubowa
Daga wannan idon da ya ƙi runtsawar
Na san kya tambaya, me ya sa hawaye?
Tunanin masoyina yaro ɗan fari
Ya min alkawari tun shekaranjiya
Nai jiransa har na gaji bai zo ba
Ya masoyi, na sani tsakanina da kai
Ba na ƙin cikan alkawarinmu ba
Baƙin duhu, hadiri, da kurayen gari
Ba za su hana ka cikan alkawari ba
Sai dai rashin lafiya, ko ma mutuwa,
Watakila su zamanto dalilin ƙin zuwa
In ko haka ne, Ya Jallah sarkin talikai
Ke ƙebe wannan bala'i daga kai nasa
Don ko in babu shi lallai babu ni
Haka kuma in babu ni, to lallai babu shi
Ya Allah, Sarki, Jallah Jalalahu
Ka bar mu, ni da shi baki ɗaya
Har ranar da ni da shi za a haɗa
Malam ya ce, 'Allah ya ba da zama lafiya.'

(Maikafi 1977: 50)

In the name of God I will begin,
Grant me good tidings and greater faith.

Ayya ra naye iraye nana ye
Arauye iye dide ayyara na ye
One day in the rainy season there was a storm
And a wind so strong it would uproot whole huts.
It was so cold and so dark,
And the night was as black as only happens in the rains,
All were long asleep and snoring,
Some in the deepest of deep sleeps.
I had not been able to shut my eyes even for a moment,
I tried and I tried but I could not,
Nothing but tears flowed from my eyes
That could not close.
I know that you, you women, will ask me why the tears?
– Thoughts of my beloved.
He promised to come to me two days ago,
I have waited and waited but he has not come.
Oh, my beloved I know that between us
There can be no broken promises.
Pitch darkness, storms, and roaming hyenas
Will never prevent you from fulfilling your promise.
Only illness or death can
Be the reason for your absence.
If that is the case, then, Oh God, the sustainer of all creation,
Protect him from this evil,
Because without him I am no more,
And without me he cannot exist.
Oh God, in your majesty,
Preserve us, both of us,
Until the day when you bring us together,
And the *malam* says, 'May God bless this union!'

(GF & SIK)

In similar vein, M. S. Ibrahim (1976) presents an extract from a song by the woman singer Zabiya Uwani Zakirai on her lover Habibu:[23]

Na tuna ran ban kwananmu
A dandali gun wasanmu
Habibu ɗan makaranta
Farin wata kal, kal, kal,
Farin wata kwana goma
Habibu mun ban kwana
Kwana bakwai ban barci ba
Ina tunanin soyayya
Habibu ɗan makaranta

An ba ni tuwo, na ce a'a
An ba ni fura, na ce a'a
An ba ni ruwa, na ce a'a
Dubi jikina na rame
Nai kwatakwal duk na bushe
Ina tunani soyayya
Habibu ɗan makaranta.

(M. S. Ibrahim 1976: 83)

I remember the day of our farewell,
On the open space where we used to play,
Habibu, the schoolboy,
The moon was clear and bright,
Ten days old.
Habibu and I said farewell to each other,
And for seven days I have not been able to sleep,
I have been thinking of love,
Habibu, the schoolboy,
They gave me one kind of food and I said no,
They gave me another kind of food and I said no,
They gave me water and I said no,
Look how thin I have become,
All skin and bone and all dried up,
Thinking of love,
Habibu, the schoolboy.

(GF & SIK)

Uwaliya Mai Amada, born around 1934 in Gezawa, was well-known in Kano before her death in the 1970s (Tanko 1990). She worked in the same tradition of *Amada* singing as Barmani Choge. According to Tanko (1990) it was at women's gatherings to undertake *dabe* 'making floors' that she was noticed for her singing, such that she began to be invited by other women to go with a small chorus of five women friends to entertain. At the age of 27 she moved to Kano with her husband who would play the *kwarya* 'gourd' while she sang until, in her heyday, her chorus consisted of ten women singing and playing in the *kidan Amada* style. Her group continued on after her death but with much less success.

In addition to these three singers there is a whole cultural world of women's song, sometimes associated with particular communal activity but also with comment upon men and their perfidious ways.[24] Some of the earliest Hausa recorded songs in roman script are expressions by women of their views and feelings. A number of such songs were transcribed and translated in Prietze (1904), including the following extract:

Tafo yaro tafo maza
Tafo yaro tafo maza!
Aradu bege zai kashe ni
Aradu aradu zai kashe ni!
Kadan ba ka zo ba, za ni mutuwa
Wasa da yaro ba ni iyawa
Wasa da wani ba ni iyawa
Kadan ban gan ka ba za ni shiga dawa
Kadan ba ka zo ba za ni kashe kaina
Zan sha∂e kaina da rawani
Ba ni so ubana
Ba ni so uwata
Ban san kowa ba sai kai, mata
kadan na gan ki da safe
Ba ni kama hankalina
Kan ka tafi ya∂i
Da kai nake mafalki
Kan ka tafi ya∂i
Ba ni ∂amnan kowa sai kai.

(adapted from Prietze 1904: 44–5)

Come young man, come quick
Come young man, come quick!
By thunder, longing will destroy me
By thunder, this thunder will destroy me!
If you do not come I will surely die
Amuse myself with a boy I can no longer
Amuse myself with another I can no longer
If I cannot see you I will go off into the forest
If I cannot see you I will kill myself
I will strangle myself with a turban
I love my father no more
I love my mother no more
I love no one except you, as a woman
If I see you in the morning
I cannot keep hold of myself
Before you went off to war
I dreamt of you
Before you went off to war
I loved no one but you.

Some of these songs reflect the views not only of women about men but, in the case of the following song, again from the early years of this century, the views of a slave-girl about men and other women:

Wakar Kuyangin Sokoto[25]

Shiririta ararra ta : kare gadon gidda yayyo
Ba ni bukinka da shara : sai ranar zua aiki im ba ka taro ka futasan

Farin wake na banza ne : ko an matsu ba a gunba tai

Bembeni ka gyara gije : kurche giddansu ta gado
Domin biri a jaye kadarko : bika da shirin tuma ya zo

Kwa ɓache ni in rama : don ba shi ka chisan ba

Anini mai kammar sissi : da tsakka ga shi fudadde

Kwabo kau mai kammar fataka : dagga tsakka ga shi fudadde
Mai-Gwanja gaton shigifa : na Mallam ɗan Majidaɗi
Mai kyautar dala da dala : na Mallam ɗan Majidaɗi
Ɗiyal laka ta banza ta : don ba ta zua ta yo wanka
Ɗiyal danƙo ta banza ta : don ba ta fitta chikkin rana
Zanchen ɗaka sai mata da miji : hainyar bissa dole sai tsuntsu

Garar ƙassa maganin ajiya : zago mai fanfatse kaya
Ba ni zua ga yan boko : gara in zo ga yan madara

Ɗan boko sai hawan doki : amma ba kuɗin Sati
Mai rai duka ma-sami ne : Zabarma akwoi biɗɗar kuɗi

Limamin giddan joji dogo ƙetare ka chiro : har ya manta wando nai

Kuku da boyi sun rantse : sai sun ɗauki 'yar Gwari
Tulu ɗai ka shain yawo : randa na chikkin ɗaki
Mai rai duka shi ɗau himma : a yi ta batun biɗɗar kuɗi
Ɗan kawo rinin Allah : madilla masoyyina
Namijin kuti mai ƙaffar kwaɓi : har ya rena mata tai
Randa na chikkin ɗaki : Allah shi ka ba ta rua ta sha
Tukuruwa mai-ƙaya ɓoye : gawo da ƙayarka ka girma

Tataka sai a ba doki : nama sai a ba zaki
Tafarnuwa ta faye yaji : amma ga maganin sanyi
Dabino farkonka ɓaure na : a chan ƙarshe ka kan zaƙi
Anini ɗan mutan Lokwaja : bana ya zo ƙassar Hausa
Kwa duke ni in rama : don ba shi ka tufasan ba.

Song of the Sokoto Slave-girl

Wasting time is an acquired art : the dog professes the nature he is heir to

I will not be at your celebration with a gift : on a working day I'll pay you threepence to come and relieve me of my work

White beans are useless : not even when desperate can you make gumba cake from them

The sunbird prepares the nest : and the dove has taken it over

The bridge can be dismantled as far as the monkey is concerned : the baboon has come ready to leap across

Whoever insults me against him will I retaliate : he is not the one who feeds me

The tenth-of-a-penny coin looks like a sixpence : but there is a hole in the middle

A penny looks like a two-shilling piece : but there is a hole in the middle

The rich kola trader near the two-storeyed house : Mr. Comfortable's man

The man who gives away two-shilling pieces : Mr. Comfortable's man

The mud-dolly is useless : she can't go and wash

The glue-dolly is useless : she can't go out in the sun

The question of which room comes next is for the wives and the husband : only the birds can take the paths above

White ants are the bane of things put in store : termites that devastate possessions

I don't go near those who are full of pretence : better to go with those who are honest

Those full of pretence may have influence : but there is no money in that

All living things need to consume : the Zabarma people are always out for money

The imam at the judge's house, 'Lofty with the grasping reach' : has left his trousers behind

The cook and the serving-boy have sworn : they must have the Gwari girl

There is one kind of water pot that travels around : another that stays indoors

All living things must work at it : concentrate on making money

The mahogany tree was dyed by God : wonderful my beloved!

The drake with the foot that stirs the mud : he even ridicules his wife

One of the pots is indoors : God gives it water to drink

The bamboo palm has hidden thorns : but you, the acacia, grow with your thorns visible

Hay is for the horse : meat is for the lion

Garlic is astringent : but it is a sure cure for the cold

The date is at first as bitter as the wild fig : only later do you become sweet

The tenth-of-a-penny coin comes from the Lokoja people : this year it came to Hausa country

Against whoever beats me will I retaliate : it is not he who clothes me.

(Furniss & Ibrahim 1991/2:49–51)

The majority of popular singers are men. In the remaining part of this chapter it is possible only to discuss some of the better-known figures from Nigeria whose music is retailed across the Hausa-speaking parts of West Africa.

Mamman Shata was born around 1925 in Musawa in northern Katsina into a nomadic Fulani family (Abdulƙadir 1975: 67-8). He did not 'inherit' the craft of singing from his father, but came to it through singing in local events, such as *kalankuwa*, until by the age of 20, and with some opposition from his family, he was making enough money at it to begin to make a living as a travelling performer. He worked for a period during the 1950s singing in the Niger Club in Kano (Abdulƙadir 1975: 84), which was the beginning of a major rise to fame. Over the years his output has been phenomenal, with constant radio and television performances in addition to record and cassette-tape sales. He himself sees only a very small proportion of the money made on the sales of his music. Nevertheless, he has become a relatively prosperous businessman with interests in hotels, farming and retail trades. Although described as a freelance singer, his output has included many songs in praise of major Nigerian figures including northern royalty. We have already seen at the beginning of this chapter how he has been used by companies to advertise their products; freelance in this context means that he is able to pick and choose his patrons, not that his work is outside the orbit of patron–client relationships *per se*. Where Shata's freedom of approach and attitude most directly manifests itself is in his willingness to take, on occasion, a contrary position to the dominant cultural values promulgated by the proponents of Islamic behavioural norms. Where poets may expatiate at length on drink and other evils, Shata says that drinking is no crime. At the same time, he sings in praise of education and hard work[26] and participates in the very traditional values of courtly praise-singing. It is this intriguing mixture of the risqué and the conventional which makes him so popular. To provide a flavour of these two sides of Shata's singing I cite an extract from his song in praise of Mamman, emir of Daura, and from his songs for Habu 'Yam Mama and in praise of drink:

Waƙar Mamman, Sarkin Daura

Rule your people with great courage since you are their king
Long live the lion, Mamman, father of Galadima, son of Musa

Hunters you have made a mistake, you have allowed the lion to mature
Aspirants to the throne, your plans have come to naught, the lion has come
    of age

In the forest there is a lion
In the forest there is a leopard
So children should keep away

The fishermen should change their tactics
Crocodile has taken control of the river
Master of Baushe son of Musa

Whenever the owner of the big fishing-net is present
Let those with smaller nets walk away
In the river there is a big fisherman
The small fishermen should look for a new river

I plead with you the people of Daura
To respect your emir and in return live a prosperous life
Whoever opposes you is doomed to failure, son of Musa
For God is on your side, son of Musa

You are blessed you are invulnerable, father of Galadima, son of Musa
Long live the lion, Mamman, father of Galadima, son of Musa

The present world is yours, so is the hereafter
No one disputes your possession of the two worlds
Since you have sown good deeds and they have sprouted

Bashari, an excellent administrator
His heart is pregnant with the fear of God
In religious matters he is exemplary
Love for brotherhood emanates from him
The whole of Daura is under your authority, son of Musa

(Abdulƙadir 1975: 296–7)

Habu 'Yam Mama

When he sought this world, and got it,
He sought for the next world, and got it.

He built a mosque so people could pray,
Then he came out and built a small nightclub,
There, close to the road, at the edge of the tarmac.

If you enter the city and say your prayers,
When you come out, there is a little nightclub,
There is beer to drink and tobacco to smoke,
There are voluptuous women too.

There are so many women there we have to choose
You take hold of them like chickens to see which are best

Which one is it, which one isn't it?
Is it the next world that should be sought for or this world?

(Abdulƙadir 1975: 321)

Wakar Giya

Ka ji karatun masu bugun ruwa	Here is the preaching of the drinkers,
Waɗanda ke zikiri a kuloniya	Those who recite their litanies at the Colonial bar.
A nan muke sallarmu ta Juma'a	That is where they do their Friday prayers,
Mu tattara kayanmu mu kai Neja	Let's gather our things and head for the Niger bar.
Ku sha ruwan ba laifi ba ne	To drink is no sin,
Ruwan na kwalaba ba laihi ba ne	Booze is no sin.
Ai kun ga Alhaji Shata sha yake	You see that Alhaji Shata also drinks.
Yara mu koma wasa kuloniya	Lads, let's go and play at the Colonial bar,
Mu tashi kana mu koma Neja	And then go on to the Niger bar,
Nan ne muke zikirinmu na Juma'a	That's where we recite our Friday litanies.
Malam ka sha mu sha ai ba laihi ba ne.	'Drink up' is no sin.
Ga taka ga tau kowa ya aje	To each his own bottle,
Sha ruwa ba laihi ba ne	To drink is no sin.

(M. S. Ibrahim 1976: 84)

(GF & SIK)

Dan Maraya was born in Bukuru, near Jos in 1946 (M. B. Umar 1985: 4). Orphaned as a very small child he was raised by the chief of Bukuru for whom Dan Maraya's father had been a *kotso* drummer. Determined to be a musician like his father he too started with the *kotso* drum but quickly switched to the small single-stringed lute, the *kuntigi*. He travelled widely following the transport drivers to Maiduguri and back. One of his earliest songs, *Karen Mota*, was about the 'vehicle dogs', the young men who accompanied professional drivers to act as labourers and assistants (Daba 1978: 208–12). Such concern, in song, with categories of ordinary people is unusual and has been a distinguishing feature of Dan Maraya throughout his career. While some songs are moralistic and highly critical of certain categories of people there is a strong sense of his concern for ordinary people: 'it can be argued that the single theme which runs throughout almost all the songs of Dan Maraya is the singer's concern and sympathy for the common poor man' (Daba 1973: 114). Such songs as *Lebura* 'Labourer', *Talakawa* 'Commoners', *Mai Akwai da Mai Babu* 'The Rich and the Poor', *Yara Manyan Gobe* 'Children, the Leaders of Tomorrow' fall into this category. At the same time he has also sung songs in praise and elegy, such as for Sarkin Shanun Mambila Barkindo, and for the Sardauna of Sokoto, Ahmadu Bello. A number of his songs are of a generally philosophical nature with a strongly didactic tone, such as *Dan Adam mai wuyar gane hali* 'Man, So Difficult to Comprehend' and *Duniya ba ki san gwani ba* ('The World which does not

Recognise Skill'), among others. Daba (1973; 1978) provides English translations of a number of Dan Maraya's songs, including the following:

Lebura	*The Labourer*
Shin ya Allah abin ƙauna,	Oh Allah the beloved
Annabin Allah abin ƙauna	Allah's Prophet the beloved, (Muhammad)
Shi lebura ma abin ƙauna.	Also the labourer should be loved.
Fatara mai sai a lalace,	Poverty causes suffering,
Ta ƙi yarda ma ka san rance,	It does not allow you to borrow,
Yunwa mai kai maza kwance,	Hunger debilitates men,
Ta kashe ba sai da aibu ba.	It kills without torture.
Yau lebura ne kamar zakka,	Today a labourer is regarded as an outcast
Aiki rani zuwa kaka,	Working from the dry up to the harvest seasons
In gwamnati za ta sa doka,	If government promulgates a law,
Shi lebura ba ya karyawa.	The labourer will never violate it.
Aiki a wuni cikin taro,	Working the whole day in public,
Ana abu sai ka ce horo,	It is executed like an order,
In dai Allah ake tsoro,	If people fear Allah,
Da lebura bai talauci ba.	A labourer will never be destitute.
Icen tumba su sare shi	Mahogany is to be cut down,
Wani za su datsa shi	Part of it they cut into pieces,
Su tara ƙasa su kwashe ta	They collect soil and remove it,
Mota ba za ta motsa ba	A motor car will never move,
In lebura bai yi turin ba.	If a labourer does not drive.
Wataran da na ɗauki motata	One day I drove my car,
Na zo yashi ya kama ta	On my way it got stuck in the sand,
Da lebura za ku sa targa	If you labourers are to strike,
Ku fito fili ku kwankwanta	To come out and lie down
Ku sauka da ni ku ce tura,	You ask me to come down and push
Motar ba za ta motsa ba	The car will not move,
Ko ni ba za ni tura ba	And I cannot push
In lebura bai yi turin ba.	If a labourer does not push.
Dubi tara gyaɗa kamar Dala,	Look at the pyramids of groundnuts like Dala hill,
Kauye da cikin Kano Jalla,	Which are a common sight in the city and village,
Su ɗauki guda su ɗora ta,	Even the last sack perfectly placed,
Amma ba za ta goce ba.	So that it will not fall down,

Jirgin ruwa in ya zo kwata,	If a ship comes to port,
Jirgin ruwa ba ya saukewa,	It cannot unload itself,
Jirgin ruwa ba ya ɗorawa,	It cannot load itself,
Lebura ne yakan sauke,	It is the labourer who unloads,
Lebura ne yakan ɗora	It is the labourer who loads,
Lebura ne yake tuƙin	It is the labourer who drives,
Da lebura zai sa targa	If he is to go on work-to-rule,
Jirgin ba za ya motsa ba.	The ship will never move.
Jirgin sama fankamin wofi,	An aeroplane is a big barrel,
Ba za ka saka ka kwashe ba	It cannot load or unload itself,
In lebura bai yi aiki ba.	If the labourer does not work.
Wai ga wani yai gidan kwano,	Here is someone who built a house with sheet metal,
Ina hauka yana yanga,	He is boasting and showing off,
In kai magana i ƙyale ka,	If you speak he does not listen to you,
Da kwanon za a ɓabɓalle,	If the sheets are to be broken into pieces,
Katakon a ciccizge,	Together with the wooden planks,
A dubi bulok a rurrushe,	And the blocks to be demolished,
A sauka da shi a tara mai	Then to leave it in one place for him,
A kira shi a ce taho ɗora,	To ask him to build it again,
Ka san ba za ya ɗora ba.	You know he is not able to do it.
Dubi nauyin goro huhu ne,	Look at the heavy sack of kola-nuts
Ya ɗauki guda a bayansa	He takes one on his back,
Shi ma ba za ya motsa ba,	It also cannot move
In lebura bai yi aiki ba.	If the labourer does not work.
Don haka nan mutanenmu,	Our people, because of all this,
Ku ɗaukaki leburorinmu,	Give our labourers a better status,
Ku agaji leburorinmu,	Help our labourers,
Ku taimaki leburorinmu,	Aid our labourers,
Kar ku tabbata ba su aikin yi.	Do not think they have nothing else to do.
Kai lebura ko waliyyi ne	Good God! the labourer is a saint,
Aikin da ike na lada ne,	The work he does is for the sake of Allah,
Ba don ƙarfen Bature ba	Not because of money,
Da don ƙarfen Bature ne	If it is because of treasures,
Da lebura bai yi aikin ba.	He will never do such a work.
Haka masu tuwo miyar kuka,	It is the same case with the *tuwo* [meal] sellers,
Dawa a surfa ta,	Corn is pounded and the bran removed,
Sannan dawa a wanke ta,	It is then washed,
A tuƙa tuwo miyar kuka	And to make *tuwo* with *kuka* [baobab leaf] soup
Mai tuwo ba za ki saida ba	The owner of *tuwo* will not sell

In lebura bai yi aiki ba.   If the labourer does not work.
Ina Lena da Yutisa?   Where are Lennards and UTC
Ja ka haɗa zuwa Janhol   And the John Holt Group?
Su ma ba za su saida ba   All these firms will not sell
In lebura bai yi aiki ba.   If the labourer does not work.
        (Daba 1978: 131–5)   (Daba 1978: 213–7)

Mai Akwai da Mai Babu[27]   *Rich and Poor*

Amma mai akwai da mai babu   Have and have not,
Duka dangantakarku daidai,   You are the same,
Allah yake faɗa haka,   It is said by Allah,
Ba ni nake faɗa haka ba,   Not me.
Da ni nake faɗa haka   If it were said by me
Da sai ku ƙaryata ni   You could accuse me of lying.

Kai mai akwai ka gane,   The rich should understand,
Idan kai gida talatin,   If you own thirty houses,
Cikin guda za ka je ka kwana,   You are to sleep in only one,
A ɗaki guda ka kan kwan,   In one room,
A kayin gado guda ɗai   On a single bed,
Haka nan wanda bai da komai,   It is so with the poor,
Gida zai je ya kwana,   He is to sleep in a house
A ɗaki guda ikan kwan,   In one room,
A gefe guda ikan kwan,   He sleeps on one side (of his mat or bed)
A kayin karauni falle,   On a single mat,
To in gari ya waye, ta nan   When it is morning
Duk dangantakarku daidai.   They are equal.

Im ba ku ɗan misali,   I cite an example for you,
Kai mai akwai ka gane,   The rich should understand,
In kana taƙama akwai ne,   That if you boast of wealth
Ba̧ ka sanya hula goma,   You can't put on ten caps,
Ai a kanka kai ɗai,   At the same time,
Ai da an gano ka,   If you do so,
Sai a ce wane ya taɓu,   You will be declared a madman,
Sai dai ka sa guda ɗai,   You can put on only one.
Haka nan wanda bai da komai,   So also the poor man,
Shi ma isa guda ɗai   One is enough for him,
Matuƙar in yana da hali,   If he has any at all,
To malam idan ka duba, ta nan   If you study this case well
Duka dangantakarku daidai.   You are all equal.

In ba ku ɗan misali,	I am giving you an example,
Da agogon jaka talatin,	A watch worth three thousand pounds
Da agogon sulai talatin,	And a watch worth thirty shillings,
In wannan iba da loto daidai,	If this one gives correct time,
Wannan iba da loto daidai,	And that one gives correct time
In za'a dai kira su,	If you are to name them both
Sai ka ji sunansu ɗai agogo.	Each will be called a watch.
Im ba ku ɗan misali,	I give you an example,
Da nonon sulai talatin,	Some milk worth thirty shillings
Da nonon kwabo talatin,	And some milk worth thirty pence
In za ka dai zuba,	When you look at it
Ai sai ku ga ai duk	You find that
Farinsu daidai.	It is equally white.
Kai mai akwai ka gane,	You rich should know that,
In kana taƙamar akwai ne	If you are boasting for wealth,
Ba ka sanya takalmi goma,	You can't wear ten pairs of shoes
A sanka kai ɗai	At a time, (if you do so),
Ai da an gano ka	As soon as you are seen
Sai a ce ga mahaukaci nan,	You will be declared a madman,
Sai dai ka sa guda ɗai,	You can only wear one pair
Haka nan wanda bai da komai,	It is so with the poor
Shi ma isa guda ɗai,	He also wears one pair,
Matuƙar in yana da hali,	If he can afford them
Malam idan ka duba, ta nan	If you study this (case)
Duka dangantakarku daidai.	You are equal.
Kai mai akwai ka gane	You, the rich, should understand that,
Im ba ka ɗan misali	I am giving an example,
Shi Allah Huwallazina	Allah the creator,
Bai da babu ɗinsa,	There is nothing he lacks
Sai dai da zuciya tai	Except that which he wishes not to have
Shim malam idan ka duba, ta nan	If you study this case, in this respect
Duka dangantakarku daidai.	You are the same.
Allah Huwallazina,	Allah the creator,
Kai mai akwai ka gane,	You, the rich, should understand,
Im ba ku ɗan misali,	I am giving you an example,
Ran komuwa ga Allah,	On the day of passing away (death)
Kai mai akwai ka gane	You, the rich, should understand,
Im ba ku ɗan misali,	I am giving you an example

Ranar komuwa ga Allah	On the day of passing away
Yadi biyar fari dai	It is only five yards of white cloth,
A cike za'a nannaɗe ka,	That you will be wrapped in,
Rami guda akan tona,	One grave will be made,
Ku tuna ba'a tona goma	Ten graves will not be dug,
Don wai kana da hali,	Simply because you are rich,
A ciki za'a turbuɗa ka	You will be buried in there,
Haka nan wanda bai da komai	It is the same case with the poor
Ran komuwa ga Allah	When passed away
Yadi biyar fari dai	It is only five white yards
A ciki za'a nannaɗe shi,	That he will be wrapped in,
Rami guda akan tona	One grave will be made
Ku tuna ba'a tona goma	Not up to ten
Don wai fa bai da komai,	Because he is poor,
Malam idan ka duba,	If you study this (case) well
Ta nan duka dangantakarku daidai.	You are equally treated.
Kai mai akwai ka gane,	You, the rich, should understand,
Im muddin kana da shi ne	If because you are rich,
Im muddin kana da shi ne,	If because you are rich,
Burinka shirya hairi	You intend to help,
Kai taimako ga kowa	You help many people,
Ka taimaka wa kowa,	You aid many people,
Ka agaza wa kowa,	You help many people,
Ka kyautata wa kowa,	You did well to many people,
Ran komuwa ga Allah	On the day of your death
Wallahi ka ji daɗi,	You will certainly be pleased,
Bayan ko sun ji daɗi.	And your children will not be destitute (after you).
Im muddin kana da shi ne,	If because you are rich,
Burinka da a ɓata,	You always want to offend people
Ba ka taimako ga kowa,	You help nobody,
Burinka cin mutunci,	Your way is to disrespect other,
Ko burinka cin amana,	Or to cheat others,
Malam a kwan a tashi,	As time goes on
Gidaje gami da mata,	Your houses and wives
Sannan gami da mota	Together with the car, (and)
'Ya'ya su zo su ƙare,	All the children may die,
Mata su zo su ƙare,	Your wives may also go,
Mota ta zo ta ƙare,	And your car is no longer,
Ka ga ran komuwa ga Allah,	Now your time comes

Kai ma ka zo ka ƙare,	You also die
Ka ga ranar da kai da babu,	You and nothing on that day
Duka Wallahi babu bambam.	Are equal and the same.
Allah Huwallazina,	Allah the creator
Allah Huwallazina	Allah the creator
Ya yi Larabawa	He created Arabs
Ya yi Ingilishi,	He created English people
Yai wo mutan Amerika,	He brought Americans into being
Ya yi Indiyawa,	He created Indians
Allah Huwallazina,	Allah the creator
Yai haka domin mu gane juna.	Did so for us to understand each other.
Amma mai akwai da babu,	The rich and the poor,
In ba ku ɗan misali,	I am giving you an example,
Shin Allah Huwallazina,	Allah the creator,
Allah ya yi Ghana,	Created Ghana
Yai Isofiya,	Created Ethiopia
Yai Nijeriyarmu mu ma,	He also created our Nigeria
Ga shi duk baƙaƙe,	All these are black nations,
Wani bai jin batun waɗansu,	But they have different languages,
Allah Huwallazina,	Allah the creator,
Yai haka domin mu gane juna.	Did so for us to understand each other.
Duka dangantakarku daidai,	You are all the same,
Allah ike faɗa haka,	This is said by Allah,
Ba ni nake faɗa ba	Not by myself
Da ni nake faɗa haka	If I said it,
Da sai ku ƙaryata ni.	You could declare me a liar.
(Daba 1978: 146–52)	(Daba 1978: 227–33)

This strong moral tone running through Dan Maraya's singing is typical of his many songs on what he sees as social problems within contemporary Hausa society. He is well known for his songs on divorce and marital breakdown, such as *Jawabin Aure* 'About Marriage', on drugs, such as *Shan Kwaya* 'Drug-taking' and a wide variety of other such themes. As Shata indicated in the quotation at the beginning of this chapter, the singer also may act to 'record events' as well as 'enlighten'. Right across the field of song and poetry we see events such as the introduction of new currency, the change from left- to right-hand drive, the events of the civil war, and the introduction of Universal Primary Education recorded, explained and celebrated time and time again. Dan Maraya marked all these events and more with a song. His concern with the problems faced by the common man meant that he was always more in sympathy with the opposition, reformist elements within northern politics. Daba (1981: 226) reports that he was a member of the Northern Elements Progressive Union (NEPU), opposed to the 'establishment' party during the 1950s and 1960s, the Northern People's Congress (NPC). Nevertheless, he appears not to have been directly involved in the production of party political songs, as were so many then and at later times,[28] his political views are expressed more through songs on, for example, the principles behind the Organisation of African Unity, and on black peoples' solidarity throughout the world (Daba 1981: 226). Never having been involved in the vilification of political opponents his lament on the death of the Sardauna Ahmadu Bello, the northern leader who both led the party to which he was opposed, and in many senses represented the solidarity of the north of Nigeria in the 1960s, remains a genuine expression of the shock that many people felt at his assassination in 1966. Overall, Dan Maraya has produced a substantial and popular corpus of song that is regularly heard on TV and radio as well as from cassette recorders in markets and public places wherever Hausa is spoken.[29]

Haruna Oji hails from Haɗeja where he was born in 1941. His very considerable popularity has been built upon his songs for particular women, Jimmai, Balaraba, Ladidi, Hadiza. Accompanying himself on the *gurmi* 'two-stringed lute' he is regularly heard on local and national radio. The texts of two of his songs, for Jimmai and for Balaraba, are given in B. Sa'id (1982b: 106–11). The following extract is from D. Ahmed (1989):

Wakar Jimmai	*Jimmai's Song*
Kullum sai mun hira	We were always talking.
A rannan ta zo hirar	One day she came to chat
Muna cikin hirarmu	And as we talked
Tambayar da na wa Aljuma	The question I asked Aljuma was,
Yaya ranki ya ɓaci	'Why are you so sad,
Kuma na ga jikinki da sanyi	And your body is so cold?'
Ta ce i Haruna	She said, 'Yes, Haruna,
Muna cikin hirarmu	We were talking
Na samu batun labari	When I heard that
An ce za ka Haɗejia	You are going to Haɗeja,
Amma sai gobe da safe	And it's tomorrow morning.'
Mun yi batun ban kwananmu	We said our farewells,
Jummai ta shiga bacci	And Jummai went off to bed.
Na dawo na kwanta	At home I went to lie down,
Ina ta tunanin zuci	Mulling things over in my mind,
Ni a rannan ban barci ba	That night I could not sleep

Ina ta tunanin Jummai
Washegari ya waye
Na tashi nan na yi salla
Sai na tashi na buɗe ƙofa
Sai na gano Aljuma
Da 'yar adakar makaranta
Sai na cane Aljuma
Gara ki je makaranta
Abin da ya dame ka
Lallai ya dame ni
Ko na je makarantar
Ba zan iya aikin komi ba
Na dinga tunanin zuci
Shi kogin soyayya
Ko ba ka sha ba ka ratsa
Na tuna 'yan nan Jummai
Ai ka ji kamannun Aljuma
Jummai ba kauri ba
Jummai ba rama ba
Jummai ba ga tsawo ba
Ba ta gajarta Jummai
Jummai ba ga fara ba
Jummai ba ga baƙa ba
Idan ka gano Aljuma
Amma samalo take Jummai
Dubi idanun Aljuma
Kamar madara nonon shanu
Ita ɗiya Aljuma
Tana tafiya Aljuma
Kun ga kamatta daban ce
Siffofinta daban ne
Ai takonta daban ne
Ko a cikin mata ma
Komai girman taro
In Jummai ba ta zo ba
Taron ba ya haske

For thinking about Jummai.
When the day dawned
I rose and said my prayers.
On opening the door I came
Face to face with Aljuma
Carrying her little school satchel.
So I said, 'Aljuma,
You had better go to school,
What troubles you also
Troubles me deeply.'
'Even if I go to school,
I won't be able to work,
I will just go on thinking.'
The river of love,
Even if you don't drink from it, wade into it.
I remember Jummai
And this is how she is.
Jummai is not fat,
Neither is she skinny.
She is not too tall,
And not too short,
She is not light-skinned,
And not very dark either.
If you see Aljuma
She is the picture of perfection.
Look at her eyes,
As white as milk.
When Aljuma
Is walking,
She looks really special,
Her features are special,
Her walk is quite different.
Among a company of women,
However big the gathering,
If Jummai is not there,
The gathering has no sparkle.

(D. Ahmed 1989)   (GF & SIK)

Garba Supa died tragically, like so many other Nigerians, in a car crash, in 1989 aged 35. Playing the *kukuma* 'small single-stringed bowed fiddle' he had accumulated a band with whom he sang praise songs, such as one for Bello Maitama Yusuf, and a number of commissioned propaganda/advertising songs such as those for the Kano State rural agricultural development project (KNARDA), and one advertising Kabo Airlines (Hamid 1992).

Ahmadu Dan Matawalle is one of the more unusual popular singers in that, while he operates with a chorus, he eschews any musical accompaniment. Furthermore, his songs are unusual in the degree to which they deploy reference to the world of birds and animals, albeit in allegorical mode.[30] M. S. Aliyu (1980) lists songs about 'traditional customs', in praise of the Sarkin Gumel (another case of a singer best known for his 'freelance' compositions also participating in the clientage of praise-singing), about farming groundnuts, about trains, and about political independence (see also F. Umar 1984). Born in 1932 in Gagulmari near Hadeja, he was blind from the age of ten. At the time when Dan Matawalle began singing, a song called *Carmama* was very popular in Kano and was becoming all the rage in Hadeja. The Emir of Hadeja banned it, apparently because the song was a girl's song which expressed bitter resentment at arranged marriages (M. S. Aliyu 1980). Responding to expressions of anger by young people in Hadeja, Dan Matawalle promised them a song they would like. His first song was about two girls, Sociri and Badawayya, and he always insisted that his songs were sung to give pleasure to people, they were not performed for money or to preach. Aliyu (1980) gives the Hausa text of Dan Matawalle's perhaps most famous song, *Wakar Tsuntsaye* 'The Song of the Birds', also discussed by F. Umar (1984). The song sets out a kingdom of the birds in which the complex hierarchies of Hausa *sarauta* 'chiefly office' systems are represented. Below is a brief extract:

Ga masu son sarauta	Here are those who want the kingship:
Kan a jima shamuwa da gaga sun zo	Straight away the stork and ibis presented themselves.
Kuma gaga ka bai sarauta	The ibis was proposed,
Sun ce gaga kadan ta san mulki	But they said, 'If ibis becomes king,
Daga 'ya'yanta babu mai jin dadai	Then nobody but her offspring will benefit.'
Tattabara sun taho da yautai	The pigeon came with the nightjar,
wai jimina za ta bai guda mulki	And the ostrich said she would make one of them king.
Tattabara aka bai sarauta	The pigeon was proposed
Domin dokinta ta bar gida	Because she was so eager to leave her house
Talakawa su gina mata soro	And have ordinary people build her a dwelling.
Yautai ka bai waziri	And the nightjar was proposed as vizier,
Sun ce yautai munafiki ne	But they said the nightjar was a hypocrite,
Wannan shi za ya bata sarkinsa	'He is the one who will ruin the king,

Mai halin kilaki shege	He is like a prostitute, the bastard,
Ɗan yawon duniya shakiyyin tsuntsu	The wandering rascal!'

Hankaka ya zo da gauraka	The pied crow came with the crane,
Jimina za ta bai guda mulki	The ostrich was to make one of them king.
Hankaka ka ba sarauta	The pied crow was proposed
Tsuntsaye sai suke ta mamakin	And the birds were amazed,
Wai wa za ya ba ɓarawo sarki	'Who would make a thief into a king?'
Sai dinya ta zo da kwarwa	The goose came with the comb-duck,
wai jimina za ta bai guda mulki	The ostrich was to make one of them king.
Dinya ka bai sarauta	The goose was proposed
Sun ce su ba za su je tafki ba	And the others said they would not go to the lake
Tsuntsun tudu su harbu da sanyi	And catch cold by the water.

Sai shirwa ta zo da tsakuwa	So the kite came with the chicken,
Jimina za ta sa guda yai sarki	And the ostrich was to make one of them king.
Sarauta ka bai wa shirwa	The kite was proposed
Tsuntsaye sun yi shawara	And the birds decided
Suna cewa ɗan fashi ba zai sarki ba	That a robber cannot be a king.

Sarauta ka bai wa borin tinke	The marabou stork was proposed,
Kowa yana faɗa ya yarda	And everyone agreed,
Har zuciyarsu ta zauna	And were happy in their hearts
Wai sun sami shugaba mai girma	To have such a magnificent king until

. . .   . . .

(M. S. Aliyu 1980: 101)   (GF & SIK)

Hamza Caji has been the subject of a study by Harun al-Rashid Yusuf (1979) which looks at his considerable influence upon a number of singers and poets.[31] Caji belongs to an earlier generation of singers than most of those considered here. He died of tuberculosis in 1946. He had worked under the patronage of the *ciroma* (later Emir) of Kano, Sanusi. Originally from Dausayi near Kano, he moved from one of the quarters inside the old city of Kano to live and sing in Sabon Gari 'in order to have the freedom to sing his songs' (Yusuf 1979: 1). Yusuf quotes Caji as having said, 'We will move to Sabon Gari where a youth can abuse the important man!' As we will see when looking at the influence of song upon poetry, people often refer to *wakar Caji* as having been the model for a particular song or poem. It is sometimes unclear whether such references are to a particular song or his style of singing in general. Yusuf is clearly of the view that it refers to a style of singing with which Hamza Caji was particularly associated, but which others also adopted. Yusuf (1979: 15–17) cites associates of Caji such as

Nagelu, 'Dan Sa'idu, Shatan Fagge, Zabiya 'yar Daudu, Barau and Daɓalo:

> Long before Hamza Caji became famous there were people who used
> to sing and drum in the style of Caji, although it was not called 'Caji'
> but something else. But these musicians were never as famous as Caji.
> The original name of *wakar Caji* was *A kwale a kwale ba a kwale ba*
> which was performed very much after the manner of the Fulani-style
> flute music of the Koranic students. Hamza changed its name to 'Caji'.
> (trans. from Yusuf 1979: 1)

While it may well be that a general style of singing is captured by the term
wakar Caji, it is undeniable that the salient characteristic picked up time and
again by other singers and poets is a particular rhythm pattern which some
have called a variation on the Arabic metre *Ramal* (Yusuf 1979: 20). The
pattern is distinctive, at least in terms of quantitative syllable-based metre,
as exemplified in the following lines from one of his songs.

Kan na mutu kun asara	– v v v – v – –
Tun da kun rasa madugun samari	– v – v v – v – – v – –
Kan na mutu kun asara	– v v v – v – –
Ni ne tutarku ku maroƙa	– – – – v – v – –
Kwana uku sai ya warke	– – v v – v – –
Kwana huɗu sai ya koma	– – v v – v – –
Kwana huɗu kan ya warke	– – v v – v – –
Kwana uku sai ya koma	– – v v – v – –
Wata rana sai a mai da zance	v v – – – v – v – –

(Yusuf 1979: 18)

If I die you will lose
Since you will have lost your leader of the young
If I die you will lose
I am your flag, you singers
After three days he was better
After four he was worse again
After four days if he recovered
Three days later he was back again
One day there will be nothing more to say.

In the above extract there are two types of line: a sequence of – v – – / – v –
– (with the variant first feet – – – / v v – – / – – v v), or a line with an additional
– v seemingly 'inserted' in the middle (– v – – / – v / – v – –). This is the
pattern which appears to recur in Caji-influenced song (see also Schuh
1988/9).

   This brief discussion of a few of the many popular freelance Hausa singers has indicated something of the range of topics and styles of performance

to be encountered.[32] In the next chapter we look at singers that are generally distinguished on the basis of being involved in patron–client relationships of particular kinds. These characterisations are made on grounds of the salient features of their corpus of song. In fact with all these categories, many singers produce a variety of different kinds of material in different contexts such that they span more than one of these groupings. Nevertheless, they are presented here in the categories most regularly attributed to them.

TIED SINGERS, SINGERS FOR COMBATANTS, FARMERS AND EMIRS

SINGING FOR COMBATANTS

Prime among the singers who have made their names from their association with famous boxers, wrestlers, hunters, and *'yan tauri* 'performers of feats of daring' are Dan Anace and Kassu Zurmi, as well as Isa Dan Makaho and others.[1]

Dan Anace's most famous songs were in praise of the famous boxer, Muhammadu Shago, who was born in Talata Mafara around 1933 (Attahiru 1989). Attahiru reports that Shago boxed for 60 years, had 1,115 bouts and was never beaten. He is said not to have used charms and other forms of protection unlike other combatants. His relationship with Dan Anace started off unpromisingly. Shago kept beating all the boxers whom Dan Anace had been supporting and Dan Anace refused to switch allegiance to him. Shago, having decided he wanted Dan Anace as his singer, was forced to enlist the help of Dan Anace's father to put pressure on him to agree. When finally Dan Anace did agree they became inseparable, going everywhere together (Attahiru 1989: 16). Dan Anace's father had been a singer for farmers in the Gandi area of Sokoto where Dan Anace was born around 1921 and Dan Anace, following in his father's and grandfather's footsteps, sang also in praise of farmers as well as other boxers, such as Ado dan Kure, Miko Dogo, and Bagobiri (Mahe 1984).[2] Here, for example is an extract, quoted in S. M. Gusau (1983), from a song in praise of a farmer, Salisu na 'Yan Tsakkuwa by Dan Anace:

Salisu ba ya jin kome
Ya saba yini dawa ko babu ruwa
Ba ya jin rana irin Sule
Sai duhu can za ya taho
Salihu ba ya jin kome
Ya saba yini dawa ko babu ruwa
Ba ya jin rana irin Sule
Sai duhu can za ya taho
Sannu ango masha rana
Ku fadi rokon iri dai munka taho
Ni ba ni son raggo
Ko dangi nai suna kuka da shiya.

(Hausa text from S. M. Gusau 1983: 104)

Salisu is impervious
He is used to working for days in the bush without water
He does not feel the heat the way Sule does
Only when darkness falls does he come home
Salihu is impervious
He is used to working for days in the bush without water
He does not feel the heat the way Sule does
Only when darkness falls does he come home
I hail you, the bridegroom who endures the heat
We have come to get seeds
I have no love for the laggard
Even his family cry over him.

Attahiru (1989) presents a transcription of Dan Anace's *Bakandamiya* 'masterpiece/central statement' (see D. Muhammad 1981) in praise of Shago from which the following is an extract:[3]

Ya lillahi ya Tabaraka Sarki
Allahu mai dare mai rana
Madalla giye baran labo hana noma
Baleri sannu mai hana karya
A gai da Duna mai hana noma
Dan Audu gazaguru
Dan namiji duniya gabanka da karfi.
Wandara ko bai kashe ba
Ya hana kwana, itatuwa abincin giwa.
Aradu kin fi bindiga zahi.
Kowa sako nadi mu koma dambe
Mun kwana muna jiran maza ba su zo ba.
Namijin duniya gabanka da karfi.
Mai roko so shikai a ce mashi ingo
Dan Sarki so shikai a ce mashi Sarki
Kyawon dan kwarai shi gaji uba nai.
Mai son miya ya auri tsohuwa
Mai son shimfida shi auri budurwa
Duk mai murnar dan kwarai shi auri Isassa
In dai ba a mace ba mai buga kawo
Al'amarin duniyag ga a rika duba
Duniya rawar 'yan mata
Na gaba shi koma baya.

(Hausa text from Attahiru 1989: 27–8)

Oh God, Oh Lord!
Lord of the night and the day
Wonderful! Bull elephant! Follower of Labo! Tilling strength destroyer!
Dark one (Shago), I greet you, dispeller of falsehood!
Hail the dark one, tilling strength destroyer!
Son of Audu, the formidable,
Son of the great one, the strong-chested!
The dodger, even when he fails to knock out,
He prevents sleep, the tree, the food of the elephant!
Thunder, more powerful than the gun!
He who wants to put on a glove, come, let's go and box!
We spent the day waiting for men but they failed to appear.
The great one, the strong-chested!
The piper is looking to be paid,
The prince is looking to become king,
The best thing a son can do is follow in his father's footsteps.
He who wants good food should marry an older woman,
He who wants a comfortable girl should marry a young girl,
He who looks for a strong son should marry a strong woman.
If we still exist, my drummer,
In this world we should be on our guard
For the world is like the dance of young women
The one in front moves to the back.

(GF & SIK)

In a later discussion we consider singers tied to royalty, but Dan Anace, who died about 1980, was additionally known for his songs in praise of Sokoto aristocratic figures such as the Sarkin Sudan na Wurno Shehu Malami, and the Sultan Attahiru III (Mahe 1984).

The popular categories that distinguish between singers on the basis of who they sing for also recognise particular styles and typical content for that particular social context, so that certain things would be said about a boxer or wrestler and other things said about a scholarly aristocrat. Nevertheless, as is demonstrated by Dan Anace among many others,[4] individual performers may move from one category to another while remaining within relationships of clientage. Furthermore the tools of the trade are transferable; the ability to put together epithetic phrases, deploy hyperbolic imagery and construct a particular characterisation of a patron, all within the framework of lead and chorus accompanied by drums or other instruments, is the key to effectiveness whatever the context.

Kassu Zurmi is another singer best known for his songs for combatants. Born around 1920 in Magarya in Kaura Namoda district (A. Magaji 1980) he sings, generally without chorus but with drum accompaniment, for hunters, boxers and thieves. Magaji indicates he would accompany hunters on an expedition into the bush, drumming their individual *take* 'epithets' and encouraging them to attack their rivals! He quotes from songs by Kassu Zurmi for boxers:

In ba maganab banza ba
Mani bai yi idon tsoro ba
Ko kusa ba shi da tsoron kowa
Kowan nune shi yana sara nai
... Bahogo na Sambo kad ka hwasa
    Bugu sai rai ya ƙare
Kahin dangim mutum su zo su
Iske ungullai na ci mai kai.

(A. Magaji 1980: 52)

Let's not talk nonsense
Mani is clearly unafraid
He shows no fear of anyone
Any who take him on are cut down
Left-handed Sambo's man fail not
Hit him till he's dead
Before his family come
And find the vultures are eating his head.

and for professional thieves:

Bari mu zo ga Isa mui mai kiɗi
Yanzu tun da wata yaɓ ɓace
Yah hwara shige wa duhu
Na san iya ɓanna ka kai.

(A. Magaji 1980: 53)

Let's go and drum for Isa
Now that the moon has gone
And disappeared into the darkness
I know you can wreak havoc.

In addition to the aforementioned Isa, Magaji cites songs by Kassu Zurmi[5] for other thieves such as Adamu Dodo, Muhammadu na Sani, Sale na Gidan Goga, Iro sai Mame and the following extract in praise of Garba zakokin Zanhwara:

Na gode ma Garba kura shegen kare
Na duhuwa mau ƙuru
Ba za ni talauci ba tun da Annan dare na biki
Wanda duy ya samu da ni
A'a ɗan duniya ka lalacewa
Wai hay ya yi kokon abin buki ya ƙare ga rai
A'a ga kan maza da sauran samu aje

Take sannu in mutum ya hwalka iso
Sata ba iko ba in mutum ya gane gudu
Tahiyakka ɗan durun uwan nan
A'a ba iko ba in mutum ya gane gudu.

(A. Magaji 1980: 211–12)

I thank Garba, the hyena, the wicked dog,
The one in the dark, the intrepid,
I will not become poor since the Lord of the Night is celebrating,
I have a share in whatever anyone gets,
It is only the vagabond
Who will complain that he has no money to celebrate with,
While there are still wealthy men,
Take care; if the owner awakes, disappear!
Theft does not give you power; if the owner sees you, run!
Run like hell, you bastard!
You have no power, if the owner sees you, run!

(GF & SIK)

Sulaiman (1983) makes the point that such songs for thieves are precisely the same kind of praise-songs as we have seen earlier, it is simply that they are for a different class of patron. Illustrating songs for thieves, Sulaiman describes a singer, Garba mai Waƙar Barayi 'Garba of the thief-songs', the son and grandson of an *imam* (in 1983 he was 35 years old), who became disenchanted with Islamic education and ran away to become an avid gambler consorting with thieves and prostitutes (Sulaiman 1983: 15). He started singing on his own in praise of a particular prostitute, but then after a period of time he had put together a group of four drummers working with him playing *kalangu*, and was launched on his career encouraging thieves.

In nac ce ɗauki kayanga ɗauki
Ka ga na sargu, yaka na bargu
Shi na ce ma kwashi ba ni kaya
Ko na ubanwa ne
Dauki ba ni in sun shiga hannu mai kalangu
Mugun hannu kai na kalu
Ba ganewa za a yi ba
Ballantana ai Shari'a duniya nan
Ko gobe Kiyama in an je.

(Sulaiman 1983: 16)

If I advise you to take these things, then take them!
You Na Sargu, come, Na Bargu,
It is him I ask to take the stuff and give it to me,
Whoever it belongs to.

Drummer, give it to me as soon as it crosses your palm,
Oh wicked hand! You, Kalu's man!
They won't find out,
And there's no chance of being brought to judgement
Here or in the Hereafter!

(GF & SIK)

The text of part of the song in praise of Sabo Wakilin Tauri by Hamisu Kano[6] was quoted in Chapter 4 (pp. 78–80) from Powe (1984). In an appendix to his dissertation, Powe provides the texts of a number of songs in praise of boxers, wrestlers, *'yan tauri* and *shanci* players,[7] including the following in Hausa and in English translation in praise of the boxer Adamu, the Red Lion, sung by Musa Zurmi.

Mai horo, kai maza ka tsoro,
Jan zaki, sa maza laɓewa!
  Mai horo ɗan da ba sake ba;
  Jan zaki mai rawa da kurwa!
Ga Ada ɗan mutuwa,
  Mai rawa da kurwa!
Ada jan zaki,
  Mai rawa da kurwa!
Ɗauko aniyya Duna, (ba mu kyauta)
  Ba mu kyauta!
Mai horo kai maza ka tsoro,
Jan zaki Duna,
  Mai rawa da kurwa!
Duna, jan zaki (kai maza),
  Mai rawa da kurwa!
  Mai horo ɗan da ba sake ba,
  Jan zaki, mai rawa da kurwa!
Ada ɗan mutuwa, wanda ba ya tausayi,
  Mai rawa da kurwa!
Halewa na gode,
  Na yaba da kyauta!
  Mai horo ɗan da ba sake ba,
  Jan zaki mai rawa da kurwa!
Caca na gode,
  Na yaba da kyauta!
  Mai horo ɗan da ba sake ba,
  Jan zaki mai rawa da kurwa!
Dawo ga faɗa Duna,
  Na yaba da kyauta!
  Mai horo ɗan da ba sake ba,

Jan zaki mai rawa da kurwa!
Dawo maye,
Dawo na Alhaji,
    Mai lafiyar gizago!
Dawo na Alhaji,
    Mai lafiyar gizago!
Ada Caca, jan zaki,
    Mai rawa da kurwa!
    Mai horo ɗan da ba sake ba,
    Jan zaki mai rawa da kurwa!

Punisher, men fear you!
Red lion, who makes men seek refuge!
    Punisher, the son who is unrelenting,
    Red lion who dances with the shadowy soul!
Here is Ada, death's son,
    Who dances with the shadowy soul!
Ada, the Red Lion,
    Who dances with the shadowy soul!
Be determined, Black Giant, (give us a gift!)
    Give us a gift!
Punisher, men fear you!
Red Lion, Black Giant!
    Who dances with the shadowy soul!
Black Giant, Red Lion (you, men)
    Who dances with the shadowy soul!
    Punisher, the son who is unrelenting!
    Red Lion who dances with the shadowy soul!
Ada, death's son, who has no pity!
    Who dances with the shadowy soul!
Halewa I thank you,
    I praise you for your gift!
    The punisher who is unrelenting,
    Red Lion who dances with the shadowy soul!
Caca, I thank you,
    I praise you for your gift!
    The punisher who is unrelenting,
    The Red Lion who dances with the shadowy soul!
Return to the fray, Black Giant,
    I praise you for your gift!
    The punisher who is unrelenting,
    The Red Lion who dances with the shadowy soul!
Return Sorcerer,
Return Alhaji's

    Hypocrite!
Return Alhaji's
    Hypocrite!
Ada Caca, Red Lion,
    Who dances with the shadowy soul!
    The punisher who is unrelenting,
    The Red Lion who dances with the shadowy soul!

(Powe 1984: 558–61)

SINGING FOR FARMERS

While Dan Anace is best known for his songs in praise of combatants, we illustrated above that he also sang for farmers. S. M. Gusau (1983) demonstrates that the pattern of overlapping categories extends in a number of directions. He points to singers who are well known for their songs for farmers and at the same time for their songs in praise of various members of the aristocracy: Jankidi (of whom more later), Maidaji Sabon Birni and Abu Dan kurma Maru; he also indicates that some also sing 'freelance' and includes Dankwairo, Illon Kalgo and Audu Wazirin dan Duna in this category. But Gusau cites Alhaji Wakkale Gusau and Daudun Kida Jan-Bako as being singers who sing exclusively for farmers. G. Umar (1986) discusses another singer who falls into this latter category, Mamman Yaro Hore, from Suru. Born around 1940, Mamman Yaro Hore is an interesting example of a person who traverses the cultural boundary between the cleric class, the *malamai*, and popular song. According to Umar writing in 1986, he both ran a Koranic school and maintained his Islamic education while also taking up singing with a group of people, closely involved in song composition, who gathered around him playing *ganga* drums. His songs were mainly for famous farmers in Gwandu. He comments, in one song, on his own position:

Malam nike don nai karatu
Ban daura ina yin kidi ba
Shige nike ban raina gado
Duk dan asali ya bar taba ni
... Allah ya nufan da kidan noma
Ban gada ba kake na niyyi.

(Umar 1986: 12)

I am a *malam* because I have studied,
I hadn't intended to take up music,
I only took it up, I did not inherit it,
Those who inherit this skill should not take issue with me,
... It is God's will that I have taken up singing for farmers,
I didn't inherit this music, I make it up for myself.

(GF & SIK)

His first well-known song was produced in response to the offer of a prize
from the Sarkin Dutsen Hore for a song in praise of a large bull; a song from
which Umar quotes:

'Yan mazan yin daji
Barkakka da rana
Maƙetaci uban aiki
Goga na Buhari
Maƙetaci na Umaru
Daji ba shi isa tai
In yai karo da tsiriri
Sayyu su yi banza.

(G. Umar 1986: 12)

Man of the countryside
I greet you.
Wicked champion of work,
Great one of Buhari,
Wicked one of Umaru,
No farm is enough for him,
When he encounters weeds,
He uproots them entirely.

(GF & SIK)

More typical of farming songs, however, would be the following extract from
an *aikin gayya* 'communal work' song quoted by Ahmadu (1986):

Bi da maza ka gyara daji ka daɗe
Gaishe ku da aiki
Mai ƙarfi da aiki
Bi da maza ka kabce daji
… Mai ƙarfi ka aiki, kai!
Ga na saraki, tsakin tama
In batun noma kai a' ubansu
In na rundanci kai a' ubansu
Inna shiga mota kai a' hukuma
Bi da maza ya gyara daji
Yo gaba dogo
Dogo mai wargi da kalmi!

(Ahmadu 1986: 40)

He who puts all men in their place! Tamer of the bush! The endurer!
I greet your toil!
The great worker!
He who puts all men in their place! Transformer of the bush!
… Only the strong can work! You!

The friend of the chiefs, tough as iron ore!
When it comes to farming, you are the greatest!
When it comes to butchering, you are the greatest!
If if comes to using vehicles, you are in authority!
He who puts all men in their place! Transformer of the bush!
Come forward, tall one!
The tall one who plays with the hoe!

(GF & SIK)

COURT PRAISE-SINGING

The tradition of courtly praise-singing goes back before the establishment of
the Sokoto Caliphate in the early years of the nineteenth century. Hiskett
provides oft-quoted examples of early praise-song, including the following
extract addressed to the chief of Gobir, Bawa Jan Gwarzo (died 1790):

Causer of terror, chief of iron ore,
Son of Alasan, owner of the drum,
Causer of terror, iron gate of the town,
Bawa, you kinsman of Magajin Gari,
His name is 'Hate-flight',
His name is 'Put-to-flight',
As for me, I do not decline to follow Bawa,
Here is my saddle, all laid out,
My bridle is here, laid out,
My spur is here, laid out,
My tethering peg is here, planted in the ground,
I lack only a horse.

(Hiskett 1975b: 3)

Despite attempts by the leaders of the Jihad and their descendants to discour-
age the praising of any figure other than the Prophet, such courtly praise-
singing has continued down the years as an integral part of the daily routine
of emirate administration. The praise-singer will appear and perform during
each public occasion, the appointment of a new official, a celebration in the
yearly calendar, or indeed simply the official movement of the emir from one
place to another. Even though much power and administration has moved
to the state and federal governments of Nigeria, the praise-singer remains
part of the trappings of constitutional monarchy. Over the years, the focus of
most attention as far as song and music are concerned has been courtly
praise-song, combining the vilification of rivals with the characterisation of
the patron in terms of power, authority, lineage, prosperity, tradition and
influence (M. G. Smith 1957). (See, for example, the monumental dissertation by S. M. Gusau (1988), the work of Besmer (1971) and King (1969)
and many other papers and BA and MA dissertations.)

Sa'idu Faru came from a warrior family and his grandfather was both a warrior and a *kurya* player. His father was a singer to Sarkin Yaƙin Banga 'military commander in Banga' and Sa'idu was born in Faru near Maradun in Sokoto State around 1932.[8] Now deceased, his first major patron was the Sarkin Kiyawan Kaura Namoda Abubakar for whom Sa'idu Faru would sing his well-known song *Gwarzon Giwa na Shamaki* 'Shamaki's Great Elephant' in his praise. In return he was rewarded with wives, houses, horses and corn (Mazawaje 1985). A period of coolness between Sa'idu Faru and his patron resulted in Sa'idu's decision to seek another patron. After a visit to Alhaji Macciɗo Sarkin Kudu, son of Sultan Abubakar III, in Mafara he switched allegiance and was appointed official singer to Alhaji Macciɗo, having been in competition with Musa Ɗankwairo for the position. The rivalry resulted in recrimination in song between them (Mazawaje 1985: 61). Satire and innuendo are equally part of the praise-singer's armoury. S. M. Gusau cites an extract from a song by Sa'idu Faru which is ostensibly praise but which Gusau (1988: 304–5) interprets as having ambiguous undertones that could be seen as indicating that Sarkin Zamfara Zurmi Alhaji Suleiman (1951–70) was packing official positions with his own cronies:

Alibawa kuna ganin fansarku wurin Sule babu dama
Giwa ta sha ruwa tai miƙa ta taushe gulbi
Kuma 'yan ɗiyanta sun shiga sun sha sun fara ƙarfi
Ga 'yan namu suna jin ƙisa ba dama su kurɓa
Sai bil-amu uban dabara
Shi ɗai yaz zo ga giwa
Albarkacinki niz zaka in sami ruwan da nis sha
Giwa ta ba shi hili ya sami ruwan da yas sha
Ya sha kuma ya ba ɗiyanai
Ya wa dangi kirari yac ce ya ƙwato da ƙarhi
Zomo yac ce tsaya shege lallashinta kay yi
In ƙarhi gaskiya na koma ɗebo gabana.

(S. M. Gusau 1988: 305)

You Alibawa people, know that you cannot overpower Sule,
The elephant has drunk and established her dominance over the river,
And her offspring have also drunk and become strong.
Other animals are thirsty but have no chance to drink.
Only the human with his cunning
Was able to come before the elephant and say,
'By your grace I come to get water to drink'.
The elephant gave him the chance to drink.
He drank, gave water to his children,
And then went to his relations boasting that by his own power he had
    obtained the water.

But the hare said to him, 'Wait, you bastard, you must have sweet-talked him!
If you are really that powerful, do it again while I watch!'

(GF & SIK)

Sa'idu Faru is generally considered to have only sung for the aristocracy and
is known to have rehearsed carefully with his younger brother Mu'azu, and
other members of his chorus, before performing in public. One of his best-
known songs is in praise of his patron Alhaji Maccido, *Wakar Mamman
Sarkin Kudu*, from which the following is an extract:[9]

Bai gadi sake ba Mamman na Baura
Toron giwa uban Bello Mado
Duk Hausa ba mai irin hankuri nai
Bajinin gidam Bello Mamman na Yari
Sarkin Kudu Maccido ci maraya
Babban dutse a hange ka nesa
A ishe ka soronka yatsar ma kowa
Dadai babu geben da kai ga gulbi
Ruwan Maliya sun wuce masu taru
Bajinin gidam Bello Mamman na Yari
Sarkin Kudu Maccido ci maraya
Fadi gaskiya Bello kai Shehu yac ce
Bari masu son duk su maishe ka yaro
Da kyauta da ilmi da neman dalili
Da gode na Allah da istingifari
Da su Bello dan Shehu yatsar ma kowa
Ka kai kamab Bello ka gadi Moyi
Saura ka kai inda Mai Hausa yak kai
Bajinin gidam Bello Mamman na Yari
Sarkin Kudu Maccido ci maraya.

He's inherited no laxity, Mamman of Baura
Bull elephant and father of Bello Mado,
Among all the Hausa there's none with his patience
Great bull of the house of Bello, Mamman of Yari,
Sarkin Kudu Maccido, destroy the undefended town.
Great rock, one first sights you in full from afar,
You're sought in your residence which surpasses all others,
Indeed there's no stream that can equal a river,
While the Red Sea itself surpasses mere fishermen's nets
Great bull of the house of Bello, Mamman of Yari,
Sarkin Kudu Maccido, destroy the undefended town.
Speak the truth, 'tis you Bello whom Shehu appointed,
Forget those who would treat you as utterly immature,
In generosity and learning, in seeking out logic,

In gratitude to God for His constant protection,
In these Shehu's son Bello exceeded all others
You've attained as did Bello, you've succeeded Moyi
You'll finally attain as the Lord of the Hausa attained,
Great bull of the house of Bello, Mamman of Yari,
Sarkin Kudu Maccido, destroy the undefended town.

(adapted from A. V. King, unpublished MS)

Ibrahim Narambaɗa (died *circa* 1960) was born in the early years of
this century in Tubali, 15 miles from Isa in what is now Sokoto State. His
mother was from a family of musicians and his father a famous wrestler
called Ibu dan Gwale (Mazawaje 1985); he had Kanuri face-markings and
Mazawaje claims that a joking relationship between Toronkawa Fulani and
Kanuri assisted Narambaɗa in his client relation with the Sarkin Gobir na
Isa Muhammad Na'ammani (emir 1927–35) and his successor Sarkin
Gobir Amadu Bawa I (emir 1935–75). Working with a chorus and *kotso*
drummers Narambaɗa was one of a number of outstanding court praise-
singers, including Jankiɗi, Ɗankwairo, Sarkin Tabshi and Sa'idu Faru, who
were particularly popular during the middle years of this century. A prolific
singer,[10] Narambaɗa's best known song is perhaps his *Bakandamiya* 'Masterpiece' also known as *Gwarzon Shamaki na Malam Toron Giwa* in praise of
Sarkin Gobir Amadu, discussed by Muhammad (1981) and S. M. Gusau
(1988), among others.[11] An extract from this song is cited in Chapter 6 in
the discussion of refrains and choruses. S. M. Gusau (1988) quotes an interesting snatch from a song by Narambaɗa in which he refers to the disap-
pointment of princes who are not chosen to succeed to the emirship:

Duk ɗan sarki da bai yi sarki ba	Any prince who does not become king,
Ko ya ta da kai da jikka dubu har aji dubu	Even if he sleeps on mountains of money,
Wannan ransa bai da haske	Will never be happy,
Shi wannan ransa bai da haske	He will surely never be happy.
(S. M. Gusau 1988: 300)	(GF & SIK)

The ability of the court praise-singer to operate as a defensive and offensive
screen between the patron and his rivals is discussed further in relation to
other singers.

Sarkin Tabshi, although a title that means simply 'chief tabshi drummer' and which therefore can be applied to many drummers, is the name
generally applied to the main praise-singer, Sarkin Tabshi Alhaji Mamman,
for the Emir of Katsina, Alhaji Usman Nagogo. Born circa 1920 in Rima,
Sokoto State, of a Fulani family from Maraɗi in Niger, Sarkin Tabshi moved
to Katsina in 1938, where he took up *tabshi* drumming as a newcomer
(Kofar Na'isa 1980). Now deceased, his repertoire of praise-songs was not
limited to his immediate patron, the Emir of Katsina (for music at the court

of Katsina, see King 1969). He accompanied Nigerian troops to Burma
during the Second World War and sang the song on Nigerian independence
quoted above (pp. 137–8). While he remained firmly within the clientage
relationship he had established with the Emir of Katsina, Usman Nagogo,
he both sang on topical subjects outside the frame of classical praise-song, a
field usually associated with 'freelance' singers such as Mamman Shata, and
also sang in praise of other northern emirs. Kofar Na'isa (1980) quotes
songs in praise of Sarkin Zazzau Alhaji Muhammadu Aminu, Sarkin
Musulmi Abubakar III, Sarkin Kano Alhaji Muhammadu Sanusi and
Sarkin Haɗeja Alhaji Haruna Abdulkadir, among others, in addition to
songs in praise of his own direct patron. This ability to sing in praise of a
number of royal patrons is alluded to in a song in praise of the present Emir
of Kano, Ado Bayero, quoted by I. Y. Yahaya:

Tunau na ji zancen mutanen Kano
Wai an yi sarkin Kano ban taho ba
Gidan Dabo kowa kaɗa mai nake
Gama ba ni sarkin kiɗan ɗai nike
Dabo an ba shi sarki Kano
To wanda yab ba shi sarki Kano
Ga shi ya ba wa Ado sarautar Kano
Usmanu an ba shi sarki Kano
To wanda yab ba shi sarki Kano
Ga shi ya ba wa Ado sarautar Kano
Sanusi ku san ya yi sarki Kano
To wanda yab ba shi sarki Kano
Ga shi ya ba wa Ado sarautar Kano.

Tunau, I have heard what the people of Kano are saying
It is reported that Kano has a new emir whose installation I did not attend
(It should be clear to everyone) that I do compose songs for all the
    descendants of Dabo
I do not restrict myself to one patron
Dabo was made the Emir of Kano
He who made him the Emir of Kano
Has now made Ado the Emir of Kano
Usman was made the Emir of Kano
He who made him the Emir of Kano
Has now made Ado the Emir of Kano
Sanusi was made the Emir of Kano
He who made him the Emir of Kano
Has now made Ado the Emir of Kano.

                                        (I. Y. Yahaya 1981: 141)

Salihu Jankidi, who died *circa* 1973, was born near Gusau in 1853(!) according to U. Zagga (1980). For 50 years, apparently, he was praise-singer to the Sultan of Sokoto, Abubakar III, developing a close joking relationship with him, both praising him and vilifying his opponents. According to Zagga (1980: 16) talking about Jankidi, 'the praise-singer is the protection between the patron and his enemies'. Jankidi became also closely involved with the entourage of the Sardauna of Sokoto, Alhaji Ahmadu Bello, the first premier of Northern Nigeria, later to be assassinated in the first military coup of 1966.

Singing in praise of him and his northern establishment party, the Northern People's Congress (NPC) during the 1950s and 1960s, Jankidi became a widely known and popular singer. Nevertheless, Zagga (1980: 72) writes that, 'in praising the king a singer must surreptitiously attack the princes', and indicates that, in a song to please the sultan, Jankidi included *habaici* 'innuendo' against the sardauna and conversely, in a song in praise of the sardauna, included *habaici* against the sultan. This two-edged sword, the skill of the praise-singer, means that the relationship between patron and client can sometimes be an uneasy one. Zagga indicates that Jankidi had four previous aristocratic patrons, such as Sarkin 'Yan Doto Abdu with whom he fell out (1980: 24), before he finally established his relationship with the sultan. Carefully rehearsing each song with his eight-man chorus, he had inherited the art/trade from his father but moved from playing the *kalangu* 'hour-glass drum', as his father had done, to *kotso* 'single membrane drum' and then to *tabshi* 'conical single membrane drum'.

Jankidi illustrates the flexibility and negotiability of the clientage relationships that distinguish 'tied' praise-singers, (and indeed clientage relationships more generally). Not only did he leave one patron for another, but he was able to exploit the interstices between one set of social and artistic obligations and another to his political and pecuniary advantage. *Habaici*, as an allusive and indirect art, is one point on a continuum that stretches to open insult, and Zagga quotes a snatch from Jankidi in ferocious mode:

Kai sautakarma sai ka yi hankali
Kun san bakauye ba kunya garai ba
Babu kunya wauta garai
Had da sa a yi mai girman damo.

(U. Zagga 1980:64)

You, big tall man, you had better watch out
Country bumpkins have no sense of shame
Shameless, and an idiot besides
He will be made to bow to the inevitable.

Musa Dankwairo was as prolific a singer, initially under the tutelage of his elder brother Kurna, as Ibrahim Narambada. The Oral Documentation

Unit catalogue lists numerous recordings of some fifty songs under his name (Oral Documentation Unit 1983).[12] Born around 1910 in Bakura district, Talata Mafara (S. M. Gusau 1988), his father moved to Maradun to become the singer for Sarkin Kayan Maradun Ibrahim (1903–23). Musa Dankwairo learnt his art from his father and from his elder brother, Abdu Kurna. Working with his elder brother in singing the praises of their patron, Dankwairo came to the attention of a member of the aristocracy who, when he was appointed Sarkin 'Yan Doton Tsafe Aliyu II in 1960, asked Abdu Kurna to give him Dankwairo as his praise-singer. Their patron, Sarkin Kayan Maradun, resisted this attempt at poaching and eventually Kurna stayed and Dankwairo went (S. M. Gusau 1983). It was not long however, before a bigger fish came along hunting in the pool and in 1962 Dankwairo met the Sardauna Ahmadu Bello. At the time there was no bigger patron and Dankwairo had clearly made it to the top when he became his client.[13] Having learnt his art within his own family, Dankwairo's group was peopled with his own sons and grandsons, Abdu, Sani, Abu and others. As he grew older his sons came more and more to the fore both in performance and in the process of composition and rehearsal. His repertoire, like that of Sarkin Tabshi, included songs on subjects other than straight praise. He sang songs for farming, for the political party the NPC, and more general topical and didactic songs. He is perhaps best remembered for his songs in praise of the Sardauna which included the following extract, quoted by Yahaya, from an elegy sung after the assassination of the Sardauna in 1966:

CHORUS: Ya wuce raini,
          Ba a yi mai shi,
          Amadu jikan Bello sadauki.
LEAD: Gungurum kashi giwa na Alu ba ka haɗuwa,
          Ko shi kaɗai ya toshi makoshi.
CHORUS: Ya wuce raini,
          Ba a yi mai shi,
          Amadu jikan Bello sadauki.
LEAD: Kai Alhaji Musa Dankwairo,
          Ka taɓa waƙar Ahmadu Bello,
          Mu yi shahada,
          Kowa bai wuce lokacinai.
          Ahmadu sadda ya yi mulki,
          Ya riƙe jama'a tai da kyawu,
          Na tare da kai bai lalace ba.
          Har yanzu na tare da kai bai lalace ba.
          Firimiyan Jihar Arewa Ahmadu,
          Abin da kai wa Nijeriya,
          Har ƙasa ta naɗe ana tuna ka.
          Amadu jikan bawan Allah,

Gamji ɗan ƙwarai, gamji ɗan ƙwarai,
Gobe Alla gafarta ma.
Malam gobe Allah gafarta ma.
Gaba ta wuce baya ad da saura,
Yanzu ku nemo wani kamatai.
Gaba ta wuce baya ad da saura,
Gobe ku nemo wani kamatai.
Ba tsoro ba karayar zucci,
Ya gwada jikan Shehu ne, Ahmadu,
Ya gwada jikan Shehu ne shi.
Shi Ahmadu ya sami duniya,
Ya kau gwada ya sami duniya,
Yai alheri, ya riƙe kanne,
Ya riƙe 'ya'ya, ya riƙe bayi,
Ya riƙe barwa da talakkawa,
Ran Juma'a da ƙarfe biyu,
Ran nan yaƙi yac ci Amadu,
Nai kuka, nay yi baƙin rai,
Nat tuna Allah, nai masa murna,
Da wulakanci, gara shahada
Ga Musulmi don ba illa ne ba.

CHORUS: Ya wuce raini,
Ba a yi mai shi,
Amadu jikan Bello sadauki.

LEAD: Bangon tama mai wuyar tsira,
Bajimin Sir Kashim, Uban Zagi,
Bello ɗan Hassan,
Mai martabar ɗan Fodiyo,
Mai martabar Abdullahi,
Mai martabar Muhui da Atto, da
Uwar Daje,
Mai martabar Ibrahimu mai ƙahon karo,
Sadauki, ɗan sadauki,
Kakanninka waliyan Allah ne,
Ba ba'a ba ko tak.
Ko lahira muna taulahin muna nan
Ta wajen hannunka da dama.

CHORUS: He doesn't tolerate insolence,
No one dare approach him with insolence,
Amadu, grandson of Bello, the brave warrior.

LEAD: You are like an elephant bone, of Alu, that cannot be swallowed,
It alone can block up the throat.

CHORUS: He doesn't tolerate insolence,
No one dare approach him with insolence,

Amadu, grandson of Bello, the brave warrior.
LEAD: You Alhaji Musa Dankwairo,
Sing a song of meditation for Ahmadu Bello,
Let us submit to the will of God,
That no one will live beyond his time.
When Ahmadu was ruling,
He took good care of his people.
None of his followers went astray.
Even now, his followers have not gone astray.
Ahmadu, the Premier of the North,
What you did for Nigeria,
Will for ever continue to be remembered.
Ahmadu, grandson of a pious one,
You are gamji (brave), a trusted son,
May God pardon you.
Malam Ahmadu, may Allah grant you his pardon.
Now let us forget the past and look forward to the future,
It remains for you now to find his replacement.
Let us forget the past and look forward to the future,
You should next find his substitute.
He was fearless, and never gave up,
He demonstrated that he was the grandson of the Shehu,
The grandson of the Shehu he was.
Ahmadu got all he wanted on earth,
And he showed his contentment by
Showing kindness, and caring for his brothers,
He cared for sons, and for slaves,
He cared for servants and all his subjects.
But, on a Friday, at 2 o'clock,
Ahmadu was overpowered by war.
I shed tears and felt the bitterness,
But I thought of God and congratulated him,
For rather than surrender and humiliation, it is better
For a Muslim to die a martyr, there is no shame attached.
CHORUS: He doesn't tolerate insolence,
No one dare approach him with insolence,
Amadu, grandson of Bello, the brave warrior.
LEAD: You are the metal wall from which nothing sprouts,
The brave bull of Sir Kashim, leader of the guards,
Bello the son of Hassan,
Inheritor of the qualities of Dan Fodiyo,
Inheritor of the qualities of Abdullahi,
Inheritor of the qualities of Muhui and Atto, and
The mother of Daje,
Inheritor of the qualities of Ibrahim, the brave fighter,

The brave warrior and son of a brave warrior,
Your grandparents were true saints,
There can be no mocking this truth.
Even in the next world we seek to be
At your right hand.

(adapted from I. Y. Yahaya 1981: 146–9)

SYMBOLS AND ALLEGIANCES

Within the extract in praise of the Sardauna quoted at the end of the previous section, we see the classic categories of aristocratic praise, the personal qualities, the relationships with underlings and clients, administrative skills, generosity, personal piety and, most importantly in the case of the Sardauna, his clinching claim to legitimate authority through his direct descent from the leader of the Jihad, Shehu Usman ɗan Fodiyo. A recurring feature of court praise-songs is the deployment of common symbols – animals, colours – in association with the person of the patron, as we see in the above extract. Umar (1984: 48) lists common symbols as follows: *giwa* 'elephant': strength and dignified authority; *zaki* 'lion': strength, courage and respectability; *doki* 'horse': influence and wealth; *kura* 'hyena': greed ferocity and threat; *jaki* 'donkey': stupidity; *rakumi* 'camel': endurance; *dila* 'jackal': cleverness; *biri* 'monkey': destruction; *mujiya* 'owl': unpopularity; *ja* 'red': danger, bravery and severity; *baki* 'black': invincibility, bad omen; *kore* 'green': fertility, agriculture; *fari* 'white': happiness, harmlessness, weakness; *ruwa* 'water': cleanliness, purity, power and prosperity. (See also Ryan (1976) on colour symbolism and King's (1969) listing of a hierarchy of animals used symbolically in Katsina court songs.)

While someone like Dan Maraya, as an independent freelance singer, is able to take whatever political line he chooses in his songs, the tensions between independence of thought and expression on the one hand and the demands of clientage relations on the other are able to create, for tied singers such as Dankwairo, pressures working in contradictory directions. Nowhere is this more clearly visible than in the case of two songs by Dankwairo, *Bashar Mai Daura* 'Bashar, Emir of Daura' and *Bakalori Dam*. In the first of the following extracts, Dankwairo, in praising the Emir of Daura, inserts his bitter complaint about forced removal and lack of compensation when the Bakalori Dam was constructed near Maradun as part of one of the many large-scale Agricultural Development Projects (ADPs) funded by the Nigerian government and international institutions during the 1980s.[14] In the second extract, clearly from a later song, Dankwairo sings the praises of the dam, and by implication the development policies that have now produced all the advantages of pipe-borne water and irrigated fields. Clearly, in whatever way Dankwairo was compensated, in time-honoured praise-singer fashion he produced the appropriate response. The extracts are taken from U. A. Ahmed (1992).[15]

Bashar Mai Daura
Kai duk martabar sarakunan na,
Tana ga hannun Bashari Sarki.
Ka zama sarki ka gama komai,
Kai ne Audu ka gaji Musa,
Kai aka tsoro wa kaka tsoro?
Yaro ba ya gardama da sarki.
....
Muhammadu sarkin imani,
Wanda bai taɓa cin zaida ba ko ɗai.
Allah shi ka aiko komi, yaƙin dam na Bakalori
Ya ci mu, to sai in faɗa ma Mamman
Ban da gida yanzu ban da gona.
Yanzu cikin damina muke ta
Shirin gyaran ɗan soron da za ni barci.
Yanzu gidan makaɗa ya zamo gulbi,
Na ƙwarai wanda adda zurfi,
Sarkawa su su kai da taru.
Sarkin Daura, ko da damina ta fi,
Ka yi ta shirin tarbon baƙinka.
Idan wasu sun koro mu, mu taso.
Ba ni zama inda ban da gona,
Ba ni zama inda ba abinci.
Ashe laifi abin faɗi tudu ne,
Sai in ka tsallake naka ka koma hangen
Na wani; ag ga wasu nan sun hana sata,
To amma yanzu ga su sun yi.

           . . .

Gaskiya ta dara ma ƙarya,
Ko gobe gaskiya ta dara ma ƙarya.
Ai ka san sai dai mu bar ma Allah,
Kowa nan hana ka gadonka,
Ka san ba ka son batunai.
Kai ku ji wai anka yi biyan itace,
Duk mangwaron da ag gidan Ɗanƙwairo,
Wai ka ji wai an cirikke.
Kai ku ji ɗan kaɗan gwame da logo,
'Yan ruwa sun shanye mana zaki.
Shi ko marai yana ta toroko,
Wai gwiba yake da haushi,
To mu dai ba mu dasa gwaiba ba,
To amma, mun dasa rakke
Sai in raken za ka sha ka kwana
Ka samu abincin karin kumallo.

Kai 'yan ruwa iri-iri ne,
Kai ku ji shi ko Uban ta kolo
Bai raga rogonmu ko kaɗan ba.
Ko da yac ci yaj ji daɗi,
Sai ya kama ba da labari,
Rogon masu kiɗan nan yana da daɗi.
A tafka ɓarna jan biri bai dara bika ba,
A ruga ɓarna jan biri bai dara bika ba.
Kai tsula na nan ɗan ƙaraminsu,
To shi ma yana ta kalla gero.
Kai wane ga ka ɗan musulmi,
Amma, sabga ya kai da arna.
Musulmi suna ta kuka da kai,
Wane ɗan kaza mai son ya ci shi ɗai.
Allah ba a yi masa dabara da musulmi
Da kafirin kowac ci amana ya yi ta kuka.
Sai in mun taru lahira daga addini,
Sai alheri tuna malam za su ka tsira.
Haliƙu mun bar maka biyab bashi,
Ga wurin da ba mu da ƙarfi.
Ya Allah ba mu gidaje, ya Allah ba mu abinci.
Sarkin Musulmi Abubakar ɗan Shehu,
Mai imani, ya ce a biya mu,
Ba hakanan ya shirya da su ba.

Bakalori Dam (abridged)
CHORUS: Aikin Dam ya fi gaban a yi mai wargi
          A yi zamzari nai aikin dam.
LEAD: Gawurtacce, ƙasaitacce, ingantacce,
          Dam na Bakalori
          Kai bari in yi masa tambura
          Yana da ƙarfi da martabobi.
          Allah mai canza zamani
          Ya canza mana wurin zama.
          Dubi gidan ɗan Kano da Kuka mai Rabo
          Na sabuwar Maradun,
          Can dauri ba mu da famfo,
          To yanzu an yi mana famfo
          Famfo har cikin gidana,
          Ku ji famfo har cikin gidana.
          Da ɓata gari da maras wayo,
          Sun iskikke maras kishin kai,
          Sun goga masa bakin tukunya.
          Ko da dai shi sheɗani

Duk mai bin shawara tai,
Sai ya goya mashi baƙin jin nai.
Muhimmancin dam na Bakalori,
Akwai yawa da dama garai,
Idan ka je ga dam na Bakalori
Ruwa nai masu kyau fari fat suke.
Mahauta duk masunta na Najeriya,
Masu kamun kifi kowace jaha sun zo,
Suna nan nuna ta kamun kifi,
Su sayat su samu abinci,
Nan ga dam na Bakalori,
Alhaji duk nan ga dam na Bakalori
Abin da ya shirya dam na Bakalori,
An yi wurin noman rani,
Akwai shinkafa akwai auduga,
Akwai masara akwai acca,
Akwai gero akwai dawa
Nan ga dam na Bakalori.
Duk shanun da suke jahar Sokoto
Dam na Bakalori ya keɓe,
Ba su ƙara zuwa cin rani,
Abinci dare da rana duk, nan ga
Dam na Bakalori, Allah duk nan
Ga dam na Bakalori.
Yana gargaɗi ga 'yan kasuwa,
Na kowace jahar Najeriya kowa
Ya zo ya ba shi goyon baya,
Ya zo ya kafa kamfanoni,
Ya zo ya kafa kamfanoni.
Gawurtacce, ƙasaitacce, ingantacce,
Dam na Bakalori
Da damina mu yi ta noma
Kuma da rani mu yi ta noma.
Allah ya kawo abinci,
Haliku ya kawo abinci.
Kogin Bunsuru da kogin Rima,
Can ma suna da dam,
Babu kamar dam na Bakalori.
Kai bari in yi masa tambura
Yana da ƙarfi da martabobi.
Ko Ɗanƙwairo mai waƙa,
Nan ne Allah ya halicce shi,
Bakin gulbin dam na Bakalori.

Ina waƙa, kuma ina ta noma.
Malaman Rima sun yi ƙwazo
Sun gina mana wurin zama.
Malaman Rima sun yi ƙwazo
Cikin aikin dam na Bakalori.

Bashar Mai Daura
All the honour of these emirs,
Rests upon Emir Bashari.
You have become emir, you hold it all,
You are Audu and you have inherited from Musa,
You are feared, but who do you have to fear?
No youth can compete with an emir.
....
Muhammad the most faithful of emirs,
Who has never cheated any of his subjects.
God decrees all, and the battle of Bakalori Dam
Has destroyed us, so I say to Mamman
That I have no home and I have no farm.
We are now in the season of rain, and we are
Trying to repair a little shelter to sleep under.
Now the drummer's home is under the river,
The deep, deep river,
Where fishermen fish with their nets.
Emir of Daura, even though the rains are full,
Make ready to receive your guests.
If we are driven out by others, we will come.
I cannot live where I have no farm,
I cannot live where I have no food.
An offence is like a hill,
Only after climbing over yours can you see
Someone else's; there are those who condemn theft
But who have themselves gone out and stolen.
                    .   .   .
Truth is better than falsehood
And on the Day of Judgement it will be so.
We have to leave everything to God,
He who denies you your inheritance,
You will not wish to hear of him again.
They say people were compensated for their trees,
But every mango tree in Danƙwairo's house
Has been destroyed,
Only the smallest remnant remains.
The water spirits have robbed us of our sweet things,

The weaver bird is boasting,
He's desperate for the guavas.
But we don't plant guavas,
We planted sugar-cane,
Unless it is sugar-cane you have for your evening meal
Then you will have something to eat the following morning.
There are many kinds of water spirits
And he, Uban ta Kolo
Has left nothing of our cassava,
As soon as he ate them and found them delicious
He started telling people about it,
'The cassava of these drummers is really delicious!'
When it comes to wreaking havoc the monkey is as bad as the baboon,
When it comes to wreaking havoc the monkey is as bad as the baboon,
Tsula, the small monkey,
Is also there, breaking the millet stalks,
You, you are a Muslim,
Yet you do as the pagans do.
The Muslims are complaining about you,
'He is the hen who eats with no one.'
You cannot outwit God, the Muslim
And the non-Muslim, whichever cheats will be sorry.
In the Hereafter it is only religion
And good deeds, remember this, that will save you.
God, we turn to You for the realisation
Of what is owed to us, on that day when all are weak.
God give us shelter, Oh God give us food,
The Sultan Abubakar, son of Shehu,
The pious, has said we should be paid,
That wasn't the arrangement he made with them.

>   (adapted by GF & SIK from U. A. Ahmed 1992: 33–42)

Bakalori Dam (abridged)

CHORUS: Dam construction must not be delayed
            It should be built on time.
LEAD: The largest, most important, most significant
            Bakalori Dam.
            Let me beat the drum for it,
            It is powerful and dignified.
            God who brings all changes
            Has changed our whole environment.
            Look at the villages of Dan Kano and Kuka, Mai Rabo
            in new Maradun.
            Before, we had no pipe-borne water,

But now we have water
Even inside my own house,
Listen, even inside my very own house.
The spoilers and the ignorant
Have joined up with the dishonourable,
And contaminated them too.
All such devils,
Those who follow their words
Support them in their evil ways.
The importance of the Bakalori Dam,
Is very great,
If you go to the Bakalori Dam, you will see
Its beautiful clear drinking water.
Butchers, and all the fishermen of Nigeria,
Fishermen from every State have come,
And here they catch their fish,
To sell and make their living,
Here at the Bakalori Dam.
Alhaji is here at the dam,
He has arranged that at the dam
There are places for dry-season farming
For rice and cotton,
Maize and wheat,
Guinea-corn and millet
Here at the Bakalori Dam.
All the cattle in Sokoto State
Can be accommodated at the dam,
They no longer have to migrate in the dry season,
There is food available every day
At the Bakalori Dam, truly, all
At the Bakalori Dam.
He is advising businessmen
From every State in Nigeria
To come and support him,
Come and establish companies,
Come and establish companies.
The largest, most important, most significant
Bakalori Dam.
In the rainy season we can farm
And in the dry season we can farm.
God has brought us food,
The Lord has provided us with food.
The Bunsuru river and the Rima river

Also now have dams,
But nothing like the Bakalori Dam.
Let me beat the drum for it,
It is powerful and dignified.
Dankwairo the singer,
Here was he born,
Beside the river that feeds the Bakalori Dam.
I sing and I farm.
The Rima Basin officials have worked hard
And made us a place to live.
The Rima Basin officials have worked hard
To build the Bakalori Dam.

(adapted from U. A. Ahmed 1992: 48–52)

These five singers, Sa'idu Faru, Narambada, Sarkin Tabshi, Jankidi and Dankwairo represent perhaps the best known of the so-called 'tied' praise-singers attached to some of the more important Hausa aristocratic courts. But they are only a very small sample of the very many singers and musicians who operate within patron–client relationships, some transient some more permanent, in Hausa communities. The catalogue of the Oral Documentation Unit (1983) from Ahmadu Bello University lists recordings from over a hundred different groups and individuals making music with voice and accompanying instruments.

8

POETRY: FORM AND BACKGROUND

Imagine a Hausa farmer living in a small hamlet in the valley of the upper Sokoto river in 1830. Of modest means he has in recent years become aware that the taxes levied upon him are now going to the new, expanding administration with its headquarters in Sokoto, some 100 miles away. Having heard how the new rulers in Sokoto have overthrown the pre-existing rulers of the Haɓe Hausa states, such as Kano and Katsina, he is impressed by their military prowess. From visitors passing through he has also heard that these new rulers are trying to put an end to the age-old corrupt practices of previous rulers and establish new rules for administrators. In a flush of enthusiasm he approaches a *malam*, a religious teacher, resident in a neighbouring community, and asks him to tell more about these new arrivals. The *malam* says that their reforming zeal is rooted in their adherence to the true faith, Islam. Not being a particularly religious person the farmer has previously left the issue of secret knowledge, medicines, spirits and the like to specialists in his community and so, thinking he will please the *malam* and perhaps better himself, he goes on to ask whether Islam is something that only specialists know about, living in town, reading and studying. But the *malam* insists that no, Islam is for all, and he claims that the original profession of faith is not difficult and the basic daily practices are available to everyone. He explains to the farmer what the basic phrases in Arabic mean, a language the farmer does not understand, and the latter thinks seriously about converting to Islam. During a period of some weeks of reflection he realises he would be in a small minority in his community, but that may work to his advantage or perhaps to his disadvantage he does not know. He eventually goes back and declares himself ready to take that leap of faith. Whether he will go on to study beyond the basics will depend on how busy he is with farming and other daily activities. Some months later, as he is now familiar with the basic practice and tenets of belief, he attends an evening gathering of other recent converts to listen to a visiting blind reciter who will tell of religious matters, not in Arabic but in their own language, Hausa. Having always had to have laborious translation and explanation of Arabic or Fulfulde on previous occasions, the prospect of immediate understanding and direct contact with this new and important world excites him. As they settle down to listen, the blind man introduces his chanted recitation by saying he will give a rendition of a Hausa poem by Muhammad Tukur, a local scholar from the same region, entitled *Bakin Mari*, 'The Black Leg-irons'. The recitation begins and, as a new believer, the farmer feels a growing sense of shock:

All mortal men, today the grave is calling,
 There is no orphan, there is no one whom (death) will leave behind.
In the place of eating *tuwo* [meal] where they played and laughed,
 There is no footprint, nay, no man, but only the hoofprint of the hartebeest,
The weaver of fine black and white cloth and the weaver of openwork cloth too,
 Are today no more, only the spider who weaves to give the monkey.
Their drummers and their trumpeters have passed on,
 The jackal and the cricket have inherited the place where (once) the *zari*
  jingled.
For death will cast us there beneath the ground,

   . . .

Our only neighbours are worms, scorpions, snakes
 With claws of iron, with deadly poison, black as black,
It is a town where there is no wind, save only that of the whirlwind,
 And an intense heat, fire that knows no respite.

   . . .

It is a town of darkness, pain and a thousand thousand torments,
 It is far from this world, they are chained there, there is no way of escape,
Their town is a town of holes and roads of fire,
 Scorpions and snakes all gather to attack,
There are certain black birds, the souls of the damned,
 They are picking them up, they take them to the fire, they do not relent.
Seven thousand and seventy wells there are, all of red fire,
 They are taken to (fiery) sepulchres, some are bound in fetters,

   . . .

Its space is large enough for fifty people, and as many as a thousand will
  be stood there,
 There will be thirst and hunger, there will be no water, not even the
  (stale) water in which grain has been washed,
They will weep tears until they weep black blood,
 The sweat will pour down like the stream from a roof guttering,
The sun burns the head, it splits the skull,
 The throbbing of it is like the beating of a drum,
The body has dried up, their guts have become emaciated,
 Their movement is like (the rattle of) hide shields, their pleasure (in
  eating) has all been used up,
Adulterers on this day will be brought in large numbers,

And each shall lick the privy parts of his companion in adultery.
There is swelling of the scrotum and veneral disease, it will afflict all the limbs,
    Blood and pus will flow, a stench will fill the place,
Let them be told that the child of adultery will trouble many, let them be warned,
    Their adornment is a gown of fire, there in chains,

. . .

They are told, 'The little pleasure (you enjoyed) has brought upon you
    Torment without end, for you failed to exercise restraint',
Their top lip shall reach above the cranium, there it is,
    The bottom lip to the navel, it is not a pleasant sight,
They are taken to the river banks, serpents attack them,
    They are taken to enclosed places (for) the torment of stoning,
They are taken to a town of cold, they all grimace (in pain),
    They are returned to the fire, they are brought back into intense cold,
They are taken back to huts where the fire oppresses them,
    Each one has his own hut, like a fowl pen,

. . .

The fiends of Hell who bind their arms back between their shoulders
    Are of such a size you would think them a hundred years old,
Seventy thousand cudgels they carry on one shoulder,
    And on the other seventy thousand hatchets.

                                         (Hiskett 1975b: 33–5)

In stunned silence people disperse. Sometimes frightened, sometimes scep-
tical, and always in turmoil the farmer returns a few days later to talk to the
malam. If this is what lies in store then what hope can there be. The *malam*
patiently explains that Hell and torment lie in wait for the sinner and the
unbeliever. On the Day of Judgement he, the farmer, as a true believer will
be judged and, depending upon his record, there may be a very different fate
that awaits him, with shady places and cool waters and many other eternal
delights in a place called Paradise. The basis of his faith should be his belief
in the one true God and his love of the Prophet. Somewhat reassured, the
farmer agrees to attend another recitation the following evening. More than
a little nervously, he and other recent converts come together to listen. The
reciter, this time an old man with palsy, says he will deliver an extract from
a poem by the leader of the Jihad, Shehu Usman ɗan Fodio, entitled
Ma'ama'are. As he begins to recite in Fulfulde, the audience asks for a translation into Hausa, which the *malam* duly provides.

I thank God, and may his blessings
    Be upon the Prophet, His Messenger.
From amongst the greatest he was chosen,
    The greatest of us and the last of his Messengers.
Muhammad, the Prophet, excels above all others,

In my heart I yearn for him.
When I drink of the water of desire,
    Then I hear nothing but words of love for him.
Appearing outside I look all around me,
    As if I might see him and hear his voice.
When I came back it was as if my origins were there,
    To him I will return and search for him.
Whether I stand or whether I sit
    It is as if I were living in his presence.
My own salutations are always as if to him,
    As if I had taken his hand in mine.
In my heart it is as if I have visited his
    Mecca, Daiba and the Raula.
If I look up I am filled with joy,
    To see and compare his inestimable worth.
When I look at the sun and its light,
    It is as if I see the beauty of the thought of him.
When I see the moon and its great beauty,
    It is as if I see the beauty of his face.
When I see the stars and the galaxies,
    It is as if I see the host of his companions.
Whenever I see a rain cloud,
    I remember the shade it provided for him.
Let alone the lightning which, when I see it,
    Is like a token of his smile.
When the storm comes down, then assuredly,
    I think of the blessings that came from his hand.
When I smell the scent of flowers,
    It is as if I catch the scent of his perfume.
When I see streams,
    I remember the stream that flowed from his hand.
When I see a well, I remember
    The well of Zamzam, it was a sign.
Whenever I see hills,
    I see his Safaa and Marwaa.
The rock of Hiraa'u was his retreat,
    And the rock of Sibiiru the site of Uhud.
With all the other hills of Mecca and Daiba,
    They are the hills that mark the old sites.
Whenever I see a dry stream bed,
    It is as if I see the wadi Akiika.
And all the other places in Mecca and Daiba,
    For those were his places.

And when I see a town, my thoughts turn
　To his Mecca and Madina.
On hearing each call to prayer,
　It is like hearing the voice of Biilaa.
When I see the ranks in prayer behind the imam,
　It is like him and his companions.
When I see reciters at their work,
　It is as if I have seen him and I am listening to him reciting.
He who yearns after Muhammad, I love him,
　It is as if I see Hassan who adored him.
When I see the books I am enraptured,
　For they are the marks of the one who loves the Sunna.
When I pass by places of learning,
　It is as if I see him and hear his voice.
When I listen to a sermon, in my heart
　It is as if I was listening to him preaching.
The night of preaching becomes
　As one when I come to hear him speak.
When I sleep I dream,
　It is as if I see his shape before me.
At first light I think of his birth,
　The dawn of his first arrival.
As each morning moves on
　I think of all his works.

(Furniss 1993b)[1]

This second experience is as deeply affecting as the first, but this time the farmer feels deeply moved by the heartfelt sense of longing and devotion expressed in the poetry. No longer gripped by a sense of shock and fear, the farmer's curiosity and interest turns to the detail of places and people referred to in connection with the Prophet, and he and his fellow members of the audience clamour to know more of the life history of the Prophet and the people who lived alongside him. And so, in this way our representative farmer begins the process of discovering the beliefs, moral codes and practices of Islam, while becoming increasingly aware of the world of Islamic learning in the care of a class of literati represented by his local guide and mentor, his *malam*.

In using this conceit of a 'representative farmer' I have tried to convey something of the power of the language of militant Islam. I would warn against reading into this device any notion of mass conversion of a homogenous rural peasantry. Society in the northern states was complex and heterogeneous, with groups and factions within the Fulani, alliances between Tuaregs and Fulani, peasant revolts such as the Satiru revolt in early 1906, schisms and a strong alternative culture in the 'pagan' world of so-called *Maguzawa* village life. Power, protection and medicine remained available through alternative channels, not only in the nineteenth century but down to the present day (see, for example, Wall 1988).

POETRY FOR A PURPOSE

For the cleric class, poetry in Hausa was a medium for the communication of Islamic ideas to the local population, and took its place alongside Arabic poetry, Fulfulde poetry, Arabic histories, biographies and treatises of many kinds which were extensively studied, copied and annotated. The significance of its being in Hausa was that it formed a key weapon in the battle for the hearts and minds of the ordinary people. That battle went on in conjunction with the military campaigns of the reformist Jihad of the early nineteenth century.[2] The clerics had well-defined categories for the content of poetry, and particular poems would deploy one or a number of such categories.[3]

The first extract by Muhammad Tukur, given above, was a typical example of *wa'azi* 'preaching/teaching' in which the torments of Hell and the delights of Paradise are described in the context of death and resurrection, the life of the true believer and that of the unbeliever. Powerful imagery provides the backdrop to injunctions and prohibitions of many kinds affecting the conduct of daily life.[4] This strongly didactic tone to *wa'azi* poetry has provided one of the most distinctive features of poetry writing down to the present day.[5]

The second extract, from *Ma'ama'are*, represents the category of poetic expression in which, by convention, the most intimate of personal statements can be made: expressions of love, adoration and praise. This category, *madahu*, 'Prophetic panegyric' drew upon many classical Arabic models including the *Burda* of al-Busiri and the *Ishriniyyat* of al-Fazazi. The expression of devotion would include an expression of unfulfilled desire to go on pilgrimage, to visit 'him' and all 'his places', along with descriptions of the miracles attributed to the Prophet that marked him out as God's Chosen One.[6] These two categories represent the core of much religious poetry both of the nineteenth century and of more recent times; the one concerned with behaviour in society in the context of reward and punishment in the hereafter, and the other with the expression of individual belief, emotion and religious commitment. Where the first draws upon the rationalist and moralistic tradition seeking to establish the *al'umma* 'the religious community', the second, while being a part of mainstream Sunni Islam, also represents the mystical tradition of thought, the Sufi way, in which esoteric knowledge and understanding awaited the individual in his pursuit of devotion to God and His Prophet. Abdullahi Bayero Yahya (1987) sees the expression of love and devotion as the central characteristic of Hausa *madahu* poetry around which other themes are deployed:

a basic characteristic of Hausa *madahu* verse, and a distinguishing feature that differentiates it from other categories of Hausa verse, is that *madahu* verse will always exhibit which I term mainstream *kauna* 'love' and supporting themes which may be regarded as aspects of, or manifestations of *kauna*. The supporting themes to appear in the Daliyya (a poem by the Shehu) are: *ziyara* 'visitation', *mu'ujizai* 'miracles',[7] *ceto* 'salvation', *haske* 'light', *fiyayye* 'excellence' and *sunna* 'the way'. (Yahya 1987: 52)

Hiskett (1975b: ch. 3) outlines other categories of religious poetry. Alongside the expression of personal devotion was the explanation of the life and times of the Prophet, a more narrative oriented style, termed *Sira*. The explanation of the principles of Islamic law were a subject categorised as *farilla* or *fikihu*. While these constituted categories within the world of poetry, they were essentially branches of Islamic religious knowledge not confined by any means to poetry. In this sense then, *fikihu*, *sira*, *tauhidi* 'theology', *nujum* 'astrology, science of the stars', *hisabi* 'numerology' and *hadith* 'traditions of the Prophet' were subjects of study and exegesis where topics could be addressed through versification (*nazm*) or in prose.[8] Poetry was, within this system, one instrument in the overall process of teaching, explanation and discussion. At the core of this didactic and purposive process was Koranic explanation (*tafsir*), an ongoing activity which was, and is, most visible during the evenings of the month of the Fast, Ramadan, when crowds gather to hear the most learned among their community provide 'interlinear' explanation of Arabic verses recited from the Holy Koran.

While religious poetry was, and in the main still is, directed at the general population through its all-pervasive didacticism, nevertheless mastery of religious knowledge was not simply or easily acquired. Typically during the nineteenth century and the first part of this century, following years of Koranic study as an *almajiri* 'student', the late adolescent or mature student (*gardi*, pl. *gardawa*) would go on to study further Arabic works of law and theology over a period of many years. Attaching himself to a particular teacher renowned for his knowledge of a particular work or works, the student would receive individual tuition and in return would help to support his *malam*'s local group of students and teachers through working land, tailoring, selling books, or some other economic activity. The dedicated student might spend years with different *malamai* in communities far away from his home, sometimes in town but also sometimes in very rural environments.[9] In either case, the religious obligation upon individuals and communities to give alms (*zakka*) would provide food and shelter for local *malamai* and their *almajirai*.

The transition from student to teacher and incorporation into the cleric class of nineteenth-century intellectuals was gradual; *malam* in one context would be *almajiri* in another. While all experts acknowledged the superiority of their own teachers in a chain of intellectual authority parallel to that of the spiritual chains (*silsila*) of saintly authority, their own reputations were based upon demonstrable piety and knowledge. The caricatures of the venal, ignorant, competitive *malam* we saw in the early prose of *Ruwan Bagaja* only serve to reinforce the converse image of the saintly, knowledgeable, humble and pious scholar. The culture controlled by this class of clerics, the world of Islamic knowledge and expertise, was, from the point of view of ordinary people, a specialised and exclusive culture, accessible only through the long process of Islamic education. Yet, at the same time, that identifiable group were, through 'vernacular' poetry and in many other ways, reaching out to ordinary people with the message of the true faith.

The message related primarily, as I have briefly indicated, to the fundamental tenets of Islam, the daily practices of prayer, and the behaviour of the believer. But that message had been formulated and spread, in northern Nigeria at least, through the reforming Jihad of Usman ɗan Fodio, and Hausa poetry reflected the broad ideals that had been formulated by the leaders of the Jihad in their many and varied writings. I cannot begin to do justice to the voluminous writings of historians and others on the ideals and arguments, trains of thought, sources, history and influences of the Jihad. Nevertheless, I will summarise some of the features, as I see them, that subsequently have been often manifest in the world of poetry writing.

The reformers had a strong commitment to the ideal of an Islamic state in which all believers, regardless of language or ethnic background, were equal. That ideal state was one in which justice prevailed, where institutions and regulations controlled the exercise of power such that oppression of the ruled by the rulers was not acceptable. The notion of an ideal state then provided the basis for an assessment of any contemporary administration to see how it measured up. If it did not, then it was legitimate, even mandatory, to oppose it and to seek its reform or overthrow. Even where an administration is Islamic, the presence of oppressive practices can lead to demands for reform that invoke the notion of the ideal state for their legitimacy. At the level not of the administration of states but of individual actions and personal responsibility, the Jihadist thinkers had emphasised an active morality, an insistence on identifying the good and the bad in the world of society and individual behaviour and thought. Regardless of whether the values were essentially puritanical or liberal, the legacy of this active moral expression was to bequeath to later generations a powerful legitimacy for ethical discourse and a wide vocabulary of publicly accepted evaluative language. This moral dimension to public discussion was, to some extent, in the control of the cleric class through its role as educators, educators not only of the urban élites but of ordinary people throughout society.[10]

The power of this sense of active commitment to Islamic ideals was very considerable. Not only has it motivated politicians and others in Nigeria down to the present day, it had far-reaching effects beyond the world of the

West African savanna in the early years of the nineteenth century. Drawing on the writings of Nina Rodrigues and Francis de Castelnau, Pierre Verger describes the slave revolts in Bahia, Brazil, during the years 1807–1835 in the following terms:

> These Bahia revolts were the doings of Muslims; they were religious wars. This was the direct repercussion of warfare which was taking place in Africa. The *Jihad*, or holy war of the Fulanis declared in 1804, and the pressure of Islam on northern Yorubaland was followed by the arrival of contingents of Hausa prisoners of war and also recently converted Yoruba Muslims.
>
> This holy war continued in Bahia in the form of revolts by slaves and even free Africans. These were the Hausa uprisings that were taking place between 1807 and 1816, and those of the Nago (Yoruba)-Malé between 1826 and 1835. (Verger 1976: 286)[11]

JIHAD POETRY

At the centre of the military and ideological skirmishes that broke out in the early years of the nineteenth century was an extended family group of organisers, writers and thinkers. Shehu Usman ɗan Fodio wrote, among other things, treatises on good governance in Arabic, such as *Bayan Wujub al-Hijra*, and poetry in Fulfulde such as the very popular *Tabbat Hakika*; his brother Abdullahi wrote an account of the Jihad (*Tazyin al-Waraqat*) and poetry; his son Muhammad Bello also wrote an account of the Jihad (*Infaq al-Maisur*) and other treatises; the Shehu's daughter, Nana Asma'u, wrote many poems. Nana's husband, Giɗaɗo, worked closely with her on many works of prose and poetry (Boyd 1989). Other members of the extended family and their descendants have been authors and translators down to the present day. The degree to which this intellectual effort was a co-operative one cannot be overemphasised. Verse written in one language by the Shehu was translated into another language by another member of the family. One member would transform verse by another member of the family out of couplets into quintains by undertaking a *takhmis* (adding an explanatory or exemplificatory preliminary three lines). Sometimes translation would render additional commentary such that the new would constitute more an alternative version of the old than a translation. S. Junaidu (1985) presents a study of Arabic verse produced by the Jihadist writers. B. Sa'id (1978) presents a voluminous collection of Jihad poetry.[12] Abdulƙadir (1980) presents roman transcriptions of some of the best known poems (see also the list of manuscripts in Boyd (1989: 159–64), and the Boyd Collection housed in the SOAS Library). Brenner and Last (1985: 436–7) point to the focus upon Arabic competence in the scholarly community in the early years of the Jihad with Hausa being the language of the 'others', the non-Muslims. Only later did Hausa come to be associated with 'Muslim society'.

In addition to members of the Fodio clan, other scholars outside the group of young radicals and outside the family were also apparently writing in Hausa at this time. Sa'idu (1981) follows Dalhatu Muhammad and others in attributing the famous religious poem, *Gangar Wa'azu* 'The Drum of Admonition', to Muhammadu na Birnin Gwari who was born circa 1758 in Katsina. Two Hausa poems attributed to him, *Wakar Dunbula* and *Wakar Kankandiro* were transcribed and translated into English in Robinson (1896). Sa'idu lists other poems by him both in Hausa and in Arabic. To have studied under the Jihadists did not necessarily mean permanent allegiance to the Jihadist cause and the Qadiri way. Rimaye (1986) claims that the Zaria scholar, Malam Shitu dan Abdurra'ufu (born 1806 according to the date contained in one of his lengthy compositions *Jiddul ajizi*), studied under the Shehu, although the Shehu died when he was 11.[13] However, he then returned to Zaria where he became deeply involved with Sufism and the Tijaniyya, composing both in Arabic and in Hausa including a further two lengthy poems, *Jimiyya* and *Wawiyya*, on Sufi religious themes.[14] Shunning all involvement in matters of state or administration he founded a school and became *imam* of a breakaway mosque in Zaria (Rimaye 1986: 6). Expression of opposition to the Sokoto Caliphate through the medium of poetry is cited by Hiskett (1975b) in connection with the leader of the Mahdists, Hayatu dan Sa'idu, a grandson of the Shehu, who wrote in 'protest against his exclusion from the Caliphate that he considered his right, and as a satire on the Sokoto establishment whose members he blamed' (Hiskett 1975b: 96).

From the dating, for example in B. Sa'id (1978), of original compositions and later translations and *takhmis* it would appear that the 1860s was a key period during which poems in Fulfulde and in Arabic were extensively translated into Hausa. Whether this represented a period of rapid Hausa-isation of Sokoto or a period of increased conversion generally within the caliphate, I am not aware.[15]

In addition to the many poems within the categories outlined earlier in this chapter,[16] an important further component within the Jihadist repertoire were poems that outlined the nature of the Shehu himself and the progress of the Jihad. The stories of campaigns and sacrifice were a significant part of the motivating factors that kept the spirit of the Jihad alive. A typical poem of this nature was by one of the Shehu's daughters, a remarkable and redoubtable figure who went on, with her female relatives, to organise a women's Islamic education movement called 'Yan Taru (Boyd 1982; 1986; 1989; Boyd and Last 1985). Nana Asma'u wrote *Wakar Al'amurran Shehu*, also known as *Wakar Gewaye* in Fulfulde in 1839 (the Fulfulde version is known as *Filitago*), and it was translated into Hausa by Isan Kware in 1865.[17] The following extract is from the English translation by A'isha Ahmed (1981):

Now, I am going to explain the practices of the Shehu
    For you to hear what was done in his time
Usmanu Fodio Shehu, the Almighty God
    Gave him to us here in Hausaland because of His mercy.
He brought the Muslims out of ignorance and darkness because
    He made everything clear for us with his light.
You should know that he called to Islam in Degel
    And also at Dauran and there at Faru, because of his zeal.
He returned again and went to the North, calling
    Until all the people answered his call.
He returned to the Fulani base at Degel and then went
    On to the Niger, giving his sermons.
The Muslim community accepted (his call) everywhere,
    Those of the East and West because of his high standing.
He overthrew (non-Islamic) customs and
    He established the Sunna, let us follow his path.
May God glorify his deeds always,
    As well as the Muslims who helped him.
He said men should make bows and quivers
    As well as swords, you hear his command.
Also horses, one should make the intention firm
    To prepare for Jihad, so he said.
Then he wrote letters everywhere to the towns,
    To inform everybody who would listen to him.
People should put on head-turbans and waist-bands,
    Everyone should make up his mind to be prepared.

       .   .   .

Victories were won there in the small villages, because
    Birnin Konni feared him and was terrified.
He left there and set out for the East,
    To the towns of Gobir, they feared him.
The king of Adar and Yunfa in truth,
    They gathered together to fight him.
There, they met Shehu at Tsuntsuwa, so it is said,
    There, God showed the people his might.
The imam Muhammad Sambo, Sa'ada and Riskuwa,
    They obtained martyrdom while helping him.
So also Zaidu and the son of Farouk, both
    Ladan as well as Nadumama, his teachers,
Many of the reciters of the Koran were killed,
    And also the students among his community.
Then he camped at Baura, everyone knows,
    There raids were carried out with all his strength.

Then Shehu travelled towards Zamfara, you hear,
    They tried to make peace with him because they feared him.
The places that resisted the Jihad were destroyed
    While he was in Remuwa, you have heard his victory.

(A'isha Ahmed 1981: 144–8)

Within the panorama of un-Islamic practices that were the focus of clerical attack, popular song was a significant target. It was inappropriate to sing the praises of any mortal other than the Prophet.[18] Hiskett (1975b: 17) cites a verse from the Arabic writer Al-Fazazi's *Ishriniyya* (*al-Wasa'il al-mutaqabbala*) 'The Twenties' that was well-known to the Jihadist writers:

To praise any other than the Chosen Prophet is to sport with the intelligence
    And worse still, it is ignorance; by uttering it a man utters obscenity.

. . .

Leave all other work to praise Muhammad
    For it is the road to salvation and its source.

and cites two Hausa verses (68, 76) from *Ma'ama'are* that echo the same sentiments:

Da mai waƙe waƙe tsaya kar ka ɓata	Those who sing should refrain from praising people,
Ga waƙar mutane yi bege ka huta	There lies perdition, be content with expressing
Madahi riƙe shi ka samu bukata	Praise of the Prophet, hold to that and your needs will be met,
Da masu fasaha su zo su gwade ta	The eloquent should come and demonstrate their skill
Zuwa ga faɗin ko sifofi nasa	In the presentation of his qualities.
Ina mai azanci bale sha'iri	Where is the eloquent one and the poet?
Na waƙa shi tambai yabon Dahiru	Let him ask to praise Dahiru,
Da begensa in baɗini zahiri	And express his longing openly and in secret,
Ina masu waƙa da masu kirari	Where are the singers and the praise-criers,
Ina matafa su bi hanya tasa.	And the itinerants? Let them follow his path.

The public presentation of the person of the *sarki* in the Haɓe courts was closely bound up with the activities of musicians, praise-criers and praise-singers. To attack singers was to attack the Haɓe courts while at the same time attacking Hausa culture, and particularly the *bori* religious system, with which music and singing were especially associated. The ideological divide, grounded in the Jihadist world-view, between orthodox expression in poetry and *hululu* 'idle chatter' and/or *bidi'a* 'innovation' in song, has its ramifications into the twentieth century, both in genre distinctions as they are perceived by practitioners and in the way in which poets have seen themselves as countering the evil influences of song. The success of the military campaigns and the establishment of Hausa/Fulani ruling groups in the major states of Hausaland owing allegiance to Sokoto did not mean that the ideological thrust of the Jihad became superfluous. For the orthodox and the reformer alike, backsliding and 'mixed Islam' could be everywhere identified. On the cultural front, praise-singing continued; *bori*, in spite of attempts to relegate it to the cultural fringes, was still practised; the cleric class still continued to contain its share of venal *malamai*, and Islamic preaching and teaching were as much required as they had been at the beginning of the century. Nevertheless, the cultural map had changed somewhat. The Jihadists and their successors had sought to establish a dominant culture which was, in the main, Islamic, serious, urban and male.[19] Frippery, licentiousness and 'idle chatter' had been supposedly relegated to the rural world, and to the worlds of women, children, and pagans. *Bori* was for prostitutes and deviant men, traditional tales were for old women and children, non-serious song was for farmers, hunters and the like, only praise-singing remained part of the dominant cultural scene, but even that had incorporated Islamic ideals and forms into its vocabulary. The typical form for the expression of dominant culture, poetry, had an extensive vocabulary of praise, praise of the Prophet, but which could also be appropriated in due course for Sufi praise of saints and for secular praise of major political figures.

The turn of the twentieth century witnessed the shock of the new and the foreign with the imposition of colonial administrations. From the perspective of poetic expression the key issues related not to military defeat or the establishment of overarching administrations over the top of Hausa/Fulani emirates by the British or French, or even the deposition of one emir and the installation of another. The threat represented by the *zuwan Annasara* 'coming of the Christians' was to Islam, Islamic education and to norms of behaviour that the cleric class had been hammering away at for decades. One can imagine the exasperation of the average *malam*, having spent years attacking the drinking of *burkutu*, *bori* music and ignorance of the faith, faced with the advent of Guinness, highlife music and Christian evangelists, aspects of the twentieth century which were rapidly identified as much with 'southern Nigerians' as with the Europeans. But responses to the arrival of Europeans varied. On the one hand a poem from the early years of this century, *Wakar zuwan Annasara kasar Hausa* 'On the Arrival of the Christians in Hausaland', attributed to the deposed Sultan of Sokoto, Attahiru Ahmadu,[20] who left Sokoto for the east and who died at the battle of Burmi on 27 July 1903,[21] attacks the Europeans:

Gudun mutuwa da son rai ag gare mu
   Da kau ƙin ƙaddara, a bi Annasara.
Ina muka yi da dama da hauni su na,
   Ku tashi mu sa gabanmu mu tsira tsara.
Idan ka ce akwai wahala ga tashi
   Lahan duka na ga masu biyan Nasara.
Idan iko kakai kak ko ƙi tashi
   Ina iko shi kai ikon Nasara.
Idan sun ba ka kyauta kada ka amsa,
   Dafi na sunka ba ka guba Nasara.
Suna foro gare mu mu bar zalama,
   Mazalunta da kansu ɗiyan Nasara.
Baƙar fitina gare su da kau makida,
   Ta ɓata dinin musulmi Annasara.
Halin da mukai ga yau aka bayyanawa
   Dalili ke ga anka sako Nasara.
Ku bar jin masu cewa ba a tashi,
   Ina halin zama ga Annasara.
Mu mai da gabanmu Makka mu zo Madina,
   Madina da Makka ɗai ab ba Nasara.
Batu na Shehu yay yi shi ba shi tashi,
   Sa'a ta ya faɗe ta ta Annasara.
Muna da nufa idan mun samu iko,
   Mu ja daga mu kore Annasara.
Idan ko sun kashe mu mu sam shahada,
   Mu zo Aljanna sai mu ishe maƙara.

(Abdulƙadir 1980: 64)[22]

We fear death and love life so much,
   Deny our destiny and follow the white man.
They stand to the left of us and to the right of us,
   Let us rise and set forth to escape.
You may say it is difficult to rise up,
   All fault lies with those who follow the white man.
If you have power, and so refuse to rise up,
   Where is your power, since it comes from the white man?
If they offer you a gift, do not accept it,
   It is poison that the white man offers you.
They are warning us not to be oppressive,
   But they themselves are acting oppressively.
They are evil and are trying, by trickery,
   To destroy the religion of Islam.
The [corrupt] nature of our society today has meant that

These white man have been imposed upon us.
Don't listen to those who say we cannot rise up,
    There is no way to stay with these white men.
Let us head for Mecca and Medina,
    Only in Medina and Mecca are there no white men.
What the Shehu said cannot be set aside,
    He has spoken of the time of the white men.
Our intention, if we have the chance,
    Is to fight off these white men.
And if they kill us we will become martyrs,
    And be in paradise where everything is permanent.

                                                    (GF & SIK)

On the other hand, the famous scholar, Imam Umaru from Salaga in Ghana,[23] produced, circa 1903 (Piłaszewicz 1975: 56), a lengthy chronicle of heroic resistance to the Europeans in West Africa, in which he talks of the fate of the same Sultan Attahiru as follows:

Anna Attahiru, jikan Atiƙu
Waliyyu-l-Lahi? Sun tasai Nasara.
Daɗa kuma ya shiri, ya bar ƙasarsa:
Shina tafiya, shina tsoron Nasara.
Kasar kuma tai ciri – birnin da ƙauye,
Ana ci: Ba mu son malakan Nasara
Daɗa Sarkin Musulmi ya yin tawaga:
Abin ga da firgita – ku, an – Nasara!
Suna bi shi awa ya ɗauki bashi
Fa ko ya zagi sarkin an-Nasara.
Yana cin zanguna har ga shi Bima.
A nan suka mai ruɗi, yaƙin Nasara.
A nan suka kas shi ranan ta juma'a,
Sa'an loton na sala, an-Nasara!
A nan aka turbuɗi Sarkin Musulmi
Day yai mutwar shahada gun Nasara.

Where is Attahiru, grandson of Atiƙu
And the Saint of God? They drove him away, the Christians
So he made preparations to leave his country:
He was travelling fearful of the Christians.
And the country became deserted – town and village,
They were saying: 'We do not want the Christians' rule'.
Then the Head of the Muslims removed his folk and property:
All this is terrible – oh you, Christians!
They were following him as if he incurred debt,
Or as if he abused the Christians' king.

He was passing through settlements till he reached Burmi.
Here they tricked him, the Christian warriors.
Here they killed him on a Friday,
During the time of prayer – oh, the Christians!
After that they buried the Head of the Muslims
Who died warring with the Christians for Islam.

(Piłaszewicz 1975: 92–3)

but concludes his poem (c. 1903) by saying:

Da babba da ƙanƙane – duk ɗai gare su,
Fa kowa shi takainai ga Nasara.
Fa ba tsoro gare su, fa babu kumya,
Fa keturmus su ke wa mutun Nasara.
Ka bar kuma taƙamar su san ka wawa,

Fa babu sina bugin shari'an Nasara.
Ka bar komi – da kurɗi, ko sarauta.
Da malantarka babu ruwan Nasara.
Fa halin Ingilishi sina da tafshi:
Suna tausai mutum – manyan Nasara.
Fa ni na gode Allah zamaninsu,
Zama dai sun riƙe ni da kew, Nasara!
Fa domina zamansu tutur shi dure,
Zama na mori mulkin Nasara.

The adult and the child are equal for them,
Everyone dances for himself in front of the Christians.
They neither fear nor feel ashamed,
They speak out bluntly to the Christians.
Stop being proud – they know you, ye fool!

It is not wise to fight the Christians' law.
Leave everything – the money and the chieftaincy.
As for your learning, it is no concern of the Christians.
The character of the English people is soft:
They have mercy on people, the big Christians.
As for me, I thank God for their times because
They have treated me kindly, the Christians.
For me their rule may last for ever
Because I feel enjoyment under the rule of the Christians.

(Piłaszewicz 1975: 106–9)[24]

This ambivalence towards things 'Western' is manifested in later poetry, particularly when debating appropriate attitudes towards Western and Islamic education. The necessity to address new and secular elements in society while maintaining the perspectives of Islamic thought meant an expansion in the range of topics addressed in poetry. A division in content and style of writing between strictly religious poetry and more secular poetry began to emerge at the beginning of this century. Many poets to this day write some-times in religious mode and sometimes in secular mode. The themes and styles of religious poetry have continued and expanded particularly with the flowering of Tijaniyya and Qadiriyya poetry-writing in the mid-1970s and 1980s.[25] One poet who embodied this ability to write on secular subjects and to address strictly religious themes in the early years of this century was the emir of Zaria, Aliyu ɗan Sidi. Aliyu ɗan Sidi was installed by the British after the deposition of the previous emir, Kwasau. The anthology of his better known poems published in 1980 (Dan Sidi 1980) includes religious poetry such as *Mu Sha Falala* and *Mu San Yarda* as well as didactic poems such as *Saudul Kulubi, Sasake*[26] and the allusive *Tabarkoko* (Dangambo 1982) and the secular *Wakar Zuwa Birnin Kano* about a 'state visit' made by him and other dignitaries to Kano for a meeting. Perhaps the best known poet who combined religious writing with a more secular style of social comment, and even humour, was Aliyu na Mangi. His most famous and lengthy poem in nine cantos is entitled *Wakar Imfiraji*. Born in 1894 (Birniwa 1981: 1), he went blind at a very early age. Nevertheless, he went on to an extensive Islamic education and to write/dictate his first classical *madahu* poem, *Kanzil Azimi* (Yakawada 1987).[27] The circumstances in which he came to compose the first part of *Wakar Imfiraji* are interesting in that they illustrate the dialogue between two aspects of Hausa culture, the specialised didactic world of poetry seeking cultural dominance and the world of incorporative popular song. The last verse of the first canto says:

Wanga talifi da na ji	This song when I heard
Waƙe waƙen masu Caji	The songs of those who sing like Caji
Nai wa 'yata ce Ajuji	I composed it for my daughter, Ajuji
Sai na sa mata Imfiraji	Then I called it Imfiraji
Mai yin ta ba zai baƙin ciki ba.	He who recites it will not be unhappy.

The story of how *Imfiraji* came to be composed is commented upon by a number of writers (U. Abdurrahman 1985; Dangambo 1973a; U. Hassan 1973a ; D. Muhammad 1979; Yakawada 1987). Birniwa (1981: 4) relates that the Ajuji referred to in the poem is the co-wife of Aliyu na Mangi's daughter, Hauwa, and both women were married at the time to a local *imam*. The women wanted a song to sing while working but felt that the 'frivolity' of the very popular Caji-type songs were not appropriate for women in the house of an *imam*. They therefore asked Aliyu na Mangi to compose for them something of 'suitable' content but in the style and metre of a Caji-type song. The 1,000 religious verses of *Imfiraji* must have been more than they bargained for.[28] Nevertheless, this anecdote encapsulates aspects of the relationship between song and poetry and the efforts of the cleric class to establish their own cultural hegemony. The form of Caji-type song is neutral, it is the content which is 'inappropriate'. Presence within the Islamic orbit, and there can be no more direct manifestation of that than being married to an *imam*, brings a need to find a substitute for the implied powerful influence of popular song. Enjoyment of singing can, it appears, still be maintained so long as the content of the song is right. Moving from racy humour to seriousness is a move in the 'right' direction. Perhaps the most significant element in the anecdote is the fact that it is the women of the household who initiate and seek the cultural transformation. Cultural dominance is not imposed by the male *malam* from outside, it is sought by the women of the household, according to the anecdote.

The question of the relationship between the rhythms of song and poetry, raised by the adoption of a Caji-type form in *Imfiraji*, has been addressed by a number of writers. On the one hand, as indicated in an earlier chapter, there are those who oppose any attempt to discuss poetry and song in terms of Arabic metres because that is perceived as implying Arabic cultural influence (Sipikin 1984). On the other there are those who have been concerned to investigate precisely what the patterns of poetry and song are and the relationships between them. In so doing they have sought to consider the appropriateness or otherwise of Xalilian Arabic descriptive techniques for the rhythms both of poetry and of song (see particularly Ɗ. Muhammad 1979; Ɗ. Muhammad 1980b; Schuh 1988; Schuh 1988/9).

While Aliyu na Mangi is perhaps best known for his religious poetry, he also composed an amusing cameo poem in which he describes the struggle between a *malam* with his flowing robes and a bicycle which is determined to entangle his robes in its chain and throw him to the ground. A neat allegory for the quandary faced by the cleric class in its handling of modernity, the poem is light, humorous and reminiscent of popular song in its picturing of the incongruous and absurd. The poem, entitled *Wakar Keke* 'Song of the Bicycle', is translated and discussed in Skinner (1970a).

The co-existence of modern secular themes with traditional religious ones in the work of a single writer brings us to the development of poetry in the last sixty years, which forms the subject of the following chapter. But before turning to that discussion I outline, in brief, the major characteristics of the form of poetry in Hausa, a subject which was adumbrated, to some extent, in the discussion in the previous chapter of how people make distinctions between song and poetry.

POETIC FORM

For many poets the first distinguishing feature of the form of Hausa poetry is not metre but rhyme (*qafiyya*). The salience of rhyming line-final sylla-

bles, often pre-pausal, is such that it is perceived as one of the most important features distinguishing poetry from song. The patterns of rhyme are the
basis of division into stanzas and there is an elegant simplicity to these patterns. The basic form is the rhyming couplet in which there is a running
rhyme of the same final cv or cvv syllable. In the *ajami* way of setting out
couplets with the two hemistichs on the same line the last syllable on the left
is identical. The last syllable of the first hemistich in the first couplet is also
often the same. The roman script way of setting it out usually indents the
second hemistich below the first:

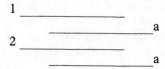

A very common form, derived from the couplet by performing *takhmis*
'making five', is the quintain or five-line verse in which a running rhyme in
the last line of each verse is combined with an internal rhyme within the first
four lines of each verse. The internal rhyme will usually differ from verse to
verse. In *takhmis*, the poet has built an internal rhyme upon the final syllable of the first hemistich in each couplet by adding the three lines that come
at the beginning of each verse.[29] Making a *takhmis* was often an activity by
one poet upon the original couplets of another poet. While the five-line
form may have originated with the practice of *takhmis*, in more recent times
poets have adopted the five-line stanza as a form for their original compositions. In *ajami* such five-line verses are set out thus, reading from right to
left:

```
a_____2        a_____1
a_____4        a_____3
      b_____5        5
c_____2        c_____1
c_____4        c_____3
      b_____5        5
```

In roman script such verses are usually set out as follows:[30]

```
1_____a
2_____a
3_____a
4_____a
  5_____b
```

While rhyme is normally carried by the final syllable it can be carried by
the repetition of a complete word or phrase. Ɗ. Muhammad (1980a) also
draws attention to the fact that there may also be tonal rhyme whereby the

same sequence of tones may be repeated in this line-final position.[31]

Rhythmic regularity in poetry is based, as indicated in Chapter 6, on the regular repetition of heavy (cvv or cvc) and light (cv) syllables. It has long been recognised that the rhythmic patterns most commonly encountered in Hausa poetry are describable in terms of Arabic metres. More recently there have been moves to describe such patterns using a system that copes more adequately with rhythms not only evident in poetry but also in song, and indeed a system that copes with patterns which are regular yet not describable at all in Xalilian terms. Others have also pointed to an indigenous Hausa system for describing rhythmic patterns.[32] Hiskett (1975b: 176) indicates that ten out of sixteen common Arabic metres are to be encountered in Hausa. In a survey of 252 poems published during the 1950s and 1960s I found that all bar 17 were identifiable as being in 9 Arabic metres with wide variation in frequency. These were the frequency figures as I found them:

Kamil	92
Mutaqarib	46
Wafir	27
Ramal	21
Mutadarik	21
Basit	9
Rajaz	9
Tawil	8
Khafif	2

(Furniss 1977: 379)

These figures would indicate that, in recent years, *Kamil* is by far and away the most common metre with *Basit*, *Rajaz*, *Tawil* and *Khafif* being rarely encountered. For the purpose of illustration, consider the following verse from a poem by Na'ibi Sulaiman Wali which is 'in *Kamil*'. Below each line I have set out the sequence of heavy and light syllables using the further indicators of 'v' for a light syllable and '–' for a heavy syllable. The line is made up of the repetition of the same 'foot', with possible variations in certain positions, the most common being the substitution of two light syllables for one heavy syllable:[33]

Tsun	tsun	da	kee	faa-	man	la-	yii	a	sa-	maa-	ni-	yaa,
cvc	cvc	cv	cvv	cvv	cvc	cv	cvv	cv	cv	cvv	cv	cvv
–	–	v	–	–	–	v	–	v	v	–	v	–

Ka-	naa	ta	shaa-	waa-	gii	ka-	naa	yin	daa-	ri-	yaa,
cv	cvv	cv	cvv	cvv	cvv	cv	cvv	cvc	cvv	cv	cvv
v	–	v	–	–	–	v	–	–	–	v	–

Ka-	naa	ta	waa-	laa-	war-	ka	baa	wa	ta	ƙan-	gi-	yaa,

cv	cvv	cv	cvv	cvv	cvc	cv	cvv	cv	cv	cvc	cv	cvv
v	–	v	–	–	–	v	–	v	v	–	v	–

Ka-	naa	ta	an-	na-	shu	waa	ka-	mar	mai	shan	gi-	yaa,
cv	cvv	cv	cvc	cv	cv	cvv	cv	cvc	cvv	cvc	cv	cvv
v	–	v	–	v	v	–	v	–	–	–	v	–

In	zaa	ka	yar-	da	tsa-	yaa	i-	nai	ma	ka	tam-	ba-	yaa.
cvc	cvv	cv	cvc	cv	cv	cvv	cv	cvv	cv	cv	cvc	cv	cvv
–	–	v	–	v	v	–	v	–	v	v	–	v	–

> Bird that planes through the sky,
> You hover and laugh,
> You do as you please without restraint,
> You express your joy like one intoxicated,
> Please pause a moment, I have a question.
>
> (first verse of Na'ibi Wali, *Maraba da 'Yanci* 'Welcome Freedom')

In this verse we see the regular repetition of a foot (– – v –) with a variation (v v – v –), and a less common shortening of the first foot to (v – v –).[34] The rhythm of the foot is conveyed through the use of the term *mutafaa'ilun* which both describes it and embodies it. Three repetitions of *mutafaa'ilun* produce a line, or in the case of couplets, a hemistich, that is in *Kamil*.

To sense the rhythm inherent in a line of poetry does not require the knowledge of such terms. Mudi Sipikin, a poet of the modern era, often composes in *Kamil* and, although he has some knowledge of the Arabic terminology, thinks of a line being 'too full' (*ya cika*) or 'being broken' (*ya karye*) depending upon whether 'errors' in the rhythm create too many or too few syllables. When assessing poems brought to him for comment he would use these terms (Furniss 1977: 72–3). Other people have other ways of describing 'wrong' patterns or 'mistakes' in metre.

The debate concerning metrical patterning in Hausa poetry has two dimensions to it. On the one hand, there is an approach which views the *Xalilian* system of Arabic metres as a more or less adequate system for describing Hausa patterns which are, like Arabic, quantitative rather than stress-based. On the other there is the approach which sees mention of the *Xalilian* system and the proposition that 'there are Arabic metres in Hausa poetry' as a form of cultural imperialism attempting to co-opt that which is indigenous in Hausa culture.[35] In some senses, therefore, the debate relates again to issues of cultural hegemony and the relationship between the cleric class and the wider society. The modern debate, however, is in a context where there are many more components in the melting pot: not simply old-style *malamai*, but also university academics, media commentators, school and college graduates, and cultural nationalists.

In addition to aspects of form, such as rhyme and metre, there are conventions concerning the structure of a poem and its style of language that mark it off both from song and from ordinary speech. These are also alluded to by people in constructing ideas of what constitute the distinguishing features of *rubutacciyar waka* 'written *waka*'. Conventionally a poem will start with a religious doxology leading on to the main subject-matter. This feature inherited from the world of religious poetry sets the 'serious' and didactic tone of much poetry. In so far as poetry is regularly chanted it also provides the necessary moments of transition, typical of orality, from ordinary speech into the 'special language' of poetry. Again, typical of orality, a closing doxology, which in religious poetry often also contained a *ramzi* (chronogram) conveying the date of composition,[36] would mark the transition back out of this 'special language'. In addition to a chronogram, a poem would often also conclude with a signature, occasionally not only by the author but, if appropriate, by the translator or *takhmis*-maker too.

Clearly, within the world of religious poetry-writing, knowledge of Arabic and of such specialised vocabulary as Sufi mystical terminology were marks of erudition. The presence of Arabic terms in a Hausa poem was a sign that the author was well versed in Islamic knowledge. Part of the aesthetics of such poetry was the presence of Arabic phrases. Appreciation of modern poetry has carried on the characteristic that erudition and the use of special, restricted, archaic language is a mark of quality in a writer. On the one hand, there is a premium, in didacticism, on simplicity and clarity in order to get across the message, on the other, allusiveness and depth are appreciated in the skilled writer. Both of these poles co-exist in the discussion of the aesthetics of poetry. In selecting poetry for publication in the main Hausa newspaper, *Gaskiya Ta Fi Kwabo*, the one-time editor, Abubakar Imam, once told me he was primarily concerned to determine whether the poet was clear and comprehensible and whether what he was saying was useful and 'the right thing'. In this context the message and its communicability were the primary considerations. On the other hand, in assessing the reasons why the poet Aƙilu Aliyu is considered perhaps the outstanding poet of the present day, scholars have pointed to his outstanding skill with language and his great knowledge of the farthest reaches of Hausa. In this case, the concentration is upon esoteric language, not primarily of Arabic but of Hausa, and yet the criteria are similar. (See, for example, Arnott 1988; D. Muhammad 1973a, 1977, 1984.) A number of studies have focused upon different aspects of style that distinguish individual writers or subcategories within the broad field of poetry.[37]

9

MODERN HAUSA POETRY

In this chapter we consider modern poetry of the last sixty years and examine the way in which, while maintaining many of the ideological characteristics we have discussed in relation to earlier poetry, it has taken on new roles, new topics and is beginning to find new forms.

Whether on religious themes or on 'secular' subjects, the cardinal feature inherited from the poetry tradition of the nineteenth century has been the strength and ubiquity of moral discourse within poetry. Coming from a culture in which overtly 'moralistic' discourse is a style of speech and writing associated with pulpits and a bygone Victorian era, the pervasive didacticism of much Hausa poetry is striking in its vigour. Poets are constantly telling people what to do, how to behave, how not to behave, what to believe, what to think, and quite often how to vote. Regardless of whether people do actually alter their patterns of behaviour and thought as a result of such upbraiding, the ubiquity and legitimacy of the poet's voice as exponent of values and of perceptions is undoubted. Right across West Africa in ascribing to 'Hausa identity', whether as 'assimilado' or as self-proclaimed 'original Hausa', one of the pieces of baggage to be carried by the cultural traveller, in addition to the language itself, is knowledge of such cultural products. Not everyone carries the same baggage – some know of Mamman Shata, some also of the religious poems of Nana Asma'u, others know perhaps only of the category of *makadan noma* 'farming musicians'.

One component which makes for the dynamic, expanding, adaptive nature of Hausa culture is, in my view, the strength of its moral discourse. It is not the nature of the actual values being expressed in any particular context, nor any suggestion that, in some way Hausa society is more 'moral' than any other society, that is at issue here. It is the fact that discussion and argument about what is right and what is wrong is the stuff of public discussion and the product of the reflection of so many writers of prose and of poetry. The language deployed in such discussion is overtly 'value-loaded' and 'moralistic'. To an outsider's ear such as mine, used to the refracted values of the advertiser's symbols and the encoded morality of novels, plays and contemporary discussion of politics and current affairs, the language of much modern Hausa poetry is reminiscent of the Victorian tract or the revivalist preacher. The power of this aspect of Hausa culture lies in its very directness and its ability to take any aspect of the social, political and cultural world of modern Nigeria and construct a characterisation of that feature, be it person, event, or idea, in which certain aspects can be unequivocally condemned and other aspects clearly endorsed.[1]

Many contradictory positions can of course be taken on any particular issue, nevertheless writer after writer deploys the same value-loaded vocabulary in pursuit of his or her own vision. One of the best expositions of a part of this vocabulary is provided by Kirk-Greene (1974) in his discussion of the concept of 'the good man' in Hausa. Personal and institutional values overtly expressed in relation to political leadership are discussed extensively by Paden (1986) in his book on the late Sardauna of Sokoto, Ahmadu Bello. The language of the good, the true, the honourable, the just, the fair, the right and the reasonable is deployed in relation to soldiering in the civil war or growing groundnuts, as it has always been in relation to the beliefs of Islam and the person of the Prophet. Conversely, the dishonourable, the reprehensible, the corrupt, the illegal and the wrong, along with a myriad other negatively loaded concepts, are words applied to drug addiction and bureaucratic corruption now as they were to un-Islamic practices in the early years of the nineteenth century.

As examples of this didacticism of modern poetry I have selected two poems that represent two aspects of twentieth-century Nigeria. Both are from a short anthology of Hausa poems entitled *Wakokin Hausa* 'Hausa Poetry' that was first published in 1957 and which has been reprinted regularly ever since.[2] The first, *Gargadi don Falkawa* 'A warning to be wakeful' by Na'ibi Sulaiman Wali[3] is a lament for the declining standards of the day and an attack upon those whose interests are in wine, women and song. The second, *Wakar Hana Zalunci* 'Poem against Oppression', by Salihu Kwantagora,[4] is a broadside against bribery, corruption and injustice. These two poems present two aspects of so much didactic poetry: morality in the world of personal behaviour and morality in the public behaviour of officialdom:

Gargaɗi don Falkawa

Subuhanallahi me za na ce?
  Zamanin nan namu ya rikice.
Mahankalta sun haukace
  Mabiya sunna sun ɗau fice.
Mai basira duk ta dakushe,
  Mai bin hanya ya karkace.
Likitan cuta mai magani,
  Cuta ta ka da shi zai mace.
Ba amana ba son gaskiya,
  Kowa sai zambace-zambace.
Ba alheri bisa zuciya,
  Kowa sai ƙullace-ƙullace.
Jahilci ya yi yawa ga ma
  Ilmin Allah ya mace,
Har an binne shi wajen gari,
  Mai zuwa nema nasa ya ɓace.
Babu mai aiki bisa zuciya
  Ɗaya, don Allah, sai don a ce.
Imani ya ƙare, ga ma
  So domin Allah ya mace,
Sai don samu don arziki,
  Yadda za a yi zance zance.
Ba a son zancen gaskiya,
  In kana yi kai ne mai fice.
Kai ne sususu sakarai,
  Wayonka kaɗan ka haukace.
In ka ce Allah, ko Annabi,
  Su ne suka ce kuma sai a ce
Kai ne ka fi kowa ko kuwa?
  Wa ya ce ka faɗa, sarkin fice?
Kowa burinsa ya san kuɗi,
  Ga gida ga mota ga mace
Ko ya hau rali sai ya kaikaice,
  Yai wajen Sabon Gari ya ɓace.
A cikin wanka a cikin diras
  Da kayan ƙwambace-ƙwambace.
Yana ta nishaɗi ga giya,
  Ya san ni'ima ya haukace.
A wajen hotel da wajen giya,
  Nan zai ƙare a gaban mace.
Sai rawa sai ihu fasiƙai,
  Gabansa gaɗi ba dakace.

A Warning to be Wakeful

Lord preserve us what shall I say?
    Our time is out of joint.
The sane have gone insane,
    Those on the path of the Sunna have gone astray.
Those with vision find they can no longer see clearly,
    Those on the right road have strayed.
The doctor with the cure for disease,
    Has been struck down and is sure to die.
There is no trust any more, no love of the truth,
    Everyone is engaged in crookedness.
There is no goodness in men's hearts,
    Everyone is involved in plots and intrigues.
Ignorance is everywhere
    And religious knowledge is dead,
Dead and buried beyond the boundaries,
    And he who seeks it is lost.
No one acts according to the dictates of their heart alone
    And in God's name, but rather for their reputation.
Faith is finished, and furthermore,
    True friendship is no more,
Friendship is just a means of gain and enrichment,
    And a way to make a name.
They don't like the truth to be told,
    If you speak it you are the one out of line.
You are the fool and the idiot,
    Naive and losing your mind.
If you say that it is God, or the Prophet,
    Who has said these things, then they reply
How is it that you are better than everyone else?
    Who told you to say these things, you freak?
Everyone is out to make money,
    Houses, cars and women.
Even out on his bicycle taking the long way round,
    Off to Sabon Gari and to lose himself.
All clean and in his smartest clothes,
    All his ostentatious finery.
His pleasure is in alcohol,
    He feels so good, it's gone to his head.
In clubs and bars,
    Is where he ends up, with a woman.
Dancing and shouting shamelessly,
    Brazen, and without a moment's pause for thought.

In sun sha sun bugu sai su yi
  Sururun zancensu a haukace.
Kyautansu maroka karuwai,
  'Yan iska 'ya'yan tarkace.
Zakka Salla duka ba su yi,
  Sai dai kyautar a fadi a ce.
Kai mutum yau ka rasa hankali,
  Ka susuce ka haukace.
Jahilci yai maka runduna,
  Ya hana ka ka san ka karkace.
Ka ki shawarto ka fandare,
  Ibilis ya sa ka karkace.
Matan kuwa su ne karuwai,
  Makiya Allah mazawa fice.
Kan dai mace ta zama karuwa,
  Ta lalace tir! Ba mace.
Ayya haka za mu yi 'yan'uwa,
  Aikinmu dukansa a barkace?
Anya haka shi ne za ya kai
  Mu limana ba wata karkace?
Ya ilahi mu Nijeriya,
  Me za mu yi ko me za mu ce?
Mu yi wa kanmu fada, mu bi gaskiya,
  Mu bi kan hanya ba karkace.
Mu tsaya tsayuwar mai yin daka,
  Lokacimmu kadan ne zai wuce.
Mu sani duk kowa za ya je
  Gun hisabi ranar gaskiya.
Na gode Allah nai yabo
  A gare shi a nan zan dakata.
Tsira da amincin Rabbana
  Ga Rasulu da ya hana yin fice.
Ka zo a cane maka wa ya yi
  Wakan nan, malam, sai ka ce
Na'ibi Wali sunansa ne,
  Kuma Kurawa unguwarsu ce.
Tamat, yau wakata ta cika,
  Allah sa mu mu bar son yin fice.[5]

Wakar Hana Zalunci

Allah Rahmanu Mafifici,
  Mai mulki tare da adalci.
Ka jikanmu ka yafe laifimmu,

When thoroughly drunk they pursue
>Their crazy foolish conversations.
Their charity goes to musicians and prostitutes,
>Delinquents and riff-raff.
They neither give alms nor pray,
>They give away only to make a reputation.
Hey, my friend, you have lost your commonsense,
>Turned into an idiot, gone mad.
Ignorance has laid seige to you
>And stopped you from seeing how you have gone wrong.
You have rejected advice and turned away,
>The Devil has set you wrong.
And these women are prostitutes,
>They reject God and embrace all that is bad.
When a woman becomes a prostitute,
>She is pitifully ruined. She is no longer a woman.
Is this the way for us, my friends,
>All our actions set at nought?
Will this path bring us
>Directly to happiness?
In God's name, we here in Nigeria,
>What can we do and what can we say?
We must be self-critical and pursue the truth,
>Follow the true path without straying.
We must, like the pounder of grain, stand firm,
>Our time is short and soon will pass.
Let us remember that everyone will come
>To the place of reckoning on that Day of Truth.
I thank God and I give praise
>To Him, and here I will stop.
May salvation and the trust of the Lord God
>Be upon his Prophet who has forbidden us to stray.
If they ask you who wrote
>This poem, then, malam, tell them
His name is Na'ibi Wali,
>And he lives in Kurawa quarter.
This is the end, and now my poem is finished,
>Lord preserve us from going astray.

Poem against Oppression

God, the Merciful, the Most High,
>The just and righteous Ruler.
Have mercy on us and forgive us our errors,

Ka rufe zunubinmu da adalci.
Ku taho ga waƙa ƙanƙanuwa,
    Zan bayyana aibin zalunci.
Shi dai zalunci cuta ne,
    Tsananin cutar har ta ɓaci.
Laifin da shi ke kai mai yinsa
    Shiga wuta to, sai zalunci.
Allahu Gwani yai alkawali,
    Zai babbaka duk mai zalunci.
Kwasshaƙe ciki da tuwon zulmu,
    Zai ɗibgi wuta a cikin ƙunci.
Zai shaƙe ciki da wuta haƙƙan,
    A gaban Sarki mara zalunci.
Kwacce rashawa ta ce cima
    Zai ɗibgi wuta a cikin ƙunci.
Muggan laifofi munana,
    Mai ja ma ƙasa wahala ƙunci,
In sun yi yawa don aibinsu,
    A cikinsu da laifin zalunci.
In mai fatawa ya zo gunka,
    Ya ce, 'Menene zalunci?'
Shaida masa yanke ka bar tsoro,
    'Saɓa wa tafarkin adalci,
Da aje abu ba ma'ajinai ba,
    To, yin haka shi ne zalunci'.
Da rashin yarda da faɗar Allah,
    Da ya ce, 'Ku kiyayi fa zalunci'.
Haka ƙetare inda ka ce a tsaya,
    Da rashin kafuwa kan inganci.
Da zamowa mai ƙaramin ƙarfi
    Gun mai ƙarfi wainar cinci.
Da rashin lura komi ya taho,
    Mai zaƙi ne ko mai ɗaci,
Da halas da haram da zuma da guba,
    Duk ɗai ne ba wani bambanci.
Karɓar rashawa kyautar hanci,
    Kirga shi ga ƙunshin zalunci.
Kowa aka ba ko wanda ya bai,
    Zunubinsu guda ba bambanci.
Haka sauƙaƙe ƙaƙƙauran sha'ani
    Domin kwaɗayin karɓar hanci;
Haka ƙarfafa sassauƙan sha'ani
    A ƙulle da sharrin ha'inci.

Cover over our sins with righteousness.
Gather round for here is a short poem,
   In which I will talk of the sin of oppression.
Oppression is a disease,
   So serious has it become that we are in crisis.
The crime which leads its perpetrator
   Straight to hell-fire is oppression.
God the Omniscient has promised
   To bake all those who oppress.
Whoever fills his stomach with the product of oppression,
   Will truly feel confinement in the fires.
He will eat his fill of hell-fire
   Before the Lord who is innocent of all oppression.
Whoever sees bribes as his meat and drink
   Will truly feel confinement in the fires.
Evil and ugly crimes,
   That bring down calamity and pressure upon the land,
If they and their evil effects are everywhere to be seen
   Then amongst them will be the crime of oppression.
If someone comes to you and asks,
   'What is oppression?'
Tell him straight, do not be afraid,
   'Straying from the path of justice,
And assigning things not to their correct places,
   Doing that is oppression.'
Failing to accept the word of God
   When He said, 'Desist from all oppression.'
Going beyond the limits that have been set,
   And failing to take a firm stand.
The small man being devoured
   By the powerful as if he were no more than a titbit.
Being unconcerned at things that happen,
   Be they sweet or bitter,
Lawful or unlawful, honey or poison,
   Treating them all alike, drawing no distinction.
Accepting bribes and corrupt gifts,
   They are all part of what makes for oppression.
He who receives or he who gives,
   Their sin is equal, there is no distinction.
Making light of something serious
   Out of a desire to be offered a bribe;
Or making too much out of a minor incident
   With intent to extort.

To, kun ga waɗannan munanan
    Abuba su ne zalunci.
Duk mai fitinan jama'a bisa kan
    B'arna har yai musu zalunci,
Ya risku cikin whala tabbas,
    Ya turmutsa kansa cikin ƙunci.
Kowai haka zai ga fa sakayya,
    Don ko ya aikata zalunci,
Duk mai aiki, mutumin kirki,
    Da yake aikinsa da adalci,
Ladansa na aikin albashi,
    Da yake amsa ya ci ba ɗaci.
Ya hanƙura kansa farin bawa,
    Wannan na tare da inganci.
Ba zai kula amsar rashawa ba,
    Balle ya zamo mai zalunci.
Ɗan sandan kirki me ya tsare
    Illa aikinsa na adalci?
Hana mai son yin laifi, laifi,
    Sai ɗan sanda mai adalci.
Haka alƙalai su ma sun san
    Mummunan aikin zalunci.
Domin shi alƙalin kirki,
    Mik kai shi ga son karɓar hanci?
Sun san kowa aka zalunta
    Don fin ƙarfi ko makirci,
In yai ƙara a wurin Allah,
    Ya ce, 'Allah mai adalci
Haƙƙina na a wuyan wane,
    Ka bi mini mai yin zalunci',
Hakika ba da daɗewa ba,
    Zai risku kawai a cikin ƙunci.
Faufau wahalar wani ba ta zama
    Hutun wani cuɗe da zalunci.
Sun san haka, to me zai kai su?
    Su tabbata Allah bai barci,
Sun san komi Allah ya faɗa
    Zai i da faɗarsa da adalci.
Kuma sun ga faɗar Allah haƙƙan,
    Me zai ruɗe su su so hanci.
Sun san a cikin Alƙurani,
    Ai an yi hanin yin zalunci.
Aya metan da guda sittin

These evil things
    Are what constitutes oppression.
Anyone who troubles others and
    Does them harm through oppressing them,
Will end up without a doubt in torment,
    Having been the cause of his own predicament.
Any who behave so will receive their just desserts
    For having acted oppressively.
The virtuous man who works,
    Carrying out his responsibilities correctly,
Is rewarded by the salary
    Which he receives to do with as he wishes.
He is content with that, as a righteous man,
    And to be so is of great importance.
He will have no interest in taking bribes,
    Let alone in acting oppressively.
What should concern the honest policeman
    Other than the honest pursuit of his duties?
To prevent the criminal from committing crime
    The only answer is an honest policeman.
Judges also know
    The evil effects of oppression.
The honest judge,
    What could lead him to want to accept a bribe?
They know that whoever is oppressed
    By superior force or by trickery,
If that person lays his complaint before God
    And says, 'Oh righteous God,
I have been grievously wronged,
    Pursue for me the one who has oppressed me',
Then soon and for sure and certain,
    The oppressor will find himself directly in torment.
Never will one man's trouble be to another man's
    Gain if oppression lies at the heart of it.
They know this to be true, so why should they do it?
    Let them be sure that God does not sleep.
They know that God's word,
    He will justly fulfil.
And they know the certainty of God's word,
    What could so delude them that they seek bribes?
They know that in the Holy Koran
    Oppressive acts have been forbidden.
It is the two hundred and sixty-first verse

Da ɗaya magana kan zalunci.
Allah ya tanadi yin ƙuna
    Da wuta ga mutum mai zalunci.
Kuma ya hana yin baiwar nasara
    Wurin jama'a mai zalunci.
Ni Salihu ga tau 'yar waƙa,
    Wajen maganar ƙin zalunci.

The latter poem, reflecting as it does the view whereby Islam is centrally concerned with social and political matters as well as matters theological, is representative of a body of poetry in which basic political values are expressed. Occasionally such sentiments are expressed in general abstract terms as, for example, in this brief extract from the end of a poem *Maraba da Soja* 'Welcome to the Soldiers' written by the early political activist and poet, Sa'adu Zungur,[6] about the return of Nigerian soldiers after the end of the second world war:

Babu amfani ga 'yanci,
In akwai halin talauci,
Babu yin zarafin aminci,
In da masu ƙwafa a zuci,
Babu kyawun shugabanci,
Sai idan da akwai adalci,
Babu amfanin zumunci,
Sai fa in da akwai karimci,
Kuma babu yawan butulci,
Babu ƙeta, ba sakarci,
Babu ketawar mutunci,
Babu mai yunwar abinci,
San nan 'yanci ya ke tsayawa.

These same sentiments were tied into the political fate of northern Nigeria in the lead up to Independence in 1960. One of the best known modern Hausa poems dating from the mid-1950s, *Arewa Jumhuriya ko Mulukiya* 'The North, Republic or Monarchy?' by Sa'adu Zungur, ends with a view that marries the fate of the North to the nature of northern society:

Domin fa Arewa da hargitsi,
    Da yawan ɓarna, ba kariya.
Matuƙar Arewa da karuwai,
    Wallah za mu yi kunyar duniya,
Matuƙar 'yan iska na gari,
    Ɗan daudu da shi da magajiya,
Da samari masu ruwan kuɗi

Which speaks of oppression.
God has prepared burning
 And fire for the person who oppresses others.
And he has refused the gift of victory
 To the people who practise oppression.
I am Salihu and this is my small poem
 About the need to defeat oppression.

Useless is freedom,
Where there is poverty;
Hopeless to look for trust,
Where there are those who hide envy in their hearts;
Worthless is the leadership,
Where there is no honesty;
Useless are close human ties,
Unless there is noble generosity.
Never while ingratitude abounds,
Never while there is malice or folly;
Never while men are scorned,
Never while they are hungry –
Never, till these are ended, can freedom endure!

(Abdulƙadir 1974: 47)

For if the North is full of dissension and wickedness,
 We lose our defence.
So long as there are prostitutes in the North,
 We shall face the world with shame;
So long as our towns are full of men of straw,
 Homosexuals and *magajiyas*,
Young men duping people with false money

Ga maroƙa can a gidan giya,
Babu shakka 'yan Kudu za su hau
   Dokin mulkin Nijeriya.
Su yi ta kau sukuwa bisa kammu, ko,
   Mun roƙi zumuntar duniya.
Matuƙar yarammu suna bara
   'Allah ba ku mu sami abin miya!'
A gidan birni da na ƙauyauka,
   Da cikin makarantun tsangaya,
Sun yafu da fatar bunsuru
   Babu shakka sai mun sha wuya.
Matuƙar da musakai barkatai,
   Da makaho ko da makauniya.
Ba mahallai nasu a Hausa duk,
   Ba mai tanyonsu da dukiya.
Birni ƙauye da garuwa
   Duk suna yawo a Nijeriya.
Kai Bahaushe bashi da zuciya,
   Za ya sha kunya nan duniya!
A Arewa zumunta ta mutu,
   Sai nashaɗi, sai sharholiya,
Sai alfahari da yawan ƙwafa,
   Girman kai, sai ƙwambon tsiya.
Camfe-camfe da tsibbace-tsibbace,
   Malaman ƙarya 'yan duniya.
Cin amana kuma da yawan riya,
   Ga hula mai annakiya.
Babu mai aiki bisa hankali,
   Da basira, don ya ga gaskiya.
Rantse-rantse da Allah yai yawa,
   Ga ƙarya, ga zambar tsiya,
Gorin asali da na dukiya,
   Sai ka ce ɗan 'Annabi Fariya',
Sai kinibibi, sai kwarmato,
   Ga gulma da son ƙullaliya.
Wagga al'umma me za ta wo,
   A cikin zarafofin duniya?
To sarakai, sai fa ku himmatu,
   Don ku gyara ƙasarku da gaskiya.

And beggars who flatter in beer-houses,
Without any doubt the men of the South will sit
   In the saddle of Nigerian rule,
And they will continually gallop over us,
   Even though we beg for peace and mercy.
So long as our boys beg with their,
   'God be generous to you, give us enough to buy soup!'
In the city and village
   And in wandering Koranic schools,
Wearing goatskins,
   Without doubt we shall suffer.
So long as cripples are to be found all over the place,
   And blind, both men and women,
Having no proper place in all Hausa country,
   No one to aid them with his wealth,
So that they wander in city and villages
   And through all the towns of Nigeria –
Kai! The Hausa has no heart
   And he will face the world with shame!
In the North, ties of kin and friendship are no more,
   Nothing but pleasure and lying words,
Boasting and covetousness,
   Pride and shameless ostentation,
Superstition and mumbo-jumbo,
   False *malams*, worldly men.
Faith not kept, abundant hypocrisy,
   The grime of sham piety on their caps –
There is none that acts with sense and with wisdom
   So that he perceives truth.
There is excess of swearing in God's name,
   Falsehood and deceitful ostentation,
Boasting of ancestry and wealth,
   Like one who claims descent from the Prophet,
Mischief-making and taletelling,
   Stirring up trouble and love of intrigue –
What will such a nation achieve
   In the affairs of the world?
And so, you rulers, you must strive
   To set your country right by truth.

                        (Abdulƙadir 1974: 95-9)

The northern fear, in the 1950s, of political domination by the South after independence is expressed here by one who was himself at one time closely allied with a 'southern' party but who moved back into the 'northern camp', albeit still opposed to the 'establishment' party of the North at the time, the Northern People's Congress (NPC) led by the Sardauna of Sokoto, and supporting the Northern Elements Progressive Union (NEPU). The interest among poets in discussing the social realities of northern society led them often more or less directly into the camps of particular northern political parties, primarily the two mentioned above, with the result that certain poets became closely identified with them. Where the NPC and NEPU represented broadly the establishment and the opposition within the north during the 1950s and 1960s (with the opposition being electorally much weaker), those two blocks broadly re-emerged in the lead up to the return to civilian rule in 1979 as the National Party of Nigeria (NPN) and the People's Redemption Party (PRP) but with additional parties having a presence in the north, such as the Greater Nigerian People's Party (GNPP). An extensive study of political poetry from these two periods has been undertaken by Birniwa (1987).[7] In the following section I discuss and illustrate only some aspects of such political poetry.

PURPOSIVE POETRY: POLITICS AND SOCIETY

Typically, and as one would expect, political poetry is heavily engaged. That engagement is, however, often reminiscent of the tone of praise-song. In Chapter 7 we have seen how the double-edged sword of praise and vilification is deployed by the praise-singer in support of the patron and in subversion of his rivals. Much political poetry is similarly focused upon the person of the party leader and sets out his claims to legitimacy, his personal qualities, and authoritative aspects of his background. The policies and programmes of the party are rarely the subject of the poet's writings. Equally, vilification of the leader of the opposing party is the other side of the hagiographical picture. In the following brief extract from a poem in praise of the Sardauna by Shekara Sa'ad we see the fate of the NPC bound up with the person of its leader, one of whose trump cards is his direct line of descent from Shehu Usman ɗan Fodio:

Zaɓe na mulkin ƙasar Nijeriya,
  Enpisi ce gaba kuma tarkace na biya.
Maƙiyanmu ko sun yarda ko da sun ƙiya,
  Enpisi sai ta mallake Nijeriya.
Ni na yi mamaki cikin Nijeriya,
  Kwaɗo ya ce shi za ya kama macijiya.
Eji da Nepu da Ensi-ensi kun jiya,
  Sai dai ku sa haƙuri ku daina hatsaniya.
In Jalla ya so Rabbu Sarkin Gaskiya,

Tutar salama za ta ja Nijeriya.
Don shugaban Enpisi ba shi da fariya,
  Sardauna Ahmadu Bello Allah ne ɗaya.
Jikan Muhammadu Huɗi mazajen duniya,
  Baƙon Madina da Makka cibin duniya.
Jikan Muhammadu Bello Shehu Firimiya,
  Jikan Muhammadu Fodiyo mai gaskiya.

(Hiskett 1977a: 56–7)

In the elections for the transfer of power in Nigeria,
  The NPC is in front and the dregs follow on behind.
Whether our enemies accept it or not,
  The NPC will rule over Nigeria.
I am amazed how here in Nigeria,
  The frog says he will catch the snake.
The AG [Action Group] and NEPU and the NCNC,
  You will just have to put up with it and stop making trouble.
If the Lord God, the King of Truth wills it
  Then the NPC flag will lead Nigeria.
The leader of the NPC is not boastful,
  The Sardauna Ahmadu Bello: there is only one God.
Descendant of Muhammadu Fodio, one of the world's great men,
  Visitor to Medina and Mecca, centre of the world.
Descendant of Muhammadu Bello, Shehu the Premier,
  Descendant of Muhammadu Fodio the honest.

Conversely, poets from the NEPU camp, such as Yusufu Kantu,[8] would vilify, with more or less veiled speech, the NPC leadership, as in this extract from his poem *Ya Allah ka ba mu Sawaba* 'God grant us Freedom':

'Ya'yan jam'iyya ta Salama,	Members of the Salama [NPC] party,
To, mun gan ku, kun yi alama,	We have seen you use the emblem
Fartanya ku ruɗi manoma,	Of the hoe in order to ensnare the farmers,
To, Allah ya ƙaddara, ku ma,	Well, God has decided that you too,
Wannan shekara ku yi noma!	This year will be back tilling the soil!
Alhaji mai gani ɗai shiyya,	Alhaji who sees only one point of view,
Ba ka cin hatsi sai doya,	You no longer eat corn, only yams,
Yau me ya rage? Sai kunya!	What is there left? Nothing but shame!
Ko ka daina yin jam'iyya?	Are you going to give up politics?
Na gan ka ba ka nuna karama!	Your powers appear to have evaporated!
Dungama, uban 'yan iska,	Fat man, worst of the delinquents,
Dodo, masu saurin duka,	Monster, quick to attack,

Yau ga zamani ya hau ka,
Ai magana kaɗan ka yi kuka,

  To kukanka ba shi isam ma!

Kai mai hankalin raƙumma,
Ɗan akuya, uban 'yan gama,

Ka kashe nagge daɗi goma,

Ka ɗau alhakin al'umma,
  Al'amarinka ba shi da dama!

'Yan birni, uban kasumba,
Tunkun, masu ƙullin taba,
Kai mai shan hayaƙin ruba,
Cima-kwance, ɗan geloba,
  Zo gafiya, mu sa ka a burma!

Karyar gatari ta ƙare,
Sai suma yake zai shure,
Yau shi ne da kansa ya sare
Kansa sabo da ɗan Banasare,
  Sun sa wanduna da kunama!

But now the time has turned against you,
A little further and you will be the one
    to cry,
And your crying will do you no good!

You, with the mind of a camel,
And a goatee beard, the worst of the
    braggarts,
You have killed the cow with the
    golden horn,
You have violated the rights of the people,
    Your plans are going nowhere!

City boys, man with the hairy cheeks,
Mongoose, one of the tobacco chewers,
You who smoke the tobacco of arrogance,
Sponger, son of a camel,
    Come rat, and we will put you in the
        trap!

The NPC's lying days are over,
It has collapsed and will surely die,
It has today cut off
Its own head because of ɗan Banasare,
The trousers they pull on still have the
    scorpion inside.

(Hiskett 1977a: 45–6)

The combative and dialogic nature of much political poetry has led to occasions where poets have entered into lengthy poetic exchanges, some in private and some in public. One of the best known involved a series of points and counter-points in the early 1950s between Mudi Sipikin,[9] then a staunch supporter of NEPU, and Mu'azu Haɗeja[10] whose allegiances lay much more closely with the NPC. Mudi also wrote a poem *Arewa Jumhuriya Kawai* 'The North – A Republic Pure and Simple', to register his disagreement with Sa'adu Zungur where Zungur had proposed a constitutional monarchy for Nigeria rather than a republic:

To, don haka ne ban yarda ba
  Bisa waƙar nan ta Sa'adiya.
Amma a wajen da ya ce kurum
  Babu damar rushe mulukiya.
Shi ne na taho zan bayyana,
  Jama'a ku taho ku ji gaskiya.
Asalin sarki ba gardama,

A cikin Daura ne kun jiya.
Da maciji ne wani mai faɗa,
 Ya fito a cikin wata rijiya.
Shi ne asalin kalmar ku san,
 Don ku gane zancen gaskiya.
Daga baya ga halin zamani
 Suka ƙara har da sarauniya.
Kuma rushe gini na mulukiya
 Ya taho mana ba wata kariya.
Ba daɗewa kan 'yan shekaru
 Za mu tsunduma kan jumhuriya.
Ingilishin nan na ƙasarmu duk
 Za su bar mana nan Nijeriya.
Watau mulkin kai za ya isa
 Mu fice daga mulkin danniya.
Na faɗa na ƙara faɗa muku
 Za mu san mulkin Nijeriya.

(Unpublished MS)

Therefore I do not agree
 With that poem by Sa'adu.
But only where he says there is
 No way to bring down the monarchical system.
That is what I have come to address,
 Come, people, and hear the truth.
The word *sarki* 'king' originates
 In Daura and was the word for
A fearsome snake
 That came out of a well [and was killed by Bagauda].
That is the origin of the word,
 I tell you so you may know the truth.
Later on as time went by
 They added another queen [Elizabeth].
The destruction of the edifice of monarchy
 Is before us and there is no getting away from it.
Within a very few years
 We will become a republic.
All the English in our country
 Will leave and give us back Nigeria.
Independence will be upon us,
 And we will be out from under oppressive rule.
I have said, and I will say again,
 We will take control of Nigeria.

While much political poetry sings the praises of the leadership of particular parties, the above extract provides a brief illustration of a poem which does in fact focus upon issues. Issues and personalities are often, of course, wrapped up together. In the following extract from a NEPU poem by Gambo Hawaja,[11] *A Yau ba Maƙi NEPU sai Wawa* 'Today only the Fool rejects NEPU', the poet addresses the issue of colonial government rules and regulations and the way in which they have affected the daily lives of ordinary people. Housing for foreigners has meant the pulling down of buildings belonging to ordinary people; those whose livelihood depended upon hunting are faced with bans and restrictions; restrictions are placed upon the gathering of wood; traditional methods of dealing with thieves are no longer permissible. In the poem these and many other injustices are laid at the door of the unholy alliance between the colonial English and their local aristocratic lackeys:

Ku dubo ƙasashe kamar namu,
A ce ba mu iko da kayanmu?
Mazaje da 'ya'ya da matanmu,
Da igwai na bauta a gindinmu,
    A yau mu ka bauta ga su, wawa!

Idan anka zo kan gidajenmu,
A ce za a zaunar da baƙinmu,
A ce du mu rurrusa soronmu,
Da mu ɗan musu sai a ɗaura mu,
    A ce mun yi laifi ga Turawa!

      . . .

Kamar dorina ma ta tafkinmu,
Kaza raƙuman nan na dajinmu,
Halas ne ga duk ɗan ƙasashenmu,
A yau ba maharbi guda namu,
    Da zai kar su in ban da Turawa!

Jama'a masifa ta same mu,
Na bautar da 'ya'yan ƙasashenmu,
Da mun sari icce a kamo mu,
A je duk a ɗaure iyalanmu,
    Ina kwanciyar hankalin kowa?

Idan ban da Enpisi, wawanmu,
A Jos ga ciyawa a dajinmu,
A ce ba mu yanka da laujenmu,
Tutur sai da famet a hannunmu,
    Harajin ciyawa ga Turawa!

. . .

Ku gane a kayin ɓarayinmu,
Da ƙarfi su ke fizge kayanmu,
Su zare wuƙaƙe su soke mu,
A ce ba mu dukansu sai kamu,
    Da hannu mu miƙa wa Turawa!

. . .

Su kan tuɓe sarki, masoyinmu,
Su sa nasu ko babu yardarmu,
Suna shuka ƙarya da sunanmu,
Suna ce da mu sun wakilce mu,
    Ashe ba su son arzikin kowa!

(Hiskett 1977a: 16—22)

Look at a country like ours,
How can we not have control over our own things?
Men, women and children
Have the shackles of slavery around their waists,
    We are even today enslaved to them!

Take, for example, our homes,
We are told there are strangers who must be housed,
And all our buildings must be razed,
At the slightest objection we are arrested,
    And charged with offending against the English!

. . .

As with the hippos in our lakes,
And the giraffes in the bush,
Any citizen had a right to them,
But now there is not one hunter
    Who can kill them other than the English!

People, a calamity has befallen us,
Whereby our citizens have been enslaved,
If we cut wood, we are arrested,
And they go and lock up our families,
    Where is peace of mind for anyone in all this?

Other than for the NPC, the fools amongst us,
In Jos the bush is full of lush grass,
But we are not allowed to use our sickles,
Only with a permit in our hands,
    The English even tax the grass!

. . .

And with the thieves amongst us,
Who take our goods by force,
And pull out their knives and stab us,
But we must not touch them, only arrest them
    And hand them over to the English!

                . . .

They depose the emirs who love us,
And appoint their nominees even if we do not agree,
They spread lies in our name,
And tell us they are representing us,
    But they have nobody else's interests at heart.

PURPOSIVE POETRY: 'THE RIGHT PATH'

The first poem presented in this chapter, *Gargaɗi don Falkawa,* represented the type of poetry which reflects upon the morality of personal behaviour and of everyday life. There are many areas of personal and social life that are treated in this didactic manner in poetry. In this discussion I can only comment upon and illustrate a small range of such issues. In the last part of this chapter I select three such issues: money, marriage and the young, and approach them through the work of two poets writing in the 1970s. In this section I address a further issue which has been a dominant theme in poetry during this century: the role and purpose of education and specifically 'Western' education.

Part of the arrangement between Lord Lugard and the northern emirs at the beginning of this century was maintainance of the system of Islamic education in the North and a discouragement of Christian missions, with their attendant schools, from establishing themselves in the North. After the Second World War it became increasingly clear to northern leaders that the imbalance that had grown up between north and south in the spread and level of western education was going to have serious consequences for the future of Nigeria. The northern leaders saw access to jobs in government and in many other sectors being filled with the only available qualified people: southerners. The northern leadership, centred on the Sardauna, in concert with the colonial administration, began a concentrated campaign to promote adult education and to expand school facilities and the numbers of children in Western-style schools. Poets turned to a theme which has kept them busy ever since. One of the first volumes of poetry published in roman script, the 1955 anthology of poems by Mu'azu Haɗeja, *Wakokin Mu'azu Hadejia,* contained three poems on the theme, validating Western education alongside Koranic education, linking 'progress' to education, and reiterating the necessity to combat the 'threat' from the south. In more recent times, the issue has been seen less in terms of the contrast between Western and Islamic education and more in terms of the value of knowledge and education in and for itself. One of the best known poems by Aƙilu Aliyu[12] is on this subject and is entitled *Kadaura Babbar Inuwa* 'The Shadiest of All, the Balsam Tree', from which this is an extract:[13]

A mazanmu har matanmu, yara da manya
   Jama'a mu san ilmi muna tarawa.
Shi ne kadaura, ilmu babbar gayya,
   Inuwa mayalwaciya wajen hutawa.
Lallai mu ja ɗamara mu miƙe sosai,
   Ba nuna lalaci da son gajiyawa.

. . .

Sai ga mutum ba ilmu, ba mulki ba,
   Shi ba kuɗi, sha'anin akwai rikitarwa.
Zai zamto ƙungurmin baƙin makwaɗaici,
   Ko ko maɗauki tun gaban miƙawa.
Karshensa dai ya zamo abokin yara,
   Ka ji ɗan kira daidai da kuka kyanwa:
'Kai, wane, ko ba ka gan ni ne ba? Wuyana!'
   Ya zam abin wasa abin tonawa.
Domin gudun haka ya kamata mu lura,
   Hanya mafi kyawo mu zam danƙawa.
Yaro marar ilmi, tasono ke nan,
   Mai toshe hanci babu numfasawa.
Lallai yana wajaba mu shiryu mu kintsu,
   A bisa tafarkin nan mafi dacewa.
Mu yi ƙoƙari, mu yi ƙoƙari, mu yi ƙwazo,
   Himma maɗaukakiya, marar rushewa;
Bisa tattalin neman sani kowanne,
   A maza da mata duk mu zam miƙewa.
Ka yi ƙoƙarin neman sani don kanka
   Da ƙasarka, aiki ne abin godewa.
Ba inda jahilci yake amfani,
   In ban da ma cuta a kan cutarwa.
Cutar rashin ilmi tana cutarwa,
   Mawuyaciyar cuta, marar warkewa.
Shin jahili, wai ransa me ya daɗa ne?
   Da zamansa ɗin nan, na ga ƙwanda macewa.
Mai bincike ya zuwa ga wannan zance,
   Neman ya san hujja, akwai amsawa.
Tirƙashi, aikin ya fi ƙarfin wasa,
   Zan ɓuntuna maka ƙyas ka san ta ƙararwa.
Hauka da jahilci suna da zumunta,
   Makusaciya ta ƙuƙut mara jayawa.
Har ma kusan in ce su, wa da ƙani ne,
   Saƙo da saƙo ne wajen haifawa.

Kai hasalin magana, tagwaye ne su,
'Ya'yan ciki daya ne, a daina rabawa.

Men and women, young and old,
   Let us garner knowledge and gather it in.
It is the copaiba balsam tree, it is our major common task,
   It is the deep shade in which we can find solace.
We must take up arms and exert ourselves,
   Showing no dilatoriness nor tendency to tire.

                    .   .   .

Behold the man lacking knowledge or position,
   Penniless and in a grievous state.
He will become a serious parasite on the resources of others,
   Taking before being offered.
He ends his days as the companion of children,
   Crying out with the plaintive miaow of the kitten,
'Hey, can't you see the position I am in! All my difficulties!'
   He has become a laughing stock.
To avoid this we must take care,
   And walk upon the right path.
The ignorant youth is like dry snot
   That blocks the nose and hinders breathing.
It is for us to act responsibly
   In this the most important of all matters.
Let us try and try and try again
   With the very greatest of efforts that will not fail.
In the search to attain mastery in all aspects of knowledge
   We must all, men and women, step forth;
Seek knowledge for your own good
   And for the good of your country, it is a worthwhile task.
Nowhere does ignorance have value,
   It merely piles ill upon ill.
The ill of ignorance is injurious,
   A terrible illness without cure.
What value can ignorance have?
   Better it die than live.
Whoever looks into this question,
   Seeking information, know that there is always an answer.
My goodness! What a task!
   I will break off the tiniest fraction for you to give away.
Ignorance and madness are closely related,
   Indivisible and interlocked;
I can almost say they are brothers,
   Consecutive siblings,

To be candid they are really twins,
Coming from the same womb, inseparable.

(GF & SIK)

Aƙilu Aliyu's renowned skill with words is apparent in the Hausa text of the poem, less so in the translation.

The didacticism that typifies so much poetry ranges, as I have indicated, across many social and political themes, both in terms of public and personal behaviour. In considering song we have seen how the patron–client relationship was extended to include the commissioning of advertising songs by companies and organisations. In similar fashion, government agencies, development corporations and others have recognised the potential of this didactic characteristic of poetry for the conveying of their own particular messages to the general public. There have been poems written and published informing people about impending currency changes, the change from left- to right-hand drive, or how elections are conducted. There is exhortation, in poetic form, not only to vote for particular parties but also to use certain kinds of modern fertilisers or to buy certain products. The following is a very brief extract from one of more than twenty poems written by Garba Ebisidi Funtuwa[14] about using chemical fertilisers; poems that were printed and distributed by the Northern Region Development Corporation based in Kaduna during the 1960s.

Kurɗin buhu ɗaya ai sule ne sha biyu,
  Ruga da sauri ka ji arha gare shi.
Takin akwai auki ƙwarai maza je sawo,
  Eka guda ɗaya ka ji za shi ishe shi.
Dukkan buhu ɗaya za shi jawo fam biyar,
  Ribarka to Malam ina ya kamarshi.
Sayi ko buhu huɗu ko biyar ka yi tanadi,
  Duk inda ya shiga ka ji je ka biɗo shi.
Je adana kafin ruwan shuka ya zo,
  In an ruwa takin ka je ka biɗo shi.

(Unpublished MS)

The cost of one sack is twelve shillings,
  Hurry, you hear how cheap it is.
It is very strong fertiliser, be quick and buy some,
  It is enough for one whole acre.
For each one sack will bring you five pounds clear profit,
  So, Malam, have you ever seen the like of it.
Buy four or five sacks to always be ready,
  Whatever it takes, go and find it.
Go and make ready before the sowing rains arrive,
  When the rains come, go and seek it out.

Clearly the didactic potential of this well-established oral and written communicative mode were being exploited to the full. The adaptation of the form to these new secular, communicative functions does not mean that the tradition of religious writing from which it originated had disappeared. On the contrary, religious poetry has continued to flourish and grow.

MODERN RELIGIOUS POETRY

While the twentieth century has seen a broadening of the range of topics addressed in poetic form, poetry has continued to be written on strictly religious themes. On the one hand the revitalisation and transformation into mass movements of the two main Sufi sects in northern Nigeria, the Qadiriyya and the Tijjaniyya, during the 1960s and 1970s engendered a flowering of poetry writing on the beliefs and practices of the sects and in praise of the saints and leaders of the organisations.[15] On the other, the two major yearly religious festivals, the *Babbar* and the *Karamar Salla*, and the *mauludi* 'birthday of the Prophet', were occasions for the production of poems in praise of the Prophet and on other religious topics.[16]

There is a very large body of modern religious poetry and I am unable to do it justice here. I have elected, instead, to cite the whole of one example of devotional poetry that mirrors the sense of deep religious commitment expressed in nineteenth-century poetry such as, for example, *Ma'ama'are*, the poem by Shehu Usman cited in the previous chapter. This poem, written in about 1970 and entitled *Allantaka* 'The Being of Allah' is by a contemporary poet, Tijjani Tukur,[17] a university graduate and one-time member of the Hikima poetry circle, *Hikima Kulob*, that had access to Kano radio under their leader, Mudi Sipikin.

Allantaka expresses Tijjani Tukur's profound religious sentiments. It is a modern example of the devotional *qasida* inherited from the religious verse tradition of the nineteenth century. *Madahu* poetry was a mainstay of the Jihadist writers and the Sufi poets of the Tijaniyya and Qadiriyya movements. Such poetry formed an outlet for the expression of personal emotion that balanced the highly didactic and purposive styles of so much nine-teenth- and twentieth- century Hausa poetry. During the recording of a recitation of this poem in 1974, tears began to roll down the cheeks of the poet as emotion welled up in him, eventually he broke off into silence for some considerable time as he struggled to recover himself and continue:

Allantaka

Allahu ni na tabbata bawanka ne,
    Tun fil azal ya Rabbi babu kamarka.
Allahu ni na gaskata tun ran nan,
    Da ka ce mu amsa Rabbi na gaishe ka.
Allahu kai ne ma kadimu Ubangiji,
    Antal baka'u gwanin isa da isarka.

Allahu babu uwa gare ka bare uba,
    Balle su ce maka wane ya saɓe ka.
Allahu balle ma su tilasta ma,
    Kuma babu su balle su zan yaddaka.

       .   .   .

Allahu na san kai kake rayawa,
    Kai ne kake kashe dukkanin bayinka.
Allahu kai ne Alfattahu a suna,
    Kai ne kake buɗi cikin yardarka.
Allahu na san arziki ba mai shi,
    Ilmi da ƙarfin zuciyar ƙaunarka.
Allahu na san kai kaɗai aka duba,
    Don babu mai su ban da kai na san ka.
Allahu ba wani mai isa ko gauƙa,
    Kuma babu mai ikon ruwa ko iska.
Allahu in duk duniya ta taru,
    Wai duk suna ƙaunar mutum ya yi harka.
Allahu na san ba shi samun komai,
    Sai dai abin da ka so ka ba shi da kanka.
Allahu in sun taru wai don ƙyama,
    Ko tuntuɓ bai yi idan a nufarka.
Allahu har ka ƙaddara masa girma,
    Komai tsiyar maƙiyansa sai ya haska.
Allahu don haka na tsaya na kwanta,
    Nai sujada roƙo nake a gare ka.
Allahu roƙona ka sa niyyata,
    Komai in nake yi ya zan dominka.
Allahu ban ilmi ka zam ƙarawa,
    Kuma sa in zam yaƙi a san girmanka.
Allahu ban haske a zuci in yarda,
    Dukkan abin da ka ƙaddaran in yabe ka.
Allahu arzurta ni kai ne nawa,
    Koren talauci don isar Kadarinka
Allahu kar ka kashe ni mai yin saɓo,
    Rufa duk asirina ka ban yardarka.
Allahu na roƙe ka ran mutuwata,
    Ka tashan nake tsoro ka sa ni in farka.
Allahu ka san masu tarkon wofi,
    Su ga wai tsirarata cikin bayinka.
Allahu komai tanadinsu kana nan,
    Ka tsare ni dukkan kunyata a gabanka.
Allahu nan kuma duniya na roƙe,
    Ka tsare ni dukkan kunyatar bayinka.

Allahu ƙarshena ya kyautu in tabbata
  Ka yarda ni bawanka ne mai sonka.
Allahu kar ka bari abokan gaba,
  Su yi gangami wai don ina saɓonka.
Allahu na roƙe ka kar ka kashe ni,
  Sai na warware bashi cikin yardarka.

. . .

Allahu ka sa kuma zuciyar koyaushe
  Kaunarka ce a ciki da son Manzonka.
Allahu ka sa kullum idan nai bauta
  A gare ka ne Allah bi gairi siwaka.
Allahu kai ne mai isa mai kyauta
  Wallahi ba na biyunka babu kamarka.
Allahu sa ni cikin maza managarta,
  Ka tsare ni sharrin dukkanin bayinka.
Allahu ni bawa ina yin saɓo,
  Kai ne kake shiriya ina roƙonka.
Allahu ya Allahu ban shiriya don,
  In guje aikin assha don girmanka.
Allahu ɗauke fargaba ko tsoro
  Daga zuciyata sai kawai tsoronka.
Allahu na roƙe ka na maimaita,
  Ka rufan asirina cikin bayinka.
Allahu ban Ludufi ka ban jurewa
  Ka ko ban amana kar ka sa ni wutarka.
Allahu na san ambatonka da daɗi,
  Wallahi ba na son in daina yabonka.
Allahu ka ban hankali da tunani
  Har ga shi na ma san ka na roƙe ka.
Allahu tun da ka ƙaddara ni na roƙa
  Na san ba za ka hana ni amsawarka
Allahu alwashinka ne na yarda
  Kuma ba saɓawa cikin zancenka.
Allahu tun da ka ce idan na roƙa
  Kai ne mafi kusa za ka ba ni da sonka.
Allahu ka ce wanda ya ƙi roƙo,
  Wannan baƙin mutakabbiri gunka.
Allahu na roƙe ka na maimaita,
  Ban duk abin da na ce bi jahi Ulaka
Allahu raina ya amince sosai
  Kuma nai zato mai kyau ina a gare ka.
Allahu da ma ka faɗa na yarda,
  A wajen zaton bawanka ne kyautarka.

Allahu ga Tijjani bawa tsantsa,
  Ya sunkuya roƙo yake a gabanka.

(Unpublished MS)

The Being of Allah

Allah, I declare myself Your slave,
  Since the beginning, Oh God, none compares with You.
Allah, I vouchsafe that since that day
  You told us to respond, Lord, I have acknowledged You.
Allah, You are the eternal, the master,
  The continuer, the Almighty.
Allah, You have no mother, nor yet a father,
  No one need tell You that someone has sinned against you.
Allah, nor can anyone prevail upon you,
  There are none such as these, nor any who would disown You.

                    .   .   .

Allah, I know You grant life
  And it is you who takes life away from all Your slaves.
Allah, you are in name the initiator,
  You are the one who opens the way with Your blessings
Allah, I know that none are wealthy;
  Or have the knowledge and the steadfastness of heart to love You,
Allah, I know to You alone one turns,
  For no one other than You can grant these things, I know it is You.
Allah, no one can boast or show superiority,
  And none have power over water and wind.
Allah, if all the world joins forces
  And says it wants a particular man to succeed,
Allah, I know he will gain nothing,
  Except that which You wish to give him Yourself.
Allah, if the world comes together in hate
  He will not even stumble, if that is your will.
Allah, if You have planned for him greatness
  Then however evil his enemies, he will shine through.
Allah, for this reason I lie here motionless,
  I prostrate myself and beg before You.
Allah, my entreaty is that You grant my wish,
  My wish that all I do is done for Your sake.
Allah, grant me knowledge, ever deeper,
  May I be always struggling to spread knowledge of Your greatness.
Allah, instil light in my heart that I may accept
  All that You have planned for me, and praise You.

Allah render me prosperous, You are mine,
  Drive poverty from me, by Your will.
Allah, do not kill me, the sinner,
  Respect my loyalty, grant me Your favour.
Allah, I beg that on the day of my death –
  I fear Your rousing me – You waken me.
Allah, You know those who lay evil traps
  Their intention is to expose my nakedness before Your slaves.
Allah, whatever they have plotted, You are there
  Protect me from all humiliation before You.
Allah, in this world I beg of You,
  Protect me from all humiliation before Your slaves.
Allah, may my end be a good one so that I may be sure
  You have accepted me as Your slave, one who loves You.
Allah, do not allow enemies
  To declare that I have disobeyed You.
Allah, I beg You not to kill me
  Until, with Your blessings, I have paid off my debts.

.   .   .

Allah, make my heart be always
  Full of love for You and Your Prophet,
Allah, grant that whenever I submit,
  It is to You, Allah, and no one other than You.
Allah, You are the all-powerful and the bestower,
  There is no second in line behind You and none like You.
Allah, place me among the good men,
  Protect me from the evil of all Your slaves.
Allah, I, the slave, am a sinner,
  You it is who makes things right, and I beg of You to do so.
Allah, Oh Allah, grant me absolution
  That I may avoid evil deeds by Your greatness.
Allah, take away fright and fear
  From my heart, other than the fear of You.
Allah, I beg of You, and I say again,
  Stand beside me, here among Your slaves.
Allah grant me goodness and forbearance,
  Grant me Your trust, throw me not upon Your fires.
Allah, I know the mention of You gives pleasure,
  By Allah, I want never to stop praising You.
Allah, grant me sense and thought
  Such that I may know You, I beg of you.
Allah, since You ordain, so I beseech You,
  I know You will not withhold Your acceptance from me.

Allah, I accept Your promise,
  And there can be no error in what You say.
Allah, since You have said that if I beg,
  You are the closest, You will bestow on me, by Your will.
Allah, You have said that he who refuses to beg
  Is the worst, the proudest, in Your eyes.
Allah, I beg You and I beg again,
  Grant me all I ask through Your grace
Allah, my mind trusts implicitly,
  I have thought well, and I am in Your hands.
Allah, You have always said, and I accept
  That Your blessings lie in the thoughts of Your slaves.
Allah, here stands Tijjani, a simple slave,
  He stoops and begs before You.

TOPICAL AND NARRATIVE POETRY

In Chapter 6, on song, Mamman Shata was quoted as saying that one of his functions was to record events of importance in his society. Precisely the same function is alluded to by poets in their discussion of their own positions. Where Jihadist poets recorded the victory of Alkalawa and others, so modern poets write upon current events combining a narrative style with elements of the didacticism or praise that we have seen earlier in this chapter. The pages of the Hausa newspaper, *Gaskiya Ta Fi Kwabo*, in the 1950s, 1960s and 1970s saw poems on constitutional conferences, on the Nigerian soldiers in Abyssinia and Burma during the Second World War, on royal visits, on northern self-government, on Nigerian independence and, as a result of a national competition, on the Nigerian civil war, as well as a host of other topics. Many poems submitted on the civil war were narrative in style,[18] however the winner of the first prize, *Jiki Magayi* 'Appearances Tell' by Aƙilu Aliyu, presented a more rhetorical tone as the following extract illustrates:

Ja kuke a shika, soja.
Jami'in a kara, saja.
Jagaban yaƙi, manja.
Jar wuta ita ce danja
  Jar baƙar mutuwa, soja.

When you pull, the other lets go, soldier.
Leader in the fight, sergeant!
Pathfinder in war, major!
A red glow, the sign of danger.
  Red, dark death, soldier!

Gaskiya a cikin taɗi
Coi kamar sukari kwandi.
Rabbana, ka yi min budi,
Kar ka sanya in faɗi,
  Za ni waƙe kan soja.

Truth in discourse is like
A dish that is sugar-sweet.
God grant that I may succeed,
That I may not fail
  In my song about the soldiers.

Babu ƙarya ba fenti,
Babu zance halbati.

I add no falsehood, no veneer,
No stupidly unlikely tales.

'Yar biyar tisi'in baiti
Mai shigen ƙamshin zaiti
   Zan yi domin ku, soja.

Ninety verses in all, each of five lines,
Whose scent is finer than eucalyptus oil,
   These I am writing for you, soldiers.

Za na yi ta da hausarmu
Tun ta kakan kakammu,

And I will declaim it in Hausa,
Our tongue since our grandfathers' grandfathers,

Har ta zo ga iyayenmu,
Mu, ɗiyammu, jiyokimmu,
   Ma yaba wa maza, soja.

Our fathers' too,
And ours, our sons' and grandsons'.
   We shall praise brave men, the soldiers.

Ba kirari, ba washi.

There will be no praise for its own sake, or
   false colouring.

Duk mawaƙi mai kishi
Zai yi wannan ba fashi
Don ya bayyana ƙaunarshi
   Gun ƙasa da maza soja.

Every patriotic poet
Will do the same unceasingly,
To show his love
   For our country and our brave soldiers.

Kash! Ina ma an yarje
In bi komai in darje,
In yi tsifa in taje.
Da fasaha ta gaje
   Tsarkake matsayin soja.

What! Would that I were able to
Cover the whole subject, combing it finely
And separating the strands,
And that my eloquence might achieve
   Clarification of the calling of the soldier.

Mai shirin tafiya aiki
Bai zama a cikin ɗaki;
Dukiya, hajjar, banki –
Kai! Rago ba ya mulki,
   Sai a ba wa maza soja.

No man who has a job to do
Will sit quietly at home;
Wealth, goods for trade, banking –
A sluggard will never come to govern.
   Leave it to the brave soldier!

Yanzu kafin in tura
Can da nesa, zan tsara
Manya-manyan in jera.
Sai a ƙarshe in ɗora
   Tarashen mabiyan soja.

Now, before I go too far
With my song, let me list
The great ones, one by one,
And afterwards I'll go on
   To all the other ranks, the soldiers.

Nai tunani na nisa
Na yi cizo, na busa.
Tambaye ni, akwai amsa
Ko a goro akwai marsa.

I have pondered and groaned
I've bitten and blown.
Ask me for there is an answer –
Even among colanuts some are better than
   others.

   To, bare a cikin soja.

   Well, much more so among soldiers.

'Yan'uwa nai tammani
Za ku ɗan saurare ni,
Don sabo da ku jijji ni
Kan abin da nake nuni
   Dangane da maza soja.

Brothers, I think and hope
You will lend me your ears for a while
And listen to me
And to what I have to say
   Concerning the brave soldiers.

Shugaba mai zamani,	Leader of the age,
Hankalina ya ba ni	My heart bids me
In yi ma wannan launi,	Make this song for you
Manjo Yaƙubu Gawwani,	Major Yakubu Gowon,
Babba, jagoran soja.	Great one, leader of soldiers.
Duniya ta shaide ka,	The world recognizes you,
Koƙari, kirki naka.	Your zeal and honesty.
Ga yawan haƙuri gunka.	Your patience is very great.
Sai ƙani ba yayanka	You have no elder, only younger brothers
Duk a gwamnonin soja.	Among all the soldier-governors.
Ba ka tsoro sai kunya.	You have no fear, only respect for others.
In mutum yai jayayya	If any man opposes you
Ko ya nuna rashin kunya,	Or acts shamelessly,
Sa shi dole ya zo hanya,	Compel him to return to the road,
Jami'in jama'ar soja.	Commander of the host of soldiers.

(Skinner and Galadanci 1973)

While such a poem is clearly topical in its content, the style is very much within the rhetoric of praise, and, in fact, in a later section switches into vilificatory mode when the subject turns to the leader of the secessionist forces, Ojukwu.[19]

An alternative celebratory style of topical poem is offered by Na'ibi Sulaiman Wali in his well-known poem *Maraba da 'Yanci* 'Welcome Freedom' written in celebration of Northern self-government in 1959.[20] The first 18 of 51 verses run as follows:

Tsuntsun da ke faman layi a samaniya,
Kana ta shawagi kana yin dariya,
Kana ta walawarka ba wata kangiya,
Kana ta annashuwa kamar mai shan giya,
In za ka yarda tsaya inai maka tambaya.

Shin me ya samu a yau a wannan duniya,
Kome a yau ya sauya kyansa farat ɗaya,
Ita duniyar duk ta yi haske bai ɗaya,
Kuma tai ƙawa tai kyau tana 'yar walƙiya,
Kome na duba yau yana yin dariya?

Ita kanta rana ta sako riga fara,
Kuma sabuwa ta lilin kamar mai takara,
Ta kore sanyi babu shi, korar kara,
Kuma ta riƙe zafinta domin hattara,
Haske kawai tsantsa ta aiko duniya.

Wata da daddare ko da taurari nasa,

Sai murmushi wannan dare, sai rausasa,
Sun kewaye shi suna ta gaɗa da kwarsasa,
Ka ce zaman ango da 'yammata nasa,
Su ba su jin bacci a yau har safiya.

Kuma rafuka shar-shar gwanin kyawun gani,
Nan ga furanni koina sun sansani,
Launi iri da iri gwanin ban kwarjini,
Kanshi yana tashi kamar a gidan yini,
Kanshin furannin nan kurum sai godiya.

Hudar furannin ka ga duk sun farfashe,
Kanshinsu ya sa koina ya ƙamsashe,
Iskar arewa tana buga wa kowashe,
Kanshi gare su kamar na almuski, ashe,
Ni'ima tana da yawa a wannan duniya!

Kuma na ga tsuntsaye suna waƙa tasu,
Ganyayyakin bishiya suna tafa musu,
Waƙa da tafi babu sulu ba musu,
Kowa ya ji su lakan yana sara musu,
Bishiyar cikin rafi tana yin rausaya.

Har ƙoramu dai ka ga sun sake gudu,
Yar-yar, kamar mai tona ramin kurkudu,
Tamkar macizai ƙanƙanana na gudu,
Jejjere an koro su sun yi wajen kudu,
Don razana a cikinsu ba mai waiwaya.

Tsuntun ina son in ji amsa ka jiya,
Shin me ya sassake su, nai maka tambaya,
Ko ni na sake ne, na ce duk duniya?
Amsar da tsuntsun nan ya ba ni farat ɗaya,
Ya ce da ni: 'yancin Arewa gaba ɗaya!'

An ce da mu ran sha biyar ga watan uku,
Shi ne watan Maris da kowa zai saku,
Mun daina kukan kaito ko na shiga uku,
Daga yau shigogo ba za ya ƙara dakan uku
A wuyanmu ba, balle ya sa mana karkiya.

Ran sha biyar Maris, alif da ɗari tara,
Hamsin idan ka tattara da guda tara,
Nauyin da ƙangin nan da ya kai gargara,
An taru an sauke shi yau bisa hattara,
Kowa ya taka ƙafarsa ba sauran ƙaya.

Akuyar da ke turke a yau ta san saki,
Kowa ya mimmiƙe ya buɗe fukafuki,
Ya yi fuffuka ya cira ya bar mutuwar jiki,
A Arewa kowa yai shirin babban biki,
Kowa ya san mu ma akwai mu a duniya.

Magana ta tsuntsun nan da ban sha'awa take,
Ga tausayi in ka ji yadda abin yake,
Ya ce da ni: 'Da can cikin keji nake,
Kullum ina tsalle ina kaɗa fuffuke,
"Yara ku bar ni na tashi ko da sau ɗaya."

Su ko suna cewa: "Haba ɗan arziki,
Ba ka gani ka sami sabon shamaki,
Kuma ga ruwan sukari da tattausan tsaki,
A ɓagas, a tun kafin ka motsa fukafuki,
Sauran da ke tashi ko sai galudaya?"'

Shi ko yana cewa: 'Da kwana kan haki,
Da zuwa wajen kiwo da motsa fukafuki,
Da haɗiɗiyar tsakuwa wajen neman tsaki,
Da ruwan cikin kwatami, da mummunan jiki,
Muddin da 'yanci sun fi daɗaɗa zuciya.'

Daga jin haka sai na yi babbar hamdala,
Na faɗi nai sujada ga wanda ya kammala,
Allahu, ba don shi ba ba wata walwala,
Ya ɗan'uwa kai ma ka ce: 'Nai hamdala,
Alhamdu na gode wa Allah Shi ɗaya.'

Ranar ta kowa ce Arewa gaba ɗaya,
Ranar bikin idin ƙasa baki ɗaya,
Mata, maza, manya da yara bai ɗaya,
A Arewa, har bare idan har ya taya,
Mulkimmu ba ƙyama ciki ba togiya.

Rana ta fansa ce ga kaka har uba,
Da sukai ta artabu da kangawa, haba,
Gindin giginyan nan ba zan mance ta ba,
Nan ne mazajen duniya suka zuzzuba,
Domin tsare 'yancin Arewa gaba ɗaya.

(MS in the author's possession)

Bird, busy with the pathways of the sky,
You hover and laugh,
You fly at ease, no barriers in your way,
Joyful as one intoxicated,

Hold still a moment, I have a question.

What has happened to the world today,
Everything suddenly looks its best,
The world itself is all bright,
And beautiful, fair and sparkling,
Whatever I look at today is laughing?

The sun is dressed in a white gown,
Of the best new linen, as if on display,
With a stick it has driven away the cold,
And yet held back its strongest heat,
Sending down to the world its purest light.

The moon and stars
Are smiling tonight, swaying gracefully,
The stars surround him, clapping coquettishly,
Like a bridegroom and his company of girls,
No wish to sleep tonight till morning comes.

The stream-beds are beautiful in their vivid green,
And all around are encampments of flowers,
A myriad exquisite colours,
And a scent wafts up like at a wedding,
The perfume of these flowers is a gift from God.

Flower buds have burst out all over,
Their scent is everywhere,
The wind from the north touches them all,
And their fragrance is like musk. My! but
This world is a bounteous place!

The birds sing and
The leaves on the trees clap in time,
A singing and a clapping in perfect harmony,
All who hear them must applaud them,
As the tree by the stream sways in time.

The rivulets have started to flow again,
Smooth as the sand sliding at a sandhopper's hole,
Like tiny snakes gliding
Perfectly aligned, driven southward,
In their fear not one turns its head.

Bird, I want to know the answer,
What, I ask, has changed them,
Or is it me, and thought it was the world?
The answer came straight back:

'Freedom for the North!'

They say that on the fifteenth of the third month,
March, we will all be released,
No longer will we bewail our misfortune, our troubles,
From this day the intruder will no longer beat down
Upon our necks, or place the yoke upon us.

On the fifteenth of March, nineteen
Hundred and fifty-nine,
The weight of the shackle that was beyond bearing,
Has, by our united efforts, been lifted,
And, as each man steps out, no more thorns lie in wait.

The tethered goat has today found release,
All may stretch their limbs or spread their wings,
Take off, fly, and leave behind the old paralysis,
Throughout the North make ready for the celebrations,
Let the whole world know we are a part of it.

The bird's reply was enough to gladden the heart,
But there was more, and moving it was too:
'I used to be in a cage,
Jumping up and down and flapping my wings,
"Please let me go, boys, just once."

But they replied: "But you are lucky,
Can't you see your brand new house,
With sweet water and soft grain
Aplenty, you don't have to move your wings,
Like the other birds who have to struggle to survive?" '

But he responded: 'Sleeping on stalks,
Going out in search of food, moving my wings,
Swallowing gravel along with the grain,
Muddy water from a puddle and being always dirty,
Are infinitely preferable, if one is free.'

When I heard this I gave thanks to God,
I fell and worshipped Him who is Perfect,
Allah, without whom there would be no answers,
You, my friend, should also say: 'I praise God,
Thanks be to God, the one God.'

It is a day for everyone in the North,
A festival day for the whole country,
Women, men, old and young,
Throughout the North, and even the interested outsider,

In our domain there is no prejudice, no holding back.

It is the day of redemption for our fathers and grandfathers,
Who endured adversity and discrimination,
Let us not forget the battle of Gindin Giginya,
There it was that the heroes marched out,
To defend the freedom of the North.

The use of imagery from the natural world is a feature of Na'ibi Wali's poetry, the best known example being the 'Song of the Rains' that has been translated and presented by Arnott (1969) and Mack (1982), among others.

Muhammad (1982) has provided evidence of a lengthy poetic epic narrative entitled the *Waƙar Tabuka* 'The Song of Tabuka' concerning one of the episodes from the life of the Prophet. However, lengthy poetic narrative is perhaps unusual in Hausa although there are some extended series of poems around a related set of themes, such as the nine cantos of *Waƙar Imfiraji* discussed in the previous chapter. Abubakar Ladan[21] has published an extensive narrative poem concerning his journeys through Africa, *Waƙar Haɗa Kan Al'ummar Afrika* 'The Poem of African Unity'.[22] Threaded through his narrative is a rhetorical theme calling upon Africa to unite.

Among new directions taken in recent years has been the publication of a volume of love poetry, *Dausayin Soyayya* edited by Bello Sa'id (1982b). Love poetry may well be a form with a much longer history but it is only with the appearance of *Dausayin Soyayya* that it has appeared in the public domain.[23] Notions of what is appropriate for public recitation, and poetry has usually involved such recitation, have led to controversy as to whether such poetry should be published. It is my impression that with a split appearing between the oral and the written representation of poetry, many new directions are being experimented with on paper that have yet to reach the 'public domain' – in this context the domain of oral recitation and audience response.

POETRY ON CONTEMPORARY SOCIAL ISSUES

In the course of research in 1973 and 1974 on the *Hikima Kulob*, a poetry circle in Kano, I found that among the members of this particular circle were three women, two of whom I was able to find and talk to at length, Hauwa Gwaram and Alhajiya 'Yar Shehu, and one, Ruƙayyatu Sabuwa Nasir, whom I was not able to contact. Hauwa Gwaram was conducting adult education classes at the old library near the emir's palace in Kano city, and much of her daily effort was expended encouraging women to come to classes while fending off the disapproval of husbands, and the barbed comments of men in general. Nevertheless, her commitment to social issues and to women's education was tangible. Beverly Mack, who made a detailed study of Hauwa Gwaram's work, as well as that of Alhajiya 'Yar Shehu and others (Mack 1981), reported that, much later on, Hauwa Gwaram effectively withdrew from poetry-writing and 'public life' to seek her own religious salvation in a life of contemplation in purdah. In contrast, Alhajiya 'Yar Shehu, working as a professional woman – she was, until her retirement, supervisor of ground staff at Kano airport – always saw her role as a sustainable one, one in which she was the equal of any other commentator upon the many issues of daily concern to ordinary people. In the ensuing discussion I have selected an unpublished poem by Alhajiya 'Yar Shehu to illustrate the way in which she sees her role as commentator upon contemporary social issues.[24] In addition I have chosen to set alongside her another poet, Ibrahim Yaro Muhammed,[25] whose output of poetry on aspects of contemporary Hausa society was prolific. This discussion draws upon a number of his unpublished poems, in addition to the poem by Alhajiya 'Yar Shehu entitled, *Wakar Gargadi* 'A Poem of Warning'.

In the remainder of this chapter I seek to give a flavour of the way in which poets survey Hausa society around them and paint pictures of the salient features of aspects of that society. At the same time the image of society thus created is strongly overlaid with evaluative assessments of what is good and what is bad. In order to illustrate this ideological process at work I have selected three themes which seem to me to recur frequently in modern poetry of social comment: money, marriage and the young.

The picture presented in these extracts reflects various features and problems of post-Independence development that are common to many Nigerian and indeed African cities over the last twenty-five years – the gathering pace of urban migration with its effects upon the rural hinterland and upon a chronically underdeveloped urban infrastructure; the rising expectations of the new generations of Nigerians who have passed into and out of Western education; the disruption of what are viewed as 'traditional' patterns of relationships between marriage partners and between parents and children; and the adoption of European styles of speech, dress and manners that further delineate the differences between the rich and the poor, the old and the young and which constitute, for the poet, the signs indicating an abandonment of 'traditional' values.

In a poem entitled, *Kudi!* 'Money!' in which Ibrahim Yaro Muhammed outlines the bad and the good characteristics of money, he starts by saying,

Yau zamanin nan namu kai,	In this day and age who are you
Waye idan dai ba kudi?	if you don't have money?
Kome kake so za ka sa-	You will get whatever you want
Mu in kana fa da su kudi.	if you have money.
Aure a yau ya munane,	Marriages are being ruined,
Me ya sa? Kul ce kudi.	why? - money.
. . .	. . .
Kowa abin da yake buka-	Everyone is out
Ta yau bara ne kan kudi.	begging for money.

Yau malamai sun bar sani,
   Don me-ye? Domin kuɗi.
Yau 'yan'uwa sun rarrabu,
   Sun bar zumunci don kuɗi.
Kuma yau shari'a ta zamo
   Galabarta yau sai mai kuɗi

. . .

Aiki ku san ya cakuɗe,
   Ya jagule domin kuɗi.
Mata na aure ba zama
   Fa na lafiya in ba kuɗi.
Wasu sun ƙi auren ma tuni,
   Me ye dalili? Ce kuɗi.
Sun je suna yin karuwan-
   Ci wai suna neman kuɗi.
Aurenmu Hausawa a yau,
   Ba so fa sai dai son kuɗi.
Shaida ta zur yau tai yawa,
   Domin kurum neman kuɗi.
Haka nan ga sata har fashi,
   Yau sun ƙazanta fa don kuɗi.
Karya da son ni wanene,
   Duk su ake yi don kuɗi.

. . .

Ba su san su bautawa ƙasa

Bautarsu yau neman kuɗi.

. . .

Haka yau musulmi yai hotel,
   Na sayar da giya domin kuɗi.
Wasu yau suna yin takidin,
   Yunwa fa domin son kuɗi.
Sun sai hatsi fa buhu buhu,
   Sun ɓoyiya ƙwalamar kuɗi.

Kai! Yau kuɗi ya 'yan'uwa
   Sun zam bala'i su kuɗi.

    (Unpublished MS)

The teachers have abandoned knowledge,
   why? – money.
The people are divided against themselves
   because of money.
In a lawsuit the judgement goes
   to him who has money.

. . .

Working practices are perverted
   by money.
Married women will not live
   peaceably if there's no money;
Some refuse to marry,
   why? – money,
They prefer prostitution
   in their search for money.
There is no love in marriage
   other than a love of money.
Bearing false witness is everywhere,
   all in the search for money.
Theft and muggings are rampant,
   all for money.
Lies and ostentation
   surround the search for money.

. . .

[There are leaders] who do not look to
   serve this country,
Their service is in search of money.

. . .

There are Muslims who have built hotels
   and bars in pursuit of money.
There are some who promote
   hunger in their search for money;
They buy up sacks of corn
   and hide them in their greed for
   money.
My! but these days, my friends,
   money has become a disaster.

The poet deplores what he sees as an avaricious materialism which has corrupted the classes of person listed in the above extract, all of whom, the poet implies, were once relatively unaffected by considerations of money and profit. Note that the poem was written in the early 1970s at a time when Nigeria was rapidly growing richer as a result of oil revenues. On the one hand, the poet talks of the destructive effect of money upon accepted social

institutions such as marriage or the law, and, on the other, he describes the
rise of illegitimate activities such as theft, the building of drinking places and
hoarding. An underlying theme in many of Ibrahim Yaro Muhammed's
poems is the creeping, pernicious effects of Europeanisation and it is the
emphasis upon money that he sees in European culture that underpins his
attack here. In the poem the author talks of the bitter aspects of money; in
contrast, later in the poem, he talks of the legitimate, praiseworthy functions
of money as follows:

Zakka ana yi 'yan'uwa,	Alms, my friends,
Sadaka ana yi bil kuɗi.	are done with money,
Haka nan masallatai duka	The building of mosques
Fa gininsu sai fa akwai kuɗi.	is done with money,
Littattafan ilmi kana	And books
Samunsu in fa akwai kuɗi.	are bought with money.
Haka nan sana'u jimlatan,	The trades and professions are pursued
Duk yi ake domin kuɗi.	in order to get money,
Noma da harkar kasuwa	Farming and trading
Duk yi ake fa a sam kuɗi.	are done for money,
Su dako da dukanci duka,	Portering and tanning are done
Me ya sa ake yi? Kuɗi.	for what? For money.
Haka nan karatun zamani,	The desire for modern education
Buri na yinsa ku ce kuɗi.	is based upon a desire for money.
Magina a yau me ye ya sa	Why do builders
Su suke gini? Domin kuɗi.	build? For money.
Wanki da ɗinki har da ƙi-	Washing, sewing and
Ra, duk ana yi don kuɗi.	smithing are done for money.

(Unpublished MS)

In this extract the pursuit of money is legitimate for religious purposes and
as the aim of traditional professions. But interestingly, the legitimate pursuit
of Western education is based not upon the search for knowledge *per se*, that
sanction being confined to the search for Islamic knowledge, but rather
upon the central role of Western education in obtaining a salaried job, the
key to advancement and financial security.

Ostentation and snobbery associated with increasing social differentiation based upon wealth is one of the themes discussed by Alhajiya 'Yar
Shehu in her poem, *Wakar Gargadi* 'Song of Warning':

Amma akwai wasu masu tarin dukiya
   Da suke ganin wai sun fi kowa duniya.
Su ba ruwansu da 'yan'uwansu bare wani,
   Sai busa hanci sai ɗagawa fariya.
Ba sa zuwa suna bare su jana'iza,
   A gidan maƙwabta ga su wai mai dukiya.

But there are those who have made money
    Who think themselves better than anyone else in the world.
Their fellow men are no concern of theirs, nor anyone else's;
    They are supercilious and boastful.
They wouldn't go to a naming-ceremony let alone a funeral.
    In their neighbours' houses they make a show of being rich.

This extract highlights the way in which the *nouveaux riches* are typically viewed as having abandoned their normal social obligations to neighbours and friends, the basis of social cohesion in a settled community. Precisely the same characteristics form part of the stereotype of the new 'contractor' class outlined so savagely in the novel *Turmin Danya* by Sulaiman Ibrahim Katsina (discussed in Chapter 2). Ostentation and competition between women is a subject also attacked by Alhajiya 'Yar Shehu:

Na zo gare ku masu yiwa ƙawa biki,
    To sai ku saurara ku ji ni gaba ɗaya.
Don ko akwai wasu masu ɓarnar dukiya,
    In sunka tashi bikin ƙawaye kun jiya.
Su sayo su tebur tangaraye har kabod,
    Da gado katifu kumbuna har taliya,
Har ma da langogi gami da akwatuna,
    Duka an cika su da zannuwa mai walƙiya.
Wai ta yiwo kaya na salla ko biki
    Na ƙawarta ko na ɗiyar ƙawarta masoyiya.
Kuma sai a dinga zuga ta wai ita ce ta fi,
    Wai ta fi wance da wance sai kuma fariya.
To in ta aure ce mijinya sai tsaye
    Hidimar ƙawa duka na wuyansa gaba ɗaya.
In ko ya dage ya ƙi ɗauka kun jiya
    Karshenta ma wataran ta bar shi gaba ɗaya.
Ko ko ta faɗa bashe bashe na zannuwa
    Ta saye su fam biyu sai ta sai da fam ɗaya.
Ko tarkacen ɗakinta duk ta sayar da su,
    Ko ma ta faɗa lunguna bin rariya.
Don Allah mata sai a bar yin fariya,
    Ita dai ƙawa an so ta don ai dariya.
An so ta domin bai wa juna shawara,
    Ku yi zantukanku akan amana kun jiya.
Fitina idan ta samu sai ki taya mata,
    Ke ma idan kin samu kui ta gaba ɗaya.

                                                    (Unpublished MS)

I turn to you women who throw parties for your girlfriends,
    Listen to what I say.

There are those who waste money
  When they set about having a party for their friends.
They go and buy tables, dressers and cupboards,
  Beds, cushions, pots and food;
Dishes and boxes
  Full of glittering cloth.
She says she's bought things for the marriage of her best friend,
  Or the daughter of her favourite friend.
And people flatter her and say she's the one with the most,
  And she's got more than so-and-so, and it's all boasting.
If she marries a man then right away
  All the obligations to her friends are round his neck.
But if he digs in and says he will not take them on
  In the end one day she leaves him.
Or she'll get into debt over the cloth that
  She buys for two pounds and sells for one.
Even the little things in her room she'll sell,
  Or end up on the streets.
In God's name, women, stop competing with each other,
  Your friend is for laughing with.
You are there to give each other advice,
  Talk to each other trustingly.
If she's in difficulty help her,
  If you have a problem, face it together.

'Yar Shehu, while she does not imply that Europeanisation is the root cause
of the behaviour she criticizes, closely parallels Ibrahim Yaro Muhammed in
attacking the excesses occasioned by access to large amounts of cash. It is
not the throwing of parties for friends that is the problem; that is precisely
one of the ways in which the sharing which she applauds can take place, it is
rather the extremes to which people go which occasions the waste she attacks so vigorously. As with Ibrahim Yaro Muhammed she also talks of the
appropriate use of wealth in the same poem:

To za na koma kan manoma kun jiya,
  Su ma akwai wasu masu ɓarnata dukiya.
[Nomau] Ka gaya mini bara ka yi ɗari shida,
  Gero da dawa dammunanka gaba ɗaya;
Wake buhu nawa ne gyaɗa nawa ne duka,
  Kuma auduga nawa ne buhunsu gaba ɗaya.
To sai na gan ka a kantuna neman dako.

              .   .   .

To na sani nomau fa ba ka shan giya,
  Kuma caca ma na san ka ba ka yin ɗaya.
Don na ji ka ce wai hatsinka da auduga,

Har ma gyaɗa duka ka sayar su gaba ɗaya.
Ko ka sayo shanu na noma duk da su,
   Ko injunan noma ka huta ɗawainiya?
Ka ce da ni ka auri jikar ci tumu

       .   .   .

Tun can da farko ta gaya maka ba ta so,
   Ba ta ɓoye kome ta gaya maka gaskiya.
Kai ne ka nace duk kuɗinka ka ba da su,
   Wai dole ne sai ka yi ko da ta ƙiya.
To kun ga sharrin ƙin tsimi da tanadi.
   Ga dai abin da ya ja ma Nomau kun jiya
Matansa 'ya'ya ba abinci bare tufa,
   Kuma har garin ma ya baro shi gaba ɗaya.

(Unpublished MS)

Let me turn to the farmers,
   Among them there are some who squander money.
[Nomau] you said to me last year that all together
   You had six hundred sheaves of millet and guinea corn;
So many sacks of beans and so many of groundnuts
   And so many sacks of cotton all in all.
I saw you looking for people to transport it.

       .   .   .

Well, I know Nomau that you don't drink
   And you never gamble.
I heard you say you had sold
   All your corn and cotton and groundnuts.
Did you buy tilling-cattle with the money
   Or machinery so you could rest from your troubles?
You said to me you wanted to marry Ci-Tumu's granddaughter.

       .   .   .

Right from the start she said she didn't want to,
   She hid nothing, she told you the truth.
You it was who insisted and gave away all your money.
   You said you would not be deflected even though she refused.
So now you see the evil of refusing to use your money wisely.
   This is how Nomau, his wives and children
Have come to be without food or clothing,
   And, in the end, have had to leave town.

Here, it is precisely the waste of scarce resources and the inability to see the need to invest in future profitability which Alhajiya 'Yar Shehu attacks. For her the wish to marry another wife should have been a second priority after reinvestment in the farm to provide the income with which to support the increased family. A second theme, to which we will be returning later, is forced marriage. Alhajiya implies that an increase in wealth produces a greater ability to force a girl to marry against her will. Whether the institution of marriage has effectively undergone radical changes over the last twenty years I do not know. But the implication from a reading of the poems of Alhajiya 'Yar Shehu and Ibrahim Yaro Muhammed would seem to be that at one time, in the poet's view, a delicate balance obtained between a girl's wishes, a prospective husband's hard-earned cash and a life of productive labour. Whereas now, a girl's wishes are readily ignored in the face of large offers of money from rich men. Furthermore, a get-rich-quick lifestyle produces frequent divorce and greater prostitution.

Relations between men and women are not the only ones that have been damaged by rampant greed. In a poem entitled, *Wakar masu Gidan Haya* 'Song of the Landlords' Ibrahim Yaro Muhammed refers to the exorbitant demands of landlords,

Ga kuɗi nan tsababa an saka,
    Mai yawa a gidajen 'yan haya.
In mutum ya bukaci shiga kuwa
    Sai su zabga kuɗi don zai haya.
Wasu ko na wata shida za su sa,
    Shekara wasu za ka biya haya
In ka ce na wata uku ne da kai
    Ko wata huɗu ba sa ƙyaliya.
Yanzu ma ba sa son wai su bai
    Wa maza sai karuwa yin haya.
Wai sun fi biyan tsadar haya
    Sun ƙarfafa hanyar kauciya.

And the rents that are demanded
    are enormous.
If a man has no alternative but to find somewhere
    Then the price starts to go up.
Some will ask for six months rent,
    Others ask for a year;
If you say you can only pay for three months
    Or four, they won't accept it.
And these days they don't let
    To men, only to prostitutes.
Because, apparently, they can pay higher rents.
    They reinforce these evil practices.

While high rents are the main point of the attack here, it is clearly implied that it is the pressure upon available accommodation that is pushing prices up. Again the poem illustrates a further feature of urban migration and the

problems of life in the modern city. And in the same poem he talks of the
pressures that tenants live under:

An tsananta an kuma ƙuntata
    Wa mutane wanda suke haya.
Ba su damar miƙe ƙafufuwa,
    Su ji ɗan sakayau a gidan haya.

Tenants are pressurized
    And harassed,
No way can they relax
    And have peace of mind in a rented
    house.

In ka ce uffan to ka sani
    Kora ce ba wata tankiya.
In kana so ma a fitar da kai,
    In ka ƙi a ma ƙullalliya.

Breathe a word and you may be certain
    You will be out on the street.
If you agree then you are out,
    And if you refuse to go then you will
    be locked up.

Wasu masu gidan da ake haya
    Ba sa son wai girka abin miya.
Wai gudunsu na kar soro ya tsa-
    Ge ko ya baƙanta baƙaƙƙiya.
In mutum ko ya saɓa lokaci
    Kwana ɗaya ko biyu kun jiya
Sai su ce kwashe kayanka duk,
    Ka fice yanzun nan don tsiya.
In ka nemi a jinkirta maka
    Sai suke fafir su sun ƙiya.

Some landlords
    Prohibit cooking in their houses,
Saying they are afraid the roof
    Will crack or become too blackened.
If a tenant is late in payment
    By just a day or two,
Then they say, 'Take your things
    And get out now';
And if you look for a delay
    They will refuse point blank.

        (Unpublished MS)

While concentrating in the main upon exploitative landlords and government responsibility he also points out the obligations upon tenants,

Ku masu haya a gidan haya,
    Kar kui raini da ɗagauniya
Ga waɗanda ke su suka mallaka.
    Ku biya su kuɗinsu kuɗin haya.
In kun ƙi biya bisa ƙa'ida

Kun kauce hanyar gaskiya.

You who rent
    Must not treat badly
Those who own the property.
    Pay them their money,
If you refuse to pay according to the
    agreement
Then you have strayed from the true
    path.

        (Unpublished MS)

In the extracts earlier from the poem by Alhajiya 'Yar Shehu, money reared
its ugly head as a destructive influence in marriage and as a factor in the occurrence of forced marriage. Marriage forced upon a girl against her will is the
theme of a poem entitled, *Waƙar Soyayya da Kiyayya* 'Song of Love and Hate'
by Ibrahim Yaro Muhammed which contains the following gruesome story,

Na samu labari na auren ƙi da an
    Yi a cikin wanin ƙauyen ƙasar nan kun jiya.

Auren da an ce an yi ba so ko kaɗan,
   Aure irin na baƙar ƙiyayyar zuciya.
Kissa ta labarin budurwa ce ku san,
   An tilasa a gare ta aure kun jiya.
Ta nuna ƙiyayya baƙa kuma zahiri,
   Ga mijin na auren nata filla filliya.
Ta dai haƙurce duk da wannan tai lumus,
   Har dai ta kai ta haifu ɗa bisa gaskiya.
Kwana da tashi ɗansu ya kai har rarrafe,
   Tafiya yana yi har da zance ɗaiɗaya.
Wata ran abin ƙaddara mijin ya shingiɗe,
   Ta ba shi kalaci yana ci shi ɗaya.
Kuma daf da shi ga ɗansa ya zauna a gun,
   Sai yai tunanin al'ajab gun zuciya.
Ya ce da matar wance da ke ce kike
   Kina baƙin ƙi yanzu sai so bai ɗaya.
Ta ce da shi ni ba ni sonka haƙiƙatan,
   Bari wai ganin mun haifu ɗa bisa gaskiya.
Ta ce da shi zan nuna ƙina gunka nan,
   Domin ka san ƙin dai yana nan bai ɗaya.
Ta tashi ta zari wanga ɗa ta kwarangwatsa
   Shi akan ƙasa ya mace a gun ba motsiya.

                                        (Unpublished MS)

I heard of a marriage made in hatred
   In one of the villages of this land.
There was not the slightest love in this marriage,
   Based upon the blackest hatred.
It's a story of a girl's first marriage
   Forced upon her.
She showed a deep, deep hatred for the man
   Quite openly, she hid nothing.
But she bore with the marriage and in time
   She gave birth to a child.
The child crawled, then walked and reached
   The stage when it began to talk.
Then one day the husband was resting
   When she brought him food.
Nearby the boy was sitting.
   A thought struck him and he said to his wife,
'You used to say you detested me
   But now there is nothing but affection.'
She replied, 'I do not love you,
   No matter that we have a child.'

She said, 'I will show you how I hate you,
  So that you will know that the hatred is still there.'
She stood, lifted the child and threw it to the ground.
  There, without moving, the child died.

Marriage, the position of women and relations between men and women in
general are topics under constant discussion in contemporary Hausa society.
Alhajiya 'Yar Shehu has not, to the best of my knowledge, written directly
upon the subject. Ibrahim Yaro's position, like that of so many male poets,
is a generally conservative one, but one based upon the belief that there are
strict rights, duties and responsibilities upon men in their dealings with
women and vice versa. He has written a number of poems along these lines
that exhort women to behave in certain ways and which attack the position
of unmarried women. An introduction to alternative viewpoints can be
found in the four papers published as 'Part 4. Women's voices: feminine
gender in ritual, the arts and media' in Coles and Mack (1991). Another
major theme of contemporary didactic poetry is young people and the relations between parents and children. This time I quote from a poem by
Ibrahim Yaro Muhammed entitled, *Mu Kula da Tarbiyyar Yara Kanana*
'Let us Look to the Care of our Children',

Da yawa a yau yara ƙanana ba a ce
  Musu tak idan har ma suna taɓewa.
Kome yake so sai ya wo shi gaba gaɗi
  Ba mai kwaɓa tar don ya zam dainawa.
Zagin mutane yau ga yara ƙanƙana
  Ya zam abin wasa wajent furtawa.
Neman kuɗi, kai, ban kwabo, kai, ban ɗari!
  Gun ƙananan yara yana caɓewa.
Yawo na banza bin gidaje, lunguna,
  Gun ƙananan yara yana munewa.
Yawon farauta 'yan'uwa a cikin gari
  Duk rariya yaranmu suna tonewa.
Bibbin cikin juji da rana ƙwal tsaka,
  Sun zam kamar kazah wajen tonawa.
Wannan abubba wanda dukka na rattaba,
  Meye ya sa yara suke shukawa?
Amsar dalilin wanga zance ba musu,
  Sakacin iyaye ne ku zam ganewa.
Domin haƙiƙa da suna yin tarbiyyar
  Yaransu, na san ba su zam taɓewa.

                                              (Unpublished MS)

Often these days children are not rebuked
  If they go astray.

They do what they want quite brazenly,
    Nobody says a word to make him stop.
Insulting people has become
    A game for them.
They are after money, 'Give me a penny, give me a ha'penny'
    So say the little children.
Running wild from house to house and through the lanes,
    Leading the little ones astray.
Hunting, my friends, through the town,
    Digging in the gutters,
Going through the rubbish piles in broad daylight.
    They are like chickens scratching about.
And all these things I have described,
    Why are the children doing them?
There is no question that the answer is
    Because of the parent's lack of care.
For if they gave them training then
    I know their children would not go astray.

The image of children and their behaviour illustrates yet another aspect of contemporary urban life – children running wild, scavenging and becoming increasingly more estranged from their parents and less amenable to parental control. The whole question of the behaviour of the younger generation is of concern to both Ibrahim Yaro Muhammed and Alhajiya 'Yar Shehu and particularly they see drink and drugs as being major social problems. In *Wakar Giya, Roka da Wiwi da Kwaya* 'The Song of Drink, Speed, Cannabis and Barbiturates', Ibrahim Yaro says:

To sai bayani ga duk masu ƙwaya
Da masu sayarwa da sha bai ɗaya
Ku daina sayarwa kuna kauce hanya,
Tana sa ku hauka da hanyar mugunya,
    Ku daina sayarwa batun gaskiya.

Ku masu sha 'yan'uwana ku taru,
Don zan bayani na shanta da shairu.
Tana sa ku hauka a sa ku a turu
A kullum a ɗaure zugundum a turu,
    Kuna zage zage batun gaskiya.

Tana sa ku yawon da babu dalili,
Tana hana barci a kowane fili,
Kwaƙwalwa ta juye cikin wanga hali,
Tana haddasa muku cutar jidali,
    Da yawo da daddare baki ɗaya.

Kuna lafiya karnuka na ta binku,
Suna yin ta haushi a nan a gare ku,
Kun zam fa tamfar ɓarayi a ranku,
Nasiha fa ku masu sha jimlarku
    Ku daina gaba ɗaya baki ɗaya

Sukan ce tana ƙara ƙarfi gare su
Ko ko tunani take sa musu,
Waɗansu su ce wai tana himmata su,
Karya suke kar ku yarda batunsu
    Sun so su ɓad da ku ne ku jiya.

Mun san tana sa ku ci babu kima,
Tana sa yawan dariya ta nadama,
Tana sa ku bori da yin homa homa,
Ta maishe ku tamfar mutane kumama,
    Dukan masu shanta ku zam tambaya.

Sai ɗan bayani akan masu roka,
Kwayar da ke sa bugu har da hauka.
Tana sa yawan ƙyalƙyalar dariyarku,
Takan sanya barci kamar an saka ka
    A ɗaki da zuffa batun gaskiya.

Akwai wanda ya sha ta yasha gumi,
Ya bugu ya kwan cikin kwatami,
Ya sha ruwan kwatamin mai ko tsami,
Da ɗoyi da wari yana hamami,
    An fid da shi nan da sassafiya.
Tana sa su zancen da babu dalili,
Suna kai da kawon da babu muhalli,
Da yawo na banza nufinsu jidali,
Cikinsu akwai wasu ma wani hali,
    Suna haukacewa ga baki ɗaya.

Da dama cikin masu shan ita roka,
Idan ka gane su kamar masu iska,
Da tarin gizo mai yawa babu wanka
Sa'an nan fa ba ƙyaun gani nan kamarka
    Baƙaƙe da tsumma suke tafiya.

                                        (Unpublished MS)

Let me speak of the pill-poppers,
The pushers and the addicts,
Stop this trade,
It makes you mad and fall into evil ways,
    Stop selling them, I speak the truth.

You who swallow them, gather round
And I will explain why taking them is evil.
They make you crazy and you will be put in the stocks like a madman,
Forever shackled to the stocks,
    Swearing all the time, I speak the truth.

They make you forever on the move,
They prevent you from sleeping,
Your mind turns in this state,
And you become ill,
    Wandering through the night.

Dogs follow you
Barking at you,
As if you were a thief.
Let me advise you –
    Give it up completely.

They say it makes them stronger,
Or helps them to think,
Others say it motivates them.
They are lying, don't believe them,
    They want to lead you astray.

We know it makes you eat and eat,
And makes you laugh in remorse,
Act possessed and boast outrageously,
It makes you feeble,
    All of you who take it.

Now let me explain the barbiturate takers,
The pills that intoxicate and send mad.
They bring on sudden uncontrollable laughter,
And send you to sleep
    As if you had been placed in a hot, hot room.

Some of them break out into a sweat when drugged,
Like a drunk they spend the night in the gutter,
Drinking in the bitter gutter-water,
Filthy and stinking,
    And then are dragged out in the morning.

The drug makes nonsense of their speech,
They come and go without purpose,
Wandering constantly looking for trouble.
Among them are those
    Who finally go mad.

Many who are on drugs
Are as if possessed,
Covered in cobwebs and unwashed.
They make a foul sight
    As they pass by in filthy rags.

The poem is directed specifically at drug abuse, but forms part of a broader
picture in which overcrowding, unemployment and the weakening of family
ties are interrelated factors along with drug abuse in the urban social decline
so clearly of concern to the poet.

    In these extracts we have moved from the young who would normally still
be under the control of their parents to the young men and women in their
twenties and thirties who gravitate to the cities and who constitute the army
of labourers living a marginal existence in the markets, lorry parks and on
building sites. The precarious nature of their existence is commented upon
by Alhajiya 'Yar Shehu in an extract below, but before we come to that let us
look at the way in which they are typically identified in a poem entitled, *Wakar
marasa Mutumci* 'Song of the Indecent Ones' by Ibrahim Yaro Muhammed:

Yaranmu duk sun ɗau ɗabi'un ɓaci,
    Sun bar ɗabi'o'inmu duk na mutumci.
Adar Nasara suke suna Turanci,
    Wai kansu ya waye fasun sam 'yanci.
Wando da ƙaton bel kamar ɗamaranci,
    Wando da lawurje fa wai ya ɓaci.
Duk riguna duk namu masu karamci
    Wasu ba su sawa sai na zamanci.
Sai kwat da wando wanda ke cacanci
Rigarsu duk ƙirjinsu ya yi tsiraici,
    Wandonsu sai sharar ƙasa ya ɓaci.
In ka yi zance nan akan Hausanci,
    Wai su su ce su sai ka zam Turanci.
Ko ko suna Hausar suna Turanci,
Sun mance harshen Hausa mai inganci.
Ni shawarata don mu samo 'yanci
    Mu riƙe dukan adarmu kada ta ɓaci.

(Unpublished MS)

Young people have taken up evil ways,
    They have abandoned all our respected traditions.
They have adopted European customs and speak English
    To indicate their worldly wisdom and their liberation.
Trousers they wear with a great big belt like a shield.
    They say their drawstring-trousers are broken.
They no longer wear our traditional clothes,

Only these modern clothes.
Preferring a jacket and trousers.
Their shirts expose their chests,
    And their trousers brush the ground.
If you speak to them in Hausa,
    They tell you to speak in English.
Or else they move from Hausa to English and back again,
    They have forgotten the importance of the Hausa language.
My advice if we are to look for liberation
    Is to hold hard to our traditions and not let them die.

The key characteristics, as far as Ibrahim Yaro Muhammed is concerned, are the visual markers of dress and deportment and the use of English combined with a conscious rejection of the Hausa language and traditions. For him the liberation so assiduously sought by the young should be obtained through rejecting rather than embracing Western styles and values. While this poem is addressed both to these young people, and to a wider audience as comment, the riposte to these remarks is, in a sense, the non-verbal statements provided precisely by the visual markers of dress. This type of message is appropriate for the written poetic form – younger poets writing in the same circle adopt a similar moral stance toward their contemporaries – other types of communication are used to reply.

    Closely related to the problems of young people in the mind of Alhajiya 'Yar Shehu is the question of the function of education in Hausa society and in the poem from which I am quoting here, *Wakar Gargadi*, written in the early 1970s, she talks at length first of restricted access to education and then the general problem of the effects of producing large numbers of young people with a relatively low level of formal education:

Duka ɗaliban da suke ƙasashen duniya
    Daga nan ƙasarmu tsaya ku bincika gaskiya.
In an kasa su ɗari, kashi casa'in duka
    'Ya'yan sarakai ko abokan dukiya.
Su ne aka tura su don neman sani,
    Haka nan abin yake ko a kowace nahiya.
'Ya'yan manoma ba su samun ci gaba
    Ko sun yo ƙwazo sai a yo musu murɗiya.
Ita gaskiya ɗaci gare ta ku tabbata,
    Amma idan an bi ta ba'a shan wuya.

Hayye iye nanaye ayyururuy yuruy

        . . .

    Kai me ya sa Kosau kake yin dariya?
Ka ce da ni an kai ka har ga uban gari,
    Wai ka ƙi ba da su Tanko har da Magajiya

Aka tilasa ka ka ba da su aka kai gari,
   Wai don su yo ilmi ka huta ɗawainiya.
Aikinka noma ka ga su ba su san shi ba,
   Su sai zama bisa kan kujera ka jiya.
Ka kai su sun gama da Piramare sun fita,
   Kuma an hana su shiga Coleji gaba ɗaya.
Har ma da Certificate Piramare sun gama,
   Kuma an rubuta sun yi passing kun jiya.
Sai anka ce musu wai akwai interview
   Interview nan ne akai musu murɗiya.
Sai anka ja su aka hau su da tambaya,
   Ko sun ci ma ai dole ne sai an biya.
To kun ga Kosau babu wanda ya san da shi,
   Kuma bai da kurɗi wanda zai yi murɗiya.
Gona guda ɗaya ga shi 'ya'ya sha biyar,
   Kuma ban da noman ba sana'a ko ɗaya.
To kun ga Tanko Magajiya duka sun rasa
   Don babu wanda ya san ubansu a duniya.
Daga nan su Mallam Tanko sai a shige gari,
   An bar uwa da uba da ɓacin zuciya.
Daga nan a faɗa kantuna har campuna,
   Har ofisoshi babu aiki ko ɗaya.
Ilmin su Tanko bai wuce na Piramare,
   Su 'yan Coleji suke buƙata kun jiya.
To kun ga shi bai zauna gun babansa ba
   Kuma nan a birnin babu aiki ko ɗaya.
Irinsu ba su ƙidayuwa a Nijeriya,
   Su yiwo Piramare ba sana'a ko ɗaya.
To kun ga guntun ilmi ba shi da fa'ida,
Kuma shi yake da yawa a nan Nijeriya.

(Unpublished MS)

Of all our students away studying in other lands,
   Far away from our country, check it and it's true,
Eighty per cent of them
   Are the sons of the aristocracy or of the wealthy.
They are the ones sent to find knowledge
   And so it is in all parts of this land.
The sons of the peasantry receive no advancement,
   If they try for it they are pushed down.
Truth is bitter, of that you may be certain,
   But to pursue it is only right.

Hayye iye nanaye ayyururuy yuruy

.   .   .

Why, Kosau, do you laugh?
You say to me you were taken right to the chief
    Because you refused to let your children Tanko and Magajiya go to
    school.
You were forced to allow them to be taken to town,
    To be educated and thus relieve you of your labours.
Your work is farming, but they know nothing about it,
    They can only sit around on chairs.
You take them and they finish primary school and are out,
    But they are prevented from going to college.
They have a 'Primary Certificate',
    And a 'Pass' is there inscribed.
They are told there will be an interview
    And it is there that all is lost.
They are bombarded with questions
    And even if they pass they must still pay up.
But, you see, Kosau has no one who knows of him,
    And he has no money with which to meet the demands.
He has one field and fifteen children,
    And apart from farming he has no other trade.
So, you see, both Tanko and Magajiya lose out
    Because no one knows their father.
Those like Tanko set off for town,
    And leave mother and father desolate in heart.
Round they go from shops to companies and offices
    Where there is no work at all.
Those like Tanko stopped at primary –
    They want college boys.
He did not stay with his father
    But here in the city there is no work at all.
The likes of Tanko are uncountable in Nigeria,
    They go through primary and are without a trade.
So, you see, a little knowledge is useless
    And there is a great deal of that here in Nigeria.

Alhajiya's critique of the implementation of educational policies during the
early 1970s raises many questions concerning Nigeria since Universal Primary
Education and places the debate about education first, in the context of the
flight from the land and the consequent scarcity of agricultural labour; and
second, in the context of the dislocation of family life and social control brought
about by the flight of the young to the cities. Where school leavers have, as they
inevitably will, a firm expectation of a job with a wage, what is the role of education in a society which needs to rely heavily upon its agricultural production?

Directly related to the plight of the half-educated in Alhajiya 'Yar Shehu's poem are the urban unemployed,

To shugabanni ya kamata ku waiwaya,
    Kui taimako gun wanda ba su da dukiya.
'Ya'yansu jikokinsu duk ku kula da su,
    In sun yi ƙwazo kar ku bar su su sha wuya.
Haka nan sana'o'i ku buɗe kamfuna,
    Har wanda za su wadaci 'yan Nijeriya.
Don ga tulin ƙatti biris ba ayyuka
    Sai tura kura ba sana'a ko ɗaya.
Haka kasuwoyi sai ka gan su da gammuna,
    Neman dako domin su samu abin miya.

To sai mu koma kan batun ƙattin da ke
    Zube ba sana'ar yi a nan Nijeriya.
In an buɗe ma'aikata ɗaya kun sani
    Ka tad da ƙato fin ɗari tun safiya.
In sun yi sa'a ma a ɗauki kamar biyar,
    Sauran a ce musu babu aiki kun jiya.
In ko ka ratsa inda ke raba ayyuka,
    Office na Labour don ka huta tambaya
Ka tad da manya har samari ga su nan,
    Domin biɗar aiki a kowace safiya.

                                   (Unpublished MS)]

Leaders of our country, you must look behind you,
    And help those who own no wealth.
You must care for their children and their grandchildren.
    If they are doing their best, don't leave them to suffer hardship.
Open new industries and new businesses
    That will enrich Nigerians.
For there are vast numbers of strong young men without work,
    All they can do is push barrows, they have no trade.
And in the markets you will see them with their headpads,
    Looking for portering jobs to make enough to eat.

Let us return to the matter of the strong young men
    Who are churned out without work here in Nigeria.
If a factory has recently opened
    You will see more than a hundred of them waiting from early in the morning.
If they are lucky then about five will be taken on,
    And to the rest they say there is no work.
If you go directly to where work is given out,
    The Labour Office, no longer to have to search,

You will find young and old there,
  Looking for work each day.

                                                    (Unpublished MS)

Alhajiya goes on to call on Nigerians to found the companies that will create the employment so badly needed.

Broadly speaking, these extracts produce a grim view of urban life in Kano. Young people with a small amount of Western education and a large appetite for Western consumer goods pouring into the cities, moving from an environment in which kin relations assist with the education of children, the provision of housing, and the regulation of marriage and labour relations to an urban environment where housing is difficult to obtain, children slip from the control of their parents, differences between the rich and the poor are greater and more obvious, and the drifting, isolated young turn to drink, drugs and a general rejection of the cultural milieu from which they originate.

In the circumstances of modern Nigeria where change is taking place very rapidly and a bewildering variety of new social phenomena are being thrown up, the poet, as we have seen through the work of these last two writers, typically maintains the dominant characteristic of the form: an overwhelming didacticism representing something close to the core of Hausa culture, a willingness and a sense of obligation to rethink the world into a framework that, I suggest, is seen as representing truth and enduring societal values.

NOTES

INTRODUCTION

1. The economist Alan Frishman estimates that from the 1991 census results for Nigeria and World Bank figures for other countries of West Africa, the Hausa-speaking population of West Africa is in excess of 50 million. This figure covers both mother-tongue speakers from the southern parts of the Republic of Niger and from the states of Sokoto, Kebbi, Katsina, Kano, Jigawa, Bauchi, Kaduna, Niger and Plateau in Nigeria, as well as second- and third-language speakers in both these same regions and in other parts of West Africa (personal communication).

2. For a discussion of Hausa society in Niger, see, for example, Baier (1980), Dunbar (1970; 1977), Echard (1978; 1989), Fuglestad (1983), Monfouga-Nicolas (1972), and G. Nicolas (1975).

3. There is a very extensive literature on the history of the Hausa states, but see, for example, D. M. Last (1967) on Sokoto; Y. B. Usman (1981) on Katsina; M. G. Smith (1960) on Zaria; and (1978) on Daura; Abdullahi Smith (1987) and M. Adamu (1978) on the Hausa states more generally; Nadama (1977) on Zamfara, Y. A. Aliyu (1974) on Bauchi; and Barkindo (1983) and Fika (1978) on Kano.

4. There is an extensive literature on economic relations between town and country and on the production and trade in agricultural commodities. See, for example, P. Hill (1972; 1977) and Hogendorn (1978).

5. Each new state produces a new set of bureaucracies providing employment for school leavers and graduates, new development opportunities for local communities and, above all, a separate slice of the federal cake.

6. See, for example, Watts (1987) and Williams (1976).

7. See, for example, Callaway (1987), Coles (1983), Coles and Mack (1991), Pittin (1979; 1983), Schildkrout (1982) and Trevor (1975).

8. For discussion of the process of 'becoming Hausa' see, for example, Salamone (1975a), and on the constitution of Hausa communities see Olofson (1976).

9. Classic studies of the invention of tradition are to be found in Hobsbawm and Ranger (1983).

CHAPTER 1

1. *Ajami* implies a language other than Arabic written in the Arabic script.

2. There is a large body of scholarship directed at the issue of the characteristics of oral style as against written style in many cultures around the world. A particularly influential figure in this field was Milman Parry whose study of the oral characteristics of Homeric verse was the cornerstone of much later work, for example by his student, Albert Lord and others. See, for example, Lord (1960; 1991) and Foley (1988).

3. See Goody (1968; 1987) and Ong (1982).
4. See, for example, Barkow (1970; 1973).
5. For an overview of 'Hausa society' see also M. G. Smith (1965; 1969).
6. See, for example, P. Hill (1976; 1977) and Lovejoy (1978; 1981; 1983; 1988).

CHAPTER 2

1. An English-language graded school-reader edition was published in 1971 by
   NNPC with the title *The Water of Cure*. The present discussion uses that title, but
   refers to the original Hausa text.
2. There is a traditional tale entitled 'Ruwan bagaja' which tells a rather different
   story of a despised girl whose visit to a well produces great and wondrous advantages while her spoilt sister's subsequent jealous visit produces calamity. See M.
   Y. Mohammed (1985).
3. East repeated in print that he thought Abubakar Imam had a real gift for story-
   telling (East 1936a) but did not elaborate further.
4. The quest theme in early Hausa novels is discussed in Sule (1986). The quest is
   a very common form worldwide. Westley (1986a), in discussing this idea in relation to Hausa tales and prose-writing, quotes Joseph Campbell on a 'universal
   monomyth' as narrative model: 'A hero sets forth from the world of common day
   into a region of supernatural wonder: fabulous forces are there encountered and
   a decisive victory is won: the hero comes back from this mysterious adventure with
   the power to bestow boons on his fellow man' (quoted in Westley 1986a: 146).
5. Westley (n.d.) relates this rivalry to a traditional Hausa story about the rivalry
   between a Katsina man and a Kano man.
6. Westley sees the episodic nature of this part of the story as one of its weaknesses.
   'These episodes, essentially unrelated to the two sets of conflicts and resolutions
   that begin and end the work, are so loosely linked that they could be rearranged
   in a completely different order with no effect on narrative continuity ... The
   result, in this case, is an episodic and poorly integrated work that is neither able
   to manipulate the advantages of orality nor the potentials of literacy' (Westley
   n.d.).
7. For discussion of oral influences on these early prose texts in Hausa see, for
   example, A. A. Abdullahi (1987), A. Magaji (1982) and Westley (1986a).
8. East repeated these sentiments in print, 'Malam Abubakar is a young Higher
   College graduate. He is one of the few who has not lost, through an intensive
   education in English, the power to express himself in his own language, and has
   already written a number of excellent books of fiction. He has, in fact, a natural
   genius for writing, and exactly the lively literary temperament which is needed
   for this kind of work. He can make the most unpromising material into a readable
   and witty article' (East 1940: 89).
9. All manuscripts submitted were published and 'prize money', such as it was, was
   distributed to all four authors (East, personal interview, June 1974).
10. An English-language graded school-reader edition was published in 1971 by
    NNPC with the title *The Adventures of the Warrior Gandoki*. A further English
    graded reader in the same series was produced in 1971 of a prose work, *Iliya Dan
    Maikarfi*, by Ahmadu Ingawa, first published in Hausa in 1951.
11. Later the first prime minister of independent Nigeria.
12. An English translation, with the same title, by Mervyn Hiskett was published by
    Longman in 1967. The story was reworked as a play in 1972 by Umaru Ladan
    and Dexter Lyndersay (first performed in December 1972 through the Centre
    for Nigerian Cultural Studies, Ahmadu Bello University, with a film version

being made of that production) and published as a Hausa playscript in 1974 by NNPC.

13. It is possible that East, in editing these first texts, worked to a target number of pages since they all come in at between 45 and 50 pages in the early editions. Cosentino (1978: 20) indicates that East had a target of 20,000 words, the same target he set for Imam in writing to him on 9 October 1934.

14. This translation of the title is from Piłaszewicz (1985: 221) and Skinner (1971a: 172).

15. Later printings of the book dropped East's name from the cover sheets. Precisely what East's role was remains unclear. On the evidence of his letters quoted above he must at least have been a zealous editor. John Tafida was working at the Literature Bureau with East while the story was being written.

16. For a discussion of bravery and bravado in this and in other early novels see Iliya (1992). F. Othman (1981) discusses in detail the prose style of *Gandoki*.

17. Referred to in Skinner (1971a: fn 5); Cosentino (1978: 24) refers to 'speculation' by Skinner which is not speculation, but information drawn from the same interview.

18. In the English-language reader an additional closure is effected by returning to the children asking about Gandoki's experiences. They laugh and say they don't believe it. I have been unable to find a Hausa edition that includes any such final section.

19. Having related the progress of the flight of his people from the British when he was 11 or 12, Bello Kagara confirms that the origin of the story, the 'reason for writing it', was their being driven out by the British (unpublished interview, November 1969).

20. The form need not be epithetically short, and Powe would claim that praise is not the primary characteristic of *kirari* (see Powe 1984: 336–7).

21. A further connection lies in the way in which the hero, Shaihu Umar, living in Rauta near where Abubakar Tafawa Balewa came from, proclaims his origins to have been much further west in Kagara, the actual birthplace of the two other authors, Abubakar Imam and his brother, Bello Kagara.

22. A comparison of the novel and the play is to be found in S. U. Dahiru (1984). In addition to the discussion of Shaihu Umar in Kirk-Greene (1974) and Westley (1986a) there are comments in Aba'ali (1982), and a comparison between *Shaihu Umar* and *The Travels of Hajji Baba* (translated from the English of James Morier) in La'ah (1972).

23. Cosentino goes on to suggest that *Shaihu Umar* is a 'literary dead end', postulating, in 1978, that '*Shaihu Umar* is likely to remain a singular example of successful prose homily in Hausa' (1978: 22). As we will see later in this chapter, prose homily did not die with *Shaihu Umar*, and is alive and well.

24. Except in one place where one of the thieves is able to perform astounding feats.

25. *Jiki Magayi* has not been translated into English. However, the story was paraphrased in English, without acknowledgement, by Cyprian Ekwensi as *An African Night's Entertainment*, see Skinner (1973).

26. A number of translations into Hausa extracted from these anthologies appeared as separate publications. In 1931, for example, *Tanimuddari* and *Saiful Muluki*, being stories from the *Thousand and One Nights*, were published under separate cover (see I. Y. Yahaya 1988/9: 79).

27. For a fuller indication of the publication of writings in Hausa covering the period see Baldi (1977) and I. Y. Yahaya (1988a).

28. Piłaszewicz, on the other hand, reports the work of Jez (1986) to the effect that in *Magana Jari Ce*:

11 stories are from *Thousand and One Nights*
2 stories are from the Indian collection *Panchatantra*
5 stories from a Persian version of the Indian collection Sukasaptati
1 story is of Persian origin
14 fables are from the brothers Grimm
2 fables are from Hans Andersen
7 short stories from *Decameron* by Boccaccio
1 based on a Biblical story
1 based on a Greek myth about the king of Macedonia
1 based on a fable by W. Hauff
34 stories were either original or derived from unknown sources

(Piłaszewicz, personal communication)

29. Analysts of the Hausa language have studied Abubakar Imam's writings extensively. Major studies of Imam's writings from a literary point of view have included those by Pweddon (1977), Westley (1986) and I. Y. Yahaya (1988/9).

30. The point is also made by Wali (1976: 17).

31. The date of the change of name from Translation Bureau to Literature Bureau is unclear. East (personal communication, 1974) placed it in 1934 (Furniss 1977: 27), I. Y. Yahaya (1988: 95) says 1933, but letters from East to Imam are still headed 'Translation Bureau' in 1935 (Mora 1989: 25).

32. A number of articles relating to the history of the Gaskiya Corporation are brought together in Hayatu (1991) along with additional information on people who have worked with the Corporation over the years. The central relationship between East and Imam, which was close and intense, is graphically illustrated through a dispute that erupted over working conditions. The relevant correspondence is reprinted in Hayatu (1991) from a chapter in Mora (1989).

33. For a survey of the kinds of material, including religious works, poetry, school books, history and books in other languages, as well as imaginative prose produced by Gaskiya and its successor NORLA, see Skinner (1970b).

34. An English-language graded-reader version was published by NNPC in 1971.

35. NORLA, with a number of divisions covering such areas as vernacular literature and school books, originated within the colonial government's adult education programme under the directorship of Wilfred Jeffries. The impetus came from Governor Sharwood-Smith, but Jeffries hived off everything except literacy classes into NORLA until excessive spending produced a crisis, as had also happened in East's time (A. Neil Skinner, personal communication).

36. Over the years there have been a number of translations into Hausa of Russian stories, published by the Progress Publishing House, Moscow, among others. For more details see Baldi (1977).

37. The dating of first publication given here varies considerably from dates given in I. Y. Yahaya (1988a). Where I have not been able to check first editions I have relied on Baldi (1977). In addition to these titles there were a number of privately published works that appeared at this time, such as *Duniya Tumbin Giwa Ce* 'The World is the Belly of an Elephant', published by its author Ibrahim Yaro Muhammed in 1975.

38. The moral qualities of the central character, Salihi, are discussed in S. Abdu (1985).

39. Modern influences in this generation of novels are discussed in Amina (1987).

40. The translation of the title *Kitsen Rogo* (lit. 'the fat on the cassava') is adopted from Piłaszewicz (1991/2: 30).

41. The condition of city life as portrayed in *Kitsen Rogo* is discussed in Ajiya (1985).

42. *Jiki Magayi* and *So Aljannar Duniya* are compared in Ubah (1989).

43. Piłaszewicz (1988c) discusses the novels of Sulaiman Ibrahim Katsina and provides some biographical information on him.
44. Translations from *Tura Ta Kai Bango* are adapted from an unpublished translation by Furniss, Green and Smith.
45. For a discussion of radical writing in the journal *Fitila* during the early 1980s see Furniss (1990).
46. See Hayatu (1991: 184–90).
47. See Furniss (1977: Chs 1 and 2; 1985) for a discussion of the economic and social background to the publishing of poetry in Hausa.
48. These organisations and others are discussed in I. Y. Yahaya (1988a: 195–200).
49. In 1993 the group consisted of the woman writer, Hajiya Balaraba Ramat (titles include *Alhaki Kwikwiyo* 'Retribution is Like a Puppy, It Follows its Owner', *Wa Zai Auri Jahila?* (2 vols) 'Who Would Marry an Ignorant Woman?', *Budurwar Zuciya* 'The Heart's Desire'), and the men, Dan Azumi Baba (titles include *Rikicin Duniya* 1, 2 and 3 'This Deceptive World', *Kyan Alkawari* 'The Good Promise', *Amintacciyar Soyayya* 'True Love', *Idan Ungulu ta Biya Bukata* 'When the Vulture is Happy'); Aminu Abdu Na'inna (titles include *So Marurun Zuciya* 1, 2 and 3 'Love is a Blister on the Heart', *Kauna Adon Zuciya* 'Love is the Heart's Decoration); and Ado Ahmad (titles include *In da So Da Kauna* 1 and 2 'When There is Love and Affection', *Hattara dai Masoya* 1 and 2 'Lovers Take Care', *Masoyan Zamani* 'Modern Lovers'), among others.
50. Abba Rufa'i indicates that some 85 titles have been recently acquired for the library of the Centre for the Study of Nigerian Languages, Bayero University (personal communication). An interesting further dimension to the 'do-it-yourself' movement in cultural production has been the emergence of a cottage industry in home-made video films which are then copied on vhs machines and sold through stalls in city and small-town markets (Barry Burgess, personal communication).

CHAPTER 3

1. See Hair (1969).
2. See I. Y. Yahaya (1988a: 36–42) for discussion of Hausa poetry attributed to the seventeenth-century scholars, Wali ɗan Marina and Wali ɗan Masani.
3. Many of the original manuscripts with accompanying transliterations in Edgar's own hand are in the National Archives in Kaduna. The Frank Edgar collection is listed as o/AR 2 and the Alder Burdon collection as o/AR 1. The author of a manuscript is frequently listed as *b. ulama'u*, Arabic 'some malams'.
4. Other volumes of translated Hausa stories include Johnston (1966), Rattray (1913) and Tremearne (1913) as well as a number of volumes in Russian translated by Olderogge, Bykova, Laptuhin and others. More recent collections include Pucheu (1982) and the collections of tales in the doctoral dissertations of S. B. Ahmad (1986), Stephens (1981) and Westley (1986a).
5 See Hallam (1966) for a discussion of the problems faced by historians when working with legendary narratives, and Hiskett (1967b) for the way in which stories of Islam percolate into the oral tradition. Hiskett distinguishes between stories about animals and stories about people, concentrating particularly upon stories relating to the coming of Islam and relations between indigenous Hausa people and outsiders. Hunwick (1991) discusses Arabic historical chronicles and the various oral versions of local 'history' in Kano.
6. Dutse (1981) uses *almara* to imply funny, non-real stories. The only distinction between *almara* and *tatsuniya* being that the former are funny and short. Katsina

(1984) uses the phrase *labarun raha* 'amusing stories'. Dutse relates a number of *almara* including the story about the European who went to the market to buy eggs. He bought a bowl of good quality eggs but needed someone to carry them home for him. Seeing a youth passing by he called him over and gestured to him to carry the bowl of eggs and follow him. In Hausa the youth asked him whether he wanted him to carry them on his head. The European said, 'Yes.' (In Hausa the verb *yas*, pronounced like the English *yes*, means 'to throw away'). The youth asked for confirmation that he really should *yas*. Assuming the youth to be rather slow in following his instructions, the European said 'Yes.' Nonplussed at this strange command, the youth flung the bowl of eggs to the floor!

7. This usage is also employed in A. Magaji (1982). Dangambo (1984b: 16) gives an example of a dilemma tale as follows. A boy and girl live in villages separated by a river. Madly in love the boy is accompanying the girl home to her village late one night. Arriving at the river bank, the boy says he will swim across to fetch a canoe in which to carry her across. Half-way across he is attacked by a huge crocodile and only just manages to make it to the opposite bank. Pulling himself out of the water he turns back to see, by the light of the moon, his lover being attacked by a leopard. What would you do in his shoes? Go back to rescue her risking death from the crocodile or leave her to the leopard?

A common form for such puzzles is illustrated by the problem of getting a hyena, a goat and corn across the river in a canoe which will only hold one at a time, when the hyena would eat the goat, and the goat eat the corn if they were left together on a river bank.

8. Other people are deploying the same terms. *Almara* and *kissa* as used by Kankiya and Sayaya (1987) conform to these definitions. Further presentation of these and other terms to the secondary-school population is to be found in the widely used textbooks by I. Y. Yahaya et al. (1992).

9. Nasr (1982) discusses the various characteristics, both good and bad, of the *malam* as represented in a number of tales. He points to the ambiguities that exist in the association, within tales, between the *malam* and Islam.

10. Karaye (1982) examines the binary systems of relationship that obtain among animals within the world of tales: predatory/non-predatory, weak/strong, light/heavy, killing by choice/killing by accident, among others. He relates these features to the nature of Hausa social relations in a society essentially divided into an aristocracy and a peasantry.

11. Gizo is often rendered as 'spider' because of the similarity between his name and *gizo-gizo*, the word for a spider. However, this view is contested, as will be evident later in this chapter.

12. Paulme (1976) discusses this and other patterns within African oral narratives. Much work has been done on the structure of oral narratives, originating with the work of Propp (1968); see Bauman (1986) and Cancel (1989), among others.

13. A major scholarly endeavour has produced a worldwide index of tale types and motifs that occur across many cultures around the world (see, for example, Aarne and Thompson 1961; Azzolina 1987; and Thompson 1955–8). Stories exemplifying common motifs are sometimes seen as representing the results of cultural diffusion and sometimes as reflective of similar discourse about the essential problems of human existence: inequality, human nature, illness; and the transitions that many societies mark in one way or another: birth, childhood, adulthood, initiation, old age, death. Bichi (1978; 1979a) has annotated a collection of Hausa folktales according to the motif indexes and tale types. Hiskett (1967b) discusses the long traditions of narrative behind the Arabic and other sources, linking Hausa stories to the motif indexes and to these ancient traditions.

14. This may be true of urban northern Nigerian culture but Stephens (1981) reports in relation to Niger that men participated more in the performance of tales.
15. The telling of tales relies upon a relaxed atmosphere between teller and audience. Hausa relations between parents and children can be quite formal (termed in Hausa *kunya* 'shame/modesty') with the result that it is quite often an older member of the household, a grandmother or aunt who tells stories to grandchildren or lateral relatives. A performance is usually during the evening after the evening meal. D. M. Haruna (1986) reports that if a *tatsuniya* is to be told during the day, then first the teller must *daure Gizo* 'tie up Gizo' which involves taking a hair of the head and throwing it up on to the straw roof of the nearest hut. Katsina (1984) says the same, adding that if this is not done then members of the audience will get lost on their way home. The contract between teller and audience, and the transition into and out of the tale are marked by variants of the introductory call and response: *ga ta ga ta nan* 'here it is, here it is' – *ta zo mu ji ta* 'let it come so we can hear it', and at the end there is a phrase pronounced by the teller to effect closure such as: *kunkurus kan kusu* 'off with the rat's head/end of story'.
16. Ibrahim Yaro Yahaya (interview, September 1989.).
17. Stephens (1981) sees the debate entrenched in the variety of meanings inherent in key symbols. She takes four core metaphors, the horse, disguised marriage partners, Dodo (the monster), and water and examines them as social metaphors exploring their many significances in some fifty-five tales recorded by her in Niger.
18. A version of 'Ta Kitse' was recorded in 1970 in Kano by I. Y. Yahaya (1972) and was the subject of his paper that examined aspects of performance style (Rufa'i 1982). This version was the subject of further discussion (Stephens 1984) which examined the symbolic elements within the tale and the parallel patterning within its episodes. An English translation (by I. Y. Yahaya) of that same version appears in Westley (1986a: 286–307) along with another version recorded on another occasion. Rufa'i's discussion is based upon a summary version in Hausa.
19. The role of Gizo in mediating a variety of contradictions in the ideology of Hausa tales is discussed in M. Karaye (1979).
20. M. Karaye (1984) points to the erroneous identification of 'Gizo' with 'spider'; Westley (1986a: 157) points to the fact that in a number of societies the spider trickster is not identified by audiences as a spider.
21. Skinner (1980: 51–101) outlines the shared core of a number of versions of the same tale while also considering the significance of variability, specifically in the cases of of four versions of 'The Girl who Married a Dodo', six versions of the 'Tar-baby', and four versions of 'The Promise to the Dodo'.

CHAPTER 4

1. There are a number of collections of Hausa 'proverbs'. From the '6,407 proverbs' in the Alder Burdon files at the National Archives in Kaduna comes the published collection by Whitting (1940); further collections were published by Prietze (1904), Kirk-Greene (1966) and Yunusa (1977), among others. In the study of oral literature the issue of considering the proverb in actual contexts of usage rather than as disembodied utterances is strongly argued. As far as I am aware, there are no case studies of actual usage in Hausa other than that by Salamone (1976). Gouffé (1981) has commented upon some of the methodological issues relating to the collection of proverbs in Hausa. A recent doctoral dissertation (Jang 1994) considers the prevalence of formal patterns in Hausa proverbs.

2. Salamone (1976) describes the role of proverbial utterances in the everyday contestations between men and women over expected roles and behaviour, working from observations of conflict between husbands and wives in Yauri, in the northwest of Nigeria.

3. Regularly repeated frames, such as those employing 'X *maganin* Y', are listed and discussed by M. B. Hassan (1982) and Yunusa (1982). Information on sentence types in *karin magana*, as well as on what Hausa people think *karin magana* are for and who uses them, is provided by C. Y. Garba (1982).

4. In one of the early collections of Hausa literature, *karin magana* that could be used as *habaici* were asterisked (Whitting and Haɗeja 1931). Gani (1984) and Waya (1990) examine phrases that are commonly deployed as *habaici* and *zambo*.

5. Some commentators (S. Ahmed 1984; Besmer 1973; A. U. Kafin-Hausa 1985; King 1967) use *take* for the instrumental phrase and *kirari* for the vocal phrase, using *waka* for the extended text in which such phrases are deployed. Powe (1984) uses *take* for the short phrase, whether vocal or instrumental, *kirari* for the longer text and *waka* for the product of performances by professional musicians. I. Bello (1985: 19) distinguishes between *take* attached to offices and *kirari* attached to individuals.

6. For a detailed discussion of Hausa musical instruments see Ames and King (1971), Kofoworola and Lateef (1987) and Besmer (1971).

7. Syllable weight is the crucial variable in the metrical system of Hausa poetry, as we shall see in a later chapter, and rests upon the fact that only three types of syllable occur in Hausa words: cv (consonant + short vowel), cvv (consonant + long vowel or diphthong), or cvc (consonant + short vowel + consonant). This three-term system resolves itself, as far as rhythm in poetry is concerned, into a two-term system of light versus heavy in which cvv and cvc are both classed as heavy syllables. When drums mark out the rhythm of speech, then, they pick up the 'lights' and 'heavies' in single or double beats.

8. The phenomenon is by no means exclusively Hausa. The English phrase 'float like a butterfly, sting like a bee' was inextricably bound up with the persona and fame of the boxer, Mohammed Ali, in very much the same way as famous Hausa boxers have their catch-phrases. In Yoruba culture identificatory-epithets piled high one upon another is an art form of great complexity and density, known in Yoruba as *oriki*; see Barber (1991). Things other than people can have epithets attached to them. Abubakar Ahmed (1980: 50) lists *kirari* for places, for example:

Kano ta Dabo ga mata ga mota	Dabo's Kano, full of women and cars
Ikko ikon Allah, sama ruwa kasa	God's only Lagos, water everywhere,
ruwa	above and below

and for animals:

nagge daɗi goma	cow with ten qualities
damo sarkin hakuri	monitor lizard the ever-patient
giwa karya itace cimarka itace	elephant the tree-breaker and tree-eater
kwaɗo ba ka mura, ba ka ciji kowa ba	frog that never catches cold or bites
sauro sa mutum ya mari jikinsa	mosquito that makes man slap himself
agwagwa mai tafiya kasaita	duck with the self-important waddle

Zarruk and Alhassan (1982) list a large number of epithets applied to 'the world'; A. U. Kafin-Hausa (1985) lists epithets for birds, animals, insects, plants, tools, weapons, foodstuffs, clothes, forms of transport, places and illnesses. Kraft (1976a) provides English glosses for a number of epithets grouped into such categories as people, food and drink, clothing, implements, conditions of life, natural phenomena, plants and places.

9. A number of BA final papers in Nigerian universities have looked at *kirari* in particular courts: Zaria (S. Ahmed 1984; H. D. Umar 1982); and Gombe (I. Bello 1985). *Kirari* as one component in the musical world of the Kano court is discussed by Besmer (1971), and similarly for Katsina by King (1969).

10. Other terms are also current. *Zabiya* is a term used of a female praise-crier (see Mack 1981: 150–7), *sankira* is a further term for this function, as is the Fulani-derived term *bambade*. A. U. Kafin-Hausa (1985) points out that proclamation and self-praise are also a part of the skills not only of court-based performers but such people as medicine-pedlars, providing the following example from a seller of medicines named Isa Kambu jikan Abdu, from Dakayyawa market:

ga mai magani uban Ladidi	here's the medicine-man, Ladidi's father
sai ni Gambo jikan Abdu	I'm the one! Gambo, Abdu's grandson
Yaro babu tambaya jaki ne!	the boy who doesn't ask questions is a donkey!
a sha magani a yi wanka!	take the medicine, wash yourself!
maganin kwarai sai gado!	real medicines are an inherited skill!
ina mai kaba ko mai dundumi	who has a pain or a nervous affliction
ko mai yawan bari ko kwantacce?	or is plagued by miscarriages or uterine problems?
su zo a ba su magani irin na sahihi	let them come and get really effective medicine
ga mai magani da sunan Allah!	Here is one who cures in the name of God!

11. I. Y. Yahaya (1979b) illustrates how riddling can be the precursor to the story in a story-telling session, a warm-up act before the main event.

CHAPTER 5

1. Kofoworola (1982; 1985a; 1985b, Kofoworola and Lateef 1987) uses the term 'performing arts' to encompass many aspects of Hausa cultural life.

2. Theatricality as constituting a broad framework for the discussion of a variety of cultural performances is deployed by Dan-Inna Chaibou (1979), whose MA thesis is extensively referred to by Beik (1987: 12–19). Unfortunately I have not had the opportunity to read Chaibou and so all references are to the discussion by Beik.

3. For further discussion of *bori* and *bori* performance, see the following: Besmer (1973; 1975; 1983), Horn (1981), Ames (1973b; Erlmann (1981; 1982a; 1982b), Greenberg (1946), King (1966; 1967), Onwuejeogwu (1969) among others.

4. Kallamu (1992). Writing in 1987 Nafada, Sadauki and Kabir indicate that NTA (National Television Authority) Kaduna was producing the TV drama shows *Tambari* and *Karambana*, radio and TV shows *Samanja* and *Kuliya Manta Sabo*; NTA Kano was producing *Taskira* and *Babarodo*, NTA Jos was producing *Tumbin Giwa* and *Karkuzu*, while the long-running *Duniya Budurwar Wawa* continued on FRCN Kaduna radio. U. A. Mohammed (1989) discusses the shows on CTV Kano: *Dan Magori, Na Duke Tsohon Ciniki* (explicitly addressed to farmers within agricultural development projects), *Dan Wanzan* and *Bakan Gizo*.

5. Three plays, *Kamar da Gaske, Mai Wasa da Maza Karya,* and *Bari Ba Shegiya Ba Ce,* from the series were published in 1980 by NNPC under the programme title and under Yusufu Ladan's name.

6. A similar character played by Kasimu Yero featured in an earlier English language TV series called 'Cockcrow at Dawn' produced by NTA Jos and may have been the inspiration for the Hausa language series (U. B. Ahmed, personal communication).

7. These same themes recur in a more ponderous way in a great deal of the didactic poetry of the twentieth century, as we see in Chapter 9. I. Y. Yahaya (1991) summarises the propagandist thrust of drama as follows: 'Enlightenment of the public on various government policies: health care; traffic law; political culture, e.g. campaigning, election procedures; population census; new forms of currency; literacy campaigns; cultural revival; discipline; combating unemployment; enlightenment on drug abuse' (Yahaya 1991: 24–5).

8. Dance, drama and mime productions from the CNCS have travelled abroad, notably the production of *Queen Amina* which was presented in Sofia, Bulgaria in 1982, and the dance-drama 'New Earth', directed by Peter Badejo, which was shown in various parts of Britain in 1987.

9. Published by Hudahuda Press in 1983 as *Amina Sarauniyar Zazzau*.

10. These developments are extensively described in Kofoworola and Lateef (1987).

11. A list of TV series and further discussion of drama groups and written plays as well as the role of sponsorship is given in I. Y. Yahaya (1991).

12. Attitudes to acting contain many of the classic contradictions of the profession. When Zagga asked the producers why the women actresses were all prostitutes by profession, she was told that husbands would never allow their wives to appear on television (N. M. Zagga 1985: 28).

13. In addition to *Magana Jari Ce*, *Ruwan Bagaja* by Abubakar Imam has been dramatised for the stage.

14. He mentions the Fagge Sodangi Dramatic Society and the Gyaranya Dramatic Society in Kano, as well as other groups such as the Tauraro Dramatic Group, the Ingarma Dramatic Group and the Janzaki Dramatic Group. He relates that a certain Malam Mamman Dan Haki was awarded a national medal on his seventieth birthday for his work with the Dan Masani Dramatic Club in Kano which appears on NTA and CTV Kano. Ado (1987) reports the existence of a drama club called Ragaya in Haɗeja. I. Y. Yahaya (1991: fn. 9), in a more comprehensive discussion, lists further groups. The degree to which these groups are active producers of plays rather than simply informal societies (of which Nigeria has a plethora) that constitute organisations for status ascription and contestation, is unclear. Kofoworola (Kofoworola and Lateef 1987: 161–3) indicates that a drama society was functioning in 1940 in Katsina and that the Daura Dramatic Society put on a production of *Bayajida* in 1949.

15. U. B. Ahmed (personal communication) considers that the oldest Hausa dramatic texts in roman script are contained in Prietze (1924/5). Ahmed entitles these texts *Turbar Tarabulus* 'The Road to Tripoli' and *Rabeh* 'Rabeh' and considers the latter to be a rare example of tragedy among Hausa dramatic forms.

16. These and other plays are summarised in Piłaszewicz (1985).

17. See the discussion of Maƙarfi's work in U. Abdurrahman (1990/1) and M. Bello (1981).

18. Discussed by U. Hassan (1972).

19. Ahmed indicates that the first of the four plays, *Bora da Mowa*, was originally written in English in 1959, and that the other three, *Malam Soko*, *Kash!* and *Buleƙe* were written in the early 1960s and staged in secondary schools. Other published Hausa plays include: *Malam Mahamman* (1974) by Bello Muhammad, *Matar Mutum Kabarinsa* (1974) by Bashari Farouk Roukbah, *Soyayya Ta Fi Kuɗi* (1982) by Hadi Abdullahi Alkanci, which was a prizewinner

in the Federal Department of Culture's 1982 competition, *Ai Ga Irinta Nan* (1988) by Umaru Danjuma Katsina, and *Gani Ga Wane* (1990), consisting of three plays: *Sai Wani Ya Rasu, Kaikayi,* and *Duniya Dauke Ni* by Abubakar Soron Dinki. As private publication has had a major role in the production of prose-writing, so there has also been some private printing of plays, such as *Na Tanko* (1979) by Ibrahim Tajo.

20. Comparison of character, moral standpoint and outcomes between plays has been a regular form of commentary in dissertation work in Nigeria. See, for example, the following: Abdulwalid (1973), Balla (1972), Dabai (1991), A. Ibrahim (1984), Ibrahim (1972), R. M. Sani (1984).

21. Beik (1984b) cites the following government statement: 'Les thèmes sont libres mais doivent s'inspirer des réalités ou aspirations Nigériennes. Les thèmes sont laissés à l'appréciation des créateurs, mais doivent s'inspirer du patrimoine culturel Nigérien. Les compositions tiendront compte des préoccupations culturelles, économiques et sociales du pays.' ('The choice of themes is free but must gain its inspiration from the real-life circumstances and aspirations of the people of Niger. The themes are left to the views of the creative people involved but must be inspired by the cultural heritage of Niger. The creative products will take account of the cultural, economic and social concerns of the country.')

22. The play is centred on Mamman Arrivé, a powerful trader with no education who has a delinquent son. The son is punished at school and Mamman Arrivé, outraged, goes through a series of confrontations with teachers, inspectors, the police, the local headman, and his friends and fellow parents. Finally, he understands his own inadequacies and the degree to which he is as much a social delinquent as his son.

23. The relationship between music and trance in *bori* is explored by Erlmann (1982b).

24. Patterns of membership vary considerably, see Besmer (1983: 14–18).

25. I. Y. Yahaya, Zariya, Gusau & 'Yar'aduwa (1992: 90) list spirits such as Sarkin Aljannu and 'Yar Fulani as benevolent white spirits and Bako and Kure as malevolent black spirits. This distinction between black and white spirits often corresponds to a distinction between Islamic and non-Islamic spirits. Besmer presents a more modulated view of the complex characteristics of spirits and the relationships between them. ·

26. Besmer (1975) discusses the distinction between *bori* 'real' and *wasa* 'entertainment' and outlines the patterning in the sequence of events in the course of a *bori* entertainment performance. Mahuta (1984) investigates the play-acting elements of *bori*.

27. Besmer employs the dominant metaphor of *bori*: the medium is the horse and the spirit is the horseman.

28. In addition to the overviews mentioned above, *'yan kama* are specifically discussed by Furniss (1991b), T. A. Gaya (1972), Gidley (1967), Kofoworola (1985b) and Yusufu (1972).

29. See S. B. Ahmad and Furniss (1994). Similar verbal routines to those employed by *'yan gambara* accompanied by rattles are performed by *'yan galura/ 'yan kacakaura/'yan buta*; see Ames and King (1971: 96–7) and Kofoworola and Lateef (1987: 95–6).

30. See particularly Kofoworola (1982), and also I. Y. Yahaya (1991).

31. They also sell antidotes and promise to remove such dangers from areas of habitation (Joe 1984). *Gardi* (sing.)/*Gardawa* (pl.) is also the term for itinerant mature Koranic students. Kofoworola (1982: 392–9) describes a group of transvestite *gardawa*, living in women's quarters, selling talismans, medicines

and prophylactics, dancing and drumming, and putting on performances with hyenas and dancing monkeys.

32. The full text is available in Furniss (1991b).

33. Yusufu quotes the *dan gambara*, Musa Maigambara of Fagge in Kano as saying: *Gambara rawar 'yan mata, ba waka ba ce, azanci ne ya yi yawa* 'Gambara is like girls dancing, it is not song, but wit and skill abound' (Yusufu 1972:2).

34 There are many studies of the political organisation and history of Hausa states; see for example D. M. Last (1967), M. G. Smith (1960 and Y. B. Usman (1981).

35. *Tashe* routines are discussed and exemplified in, among others, G. Abdu (1981), Y. Ahmed (1984), Alhamdu (1973), M. I. Aliyu (1987), M. S. Bello (1986), A. U. N. Bunza (1984), Jibrin (1985), A. A. Kafin-Hausa (1983), A. M. Malumfashi (1984), A. B. K. Mohammed (1986), I. Y. Yahaya (1984a: 1991) and A. B. Yusuf (1986).

CHAPTER 6

1. For further discussion of Mamman Shata and his songs see also Dangambo (1973b; 1979), Alhaji Garba (1982), and Kang (1982). Abdulkadir (1982) considers the occasions (weddings, installations of an office-holder) upon which someone like Shata will perform.

2. Music and song, and praise-song in particular, featured as aspects of pre-Jihad society that were condemned by the Islamic reformers. B. Sa'id (1978) quotes a verse written by Maryamu, one of the daughters of Shehu Usman dan Fodio, from a poem, *Lokacin Sudaniyya za ta tashi* 'When the Sudan will Rise Up':

Bari ci ka ƙoshi ka tashi ka zo wurin zambo	Don't fill your stomach and then go talking ill of others,
Dara duk da caca, ja ba na shawarsu in dubo	Going where there is gaming and gambling, I don't like to go where these things happen,
Goge da molo ka barsu ka bar zuwa tarbo	The playing of fiddles and guitars, stay clear of them,
Bari shaye-shayen majisawan da babu rabo	Don't indulge in pagan drinking in which there is no benefit.
(Sa'id 1978: vol. 2, 365)	(GF & SIK)

Shata's insistence on his didactic function stands as a counter to those who, following Maryamu, would dismiss song as *hululu* 'idle chatter'.

3. Shata himself, along with Dan Maraya and others have been used as product advertisers. M. S. Ibrahim (1976) quotes from a song by Shata selling APC, an aspirin compound for the Paterson Zochonis company:

Magungunan zamani yau	Among today's modern medicines
Ba kamar episi mai giwa	There's none like APC with the elephant emblem,
Ciwon kai ko ciwon ƙirji	For headache or chest pain,
Ko da mura ta zama mashaƙo	Or for a cold or sore throat,
Ko ko baya ya ɗaɗɗaure	Or back pain.
Ku biɗo episi mai giwa	Seek out APC with the elephant emblem,
Sha yanzu nan magani yanzun nan	Take it now and be cured now,
Sai efisi mai giwa	APC is the only one!
(M. S. Ibrahim 1976: 71)	(GF & SIK)

4. See for example the collection of songs in praise of the Sardauna Sir Ahmadu

Bello in Paden (1986) and the discussion of political poetry in Birniwa (1987), M. B. Hassan (1980), Hiskett (1977a) and Suru (1980).

5. A variety of English terms are used: written as against oral poetry, written as against oral song, and a distinction between popular verse and Islamic verse (see, for example, Hiskett 1975b).

6. See D. Muhammad (1979: 87–9; 1980) for an introduction to this issue.

7. Umar makes the following comment, 'Hausa court songs have no fixed opening or closing doxologies, but are characterized by alternating irregular stanzas and an unchanging refrain. The irregularity of the stanzas is so apparent that a stanza may have as many as 50 lines while others, within the same song, have no more than ten lines. In Dankwairo's song for Sarkin Kano, for example, one stanza has 98 lines while all the others have less than ten except for one stanza which has 15 lines' (M. B. Umar 1984: 38).

8. The most comprehensive discussion of traditional courts and their praise-singers/musicians is to be found in S. M. Gusau (1988). There are a bewildering variety of drums, wind, stringed and other instruments used in northern Nigeria. One of the most comprehensive presentations is in Ames and King (1971), but see also Lateef in Kofoworola and Lateef (1987), and Krieger (1968) for excellent line drawings, as well as Ames (1965), Besmer (1971), King (1969), and I. Y. Yahaya (1983/5).

9. The question of what constitutes a line is a complex one relating to the relation between interpause verbal phrases and musical measures. See, for example, the discussion in Besmer (1970) and in King (1981). In this extract from the beginning of the song the refrain is first set for the audience by the lead singer and repeated by the chorus before the main verses begin. This is a commonly encountered pattern in song, similar to establishing the running rhyme in poetry by being employed throughout the whole of the first verse.

10. In addition, King illustrates various kinds of refrain as well as abbreviation and extension in refrain.

11. *Bakandamiya* (*kandama* (verb) 'to supply an abundance of') is an important concept in relation to singers and poets. Muhammad (1981) has explored the concept in detail. Sometimes rendered as 'masterpiece' the notion can also cover the idea of an intimate compilation of a singer/poet's most favourite themes and motifs, his own personal statement and piece of self-assertion, or indeed simply his most famous song.

12. The *tabshi* drum is typically used for royalty and was also used extensively by the tied group led by Aliyu dan Dawo. A number of musical instruments including the drum *tambari*, the horn *kakaki* and the oboe-like *algaita* are exclusively used for royalty. For a discussion of these and other instruments see Ames and King (1971) and Krieger (1968).

13. The *kotso* drum was also the favoured instrument of Dankwairo's group.

14. Also known as *sankira*, *bambade* (from Fulfulde) or simply *maroki*; see also Gidley (1975) and Chapter 4, n. 10.

15. There have been a number of famous *goge* players in addition to Garba Liyo from Funtuwa, amongst them Sarkin Goge Mudu in Zaria, Mamman Duka in Kano and Alhaji Babba mai Goge (born 1918), who performed with four *kwarya* drummers, six male and six female dancers, as well as a chorus. Women were the most famous subjects of his songs, including those entitled 'Hawwa Fulani' and 'Hajiya Yar Mamman' (Yakubu 1981).

16. Hausa has a high tone ('), a low tone (`), and a combined falling tone (^) apparent on vowels and occasionally on nasals. Downdrift is a phenomenon stretching

over the length of a phrase whereby the pitch level progressively drops towards the end of a statement.

17. For an introduction to Arabic metres see, for example, Galadanci (1975), Schuh (1988) and Wright (1967); see also the discussion in Chapter 8.

18. See, for example, Sipikin (1984) and the comments in Furniss (1977: 71–3) and Schuh (1988: 22–68).

19. Aminu lists the following *gimshikai*: *aiyaaranaayee* (– – v – –), *aiyaarayee* (– – v –), *aiyee* (– –), *arauyee* (v – –), *iyee* (v –), *yaarayee* (– v –); and the following *mataimaka*: *aralliyellee* (v – v – –), *dariyee* (v v –), *didee* (v –), *dideedee* (v – –), *ee* (–), *iyaara* (v – v), *naanaayee* (– – –), *naayee* (– –). He goes on to illustrate sequences of such components, equivalent to metres, called *naadiran, sauki, wuya, gaada, tsaka-tsaki, gan-tilo,* and *bakandamiya.* It is not clear from his discussion whether there are systematic combinations or whether there is free choice to combine such words in any way so long as it represents the overall pattern of the line. For example, he describes the same sequence in the 'metre' *sauki* (– – v – – – v –, which would be recognized as *kaamil* in Xalilian terms) by both of the following: *aiyaarayee aiyaarayee,* and *aiyaarayee aiyee didee.*

20. Known popularly on her tapes and on radio as Binta Zabiya, she is probably the same singer as 'Binta Katsina' referred to by Mack (1983). *Zabiya* is a term used for an emir's female praise-singer, see Mack (1981; 1983: 16–17).

21. The issue of the various statuses of women is a complex one. Dominant male cultural values prescribe *aure* 'marriage' as an honourable estate for a woman and in contrast the term *karuwa* is sometimes applied generally to unmarried women, often rendered oversimplistically as 'prostitute' in English. In fact there are a variety of independent and semi-independent statuses of women; see for example the discussions in Callaway (1987), Coles and Mack (1991) and Pittin (1979), among others.

22. Extracts from songs by Barmani Choge are presented in Mack (1986) and (1983).

23. B. Sa'id (1982b: iv) indicates that this song was originally written by Yusufu Ladan and then sung by Uwani Zakirai, an unusual procedure in Hausa. A different version of this text is given in Sa'id (1982b: 113–15).

24. For further discussion of women's song, in addition to earlier citations in this section, see Bagudo (1985), Maikafi (1977), F. Othman (1979), Hauwa Yusuf (1988) and the writings of Bichi on wedding songs (1973; 1975; 1979b; 1985).

25. The colon marks a caesura in the line as indicated in the original text.

26. See Abdulƙadir's translation of Shata's song 'Work Hard and Pursue Education' (Abdulƙadir 1975: 319–20).

27. This title, derived from the first line, is as given by Daba. M. B. Umar (1985: 57) calls the song *Duka Dangantakarku Daidai.*

28. Mashi (1986) discusses the political allegiances and political songs of various singers.

29. M. B. Umar (1985: 68–70) lists some 75 songs as of 1985.

30. Reference to the natural world, whether pastoral or allegorical, is unusual in Hausa song and poetry. A. K. Tukur (1982) discusses some ten poems and songs which feature, for example, a dove (song by Haruna Oji), a racehorse (song by Narambada), a scorpion (song by Garba Mai Tandu Shinkafi), cattle (poem by Aƙilu Aliyu) and biting ants (poem by Adamu Sandalo Sudawa).

31. See also A. I. Karaye (1974) on Hamisu Mai Ganga.

32. For discussion of the singers Ibrahim na Habu and Audu Karen Gusau see S. M. Gusau (1983); for Dan Kurji see I. Musa (1982); for Isa Mai Kukuma see S. B. Aliyu (1986); and for Lawan Gajere Mai Goge see A. G. Dutse (1991). Recordings

of a large number of tied and freelance singers have been collected in the Oral Documentation Unit (Oral Documentation Unit 1983) attached to the Department of Nigerian and African Languages, Ahmadu Bello University. A number of other recordings are also held at the Centre for the Study of Nigerian Languages, Bayero University. While this book was in press I became aware of the excellent work on composition technique by De Campos (1994) to which the reader should refer.

CHAPTER 7

1. Powe (1984) discusses in detail the way in which epithets constitute the components from which *kirari* as extended texts are constructed and the range of songs that are found in the world of 'combat literature'.
2. See also I. Mohammed (1977).
3. A further extract with English translation is given in D. Muhammad (1981: 67–8)
4. See also, for example, S. S. Usman (1990) on the singer Ibrahim dan Gulbi from Talata Mafara; and S. M. Gusau (1983) and Kankara (1983) on Isa dan Makaho and Dan Balade Morai.
5. See also M. A. Zurmi (1986) for other songs by Kassu Zurmi.
6. M. S. Aliyu (1980) has the name Hamisu Mai Ganga rather than Hamisu Kano as the singer of the song in praise of Sabo Wakilin Tauri.
7. See also Zango (1983).
8. See S. M. Gusau (1988) and Dutsin-Ma (1981).
9. An extract with English translation is given in King (1981: 133–5). The extract given here is from an unpublished manuscript in the author's possession by A. V. King dating from about 1972.
10. The catalogue of the Oral Documentation Unit, ABU, Zaria lists many recordings of 39 major songs.
11. Muhammad points out that this praise-song, which exhibits the usual lead and refrain format also ends each line with an identical sequence of tones: Lo-Hi-Hi-Hi, a feature he has described for poetry as 'tonal rhyme' (D. Muhammad 1980a). I. Zurmi (1981) discusses in detail patterning and the interleaving between lead and chorus in Narambada's songs. Udu (1972) compares two songs in praise of Sarkin Gobir na Isa Amadu, the one by Narambada the other by Aliyu dan Dawo. And see also Al-Hassan (1979).
12. A considerable number of songs by Dankwairo are transcribed in D. H. Yahaya (1991); see also Modibbo (1989) and S. M. Sa'id (1981).
13. Poaching, and allegiance-switching is also described by Haliru (1983) in relation to the praise-singer Aliyu dan Dawo (d. 1966, father of another well-known singer Sani Aliyu dan Dawo; see Malikawa-Sarari (1982)), who was invited by Sarkin Augi of Argungu to visit him after seeing him perform in Sokoto at the celebrations in honour of the appointment of Abubakar III as Sultan of Sokoto. Aliyu dan Dawo asked his patron, Ardo Mamman of Yauri, for permission to visit Sarkin Augi. He was given permission and never returned (Haliru 1983: 4).
14. Peasants from Dosara village occupied the dam site in protest and peasants from Birnin Tudu refused to be evacuated from their village. 'Police action' early on the morning of Saturday, 24 April 1980 resulted in a hundred deaths according to U. A. Ahmed (1992: 55), and that night houses in Birnin Tudu were set alight by intruders. The report in *West Africa* of 12 May 1980 indicated 14 dead, several others injured and 200 'rioting villagers' arrested. Watts (1983: 508), citing the same source, reported 200 farmers killed.
15. See also the texts of Hausa songs on famine in Watts (1983: 515–20).

CHAPTER 8

1. The poem *Ma'ama'are* was orginally composed in couplets in Fulfulde circa 1791 (Abdullahi Bayero Yahya 1987). The Hausa translation that subsequently circulated widely in Nigeria was undertaken in 1868 by Isan Kware. An expanded five-line version, a *takhmis*, was produced by Abdullahi Mai Boɗinga in 1886. An edition with commentary was presented in Hiskett (1977c), an English translation and commentary are to be found in Abdullahi Bayero Yahya (1987) and in Furniss (1993b), and translated extracts are also in Boyd and Furniss (1995). The couplets presented here from Furniss (1993b) are the last two lines of five-line verses from the edition in Hiskett (1977c).

2. For discussion of the Jihad see Adeleye (1971) and Last (1967), among others.

3. For a detailed presentation of such categories see Hiskett (1973; 1975b).

4. A detailed and comprehensive study of the nature of Hausa *wa'azi* verse is provided by Dangambo (1980b). The injunctions and prohibitions relating to marriage, inheritance, theft, prayer and many other aspects of life are enshrined in Islamic law, the *Shari'a*, and derive ultimately from the Koran and the traditions of the Prophet (*hadith*).

5. For discussion of the didactic nature of modern verse see, for example, Furniss (1977; 1978; 1982; 1988b; 1989; 1993a).

6. Extensive discussion of representative examples of this category of Hausa poetry is to be found in Abdullahi Bayero Yahya (1987).

7. The knowledge of miraculous events in the life of the Prophet, which figured strongly in Sufi poetry, is summarised by Abdullahi Bayero Yahya (1987) in discussing the *mu'ujizai* dealt with by the Shehu in the poem *Daliyya*:

   the miracle of an army of angels as an aid to the Prophet in his encounter with the infidels; earlier divine books – Torah, psalms and the New Testament – describing the Prophet by enumerating his qualities; the miracle of the udder of the ewe flowing with abundant milk; of the pebbles glorifying Allah and the flowing of water from the Prophet's fingertips; the miracle of the speech of the wolf and the deer; the speech of the monitor lizard and the bowing down of the trees in obedience to the Prophet; the speech of an infant and the swelling up of a small object on account of the Prophet's spittle; the provision of shade to the Prophet by the cloud and the protection by the dove; the miracle of the spider covering the cave in which the Prophet stayed so as to deceive the enemies; the cry of grief of the palm-tree stump; the miracle of the Prophet's touching something small thereby increasing it in size; at his birth the palace of Kisra was razed; another miracle of the Prophet's birth when the river in the land where Kisra ruled dried up and the altar fire which they worshipped was miraculously quenched; at birth the Prophet came complete with circumcision and umbilical cord already cut. (Yahya 1987: 47–8).

8. Certain Islamic scholars in northern cities had been well-known prior to the Jihad. People in Katsina revere the scholars Dan Masani and his more famous pupil, Dan Marina who were based in Katsina in the seventeenth century. Hiskett (1984a) refers also to eighteenth century scholars in Borno and elsewhere; see also M. S. Ibrahim (1982a; 1982b). As with the Jihad writers, the question of whether they composed in Hausa or were later translated and paraphrased into Hausa remains an open question. See also, for an introduction to Jihad and pre-Jihad history, Adeleye (1985), Hunwick (1984),and M. Last (1974), among many others.

9. Sa'idu (1981) describes the training of the famous eighteenth-century scholar, Muhammadu na Birnin Gwari, as having involved 10 years in Katsina, then 5

years in Borno, 7 in Kano, 9 in Zaria, 8 more in Katsina, 3 in Sokoto (after its establishment by the Jihadists) and a year in Kwantagora and Yawuri before finally settling as a famous *malam* in Birnin Gwari, where he stayed until his death in the middle of the nineteenth century.

10. It is arguable whether, in early nineteenth-century Hausaland, the structure of Hausa society, rather than consisting of an aristocracy and peasantry with an intermediate, urban-based cleric class, was not in fact a peasantry and a single élite, the cleric class, with a variety of relations, slave to slave-owner, patron to client, landowner to tenant, etc., obtaining between them. In discussing the poem *Daliyya* by the Shehu, Abdullahi Bayero Yahya (1987) comments on the rise of the cleavage between the cleric class and 'indigenous African culture':

> Thus the *Daliyya* is to be seen, in some measure, as an expression of the cultural tension that existed in the second half of the 18th century A.D. and at the beginning of the 19th century A.D. between the exotic culture of Islam and the indigenous African culture of the Sudan. This tension, of course, has continued to exist to the present day. Another aspect of the same phenomenon, the confrontation between Islam and indigenous African culture, may also be recognised in this early poem of the so-called Fulani reform movement. It is the cleavage that had by this time emerged between the literate and the illiterate. Clearly, the *Daliyya* is a highly literate production in a social and intellectual milieu that was very largely illiterate, or rather pre-literate; and what it points to is the emergence in the second half of the 18th century A.D. in Hausaland, of a self-conscious and increasingly assertive intellectual elite whose elitism rested on their possession of Islamic literacy. This class confrontation, between a fully literate Islamic literate class and a still pagan or only superficially Islamized class retaining strong ties with the non-Islamic indigenous cultural tradition, has also persisted to the present day and some consider that it manifested itself in the recent Mai Tatsine uprisings. (Yahya 1987: 79)

11. Subsequent to the quelling of revolts, investigations were conducted into who and what lay behind them. Using documentary evidence from the investigators, Verger describes the malamaic culture which was so impenetrable to the investigators and which was a unifying and motivating factor among slaves who were Yoruba, Hausa or from a variety of other backgrounds:

> The searches of the quarters of slaves and emancipated Africans led to the discovery of numerous papers and pamphlets covered with 'Harabic' letters or 'Arabic-like writings' or in 'hieroglyphics' or 'unknown letters'. They were in fact inscriptions extracted from the Koran, which when placed in small leather bags served as talismens for the insurgents and other Africans. Tablets were found which were thought to have been made for typographic or lithographic printing but which were actually used by the lettered men to teach the verses of the Koran to their pupils, and resembled those used in many Koranic schools of today. In their ignorance the police thought that they were papers in unknown writing through which the insurgents communicated among themselves, the proof of which seemed to be the finding of papers and books covered with this same mysterious writing at several places which were searched. As a result, for several months any African discovered in possession of one of these papers ... was deported if he was a freedman and given several hundred whip-lashes in the public square if he was a slave ... The entire enquiry showed the importance of the role played by a certain number of literate Hausa, Tapa and Nago (Yoruba) who were the teachers of emancipated slaves, most of whom were Nago ... One of the papers, signed Mala

Abubakar, was a sort of proclamation calling upon them to unite, and stating that no ill could befall them along the way... Thus the police made every effort to jail all the 'teachers of the Koranic schools' who were to their mind nothing but dangerous agitators. Some of them were emancipated blacks who had acquired certain means; others were slaves whose intelligence and moral values were many times superior to those of their owners ... All the Muslim teachers who were identified and found guilty were considered to be the leaders of the insurrection. (Verger 1976: 298–300)

12. B. Sa'id (1978) presents many Jihadist poetic texts in his thesis, including many by immediate members of the Shehu's family or close associates: 25 attributed to the Shehu, 8 by his brother Abdullahi, 17 by his daughter Nana Asma'u, 7 by his youngest son Isan Kware, 3 by Maryamu 'Yar Shehu, and some by others closely associated with the family.

13. Danlami (1992) situates Shitu ɗan Abdura'ufu much earlier, having been born in 1757 in Gobir and only moving to Zaria in 1806 (d. 1837). He further indicates that *Jiddul ajizi* was written in Arabic and only later translated into Hausa, and gives a roman transcription of its 1,200 verses. See also M. S. Ibrahim (1982b) and Kani (1978).

14. Hiskett (1975b: 80–90) provides English translations of extracts from the poetry of Malam Shitu in a chapter on mystical verse. See also Hiskett (1980).

15. Murray Last (personal communication) comments upon the growth of the Tijaniyya, and therefore spread of Tijani literature, and the possibility of a perceived need in Sokoto at this time to protect and enhance the Qadiri position.

16. This discussion selects certain aspects of reformist poetry for attention. English-language summaries and overviews of nineteenth century poetry are provided by Hiskett (1975b) and Piłaszewicz (1985), among others, to whom the reader should refer for a fuller discussion.

17. A major study and translation of the writings of Nana Asma'u is currently in preparation by Jean Boyd and Beverly Mack. See also Mukoshy (1979). Hiskett (1975b: 133–5) provides an English translation of a further part of this poem.

18. Boyd (personal communication) indicates that Nana, daughter of the Shehu, wrote seventeen elegies praising men and women for the contributions they had made to the community. Nana says in 'Lamentation for Ayesha', 2, v. 13: 'And it is no sin to make a lamentation, For Abu Sufiyan elegized the Prophet Muhammad after his passing'; see also Boyd and Mack's translations of the complete poetic works of Nana Asma'u (Boyd and Mack, forthcoming).

19. There was a legitimate place for women in this world-view and it was not exclusively subservient. The figure of the daughter of the Shehu, Nana Asma'u (and others among her female relatives), became an important symbol of female scholarship, piety and leadership. The Shehu had written on the importance of Islamic education for women. Nana Asma'u represented not only the 'educated woman' but also, through her leadership of the 'Yan Taru movement, a woman who was organisationally active. Boyd writes: 'Muhammad Tukur wrote a work in Arabic called "The means of helping brothers towards legitimate social relationships with women", and the Shehu's early Fulfulde poetry on men's behaviour, women's behaviour, the behaviour of married couples, etc., seems to support the view that the Qadiriyya at Degel honoured pious women and afforded them a place in the public life of the community' (personal communication).

20. The authorship of this poem is disputed. Abdulƙadir (1980) gives a roman transcription and attributes it to Sultan Attahiru. A. B. Yahya (1990) relies on an attribution by S. W. Junaidu (1990) to one Malam Labbo ɗan Mariya Kwasare.

21. See Muffett (1964), among others.

22. For further discussion of this poem and an additional translated extract see Hiskett (1984a: 269–71).

23. Alhaji Umaru was a writer and poet of great renown. Based in Ghana he was conversant with most of the major events in the Western Sudan in the 1880s and later, and wrote extensively on a wide variety of topics. The major collection of his works is in the archives in Legon, Ghana; however through his work with the German scholar-travellers, Mischlich and Krause, a large amount of his work was made available at the beginning of this century. For subsequent studies of the man and his work, see among others, Duffill (1986), Ferguson (1973), Herman (1982), Hodgkin (1966), Martin (1967), Piłaszewicz (1974; 1975; 1981; 1982; 1993), Reichmuth (1993), Sölken (1959; 1970), Wilks (1963) and Wilks & Goody (1968).

24. Hiskett (1984a: 262–6) discusses this poem at some length, providing further translated extracts.

25. See, for example, Kabara (1974) on the poetry written by the leader of the Qadiriyya, Nasiru Kabara; and Paden (1965; 1973a).

26. Hiskett calls this poem *Wakar Ajuza* 'Song of the Old Hag' and relates it to the tradition of personifying the world as an old woman (Hiskett 1975b: 83–5). See also Haruna-Soba (1982) and Skinner (1971b).

27. Other religious poems include *Kasbur Raga'ibu, Nuniyatul Amdahi* and *Taisirul Manami*.

28. The strongly Sufi elements in *Imfiraji* have been examined by U. Abdurrahman (1985; n.d.). Cantos 2 and 3 are translated and annotated in Birniwa (1981). A. Neil Skinner has been involved in the production of a translation of cantos 2–7 with a number of collaborators. That translation exists only in manuscript form, as far as I am aware.

29. Other rarer techniques of expansion are mentioned in Hiskett (1975b: 174–5)

30. There have been occasions when printers in Nigeria have misread *ajami* manuscripts and read the sequence vertically to produce versions in which the lines have been set out wrongly as 1, 3, 2, 4, 5.

31. See also Ruma (1983) and B. Sa'id (1983/5)

32. For discussion of the Xalilian system as applied to Hausa and alternative approaches see, for example, the following: Arnott (1969; 1975), Badawi (1979), S. A. Bayero (1970), Galadanci (1975), Greenberg (1949; 1960), Hiskett (1975b), I. Junaidu (1981b; 1982; 1988), Kafin-Hausa (1983), King and Ibrahim (1968), McHugh and Schuh (1984), 'D. Muhammad (1977; 1979), B. Sa'id (1978), Schuh (1985; 1988; 1988/9; 1989), Sheshe (1977), A. U. Tijjani (1983), A. B. Zaria (1973) and M. S. Zaria (1978).

33. In the following example words appearing to start with a vowel in fact start with a consonantal glottal stop, which is not marked in the roman orthography.

34. The existence of this last variation might lead one to examine whether the poem is in *Rajaz*, a metre which deploys this foot, however the vast bulk of the poem deploys the first two feet given here, feet that are typical of *Kamil*.

35. Where Galadanci (1975) takes the former position and Sipikin (1984) the latter, the middle ground sees Hausa poets using metres which are historically derived from the Arabic canon but which are now integrated into Hausa poetics (Schuh, personal communication). Schuh sees the degree of that integration in the fact that few Hausa poets have any explicit knowledge of the *Xalilian* system and in the way that Hausa poets 'do many things in the historically Arabic meters that would not have been possible for Arabic poets, e.g. allowing series of three or more long syllables or three or more short syllables, allowing – v – v v feet in *Ramal*, or allowing v – v – in *Kamil*, at least line initial' (personal communication).

36. See Hiskett (1975b: 169–73) for an explanation of *ramzi* or chronograms.
37. For discussions of style see, for example, the following: U. Abdurrahman (n.d.), Arnott (1969; 1975), Bagari (1988), CSNL (1977), Furniss (1977; 1982; 1984a), Hiskett (1975b; 1977a; 1977b; 1977c; 1982; 1984b), Mack (1982), D. Muhammad (1973a; 1977; Muhammad 1978a; 1982; 1985), Muhtar (1984), Omar (1983), Piłaszewicz (1985), B. Sa'id (1975; 1984) and Abdullahi Bayero Yahya (1987).

CHAPTER 9

1. A detailed examination of this process to be seen in the language of poetry is provided in Furniss (1977), an abridged version of which is shortly to be published as *Ideology in Practice: Hausa Poetry as Exposition of Values and Viewpoints* in the series Westafrikanische Studien: Frankfurter Beiträge zur Sprach- und Kulturgeschichte (Cologne: Rüdiger Köppe Verlag).
2. The 1957 edition contained, in addition to the two cited here, the following poems: *Wakar damina* 'Song of the Rains' by Na'ibi Sulaiman Wali; *Mu sha falala* 'Let us Drink the Water of Plenty' by the Emir of Zaria, Aliyu Dan Sidi; *Wakar uwar mugu* 'The Mother of all Evil' by Hamisu Yadudu Funtuwa; *Munafunci da annamimanci* 'Hypocrisy and Mischief-making' by Salihu Kwantagora; *Wakar sha'anonin duniya* 'The Way of the World' also by Salihu Kwantagora; *Tabban Hakikan* 'For Sure and Certain' by the leader of the nineteenth-century Jihad, Shehu Usman dan Fodio. An earlier, rather different, edition first appeared in 1956 containing the following additional poems: *Wakar batu* 'Matters of Concern' (later to be referred to as *Wakar tabarkoko* in Dan Sidi (1980)) by Aliyu Dan Sidi; *Wakar masu aikin jirgi* 'Poem of the Railway Workers' attributed to Bello Sakkwato; *Birnin Kano* 'The City of Kano' also attributed to Bello Sakkwato.
3. Na'ibi Wali was born in Kano in 1928. After graduating from the School for Arabic Studies in 1949 and a spell as a primary-school teacher, he went for further training to the Sudan from where he returned to take up a job in charge of Arabic book publication at NORLA (Northern Region Literature Agency) in Zaria until 1960. After working as secretary to the Hausa Language Board, he spent the early 1970s at the headquarters of adult education in Kano State. He reached retirement age as a judge of the Shari'a court but continued to work after retirement with the Islamic Foundation in Kano. For further discussion of Na'ibi Wali and his poetry, see Abdulkadir (1971a), Arnott (1969), Furniss (1977), King and Ibrahim (1968), Mack (1982), Schuh (1985) and Yakasai (1984).
4. Salihu Kwantagora was born in Kwantagora in 1929. After his father's death he was sent to study in Zaria with a Malam Baba who introduced him to the pleasures of poetry writing. His poetry was regularly published in the Hausa newspaper from 1949 onwards and he moved on to become a regular broadcaster with Radio Kaduna, and was subsequently employed at the NNPC publishing house in Zaria. In addition to his poetry in anthologies and in the newspaper, a collection of his poems, entitled *Kimiyya da Fasaha* was published by NNPC in 1972.
5. The Hausa text differs slightly from that published in *Wakokin Hausa*. Amendments have been made on the basis of corrections provided by Na'ibi Sulaiman Wali to D. W. Arnott circa 1970.
6. Sa'adu Zungur (1915–58) was born in Zungur near Bauchi. He graduated from Katsina College in 1929 and went to Yaba College, Lagos, from 1929 to 1934, the first northerner to gain admission there. An influential and charismatic figure, he represented a northern educated radicalism unusual in its day. His

political thinking influenced major figures such as Aminu Kano and a generation of younger intellectuals such as the poet, Mudi Sipikin, and others who formed the backbone of the opposition to the emerging establishment party in the north in the 1950s, the Northern Peoples Congress (NPC). Disillusionment with southern allies at one stage produced an ambiguous accommodation with the northern emirs, expressed in the poem, *Arewa, Jumhuriya ko Mulukiya* 'The North, Republic or Monarchy?', which Aminu Kano ascribed to Zungur's need to return to his roots (interview, October 1973). Zungur's poetry and his political thinking have been discussed in, for example, the following: Abdulƙadir (1974), Arnott (1975), A. S. Gaya (1972), Hiskett (1975a), Kano (1973) and A. Yusuf (1972).

7. Further studies of political poetry include: M. B. Hassan (1980), Hiskett (1977a), A. U. Kafin-Hausa (1976), Lawan (1983) and Suru (1980).

8. Yusufu Kantu, an Islamic teacher, was born in Isa in 1933. Having been a supporter of NEPU in the 1950s when he wrote this poem, he moved to support the GNPP and then the NPN in the 1979–83 civilian-rule period. Sharifai (1981) lists the titles of many of his poems, some of which are religious poems built on local *bori* song tunes. Sharifai also discusses public competitive verse-making between Yusufu Kantu and Malam Bawa Sha'iri and exchanges of letters in poetic form. See also CSNL (1979).

9. Sipikin indicates he still has the texts of the exchanges dating from 1951. Some extracts from the exchanges were reproduced in Diso (1979). Sipikin was born in 1930 in Kano into a family originally from Haɗeja (CSNL 1977: 30). During his early '*boko*/Western' education acquired through evening classes he came into contact with Maitama Sule, Aminu Kano, Sa'adu Zungur and other early NEPU figures. His prolific pen produced much poetry over the years, some of which was published by the NNPC in 1971 as a volume of early and later poetry entitled *Tsofaffin Waƙoƙi da Sababbin Waƙoƙi na Alhaji Mudi Sipikin*. He founded a poetry society in Kano entitled the *Hiƙima Kulob* which provided poets, particularly younger poets, with the opportunity during the 1970s to broadcast their poetry during a weekly programme each Thursday on Kano Radio. The *Hiƙima Kulob* functioned as a meeting place in which Mudi Sipikin interacted with other members of the club, discussing issues of content, form and performance. Another poetry circle, *Hausa Fasaha*, under the leadership of Aƙilu Aliyu, listed among its members in the mid-1970s, poets from many parts of the north, but did not appear at that time to function as an ongoing discussion forum. For discussion of the *Hiƙima Kulob* see Alhaji (1973) and Furniss (1977; 1984b; 1985).

10. Mu'azu Haɗeja was born into the Haɗeja royal family around 1915. From Kano Middle School he went on to Katsina College and from there to a teaching job in Ringim (Magashi 1974). In Ringim he became a close friend of one of the Kano princes, the Tafida. When the Ciroma, Sanusi, rather than the Tafida, became emir, Mu'azu was transferred to Kano to become a visiting teacher there. He moved in royal circles in Kano (Omar 1983: 6) and, while apparently never formally a member of the NPC, was clearly viewed as a supporter, particularly in his attacks upon so-called radicals within NEPU. A collection of his poems was among the earliest to be published by the Gaskiya Corporation (1955). English translations of his poems are to be found in Omar (1983). He died in 1958.

11. Gambo Hawaja was born in 1914, a Fulani from Takai, who, after a Koranic education in Haɗeja, settled as a dealer in kerosene and oil in Jos where he stayed for the rest of his life (Dagaceri 1990). He was a stalwart supporter of NEPU who became well known for his political poems attacking the NPC and proclaiming the merits of NEPU. Dagaceri (1990) lists a number of his best-known poems providing the texts of some in an appendix. Gambo Hawaja died in 1985.

12. Akilu Aliyu is perhaps the greatest poet of modern times. Renowned for his wit, deep knowledge of Hausa and original mind, he hails from Jega in Sokoto State where he was born around 1912 (I. Junaidu 1981a: vii). His family occupation was the making of horse apparel. At the age of about 15 he arrived in Kano to study under one of the Tijani *malam*s. Subsequently he followed his *malam* to Borno where he stayed for some 23 years until 1959 (CSNL 1977: 53). His staunch support for NEPU in Borno involved refusing to teach according to native authority instructions and therefore subsequent imprisonment. On his release he fled to Kano where he has stayed to this day. A major study of Akilu Aliyu and his art has been undertaken by Muhammad (1977), and further studies of him and his poetry include: T. Aliyu (1974), Arnott (1988), G. U. Gusau (1988), I. Junaidu (1981a), A. U. Kafin-Hausa (1983), Lere (1985), D. Muhammad (1973a; 1984), Ringim (1973a) and Skinner & Galadanci (1973).

13. Editions differ on the text of this poem as between (CSNL 1977) and the collection of Akilu Aliyu's poetry published as *Fasahar Akiliya* by the NNPC (1977). This extract is based upon a manuscript in the author's possession.

14. Garba Ebisidi was born in Funtua in 1932. After some Koranic education and primary school he acted as sales representative for the Hausa newspaper, *Gaskiya Ta Fi Kwabo*. He submitted poems on farming that were published by the newspaper in the late 1940s and 1950s. In the 1950s he was directly employed by the Agriculture Department as a propagandist. The agricultural extension unit at Samaru, Zaria would regularly send him to recite on farming topics on Radio Kaduna (Kofar Sauri 1982: 2–4). He once found himself being driven out of one particular village by the local farmers: 'Garba Ebisidi began reciting when all of a sudden they just went crazy, throwing stones at him and burning their cars (the extension workers). He said that on that day he ran fifty miles and they had to spend a week pulling the thorns out of his feet. The officer in charge of chemical fertiliser extension work told him he should write down what had happened to him for the record. And then we would make sure that when those who drove us out came with their money then we would get our own back and no mistake!' (trans. from Kofar Sauri 1982: 6–7). Garba Ebisidi died in 1980.

15. On the reform of the Tijaniyya and the Qadiriyya see Paden (1973b). Paden also discusses sect literature in Paden (1965; 1973a).

16. During the 1950s and 1960s a considerable number of 'Prophet's birthday' poems were published in the columns of the main Hausa language newspaper, *Gaskiya Ta Fi Kwabo* (see, for example, the list in Furniss 1977: App. 3). There are a number of studies of modern religious poetry and poets who are best known for their religious writings. Thematic studies of note include: U. Abdurrahman (1985; n.d.), A. M. Bunza (1985), Dangambo (1980a; 1980b), Dunfawa (1990), Hiskett (1980; 1982; 1984), (Piłaszewicz (1992a; 1992b) and Hafiz Yusuf (1992). Contemporary poets known particularly for their religious writings include the leader of the Qadiriyya sect in Kano, Nasiru Kabara (Kabara 1974); a number of descendants of the *waziri* Gidado of Sokoto: Sambo Wali Gidadawa (W. Dahiru 1989; Sanka 1983), Bello Alkali Gidadawa (Alkali 1982; Abdullahi Bayero Yahya 1983), Aliyu Maikudu Gidadawa (Kaura 1983), as well as a number of poets whose corpus includes a fair proportion of religious poems, such as Sani Mandawari (Mu'awiya 1990), Umaru wazirin Gwandu (Ikara 1983), Haliru Wurno (M. A. Ibrahim 1984) and the woman poet Hasana Ahmad Sufi (Babba 1986), among others.

17. Tijjani Tukur was born in Yola ward in Kano, Nigeria, in 1937. He attended the Shahuci Judicial School until 1957 and then, after a period working in the Survey Department, took up an appointment teaching at the Gidan Makama primary

school. In 1966 he entered the School for Arabic Studies and took a course in Higher Islamic Studies. After the School for Arabic Studies he went on to the University completing a degree in Hausa in 1974 at Abdullahi Bayero College. After teaching at a number of advanced teachers' colleges, he worked with the Ministry of Education in charge of Arabic teaching at primary level (Dutsi 1992). Tijjani Tukur has developed a reputation as a poet of considerable ability with published poems in a number of books, anthologies and journals. Dutsi provides a list of poems by Tijjani Tukur and the texts of some. Tijjani Tukur was for a period in the mid-1970s the secretary of the Hikima Kulob. See also CSNL (1979) and Furniss (1977).

18. For discussion of Hausa poems on the Nigerian civil war see Dangambo (1984a), and Furniss (1991c).

19. The 'mirror-image' relationship between praise and vilification is illustrated in Furniss (1988).

20. The poem was printed in the first issue of the journal *Harsunan Nijeriya*, with an accompanying brief commentary by Dandatti Abdulkadir (1971).

21 Abubakar Ladan was born in Zaria in 1935 (A. I. Malumfashi 1980). After leaving school he went to work with the Ministry of Health. A supporter of the NPC in the 1950s he is best known for his extensive travels through Africa and the record he has kept in verse of his experiences. A brief biography is provided by Ibrahim Yaro Yahaya in the introduction to Abubakar Ladan's book of poetry referred to in the text.

22. Published by Oxford University Press as a booklet in 1976.

23. See also Lawal (1990).

24. Beverly Mack was instrumental in bringing to publication an anthology of the poetry of Hauwa Gwaram and Alhajiya 'Yar Shehu entitled *Alkalami a Hannun Mata*, published in 1983 by NNPC. Further commentary upon poetry by women is to be found in Mack (1983; 1986).

25. Born in 1948, Ibrahim Yaro Muhammed was working in Kano as a clerk for the trading company SCOA during the early 1970s. Originally from Nguru, a small town northeast of Kano, he lived in Dakata, one of the fast growing dormitory suburbs built around earlier villages to the east of the commercial areas of Kano (personal communication, 27 March 1987). A prolific writer, he had a first volume of poetry published in 1974 by the Northern Nigerian Publishing Company entitled, *Wakokin Hikimomin Hausa* 'Poems of Hausa Wisdom'. The bulk of the poems in the volume are either religious in theme or are extended alliterative verses in metre and rhyme. He has, however, written extensively about social relations both in his immediate environment and in Hausa society at large.

BIBLIOGRAPHY

HAUSA TEXTS CITED

For a more extensive bibliography of creative writing in Hausa, see Baldi (1977), Skinner (1975) and particularly I. Y. Yahaya (1988a).

Ai Ga Irinta Nan, Umaru Ɗanjuma Katsina, Ibadan: University Press, 1988.
Alhaki Kwikwiyo, Hajiya Balaraba Ramat, Kano: private publication, 1990.
Alkalami a Hannun Mata, Hauwa Gwaram and Alhajiya 'Yar Shehu, Zaria: NNPC, 1983.
Amadi Na Malam Amah, Magaji Ɗambatta, Zaira: NNPC, 1980.
Amina Sarauniyar Zazzau, Umaru Balarabe Ahmed, Zaria: Hudahuda Press, 1983.
Amintacciyar Soyayya, Ɗan Azumi Baba, Kano: private publication, 1991.
Bala da Babiya, Nuhu Bamalli, Zaria: Gaskiya Corporation, 1950.
Bayan Wuya Sai Daɗi! Azbinawa Sun Je Neman Rijiyar Kudi, Abdulmalik Mani, Zaria: NORLA, 1954.
Bora da Mowa, Umaru Balarabe Ahmed, Zaria: NNPC, 1972.
Budurwar Zuciya, Hajiya Balaraba Ramat, Kano: private publication, 1990.
Da'u Fataken Dare, Tanko Zango, Zaria: NORLA, 1952.
Dare Ɗaya, Abdullahi Ka'oje, Zaria: NNPC, 1973.
Daren Sha Biyu ['Twelfth Night'], Ibrahim Yaro Yahaya (trans.), Zaria: NNPC, 1971.
Dausayin Soyayya, Bello Sa'id (ed.) Lagos and Zaria: NNPC for Nigeria Magazine, 1982.
Duniya Tumbin Giwa Ce, Ibrahim Yaro Muhammed, Kano: private publication, Zaria: Evans Brothers, 1975.
Fasahar Akiliya, Aƙilu Aliyu, Zaria: NNPC, 1977.
Gandoki, Bello Kagara, Zaria: Literature Bureau, 1934p repr. 1972.
Gangar Wa'azu, Muhammadu Na Birnin Gwari, Zaria: Gaskiya Corporation, 1969.
Gani Ga Wane, Abubakar Soron Ɗinki, Zaria: NNPC, 1990.
Gogan Naka, Garba Funtuwa, Zaria: Gaskiya Corporation, 1952.
Hattara Dai Masoya, Ado Ahmad, Kano: private publication, n.d.
Idan Ungulu ta Biya Bukata, Ɗan Azumi Baba, Kano: private publication, 1993.
Idon Matambayi, Muhammadu Gwarzo, Zaria: Literature Bureau, 1934.
Iliya Ɗan Maiƙarfi, Ahmadu Ingawa, Zaria: NORLA, 1951.
Imfiraji, Aliyu na Mangi, 9 vols. Zaria: NNPC, 1959.
In Da So Da Kauna, Ado Ahmad, Kano: private publication, 1991.
Jatau Na Kyallu, Shu'aibu Maƙarfi, Zaria: Gaskiya Corporation, 1960.
Jiki Magayi, John Tafida and Rupert East, Zaria: Literature Bureau, 1934.
Kimiyya da Fasaha, Salihu Kwantagora, Zaria: NNPC, 1972.
Kitsen Rogo, Abdulƙadir Ɗangambo, Zaria: NNPC, 1978.
Kulba Na Barna, Umaru Ɗanjuma Katsina, Zaria: NNPC, 1979.
Kyan Alkawari, Ɗan Azumi Baba, Kano: private publication, 1992.

Karamin Sani Kukumi Ne, Abubakar Imam and Rupert East, Zaria: Gaskiya Corporation, 1944.

Karshen Alewa Kasa, Bature Gagare, Lagos and Zaria: NNPC for Nigeria Magazine, 1982.

Kasbur Raga'ibu, Aliyu na Mangi, Zaria: Gaskiya Corporation, 1966.

Kauna Adon Zuciya, Aminu Abdu Na'inna, Kano: private publication, 1991.

Labaru Na Da Da Na Yanzu, Charles Whitting and Muhammadu Hadeja, Zaria: Translation Bureau, 1931.

Litafi na Tatsuniyoyi na Hausa, Frank Edgar, Belfast: W. Erskine Mayne, 1911–13.

Ma'ama'are, Usman Dan Fodio, Zaria: Gaskiya Corporation, 1959.

Magana Jari Ce Abubakar Imam, 3 vols, Zaria: Literature Bureau, 1938/9.

Malam Inkuntum, Alhaji Dogondaji, Zaria: NORLA, 1955.

Malam Mahamman, Bello Muhammad, Zaria: NNPC, 1974.

Mallakin Zuciyata, Sulaiman Ibrahim Katsina, Zaria: NNPC, 1980.

Masoyan Zamani, Ado Ahmad, Kano: private publication, 1993.

Matar Mutum Kabarinsa, Bashari Farouk Roukbah, Zaria: NNPC, 1974.

Matsolon Attajiri ['Merchant of Venice'], Dahiru Idris (trans.), Zaria: NNPC, 1981.

Mutanen Kogo (People of the Cave), Ahmed Sabir (trans.), Ibadan: Oxford University Press, 1976.

Na Tanko, Ibrahim Tajo, Kano: private publication, 1979.

Nagari Na Kowa, Jabiru Abdullahi, Zaria: Gaskiya Corporation, 1968.

Nuniyatul Amdahi, Aliyu na Mangi, Zaria: NNPC, 1972.

Rikicin Duniya, Dan Azumi Baba, Kano: private publication, 1990.

Ruwan Bagaja, Abubakar Imam, Zaria: Literature Bureau, 1934.

Shaihu Umar, Abubakar Tafawa Balewa, Zaria: Literature Bureau, 1934.

Sihirtaccen Gari, Amadu Katsina, Zaria: Gaskiya Corporation, 1952.

Six Hausa Plays, Rupert East, Zaria: Literature Bureau, 1936.

So Aljannar Duniya, Hafsatu Abdulwahid, Zaria: NNPC, 1980.

So Marurun Zuciya, Aminu Abdu Na'inna, Kano: private publication, 1991.

Soyayya Ta Fi Kudi, Hadi Abdullahi Alkanci, Zaria: NNPC, 1982.

Tabarmar Kunya, Adamu Dan Goggo and David Hofstad, Zaria: NNPC, 1969.

Tauraruwa Mai Wutsiya, Umaru Dembo, Zaria: NNPC, 1969.

Tauraruwar Hamada, Sa'idu Ahmed, Zaria: Gaskiya Corporation, 1965.

Tsofaffin Wakoki da Sababbin Wakoki na Alhaji Mudi Sipikin, Mudi Sipikin, Zaria: NNPC, 1971.

Tsumangiyar Kan Hanya, Musa Mohammed Bello, Lagos and Zaria: NNPC for Nigeria Magazine, 1982.

Tura Ta Kai Bango, Sulaiman Ibrahim Katsina, Zaria: NNPC, 1983.

Turmin Danya, Sulaiman Ibrahim Katsina, Lagos and Zaria: NNPC for Nigeria Magazine, 1982.

Uwar Gulma, Mohammed Sada, Zaria: NNPC, 1968.

Wa Zai Auri Jahila?, Hajiya Balaraba Ramat, Kano: private publication, 1990.

Wakar Hada Kan Al'ummar Afirka, Abubakar Ladan, Ibadan: OUP, 1976.

Wakokin Aliyu Dan Sidi, Sarkin Zazzau, Aliyu Dan Sidi, Zaria: NNPC, 1980.

Wakokin Hausa [anthology], *Gargadi don Falkawa, Damina, Hana Zalunci, Mu Sha Falala, Uwar Mugu, Munafunci da Annamimanci, Sha'anonin Duniya, Tabbat Hakikan,* Zaria: Gaskiya Corporation, 1957.

Wakokin Hikima, Ibrahim Yaro Yahaya (ed.) Ibadan: Oxford University Press, 1975.

Wakokin Hikimomin Hausa, Ibrahim Yaro Muhammed, Zaria: NNPC, 1974.

Wakokin Mu'azu Hadeja, Mu'azu Hadeja, Zaria: Gaskiya Corporation, 1955.

Wakokin Sa'adu Zungur, Sa'adu Zungur, Zaria: Gaskiya Corporation, 1955.

Wasan Marafa, Abubakar Tunau, Zaria: Gaskiya Corporation, 1949.
Zababbun Wakokin Da Da Na Yanzu, Dandatti Abdulkadir, Lagos: Nelson, 1979.
Zabi Naka, Munir Muhammed Katsina, Lagos and Zaria: NNPC for Nigeria Magazine, 1982.
Zamanin Nan Namu, Shu'aibu Makarfi, Zaria: NORLA, 1959.

GENERAL BIBLIOGRAPHY

Aarne, A. A. and Stith Thompson (1961), *The Types of the Folktale: a Classification and Bibliography.* Folklore Fellows Communications vol. 1, Helsinki: Folklore Society. 184.
Aba'ali, Rabi'u M. (1982), 'Jigogin Shaihu Umar: dangantakarsu ga halayyar zaman Hausawa da abokan huldarsu', BA final paper, University of Maiduguri.
Abalogu, U. N. , G. Ashiwaju and R. Amadi-Tshiwala (eds), (1981), *Oral Poetry in Nigeria.* Lagos: Nigeria Magazine.
Abdu, Garba (1981), 'Wasannin kwaikwayon baka na Hausa', BA final paper, University of Sokoto.
Abdu, Sade (1985), 'Adabi madubin al'umma: nazarin halayen Hausawa ta fuskar Salihi na cikin littafin Nagari na Kowa', BA final paper, Bayero University.
Abdu, Yusha'u (1985), 'Tasirin waka ga al'umma: gudunmawar rubutattun wakoki ga rayuwar Hausawa', BA final paper, Bayero University.
Abdulkadir, Dandatti (1971a), 'Bayani kan "Maraba da 'Yanci"', *Harsunan Nijeriya* 1: 36–9.
Abdulkadir, Dandatti (1971b), 'Modern Hausa poetry by Sa'ad Zungur', MA thesis, University of Wisconsin, Madison.
Abdulkadir, Dandatti (1974), *Poetry, Life and Opinions of Sa'adu Zungur.* Zaria: NNPC.
Abdulkadir, Dandatti (1975), 'The role of an oral singer in Hausa/Fulani society: a case study of Mamman Shata', PhD thesis, Indiana University.
Abdulkadir, Dandatti (1976), 'The role of a Hausa poet', *Harsunan Nijeriya* 6: 1–20.
Abdulkadir, Dandatti (1980), *Zababbun Wakokin Da da na Yanzu.* Lagos: Nelson.
Abdulkadir, Dandatti (1981), 'Oral composition: a historical appraisal', in U. N. Abalogu, G. Ashiwaju and R. Amadi-Tshiwala (eds), *Oral Poetry in Nigeria,* pp 18–36. Lagos: Nigeria Magazine.
Abdulkadir, Dandatti (1982), 'The social settings and occasions for oral poetry in Hausa/Fulani society', in Herrmann Jungraithmayr (ed.), *The Chad Languages in the Hamitosemitic-Nigritic Border Area (Papers of the Marburg Symposium, 1979),* pp 233–43. Berlin: Dietrich Reimer.
Abdulkadir, Dandatti (1984), 'Dangantakar labarun gargajiya da al'umma', in I.Y. Yahaya and A. Rufa'i (eds), *Studies in Hausa Language, Literature and Culture: Proceedings of the First International Hausa Conference, July 1978,* pp 194–202. Kano: Bayero University.
Abdullahi, Abba Ahmed (1987), 'Tasirin adabin baka kan kagaggun littafan zube na gasa ta farko (1933)', BA final paper, Ahmadu Bello University.
Abdullahi, A.G.D. (1984), 'Tasirin al'adu da dabi'u iri-iri a cikin "Tauraruwa mai Wutsiya"', in I.Y. Yahaya and A. Rufa'i (eds), *Studies in Hausa Language, Literature and Culture: Proceedings of the First International Hausa Conference, July 1978,* pp 237–43. Kano: Bayero University.
Abdullahi, Jabiru (1968), *Nagari Na Kowa.* Zaria: Gaskiya Corporation.
Abdulraheem, O. (1979), 'Myths of hierarchy and stability in an Islamic polity: the example of Shehu Umar', *Kano Studies* (New Series), 1(4): 142–5.
Abdulwahid, Hafsatu (1980), *So Alijannar Duniya.* Zaria: NNPC.

Abdulwalid, Talle F. (1973), 'The role of women as portrayed in Hausa drama', BA final paper, Bayero University.

Abdurrahman, Mohammed Shafi'i (1983), 'Nazari akan tatsuniyoyin Hausa da na Nufanci', BA final paper, University of Sokoto.

Abdurrahman, Umar (1985), 'Elements of Sufism in Na Mangi's poetry, especially in his use of metaphor and images', MA thesis, University of Wisconsin, Madison.

Abdurrahman, Umar (1990/1), 'Traditionalism versus modernism in Shu'aibu Maƙarfi's "Zamanin Nan Namu [These Times of Ours]"', Harsunan Nijeriya 15: 16–25.

Abdurrahman, Umar (n.d.), 'Use of images and metaphors to illustrate themes in Aliyu na Mangi's Sufi poetry', unpublished paper, University of Wisconsin, Madison.

Abubakar, Dembo Lere (1982), 'Nazarin tatsuniyar Hausa', BA final paper, University of Sokoto.

Abubakar, Hamisu (1990), 'Kwatanta tsofaffin littattafan zube da sababbin littattafan zube na Hausa', BA final paper, Bayero University.

Abubakar, Hassan Sani (1991), 'Shehu Ajilo Danguzuri: rayuwarsa da ayyukansa', BA final paper, Bayero University.

Adamu, Mahdi (1978), The Hausa Factor in West African History. Zaria: Ahmadu Bello University Press.

Adamu, Rakiya (1991), 'Malam ko wani dodo: bayanin rayuwa da ayyukan sarkin bori Sule', BA final paper, Bayero University.

Adamu, Salisu (1985), 'Saƙon Magana Jari Ce ga jama'a', BA final paper, University of Maiduguri.

Adeleye, R. A. (1971), Power and Diplomacy in Northern Nigeria 1804–1906. London: Longman.

Adeleye, R. A. (1985), 'Hausaland and Borno 1600–1800', in J. F. A. Ajayi and Michael Crowder (eds), History of West Africa (3rd ed.), pp 577–623. London: Longman.

Ado, Rabi'u (1987), 'Alaƙar wasannin kwaikwayo ga wasu hanyoyin rayuwar al'ummar Hausa', BA final paper, Bayero University.

Ahmad, Ado (1991), In Da So Da Kauna. Kano: private publication.

Ahmad, Ado (1993), Masoyan Zamani. Kano: private publication.

Ahmad (Ado) (n.d.), Hattara Dai Mosoya. Kano: private publication.

Ahmad, Mustapha (1987), 'The use of figures of speech in the works of Sa'adu Zungur', BA final paper, Bayero University.

Ahmad, Sa'idu Baɓura (1981), 'Structure, meaning and cultural reflection in oral narrative: a case study of Hausa tatsuniya', MA thesis, Bayero University.

Ahmad, Sa'idu Baɓura (1986), 'Narrator as interpreter: stability and variation in Hausa tales', PhD thesis, University of London.

Ahmad, Sa'idu Baɓura (1989), 'Stability and variation in Hausa tales', African Languages and Cultures 2(2): 113–131.

Ahmad, Sa'idu Baɓura and Graham Furniss (1994), 'Pattern, interaction and the non-dialogic in performance by Hausa rap artists', Oral Tradition 9(1): 113–35.

Ahmadu, Garba Mohammed (1986), 'Aikin gayya da waƙoƙinsa', BA final paper, Ahmadu Bello University.

Ahmed, Abubakar (1980), 'Matsayin kirari a adabin baka na Hausa', BA final paper, Bayero University.

Ahmed, A'isha (1981), 'An anthology of the verse of Nana Asma'u', MA thesis, School of Oriental and African Studies, University of London.

Ahmed, Danjuma (1989), 'Nazari akan rayuwar Alhaji Haruna Uji da waƙoƙinsa na soyayya', BA final paper, Bayero University.

Ahmed, Sa'idu (1965), *Tauraruwar Hamada*. Zaria: Gaskiya Corporation.

Ahmed, Shuaibu (1984), 'Take a fadar Zazzau', BA final paper, Ahmadu Bello University.

Ahmed, Umar A. (1992), 'Food poetries [sic], from Sokoto: analysis of some famine songs', BA final paper, University of Sokoto.

Ahmed, Umaru Balarabe (1972), *Bora da Mowa*. Zaria: NNPC.

Ahmed, Umaru Balarabe (1983), *Amina Sarauniyar Zazzau*. Zaria: Hudahuda Press.

Ahmed, Umaru Balarabe (1985), *Nau'o'in Wasannin Kwaikwayon Hausawa: A Taxonomy of Hausa Drama*. Zaria: Ahmadu Bello University Press.

Ahmed, Umaru Balarabe (1987), 'Muhammad Agigi's trans-saharan saga by Haji Ahmadu Kano: a critique of an early (1902), Hausa dramatic literature', in *Fourth International Conference on Hausa Language, Literature and Customs*. Bayero University: Centre for the Study of Nigerian Languages.

Ahmed, Ya'u (1984), 'Wasan tashe a Azare', BA final paper, University of Sokoto.

Ainu, Hamza A. (1984), 'Rayuwar Ibrahim Khalilu da waƙoƙinsa', BA final paper, University of Sokoto.

Ajiya, Abdullahi Baba (1985), 'Rayuwar mutanen birni ta zamani a arewancin Nijeriya: bincike kan "Kitsen Rogo" na Abdulƙadir Dangambo', BA final paper, University of Maiduguri.

Alhaji, Usman (1973), 'Alhaji Mudi Sipikin: rayuwarsa da waƙoƙinsa', BA final paper, Bayero University.

Alhamdu, Dauda ibn (1973), 'Tashe musamman na ƙasar Kano', BA final paper, Bayero University.

Al-Hassan, Bello Sodangi Yaro (1979), 'Narambaɗa da waƙoƙinsa', BA final paper, Bayero University.

Aliyu, Aƙilu (1977), *Fasahar Aƙiliya*. Zaria: NNPC.

Aliyu, Mohammed Abba (1982), 'Matsayin wasan kwaikwayo a rayuwar Hausawa', BA final paper, University of Sokoto.

Aliyu, Muhammad Sani (1980), 'Ahmadu Danmatawalle da waƙoƙinsa', BA final paper, Bayero University.

Aliyu, Muhammad Sani (1982), 'Shortcomings in Hausa society as seen by representative Hausa Islam poets from ca. 1950 to ca. 1982', MA thesis, Bayero University.

Aliyu, Musa Idris (1987), 'Wasannin kwaikwayo na yara', BA final paper, Ahmadu Bello University.

Aliyu, Sule Baba (1986), 'Alhaji Isa maikukuma Minna da waƙoƙinsa', BA final paper, University of Sokoto.

Aliyu, Tijjani (1974), 'Rayuwa da ayyukan Aƙilu Aliyu', BA final paper, Bayero University.

Aliyu, Y. Abubakar (1974), 'The establishment and development of emirate government in Bauchi, 1805–1903', PhD thesis, Ahmadu Bello University.

Alkanci, Hadi Abdullahi (1982), *Soyayya Ta Fi Kuɗi*. Zaria: NNPC.

Alƙali, Mahbub Amin (1982), 'Rayuwar Alhaji Bello Alƙali Giɗaɗawa Sakkwato da waƙoƙinsa', BA final paper, University of Sokoto.

Ames, David W. (1965), 'Hausa drums of Zaria', *Ibadan* 21: 62–80.

Ames, David W. (1968), 'Professionals and amateurs: the musicians of Zaria and Obimo', *African Arts* 1: 40–45; 80–84.

Ames, David W. (1970), 'Urban Hausa music', *African Urban Notes* 5(4): 19–24.

Ames, David W. (1973a), 'Igbo and Hausa musicians: a comparative examination', *Ethnomusicology* 17(2): 250–78.

Ames, David W. (1973b), 'A sociocultural view of Hausa musical activity', in Warren L. D'Azevedo (ed.), *The Traditional Artist in African Societies*, pp 128–61.

Bloomington and London: Indiana University Press.

Ames, David W., Edgar A. Gregersen and Thomas Neugebauer (1971), 'Taaken samarii: a drum language of Hausa youth', *Africa* 41(1): 12–31.

Ames, David W. and Anthony V. King (1971), *Glossary of Hausa Music and its Social Context*. Evanston, Ill.: Northwestern University Press.

Amina, Abdullahi (1987), 'Zamananci a ƙagaggun littafan zube na gasa ta biyu (1979) ', BA final paper, Ahmadu Bello University.

Aminu, Mamudu (1984), 'Muhimmancin maroƙan baka a ƙasar Hausa', in I. Y. Yahaya and A. Rufa'i (eds), *Studies in Hausa Language, Literature and Culture: Proceedings of the First International Hausa Conference, July 1978*, pp 203–24. Kano: Bayero University.

Aminu, Mamudu (1993), *Ma'aunin Wakokin Baka na Hausa*. Kano: private publication.

Arnott, D. W. (1969), 'The song of the rains', *African Language Studies* 9: 120–47.

Arnott, D. W. (1975), 'Waƙar 'Yancii: its form and language', *African Language Studies* 16: 25–36.

Arnott, D. W. (1988), 'Aƙilu Aliyu, wordsmith: some aspects of the language of his poetry', in Graham Furniss and Philip J. Jaggar (eds), *Studies in Hausa Language and Linguistics: in honour of F. W. Parsons*, pp 151–67. London and New York: Kegan Paul International in association with the International African Institute.

Ashcroft, Bill, Gareth Griffiths and Helen Tiffin (1989), *The Empire Writes Back: Theory and Practice in Post-Colonial Literatures*. London: Routledge.

Attahiru, Abdullahi Ahmed (1989), 'Nazari akan muhimmancin Shago wajen bunƙasa wasan dambe a arewacin Najeriya', BA final paper, University of Sokoto.

Auta, Aminu Lawal (1986), 'Gudummawar waƙoƙin makaɗan baka dangane da adana tarihi', MA thesis, Bayero University.

Awde, Nicholas (1988), 'A Hausa language and linguistics bibliography 1976–86, (including supplementary material for other years)', in Graham Furniss and Philip J. Jaggar (eds), *Studies in Hausa Language and Linguistics: in honour of F. W. Parsons*, pp 253–78. London and New York: Kegan Paul International in association with the International African Institute.

Azzolina, D. S. (1987), *Tale Type- and Motif-Indexes: an Annotated Bibliography*. New York: Garland.

Baba, Dan Azumi (1990), *Rikicin Duniya*. Kano: private publication.

Baba, Dan Azumi (1990), *Amintacciyar Soyayya*. Kano: private publication.

Baba, Dan Azumi (1990), *Kyan Alkawari*. Kano: private publication.

Baba, Dan Azumi (1990), *Idan Ungulu ta Biya Bukata*. Kano: private publication.

Babalola, Adeboye (1971), 'A survey of modern literature in the Yoruba, Efik and Hausa languages', in B. King (ed.), *Introduction to Nigerian Literature*, pp 57–63. Lagos: Evans.

Babba, Gambo U. (1986), 'Hajiya Hasana Ahmad Sufi da ayyukanta', BA final paper, Ahmadu Bello University.

Badawi, Ali Ahmed (1979), 'Karin waƙa a harshen Hausa (a study of Hausa verse prosody)', BA final paper, Ahmadu Bello University.

Badejo, Peter (1980), 'Bori spirit possession religion as a dance event: a pre-Islamic Hausa phenomenon', MA thesis, University of California, Los Angeles.

Bagari, Dauda Muhammad (1988), 'The use of linguistic devices in Hausa poetry', in Graham Furniss and Philip J. Jaggar (eds), *Studies in Hausa Language and Linguistics: in honour of F. W. Parsons*, pp 168–80. London and New York: Kegan Paul International in association with the International African Institute.

Bagaye, Yakubu L. Ibrahim (1992), 'Nazarin karin magana mai labari', BA final paper, University of Sokoto.

Bagudo, Fatima Abubakar (1985), 'Waƙoƙin mata na daɓe da daka a Sakkwato', BA final paper, University of Sokoto.

Baier, Stephen (1980), *An Economic History of Central Niger*. Oxford: Clarendon Press.

Bakhtin, M. (1966), *Rabelais and His World*. Cambridge, Mass.: MIT Press.

Bakhtin, M (1981), *The Dialogic Imagination: Four Essays*. Austin: University of Texas Press.

Bala, Salamatu Lami (1982), 'Karin magana', BA final paper, Ahmadu Bello University.

Balarabe, Abubakar (1980), 'Rayuwar Garba Gwandu da waƙoƙinsa', BA final paper, University of Sokoto.

Baldi, Sergio (1977), *Systematic Hausa Bibliography*. Rome: Istituto Italo-Africano.

Balewa, Abubaker Tafawa (1934), *Shaihu Umar*. Zaria: Literature Bureau.

Balla, Zilai Y. (1972), 'Comparing Uwar Gulma and Zamanin Nan Namu', BA final paper, Bayero University.

Bamalli, Nuhu (1950), *Bala da Babiya*. Zaria: Gaskiya Corporation.

Bappa, M. S. (1985), 'Roƙo: tradition and change in a Hausa theatrical form', MA thesis, Ahmadu Bello University.

Barber, Karin (1991), *I Could Speak Until Tomorrow: Oriki, Women and the Past in a Yoruba Town*. Edinburgh: Edinburgh University Press and Washington DC: Smithsonian Institution Press for the International African Institute.

Barber, Karin (1995), 'African language literature and post-colonial criticism', *Research in African Literatures*.

Barkindo, Bawuro M. (ed.), (1983), *Studies in the History of Kano*. Ibadan: Heinemann.

Barkow, Jerome (1970), 'Hausa and Maguzawa: processes of group differentiation in a rural area of North-Central State of Nigeria', PhD thesis, University of Chicago.

Barkow, Jerome (1973), 'Muslims and Maguzawa in North-Central State, Nigeria: an ethnographic comparison', *Canadian Journal of African Studies* 7(1): 59–76.

Bauman, Richard (1986), *Story, Performance and Event: Contextual Studies of Oral Narrative*. Cambridge: Cambridge University Press.

Bayero, Shehu (1971), 'Topical poems', BA final paper, Bayero University.

Bayero, S. A. (1970), 'Prosody for Hausa poetry', *Nigeria Magazine* 104: 31–3.

Beik, Janet (1984a), 'Hausa theatre in Niger: a contemporary oral art', PhD thesis, University of Wisconsin, Madison.

Beik, Janet (1984b), 'National development as theme in current Hausa drama in Niger', *Research in African Literatures* 15(1): 1–24.

Beik, Janet (1986), 'Plays without playwrights: the community creation of contemporary Hausa theatre in Niger', in Ellen Julien, Mildred Mortimer and Curtis Schade (eds), *African Literature in Its Social and Political Dimensions*, pp 23–32. Washington, D.C.: Three Continents Press.

Beik, Janet (1987), *Hausa Theatre in Niger: A Contemporary Oral Art*. New York and London: Garland.

Beik, Janet (1991), 'Women's roles in the contemporary Hausa theater of Niger', in Catherine Coles and Beverly Mack (eds), *Hausa Women in the Twentieth Century*, pp 232–430, Madison: University of Wisconsin Press.

Bello, Giɗaɗo (1976), 'Yabo, zuga da zambo a waƙoƙin sarauta', *Harsunan Nijeriya* 6: 21–34.

Bello, Ibrahim (1985), 'Take da kirari a fadar Gombe', BA final paper, Ahmadu Bello University.

Bello, M. (1981), 'Hoton rayuwa cikin wasan kwaikwayo: misalai daga Shu'aibu Maƙarfi', *Harsunan Nijeriya* 11: 91–106.

Bello, Muhammadu Sani (1986), 'Tanade-tanaden gina 'yan wasa a aikataccen wasan kwaikwayo', BA final paper, Bayero University.

Bello, Musa Mohammed (1982), *Tsumangiya Kan Hanya*. Lagos and Zaria: NNPC. for Nigeria Magazine.

Bello, Zainab Ibrahim (1991), *Wasannin Tashe a Kasar Hausa*. Kano: History and Culture Bureau.

Besmer, Fremont E. (1970), 'An Hausa song from Katsina', *Ethnomusicology* 14(3): 418–38.

Besmer, Fremont E. (1971), 'Hausa court music in Kano, Nigeria', PhD thesis, Columbia University.

Besmer, Fremont E. (1973), 'Praise-epithets and song texts for some important bori spirits in Kano', *Harsunan Nijeriya* 3: 15–38.

Besmer, Fremont E. (1975), '"Boori": structure and process in performance', *Folia Orientalia* 16: 101–30.

Besmer, Fremont E. (1983), *Horses, Musicians and Gods: the Hausa Cult of Possession Trance*. South Hadley (Mass): Bergin and Garvey.

Bichi, Abdu Yahaya (1973), 'Wakokin bikin aure', BA final paper, Bayero University.

Bichi, Abdu Yahaya (1975), 'Wakokin aure a kasar Hausa', *Harsunan Nijeriya* 5: 41–53.

Bichi, Abdu Yahaya (1978), 'An annotated collection of Hausa folktales from Nigeria', MA thesis, Indiana University, Bloomington.

Bichi, Abdu Yahaya (1979a), 'Cultural reflection in Hausa folklore', *Harsunan Nijeriya* 9: 99–111.

Bichi, Abdu Yahaya (1979b), *Wakokin Bikin Aure*. Lagos: Thomas Nelson.

Bichi, Abdu Yahaya (1983/5), 'The meaning and functions of Hausa riddles', *Harsunan Nijeriya* 13: 33–48.

Bichi, Abdu Yahaya (1985), 'Wedding songs as regulators of social control among the Hausa of Nigeria', PhD thesis, University of Pennsylvania.

Birnin Kudu, Umaru Sani (1984), 'Takaitaccen nazari kan bori a kasar Hausa', BA final paper, Ahmadu Bello University.

Birniwa, Haruna Abdullahi (1981), 'The Imfiraji 1 and V of Aliyu na Mangi', MA thesis, SOAS, University of London.

Birniwa, Haruna Abdullahi (1987), 'Conservatism and dissent: a comparative study of NPC/NPN and NEPU/PRP Hausa political verse from ca. 1946 to 1983', PhD thesis, University of Sokoto.

Boyd, Jean (1982), 'The contribution of Nana Asma'u Fodio to the Jihad of Shehu dan Fodio, 1820–65', MPhil thesis, Polytechnic of North London.

Boyd, Jean (1986), 'The Fulani women poets', in Mahdi Adamu and A. H. M. Kirk-Greene (eds), *Pastoralists of the West African Savanna*, pp 127–42. Manchester: Manchester University Press for the International African Institute.

Boyd, Jean (1989), *The Caliph's Sister. Nana Asma'u, 1793–1865: Teacher, Poet and Islamic Leader*. London: Frank Cass.

Boyd, Jean and Graham Furniss (1995), 'Mobilise the people: the qasida in Fulfulde and Hausa as purposive literature', in Christopher Shackle and Stefan Sperl (eds), *Qasida Poetry in Islamic Asia and Africa: Vol.1: Classical Traditions and Modern Meanings*, Leiden: Brill.

Boyd, Jean and Murray Last (1985), 'The role of women as "agents religieux" in Sokoto', *Canadian Journal of African Studies* 19(2): 283–300.

Boyd, Jean and Beverly B. Mack (forthcoming), *The Collected Works of Nana Asma'u*.

Brenner, Louis and Murray Last (1985), 'The role of language in West African Islam', *Africa* 55(4): 432–46.

Buhari, Ibrahim Maigari (1988), 'Nazarin jigogin wasu kagaggun labaran Hausawa', MA thesis, Bayero University.

Bungudu, Yusuf Abubakar (1990), 'Muhammadu Auwalu Isa Bungudu da wakokinsa', BA final paper, University of Sokoto.

Bunza, Aliyu Muhammad (1985), 'Tasirin addinin musulunci cikin rubutattun waƙoƙin Hausa', BA final paper, University of Sokoto.

Bunza, Abdullahi U. N. (1984), 'Wasannin Tashe a gundumar ƙasar Gwandu', BA final paper, University of Sokoto.

Batagarawa, Aminu Galadima (1983), 'Waƙoƙin Shehu Alkanci', BA final paper, Ahmadu Bello University.

Callaway, Barbara (1987), *Muslim Hausa Women in Nigeria*. Syracuse, New York: Syracuse University Press.

Cancel, Robert (1989), *Allegorical Speculation in an Oral Society: The Tabwa Narrative Tradition*. Berkeley: University of California Press.

Caron, Bernard (1985), *Contes Haoussa* ['Tales from Niger']. Paris: CILF-EDICEF.

Chaibou, Dan-Inna (1979), 'La théâtralité en pays Hawsa', Mémoire de Maîtrise, Université Nationale de Côte d'Ivoire.

Chinweizu, Onwuchekwa Jemie and Ihechukwu Madubuike (1985), *Toward the Decolonization of African Literature: African Fiction and Poetry and their Critics*. London: Kegan Paul International.

Clark, Trevor (1991), *A Right Honourable Gentleman: Abubakar from the Black Rock*. London: Edward Arnold.

Cohen, Abner (1969), *Custom and Politics in Urban Africa: A Study of Hausa Migrants in Yoruba Towns*. London: Routledge and Kegan Paul.

Coles, Catherine M. (1983), 'Muslim women in town: social change among the Hausa of Northern Nigeria', PhD thesis, University of Wisconsin, Madison.

Coles, Catherine M. and Beverly Mack (eds), (1991), *Hausa Women in the Twentieth Century*. Madison: University of Wisconsin Press.

Cosentino, Donald J. (1978), 'An experiment in inducing the novel among the Hausa', *Research in African Literatures* 9(1): 19–30.

Crow, Brian and Michael Etherton (1979), 'Wasan Manoma: a community theatre in the Soba District, Kaduna State', *Savanna* 8(1): 5–12.

CSNL (1977), *Waka a Bakin Mai Ita*, Vol. 1. Zaria: NNPC.

CSNL (1979), *Waka a Bakin Mai Ita*, Vol. 2. Zaria: NNPC.

Daba, Habibu Ahmed (1973), 'Danmaraya mai kuntigi da waƙoƙinsa', BA final paper, Bayero University.

Daba, Habibu Ahmed (1978), 'Hausa oral poetry: a case study of Dan Maraya Jos', MA thesis, University of Khartoum.

Daba, Habibu Ahmed (1981), 'The case of Dan Maraya Jos: a Hausa poet', in U. N. Abalogu, G. Ashiwaju and R. Amadi-Tshiwala (eds), *Oral Poetry in Nigeria*, pp 209–29. Lagos: Nigeria Magazine.

Dabai, Lawal Mu'azu (1991), 'Kwatance tsakanin Zaman Duniya Iyawa Ne da Kulɓa na Barna', BA final paper, Bayero University.

Dabo, Suleiman Mijinyawa (1986), 'Tahaƙiƙiyar waƙar Bagauda ta Kano daga birnin Zazzau', BA final paper, Ahmadu Bello University.

Dagaceri, Mohammed K. (1990), 'M. Gambo Hawaja Jos da waƙoƙinsa', BA final paper, Bayero University.

Dankoussou, I. and A. Mahamman (n.d.), *Baakii Abim Maganaa*. Niamey: Centre Régional de Documentation pour la Tradition Orale.

Daura, Hauwa Ahmed R. (1985), 'Tasirin adabin baka ga rubutattun wasannin kwaikwayo', BA final paper, Ahmadu Bello University.

Daura, Ramlatu Jibir (1983), 'Kayadadden karin sauti a Hausa', BA final paper, Ahmadu Bello University.

Dawaki, Alhassan M. (1974), 'Alhaji Danƙwairo Maradu: rayuwarsa da waƙoƙinsa', BA final paper, Bayero University.

De Campos, Bettina (1994), *Die Kompositionstechnik der Hausa Sängerpoeten: Inter-*

relation von Funktion und Form in einem Genre westafrikanischer Oralliteratur. Hamburg and Münster: LIT Verlag.

Dembo, Umaru (1969), *Tauraruwa Mai Wutsiya*. Zaria: NNPC.

Diso, Daiyabu Miko (1979), 'A case study of Mudi Sipikin: his life, works and contribution towards Hausa literature', BA final paper, Bayero University.

Djedje, Jacqueline Cogdell (1978), 'The one-string fiddle in West Africa: a comparison of Hausa and Dagomba traditions', PhD thesis, University of California, Los Angeles.

Djedje, Jacqueline Cogdell (1982), 'The concept of patronage: an examination of Hausa and Dagomba one-string fiddle traditions', *Journal of African Studies* 9(3): 116–27.

Dogondaji, Alhaji (1955), *Malam Inkuntum*. Zaria: NORLA

Duffill, M. B. (1985), *The Biography of Madugu Mohamman mai Gashin Baki*. Los Angeles: Crossroads Press.

Duffill, M. B. (1986), 'Hausa poems as sources for social and economic history', *History in Africa* 13: 35–88.

Dunbar, Roberta A. (1970), 'Damagaram (Zinder, Niger), 1812–1906: the history of a central Sudanic kingdom', PhD thesis, University of California, Los Angeles.

Dunbar, Roberta A. (1977), 'Slavery and the evolution of nineteenth-century Damagaram', in Suzanne Meiers and Igor Kopytoff (eds), *Slavery in Africa: Historical and Anthropological Perspectives*, pp 155–77. Madison: University of Wisconsin Press.

Dunfawa, Atiku Ahmed (1983), 'Da da ido', BA final paper, University of Sokoto.

Dunfawa, Atiku Ahmad (1990), 'Gudummawar masu darika wajen habaka rubutattun waƙoƙin Hausa (the contribution of Islamic Sufi orders to the development of Hausa written poetry)', MA thesis, Ahmadu Bello University.

Dutse, Abdu Garba (1991), 'Rayuwa da ayyukan Malam Lawan Gajere, malam mai goge', BA final paper, Bayero University.

Dutse, Garba Shehu (1981), 'Almara a ƙasar Hausa', BA final paper, Bayero University.

Dutsi, Yakubu Maina (1992), 'Rayuwa da ayyukan Malam Tijjani Tukur Yola', BA final paper, Bayero University.

Dutsin-Ma, Lawal Umar (1981), 'Sa'idu Faru da waƙoƙinsa', BA final paper, Ahmadu Bello University.

Dahiru, Gambo (1990), 'Maidaji Sabon Birni da waƙoƙinsa', BA final paper, Bayero University.

Dahiru, Sa'idu Umar (1984), 'Kwatanta labarin Shaihu Umar wasan kwaikwayo da zube', BA final paper, Ahmadu Bello University.

Dahiru, Wali (1989), 'Sharhi da nazari kan waƙoƙin wayar da kai na Sambo Wali Gidaɗawa', BA final paper, University of Sokoto.

Dambatta, Magaji (1980), *Amadi Na Malam Amah*. Zaira: 1980.

Dan Fodio, Usman (1959), *Ma'ama'are*. Zaira: Gaskiya Corporation.

Dan Goggo, Adamu and David Hofstad (1969), *Tabarmar Kunya*. Zaira: NNPC.

Dan Sidi, Aliyu (1980), *Waƙoƙin Aliyu Dan Sidi, Sarkin Zazzau*. Zaria: NNPC.

Dan-Musa, Mu'azu Aliyu (1990), 'Nazari akan yadda mawaƙan baka ke aiwatar da waƙoƙinsu', BA final paper, Bayero University.

Dangambo, Abdulƙadir (1973a), 'Alhaji Aliyu Namangi da waƙoƙinsa', BA final paper, Bayero University.

Dangambo, Abdulƙadir (1973b), 'Shata da waƙoƙinsa', BA final paper, Bayero University.

Dangambo, Abdulƙadir (1974), 'Nazari akan "Nagari na Kowa" na Jabiru Abdullahi', *Harsunan Nijeriya* 4: 27–36.

Dangambo, Abdulƙadir (1978), *Kitzen Rogo*. Zaria: NNPC.

Dangambo, Abdulƙadir (1979), 'The use of Kiraari and Taakee in Hausa oral praise songs (Shata, Narambaɗa and Sa'idu Faru)', *Nigeria Magazine* 128–9: 89–99.

Dangambo, Abdulƙadir (1980a), 'The "signs of the Hour" among the Muslim Hausa, with special reference to their verse', *Kano Studies* 2(1): 150–61.

Dangambo, Abdulƙadir (1980b), 'Hausa wa'azi verse from ca. 1800 to ca. 1970: a critical study of form, content, language and style', PhD thesis, University of London.

Dangambo, Abdulƙadir (1982), 'Rikiɗar azanci: siddabarun salo da harshe cikin "Tabarƙoko"; tahamisin Aliyu ɗan Sidi, sarkin Zazzau', in I. Y. Yahaya, A. Rufa'i and A. Abu-Manga (eds), *Studies in Hausa Language, Literature and Culture: Proceedings of the Second International Hausa Conference, April 1981*, pp 191–234. Kano: Bayero University.

Dangambo, Abdulƙadir (1984a), 'The Nigerian Hausa Civil War poems', in I.Y. Yahaya and A. Rufa'i (eds), *Studies in Hausa Language, Literature and Culture: Proceedings of the First International Hausa Conference, July 1978*, pp 452–69. Kano: Bayero University.

Dangambo, Abdulƙadir (1984b), *Rabe-raben Adabin Hausa da Muhimmancinsa ga Rayuwar Hausawa*. Kano: Triumph.

Dangambo, Abdulƙadir (1996), *Gadon Fede Adabin Hausa: Hanyoyin Nazarin Waka da kagaggun labarai da Wasan Kwaikwayo*. Kano: Dar-Al-Arabia Nigeria.

Danjuma, Maigari Salihu (1982), 'Rabe-raben waƙoƙin Hausa da tasirinsu ga rayuwa a ƙasar Hausa', MA thesis, Bayero University.

Dankiri, Umaru Rabi'u (1980), 'Nazarin wasan kwaikwayo a Hausance', BA final paper, Bayero University.East, Rupert M. (1936a), 'A first essay in imaginative African literature', *Africa* 9(3): 350–7.

Danlami, Kabiru Alhaji (1992), 'Juyar waƙar Jiddul'ajizi ta malam Shitu ɗan Abdurra'uf daga ajami zuwan Hausan boko', BA final paper, Ahmadu Bello University.

Dinki, Abubakar Soron (1990), *Gani Ga Wane*. Zaria: NNPC.

East, Rupert M. (1936b), *Six Hausa Plays*. Zaria: Literature Bureau.

East, Rupert (1940), 'A Hausa Journal', *Oversea Education* 11(2): 83–90.

East, Rupert M. (1943), 'Recent activities of the Literature Bureau, Zaria, Northern Nigeria', *Africa* 14(1): 71–7.

East, Rupert (1946), 'An experiment in colonial journalism', *African Affairs* 45: 80–7.

East, Rupert M. (1949), 'The translation of ideas', *Proceedings of the Third International West African Conference*: 45–51.

Echard, Nicole (1978), 'La pratique religieuse des femmes dans une société d'hommes: les Hausa du Niger', *Revue française de sociologie* 19(4): 551–62.

Echard, Nicole (1989), *Bori: Génies d'un culte de possession hausa de l'Ader et du Kurfey (Niger)*. Paris: Institut d'Ethnologie.

Edgar, Frank (1911–13), *Litafi na Tatsuniyoyi na Hausa*. Belfast: W. Erskine Mayne.

Edgar, Frank (1924), *Dare Dubu da Daya*. 2 vols. Lagos: C. M. S. Bookshop.

Erlmann, Veit (1981), 'Data on the sociology of Hausa musicians in the valley of Maradi (Niger)', *Paideuma* 27: 63–110.

Erlmann, Veit (1982a), 'Musik und trance: symbolische aspekte des bori bessessenheitskultes der Hausa in Maradi (Niger)', *Africana Marburgensia* 15: 3–24.

Erlmann, Veit (1982b), 'Trance and music in the Hausa boorii spirit possession cult in Niger', *Ethnomusicology* 26(1): 49–58.

Ferguson, D. E. (1973), 'Nineteenth-century Hausaland, being a description by Imam Imoru of the land, economy, and society of his people', PhD thesis, University of California, Los Angeles.

Fika, Adamu (1978), *The Kano Civil War and British Over-rule*. Ibadan: Oxford University Press.

Foley, John Miles (1988), *The Theory of Oral Composition: History and Methodology*. Cambridge, Mass.: Harvard University Press.

Fuglestad, Finn (1983), *A History of Niger, 1850–1960*. Cambridge: Cambridge University Press.

Funtuwa, Garba (1952), *Gogan Naka*. Zaria: Gaskiya Corporation.

Furniss, Graham (1977), 'Some aspects of modern Hausa poetry: themes, style and values with special reference to the "Hikima" poetry circle in Kano', PhD thesis, University of London.

Furniss, Graham (1978), 'The application of ethics in contemporary Hausa didactic poetry', *African Languages/Langues africaines* 4: 127–39.

Furniss, Graham (1982), 'Aspects of style and meaning in the analysis of a Hausa poem', *Bulletin of the School of Oriental and African Studies* 45(3): 546–70.

Furniss, Graham (1983), 'Hausa literature', in Bernth Lindfors (ed.), *Research Priorities in African Literature*, pp 62–74. Oxford: K. G. Saur Verlag & Hans Zell.

Furniss, Graham (1983/5), 'A provisional bibliography of commentary and critical writing on Hausa literature: 1940–1984', *Harsunan Nijeriya* 13: 93–103.

Furniss, Graham (1984a), '"The Way of the World": the interplay of meaning and form in the interpretation of a Hausa poem', *Research in African Literatures* 15(1): 25–44.

Furniss, Graham (1984b), 'Some constraints upon the writing and dissemination of modern Hausa poetry', in I. Y. Yahaya and A. Rufa'i (eds), *Studies in Hausa Language, Literature and Culture: Proceedings of the First International Hausa Conference, July 1978*, pp 436–51. Kano: Bayero University.

Furniss, Graham (1985), 'Réflexions sur l'histoire récente de la littérature Haoussa', *Bulletin de l'AELIA* 8: 123–31.

Furniss, Graham (1988a), 'The language of praise and vilification: two poems by Muhammadu Audi of Gwandu about Abubakar, emir of Nupe', in Graham Furniss and Philip J. Jaggar (eds), *Studies in Hausa Language and Linguistics: in honour of F. W. Parsons*, pp 181–201. London and New York: Kegan Paul International in association with the International African Institute.

Furniss, Graham (1988b), 'Money, marriage and the young as issues in modern Hausa poetry', *African Languages and Cultures* 1(1): 45–60.

Furniss, Graham (1989), 'Typification and evaluation: a dynamic process in rhetoric', in Karin Barber and P. F. de M. Farias (eds), *Discourse and its Disguises: the Interpretation of African Oral Texts*, pp 24–33. Birmingham: Centre of West African Studies.

Furniss, Graham (1990), 'Fitila, une nouvelle revue radicale haoussa', *Politique Africaine* 37: 102–7.

Furniss, Graham (1991a), '"De la fantaisie à la réalité dans la littérature haoussa en prose" suivi de "Pourquoi étudier la poésie haoussa?"' (Travaux et Documents 31). Bordeaux: Centre d'Etude d'Afrique Noire.

Furniss, Graham (1991b), 'Burlesque in Hausa: "And my text for today is food" said Mr Matches', in Paul Baxter and Richard Fardon (ed.), *Voice, Genre, Text: Anthropological Essays in Africa and Beyond (Bulletin of the John Rylands University Library of Manchester* 73, 3*)*, pp 37–62.

Furniss, Graham (1991c), 'Hausa poetry on the Nigerian civil war', *African Languages and Cultures* 4(1): 21–8.

Furniss, Graham (1991d), 'Standards in speech, spelling and style – the Hausa case', in N. Cyffer, K. Schubert and H.-I. Weier (eds), *Language Standardization in Africa*, pp 97–110. Hamburg: Helmut Buske.

Furniss, Graham (1992), 'A note on Hausa literature and R. C. Abraham', in Philip J. Jaggar (ed.), *Papers in Honour of R. C. Abraham (African Languages and Cultures Supplement* 1*)*, pp 43–50. London: SOAS.

Furniss, Graham (1993a), 'Hausa poetry', in Alex Preminger and T. V. F. Brogan (eds), *The New Princeton Encyclopedia of Poetry and Poetics*, pp 496–7. Princeton: Princeton University Press.

Furniss, Graham (trans.), (1993b), 'Ma'ama'are', in Stefan Sperl (ed.), *Qasida: The Literary Heritage of an Arabic Poetic Form in Islamic Africa and Asia*, Vol. 2: *Anthology*, pp 204–45. London: Centre of Middle East Studies, School of Oriental and African Studies.

Furniss, Graham and Yunusa Dayyabu Ibrahim (1991/2), 'An early twentieth-century Hausa song: "Waƙar kuyangin Sokoto"', *Harsunan Nijeriya* 16: 47–60.

Furniss, Graham and Philip J. Jaggar (eds), (1988), *Studies in Hausa Language and Linguistics*. London and New York: Kegan Paul International in association with the International African Institute.

Gafai, Abdulkadir Lawal and Abubakar Usman (1990), 'Wasan Baura', BA final paper, University of Sokoto.

Gagare, Bature (1982), *Karshen Alewa Kasa*, Lagos and Zaria: NNPC for Nigeria Magazine.

Galadanci, M. K. M. (1975), 'The poetic marriage between Arabic and Hausa', *Harsunan Nijeriya* 5: 1–16.

Gani, Safiya Shehu (1984), 'Habaici', BA final paper, Ahmadu Bello University.

Garba, Abdullahi (1986), 'Nazarin waƙoƙin Sani Ibrahim Musawa', BA final paper, Ahmadu Bello University.

Garba, Alhaji (1982), 'Mamman Shata da waƙoƙinsa', BA final paper, Ahmadu Bello University.

Garba, Calvin Y. (1982), 'A linguistic analysis of Hausa karin magana', MA thesis, Bayero University.

Garba, Calvin Y. (1984), 'Socio-linguistic implications of the oral transmission of Hausa culture', in I. Y. Yahaya and A. Rufa'i (eds), *Studies in Hausa Language, Literature and Culture: Proceedings of the First International Hausa Conference, July 1978*, pp 470–7. Kano: Bayero University.

Garba, Rabi'u (1992), 'Waƙoƙin Mandiri', BA final paper, Ahmadu Bello University.

Gaya, Ahmed Sule (1972), 'A comparison between Mu'azu Haɗeja and Sa'adu Zungur', BA final paper, Bayero University.

Gaya, Tijjani Aliyu (1972), 'Malam Ashana da 'Yan Kamancinsa', BA final paper, Bayero University.

Gérard, Albert S. (1981), *African Language Literatures: An Introduction to the Literary History of Sub-Saharan Africa*. London: Longmans.

Gidley, C. G. B. (1965), 'Mantanfas – a study in oral tradition', *African Language Studies* 6: 32–51.

Gidley, C. G. B. (1967), ''Yankamanci – the craft of the Hausa comedians', *African Language Studies* 8: 52–81.

Gidley, C. G. B. (1970), 'Maiwutsiya: the comet myth among the Hausa', *African Language Studies* 11: 183–90.

Gidley, C. G. B. (1974), 'Karin magana and azanci as features of Hausa sayings', *African Language Studies* 15: 81–96.

Gidley, C. G. B. (1975), 'Roƙo: a Hausa praise crier's account of his craft', *African Language Studies* 16: 93–115.

Goody, Jack (ed.), (1968), *Literacy in Traditional Societies*. Cambridge: Cambridge University Press.

Goody, Jack (1987), *The Interface between the Written and the Oral*. Cambridge: Cambridge University Press.

Gouffé, Claude (1981), 'Comment recueillir et éditer les proverbes haoussa, quelques suggestions pratiques', in *Itinérances: à la mémoire de P. F. Lacroix*, pp 116–35. Paris: Société des Africanistes.

Greenberg, Joseph H. (1946), *The Influence of Islam on a Sudanese Religion*. New York: Monographs of the American Ethnological Association, 10.

Greenberg, Joseph H. (1949), 'Hausa verse prosody', *Journal of the American Oriental Society* 69: 125–35.

Greenberg, Joseph H. (1960), 'A survey of African prosodic systems', in S. Diamond (ed.), *Culture in History*, pp 925–50. New York: Columbia University Press.

Gumel, Muhammad Ahmad (1992), 'Tarbiyya da dangoginta a waƙoƙin makaɗan baka na Hausa', MA thesis, Ahmadu Bello University.

Gusau, Garba Hassan (1972), 'Hausa poetry', BA final paper, Bayero University.

Gusau, Garba Umaru (1988), 'Hasashen Basakkwace a bambancin karin harshen Hausa cikin waƙoƙin Alhaji Aƙilu Aliyu', BA final paper, University of Sokoto.

Gusau, Sa'idu Muhammadu (1983), 'Waƙoƙin noma na baka: yanaye-yanayensu da jigoginsu musamman a Sakkwato', 2 vols, MA thesis, Bayero University.

Gusau, Sa'idu Muhammadu (1988), 'Waƙoƙin makaɗan fada: sigoginsu da yanayinsu, musamman a ƙasar Sakkwato', PhD thesis, Bayero University.

Gwaram, Hauwa and Alhajiya 'Yar Shehu (1983), *Alƙalami a Hannun Mata*. Zaria: NNPC.

Gwari, Muhammadu Na Birnin (1969), *Gangar Wa'azu*. Zaria: Gaskiya Corporation.

Gwarzo, Muhammadu (1934), *Idon Matambayi*. Zaria: Literature Bureau.

Haɗeja, Mu'azu (1955), *Waƙoƙin Mu'azu Haɗeja*. Zaria: Gaskiya Corporation.

Hair, P. E. H. (1969), *The Early Study of Nigerian Languages*. Cambridge: Cambridge University Press.

Haliru, Altine (1983), 'Aliyu Ɗandawo da waƙoƙinsa', BA final paper, University of Sokoto.

Hallam, W. K. R. (1966), 'The Bayajida legend in Hausa folklore', *Journal of African History* 7(1): 47–60.

Hamid, Mahmoud Farouk (1992), 'Garba Supa: rayuwarsa da waƙoƙinsa', BA final paper, Bayero University.

Hamisu, Mohammed (1986), 'Roƙon ruwa', BA final paper, Ahmadu Bello University.

Hamza, Wada (1985), 'Narrative as a mirror of Hausa social relationships', MA thesis, Ahmadu Bello University.

Haruna, Aminu (1985), 'Amfani da salon neman haihuwa a rubutun zube na Hausa', BA final paper, Ahmadu Bello University.

Haruna, Danjuma Mohammed (1986), 'Tatsuniyoyi: ɗaya daga cikin nau'o'in adabi na Hausa da amfaninsu', BA final paper, University of Sokoto.

Haruna-Soba, F. B. (1982), 'Waƙoƙin sarkin Zazzau Aliyu ɗan Sidi', BA final paper, Ahmadu Bello University.

Hassan, Muhammadu Babanzara (1980), 'A critical study of specimens of Hausa political verse relating to the 1979 general election in Nigeria', MA thesis, SOAS, University of London.

Hassan, Muhammadu Babanzara (1982), 'Karin magana da salon magana', in I. Y. Yahaya, A. Rufa'i and A. Abu-Manga (eds), *Studies in Hausa Language, Literature and Culture: Proceedings of the Second International Hausa Conference, April 1981*, pp 163–78. Kano: Bayero University.

Hassan, Usman (1972), '"Uwar Gulma" ko "Shawuya Halima"?', *Harsunan Nijeriya* 2: 46–52.

Hassan, Usman (1973a), 'Alhaji Aliyu Namangi (a survey of his biography, the sources and features of his major works)', BA paper 5 dissertation, Bayero University.

Hassan, Usman (1973b), 'Tarihin rubuce-rubucen Hausa tun farkon ƙarni na sha tara (History of Hausa literature since early nineteenth century)', BA paper 3 dissertation, Bayero University.

Hausa Studies Association/Kungiyar Nazarin Hausa (n.d.), *Tsarin Kamus na Kebabbun Kalmomi na Ilimin Harsuna da Adabi*. Zaria: Ahmadu Bello University.

Hayatu, Husaini (ed.), (1991), *50 Years of Truth: The Story of Gaskiya Corporation 1939–1991*. Zaria: Gaskiya Corporation.

Herman, Jerzy (1982), ' "In the Name of God, I a Slave": a Hausa homily in verse from the manuscript IASAR/334', *Africana Bulletin* 31: 147–216.

Hill, Clifford Alden (1972), 'A study of ellipsis within Karin Magana: a Hausa tradition of oral art', PhD thesis, University of Wisconsin, Madison.

Hill, Clifford Alden and S Podstavsky (1976), 'The interfacing of language and music in Hausa praise-singing', *Ethnomusicology* 20(3): 535–40.

Hill, Polly (1972), *Rural Hausa: A Village and a Setting*. Cambridge: Cambridge University Press.

Hill, Polly (1976), 'From slavery to freedom: the case of farm-slavery in Nigerian Hausaland', *Comparative Studies in Society and History* 18(3): 395–426.

Hill, Polly (1977), *Population, Prosperity and Poverty: Rural Kano 1900 and 1970*. Cambridge: Cambridge University Press.

Hiskett, Mervyn (1964/5), 'The "Song of Bagauda": a Hausa kinglist and homily in verse', *Bulletin of the School of Oriental and African Studies* 27(3): 540–67; 28(1): 112–35; 28(2): 363–85.

Hiskett, Mervyn (1966), 'Hausa literature', in *Encyclopedia of Islam*, Leiden: Brill.

Hiskett, Mervyn (1967a), 'The Arab star-calendar and planetary system in Hausa verse', *Bulletin of the School of Oriental and African Studies* 30(1): 158–76.

Hiskett, Mervyn (1967b), 'Some historical and Islamic influences in Hausa folklore', *Journal of the Folklore Institute* 4(2/3): 145–61.

Hiskett, Mervyn (1970), 'Mamman Konni: an eccentric poet and holy man from Bodinga', *African Language Studies* 11: 211–29.

Hiskett, Mervyn (1971), 'The "Song of the Shaihu's Miracles": a Hausa hagiography from Sokoto', *African Language Studies* 12: 71–107.

Hiskett, Mervyn (1973), 'The origins, sources and form of Hausa Islamic verse', *Spectrum* 3: 127–53.

Hiskett, Mervyn (1975a), 'The development of Sa'ad Zungur's political thought from Maraba da Soja , through Arewa Jumhuriya ko Mulukiya to Wakar 'Yanci', *African Language Studies* 16: 1–23.

Hiskett, Mervyn (1975b), *A History of Hausa Islamic Verse*. London: SOAS.

Hiskett, Mervyn (1977a), *An Anthology of Hausa Political Verse (Hausa Texts Edited and Annotated)*. London: Department of Africa, SOAS.

Hiskett, Mervyn (1977b), *The Hausa Kashif al-Ghumma fi Ighatha al-fayda of Mijinyawa na Atiku (Edited and annotated Texts)*. London: Department of Africa, SOAS.

Hiskett, Mervyn (1977c), *The Ma'ama'are of Shehu Usuman dan Fodio as rendered into Hausa by Malam Isa (Ajami Text and Roman Transcription)*. London: Department of Africa, SOAS.

Hiskett, Mervyn (1980), 'The "community of grace" and its opponents, the "rejecters": a debate about theology and mysticism in Muslim West Africa with special reference to its Hausa expression', *African Language Studies* 17: 99–140.

Hiskett, Mervyn (1982), 'Towards a comparison of theme and style in the Hausa verse categories of wa'azi and madahu', in I. Y. Yahaya, A. Rufa'i and A. Abu-Manga (eds), *Studies in Hausa Language, Literature and Culture: Proceedings of the Second International Hausa Conference, April 1981*, pp 417–48. Kano: Bayero University.

Hiskett, Mervyn (1984a), *The Development of Islam in West Africa*. London: Longman.

Hiskett, Mervyn (1984b), 'The imagery of light and associated ideas in Hausa Islamic verse', in I. Y. Yahaya and A. Rufa'i (eds), *Studies in Hausa Language,*

Literature and Culture: Proceedings of the First International Hausa Conference, July 1978, pp 426–35. Kano: Bayero University.

Hiskett, Mervyn (1985), 'Enslavement, slavery and attitudes towards the legally enslavable in Hausa Islamic literature', in John Ralph Willis (ed.), *Slaves and Slavery in Muslim Africa*, pp 106–24. London: Cass.

Hobsbawm, E. and T. Ranger (eds), (1983), *The Invention of Tradition*. Cambridge: Cambridge University Press.

Hodge, Carleton (1976), 'Ajami literature: a proposal', *Language Sciences* 41: 35–7.

Hodgkin, T. (1966), 'The Islamic literary tradition in Ghana', in I. M. Lewis (ed.), *Islam in Tropical Africa*, pp 442–60. London: Oxford University Press for the International African Institute.

Hogendorn, J. (1978), *Nigerian Groundnut Exports: Origins and Early Development*. Zaria: Ahmadu Bello University Press.

Horn, Andrew (1981), 'Ritual, drama and the theatrical: the case of Bori spirit mediumship', in Y. Ogunbiyi (ed.), *Drama and Theatre in Nigeria: A Critical Source Book*, pp 181–202. Lagos: Nigeria Magazine.

Hunter, Linda (1981), 'Language attitudes in Hausa literature', *Harsunan Nijeriya* 11: 67–74.

Hunwick, John (1984), 'Songhay, Borno and the Hausa states 1450–1600', in J. F. A. Ajayi and Michael Crowder (eds), *History of West Africa* (Vol. 1, 3rd ed.), pp 323–371. London: Longman.

Hunwick, John (1991), 'Constructing an "historical" past: Arabic chronicles and African oral tradition in Kano (Nigeria)', unpublished manuscript, Department of History, Northwestern University.

Ibrahim, Abdu (1984), 'Jigo da salon sarrafa harshe a "Zamanin Nan Namu" da "Jatau na Kyallu" ', BA final paper, Ahmadu Bello University.

Ibrahim, Mohammed Aminu (1984), 'Alƙali Alhaji Haliru Wurno da waƙoƙinsa', BA final paper, University of Sokoto.

Ibrahim, Mohammed Danlami (1983), 'Waƙoƙin karuwanci', BA final paper, Ahmadu Bello University.

Ibrahim, Mohammed Sani (1976), 'Kowa ya sha kiɗa, abinsa ya bayar: nazari kan waƙoƙin makaɗan sarauta da makaɗan jama'a', BA final paper, Bayero University.

Ibrahim, Mohammed Sani (1982a), 'Adabin gargajiya na Hausa kafin da kuma bayan Musulunci', in I. Y. Yahaya, A. Rufa'i and A. Abu–Manga (eds), *Studies in Hausa Language, Literature and Culture: Proceedings of the Second International Hausa Conference, April 1981*, pp 99–132. Kano: Bayero University.

Ibrahim, Mohammed Sani (1982b), 'Rubutattun Waƙoƙin Hausa kafin zamanin Shehu Usman ɗan Fodio', *Harsunan Nijeriya* 12: 93–104.

Ibrahim, Muhammadu Sani (1983), *Kowa Ya Sha Kiɗa*. Zaria: Longman Nigeria.

Ibrahim, Zakari (1972), 'Comparison of Uwar Gulma with Tabarmar Kunya', BA final paper, Bayero University.

Idi, Aminu (1982), 'Bukukuwan al'adun gargajiya a ƙasar Kano da Sakkwato', BA final paper, University of Sokoto.

Idris, Dahiru (trans.) (1981), *Matsolon Attajiri* ['Merchant of Venice'], Zaria: NNPC.

Ikara, Abdullahi Tanko (1983), 'Umaru wazirin Gwandu da waƙoƙinsa', BA final paper, Ahmadu Bello University.

Iliya, Rakiya Muhammad (1992), 'Jigon jarunta a uku daga littattafan NORLA', BA final paper, University of Sokoto.

Imam, Abubakar (1934), *Ruwan Bagaja*. Zaria: Literature Bureau.

Imam, Abubakar (1938/9), *Magana Jari Ce*. 3 vols. Zaria: Literature Bureau.

Imam, Abubakar and Rupert East (1944), *Karamin Sani Kukumi Ne* Zaria:Gaskiya Corporation.

Ingawa, Ahmadu (1951), *Iliya Dan Maiƙarfi*. Zaria: NNPC.

Institute of Education, Ahmadu Bello University (1979), *Karatu da Rubutu a Harshen Hausa: Jagorar Ka'idojin Rubutun Hausa/ A Guide to Hausa Orthography*. Nigeria: Thomas Nelson.

Isah, Abdulmumini (1991), 'Alhaji Dahiru Musa Jahun Bauchi: rayuwarsa da ayyukansa', BA final paper, Bayero University.

Jaggar, Philip J. (1994), *The Blacksmiths of Kano: A Study in Tradition, Innovation and Entrepreneurship in the Twentieth Century*. Cologne: Rüdiger Köppe Verlag.

Jang, Tae-Sang (1994), 'Balance and bipartite structure in Hausa proverbs', PhD thesis, University of London.

Jez, Beata (1986), 'Fukcjonowanie watkow obcych w dziele *Magana Jari Ce* A. A. Imama ['Functioning of the foreign plots in the work *Magana Jari Ce* by A. A. Imam'], MA thesis, University of Warsaw.

Jibril, M. Munzali (1974), 'Northern Nigeria: literature and the English language', *Kano Studies* (New Series), 1(2): 37–44.

Jibrin, Kabir Tandama (1985), 'Bambancin wasa da wasan kwaikwayo', BA final paper, Ahmadu Bello University.

Joe, Audu Yusuf (1984), 'Hausa folk theatre and occupational groups: some examples in Zaria, Kaduna State', MA thesis, Ahmadu Bello University.

Johnston, H. A. S. (1966), *A Selection of Hausa Stories*. Oxford: Clarendon Press.

Junaidu, Isma'il (1976), 'Ciza ka Busa (poems),', BA final paper, Bayero University.

Junaidu, Isma'il (1981a), *Ciza Ka Busa*. Zaria: Longman Nigeria.

Junaidu, Isma'il (1981b), 'Preliminary study on phonological constituents of the Hausa metre', *Harsunan Nijeriya* 11: 25–42.

Junaidu, Isma'il (1982), 'Muhimmancin nazarin sautin rubutattun waƙoƙi', in I. Y. Yahaya, A. Rufa'i and A. Abu-Manga (eds), *Studies in Hausa Language, Literature and Culture: Proceedings of the Second International Hausa Conference, April 1981*, pp 21–32. Kano: Bayero University.

Junaidu, Isma'il (1988), 'Linguistic analysis of Hausa meter', *Research in African Literatures* 19(3): 350–64.

Junaidu, S. W. (1990), 'Resistance to Western culture in the Sakkwato Caliphate: a lesson to generations yet unborn', in Ahmad Mohammed Kani and Kabir Ahmed Gandi (eds), *State and Society in the Sokoto Caliphate*, pp 238–52. Sokoto: Usmanu Danfodiyo University.

Junaidu, Sambo (1985), 'The Sakkwato legacy of Arabic scholarship in verse between 1800–1890', PhD thesis, University of London.

Kabara, Garba Ahmed (1974), 'Life and Hausa poetry of Alhaji Nasiru Kabara, Kano', BA final paper, Bayero University.

Kafin-Hausa, Abubakar Adamu (1983), 'Hausa folk festivals: a study of a selection of seasonal ceremonials from the north-east of Kano', MA thesis, Ahmadu Bello University.

Kafin-Hausa, Abdullahi Umar (1976), 'Jiya da Yau (political poems),', BA final paper, Bayero University.

Kafin-Hausa, Abdullahi Umar (1982), 'Ma'ana da amfanin kirari a Hausa', in I. Y. Yahaya, A. Rufa'i and A. Abu-Manga (eds), *Studies in Hausa Language, Literature and Culture: Proceedings of the Second International Hausa Conference, April 1981*, pp 133–40. Kano: Bayero University.

Kafin-Hausa, Abdullahi Umar (1983), *Jiya da Yau*. Zaria: Longman Nigeria.

Kafin-Hausa, Abdullahi Umar (1985), 'Kirari a Hausa, matsayinsa da yanayinsa', MA thesis, Ahmadu Bello University.

Kagara, Bello (1934), *Gandoki*. Zaria: Literature Bureau.

Kaigama, Muhammadu (1976), 'Kwatantawa tsakanin rubutattun waƙoƙin Hausa da na Fulatanci', BA final paper, Bayero University.

Kallamu, Danbaba (1992), 'Rayuwa da ayyukan Alh. Usman Baba Fategi (Samanja mazan fama), musamman a kan shirin "Duniya Budurwar Wawa" da "Samanja Mazan Fama"', BA final paper, Bayero University.

Kang, Winifred C. (1982), 'Sembene Ousmane and Mamman Shata, the oral and written word in West African literature (Nigeria, Senegal)', PhD thesis, University of California.

Kani, A. M. (1978), 'Literary activities in Hausaland in the late 18th and early 19th centuries', MA thesis, Ahmadu Bello University.

Kankara, Musa Mohammed S. (1983), 'Damben gargajiya da wakokinsa', BA final paper, Ahmadu Bello University.

Kankiya, Ibrahim Ja'afaru and Abubakar Sani Sayaya (1987), 'Tasirin tatsuniya akan rubutun zube na Hausa', BA final paper, University of Sokoto.

Kano, Aminu (1973), *Rayuwar Ahmad Mahmud Sa'adu Zungur*. Zaria: NNPC.

Kano, Mamman (1924), *Dare Dubu da Daya* (Vols III and IV). Lagos: C.M.S. Bookshop.

Ka'oje, Abdullahi (1973), *Dare Daya*. Zaria: NNPC.

Karofi, Dauda Sulaiman (1980a), 'Mabarata: tasirinsu da gudummawarsu a kan adabin Hausa', BA final paper, Ahmadu Bello University.

Karofi, Dauda S. (1980b), 'Sara: sigarta da yaɗuwarta', *Harsunan Nijeriya* 10: 103–14.

Katsina, Amadu (1952), *Sihirtaccen Gari*. Zaria: Gaskiya Corporation.

Katsina, Munir Muhammed (1982), *Zabi Naka*. Lagos and Zaria: NNPC for Nigeria Magazine.

Katsina, Sulaiman Ibrahim (1980), *Mallakin Zuciyata*. aria: NNPC.

Katsina, Sulaiman Ibrahim (1982), *Turmin Danya*. Lagos and Zaria: NNPC for Nigeria Magazine.

Katsina, Sulaiman Ibrahim (1983), *Tura Ta Kai Bango*. Zaria: NNPC.

Katsina, Umaru Danjuma (1979), *Kulba Na Barna*. Zaria: NNPC.

Katsina, Umaru Danjuma (1988), *Ai Ga Irinta Nan*. Ibadan: University Press.

Katsina, Yahaya Aliyu (1984), 'Labarun raha da muhimmancinsu ga Hausawa', BA final paper, Ahmadu Bello University.

Kauru, Abubakar Umaru (1991), 'Dangantaka da banbance-banbance tsakanin rubutaccen wasan kwaikwayo da na rediyo', BA final paper, Ahmadu Bello University.

Keffi, Muhammadu (1974), 'Tarihin Abdurrahaman Galadiman Kotso', BA final paper, Bayero University.

King, Anthony V. (1966), 'A Boori liturgy from Katsina: introduction and Kiraarii texts', *African Language Studies* 7: 105–25.

King, Anthony V. (1967), 'A Boori liturgy from Katsina', *African Language Studies* (Supplement 7): 1–157.

King, Anthony V. (1969), 'Music at the court of Katsina – gangaa and kaakaakii', 3 vols, PhD thesis, University of London.

King, Anthony V. (1981), 'Form and functions in Hausa professional songs', in U. N. Abalogu, G. Ashiwaju and R. Amadi-Tshiwala (eds), *Oral Poetry in Nigeria*, pp 118–35. Lagos: Nigeria Magazine.

King, Anthony V. and R. Ibrahim (1968), '"The Song of the Rains": metric values in performance', *African Language Studies* 9: 148–55.

Kirk-Greene, A. H. M. (1966), *Hausa Ba Dabo Ba Ne*. Ibadan: Oxford University Press.

Kirk-Greene, A. H. M. (1974), *Mutumin Kirkii: The Concept of the Good Man in Hausa (Hans Wolff Memorial Lecture)*. Bloomington, Ind.: African Studies Program.

Kirk-Greene, A. H. M. and Paul Newman (1971), *West African Travels and Adventures: Two Autobiographical Narratives from Northern Nigeria*. New Haven and London: Yale University Press.

Kofoworola, Ziky O. (1977), 'A comparative analysis of the development of drama in Kaduna State and in medieval and early Renaissance Europe', MA thesis, Ahmadu Bello University.

Kofoworola, Ziky O. (1980/2), 'A general survey of folk-theatre and traditions among the Hausa and some other ethnic groups in the northern states of Nigeria: research report and documentation', Centre for Nigerian Cultural Studies, Ahmadu Bello University.

Kofoworola, Ziky O. (1981a), 'The Hausa example', in U. N. Abalogu, G. Ashiwaju and R. Amadi-Tshiwala (eds), Oral Poetry in Nigeria, pp 290–308. Lagos: Nigeria Magazine.

Kofoworola, Ziky O. (1981b), 'Traditional forms of Hausa drama', in Y. Ogunbiyi (ed.), Drama and Theatre in Nigeria: A Critical Source Book, pp 164–80. Lagos: Nigeria Magazine.

Kofoworola, Ziky O. (1982), 'Hausa performing arts and the emir's court', PhD thesis, Ahmadu Bello University.

Kofoworola, Ziky O. (1985a), 'Hausa performing arts: a critical analysis of sources, concepts, forms and production techniques', unpublished manuscript, Ahmadu Bello University.

Kofoworola, Ziky O. (1985b), 'Origins, forms and styles in Hausa performing arts: case study of 'Yan Gambara and 'Yan Hoto', Nigeria Magazine 53(3): 9–16.

Kofoworola, Ziky O. and Y. Lateef (1987), Hausa Performing Arts and Music. Lagos: Nigeria Magazine.

Koko, Hadiza Salihu (1989), 'Karin magana a hannun mata a garin Sakkwato', BA final paper, University of Sokoto.

Koko, Tukur Umar (1988), 'Buɗkasar adabin Hausa wanda gidan Rima Radiyo na Sakkwato ke yi', BA final paper, University of Sokoto.

Kraft, Charles H. (1976a), 'An ethnolinguistic study of Hausa epithets', in Larry M. Hyman, Leon C. Jacobson and Russell G. Schuh (eds), Papers in African Linguistics in Honor of Wm E. Welmers (Studies in African Linguistics, Supplement 6), pp 135–46.

Kraft, Charles H. (1976b), 'Toward an ethnography of Hausa riddling', Folia Orientalia 17: 231–43.

Krieger, Kurt (1968), 'Musikinstrumente der Hausa', Baessler-Archiv (New Series), 16: 373–430.

Kudan, M.B.Turaki (1987), 'Kwatanta jigogin ƙagaggun labarun gasa', BA final paper, Ahmadu Bello University.

Kumbotso, Umar Shukuranu Nuhu (1992), 'Auwalu Isa Bunguɗu: rayuwarsa da aiyukansa', BA final paper, Bayero University.

Kwantagora, Salihu (1972), Kimiyya da Fasaha. Zaria: NNPC.

Kwarin Ganuwa, Sulaiman Lawali and Abdullahi Liman Yabo (1989), 'Jigo da salon waƙoƙin maza: 'yan tauri da ɓarayi', BA final paper, University of Sokoto.

Karaye, Ahmed Isihaƙ (1974), 'Alhaji Hamisu Mai Ganga sarkin kiɗa: rayuwarsa da waƙoƙinsa', BA final paper, Bayero University.

Karaye, Maikuɗi (1979), 'Structural characteristics of the Gizo in Hausa folktales', MA thesis, University of Khartoum.

Karaye, Maikuɗi (1982), 'The structural study of African oral narratives: evidence from Hausa', Harsunan Nijeriya 12: 47–60.

Karaye, Maikuɗi (1984), 'Beyond the illusive cobwebs of the Spider [sic],', in I. Y. Yahaya and A. Rufa'i (eds), Studies in Hausa Language, Literature and Culture: Proceedings of the First International Hausa Conference, July 1978, pp 478–96. Kano: Bayero University.

Kaura, Hamzat Ibrahim (1983), 'Rayuwar Aliyu Maikudu Gidadawa da waƙoƙinsa', BA final paper, University of Sokoto.La'ah, Linus Achi (1972), 'A comparison of two novels: Shaihu Umar and Yawon Duniya Hajji Baba', BA final paper, Bayero University.

Kofar Na'isa, Shehu Zubairu (1980), 'Sarkin Taushi's oral poems: literary and prosodic analysis', BA final paper, Bayero University.

Kofar Sauri, Haladu Ashiru (1982), 'Alhaji Garba Ebisidi da waƙoƙinsa', BA final paper, Ahmadu Bello University.

Ladan, Abubakar (1976), *Waƙar Haɗa Kan Al'ummar Afirka*. Ibadan: Oxford University Press.

Ladan, Umaru (1974), 'Drama and performance in the northern states', MA thesis, University of Leeds.

Last, D. M. (1967), *The Sokoto Caliphate*. London: Longman.

Last, Murray (1974), 'Reform in West Africa: the Jihad movements of the nineteenth century', in J. F. A. Ajayi and Michael Crowder (eds), *History of West Africa* (Vol.2, 1st ed.), pp 1–29. London: Longman.

Lawal, Nuhu (1990), 'Soyayya gamon jini: nazari akan rubutattun waƙoƙin soyayya', BA final paper, Bayero University.

Lawan, Mohammed (1983), 'Waƙoƙin siyasa na Hausa', BA final paper, Bayero University.

Leben, William R. (1983), 'On the correspondence between linguistic tone and musical melody', unpublished manuscript, Department of Linguistics, University of Stanford .

Lere, Ahmed Isah (1985), 'Tsokaci kan waƙoƙin Fasaha Aƙiliya da wasunsu', BA final paper, Ahmadu Bello University.

Liman, M. T. A. (1984), 'Dangantakar adabin Hausa da adabin Larabci', in I. Y. Yahaya and A. Rufa'i (eds), *Studies in Hausa Language, Literature and Culture: Proceedings of the First International Hausa Conference, July 1978*, pp 175–93. Kano: Bayero University.

Lord, Albert B. (1960), *The Singer of Tales*. Cambridge: Cambridge University Press.

Lord, Albert B. (1991), *Epic Singers and Oral Tradition*. Ithaca, New York: Cornell University Press.

Lovejoy, Paul E. (1978), 'Plantations in the economy of the Sokoto Caliphate' *Journal of African History* 19: 341–68.

Lovejoy, Paul E. (1980), *Caravans of Kola: The Hausa Kola Trade 1700–1900*. Zaria: Ahmadu Bello University Press.

Lovejoy, Paul E. (1981), 'Slavery in the Sokoto Caliphate', in Paul E. Lovejoy (ed.), *The Ideology of Slavery in Africa*, pp 201–43. Beverly Hills: Sage.

Lovejoy, Paul E. (1983), *Transformations in Slavery: A History of Slavery in Africa*. Cambridge: Cambridge University Press.

Lovejoy, Paul E. (1986), *Salt of the Desert Sun: A History of Salt Production and Trade in the Central Sudan*. Cambridge: Cambridge University Press.

Lovejoy, Paul E. (1988), 'Concubinage and the status of women slaves in early colonial Northern Nigeria', *Journal of African History* 29: 245–66.

Lubeck, Paul (1986), *Islam and Urban Labour in Northern Nigeria: The Making of a Muslim Working Class*. Cambridge: Cambridge University Press.

McHugh, Brian and Russell G. Schuh (1984), 'The Performance of Hausa Written Poetry', Paper presented at the African Studies Association, Los Angeles.

Mack, Beverly B. (1981), ' "Waƙoƙin Mata": Hausa women's poetry in Northern Nigeria', PHD thesis, University of Wisconsin, Madison.

Mack, Beverly B. (1982), 'Metaphor and metonymy in Na'ibi Wali's "Waƙar Damina" ("Song of the Rains")', *Research in African Literatures* 13(1): 1–30.

Mack, Beverly B. (1983), ' "Waƙa Daya Ba Ta Kare Niƙa – One Song Will Not Finish the Grinding": Hausa women's oral literature', in Hal Wylie, Eileen Julien and Russell J. Linneman (eds), *Contemporary African Literature*, pp 15–46. Washington, DC: Three Continents Press.

Mack, Beverly B. (1986), 'Songs from silence: Hausa women's oral poetry', in Carole Boyce Davies and Anne Adams Graves (eds), *Ngambika: Studies of Women in African Literature*, pp 181–90. Trenton, New Jersey: Africa World Press.

Mack, Beverly B. (1988), 'Hajiya Madaki: a royal Hausa woman', in Patricia Romero (ed.), *Life Histories of African Women*, pp 47–77. Atlantic Highland, New Jersey: Ashfield Press.

Madauci, Ibrahim, Yahaya Isa and Bello Daura (1968), *Hausa Customs*. Zaria: NNPC.

Magaji, Ahmed (1980), 'Nazari akan rayuwa da waƙoƙin Alhaji Kassu Zurmi', BA final paper, Bayero University.

Magaji, Ahmed (1982), 'Tasirin adabin baka akan rubutattun ƙagaggun labarai', MA thesis, Bayero University.

Magaji, Usman (1987), 'Tasirin Turanci a rubutattun wasannin kwaikwayo', BA final paper, Ahmadu Bello University.

Magashi, Garba Mohammed (1974), 'The life and poems of Mu'azu Hadeja', BA final paper, Bayero University.

Mahe, Abubakar (1984), 'Alhaji Dan'anace da waƙoƙinsa', BA final paper, University of Sokoto.

Mahmoud, Ibrahim (1972), 'The phenomena of kirari in Hausa society', BA final paper, Bayero University.

Mahmud, Tijjani (1972), 'A comparative study on 19th and 20th century Hausa poems', BA final paper, Bayero University.

Mahuta, Othman Yusuf (1984), 'Taƙaitaccen nazari akan bori wasan kwaikwayo ne?', BA final paper, Ahmadu Bello University.

Maikafi, Shekarau Umar (1977), 'Nazari akan waƙoƙin matan Hausawa na gargajiya', BA final paper, Bayero University.

Majiya, Muhammad Magaji (1986), 'Malam Alhaji Mazuga da waƙoƙinsa', BA final paper, University of Sokoto.

Maƙarfi, Shu'aibu (1959), *Zamanin Nan Namu*. Zaria: NORLA.

Maƙarfi, Shu'aibu (1959), *Jatau Na Kyallu*. Zaria: Gaskiya Corporation.

Malikawa-Sarari, Idi Bala (1982), 'Sani Aliyu Dandawo da waƙoƙinsa', BA final paper, Ahmadu Bello University.

Malumfashi, Adamu Ibrahim (1980), 'Abubakar Ladan da waƙoƙinsa', BA final paper, Bayero University.

Malumfashi, Abdulazizu Mu'azu (1984), 'Tashe a Kano, Katsina da Zariya', BA final paper, Ahmadu Bello University.

Malumfashi, Adamu Ibrahim (1985), 'Asali da haɓakar rubutattun wasannin kwaikwayo na Hausa', MA thesis, Ahmadu Bello University.

Mangafi, Bala Lawal (1985), 'Waƙar Gagara Karya Sadauki ta marigayi Buda Dantanoma', BA final paper, Ahmadu Bello University.

Mangi, Aliyu na (1959), *Imfiraji*. 9 vols. Zaria: NNPC.

Mangi, Aliyu na (1966), *Kasbur Raga'ibu*. Zaria: Gaskiya Corporation.

Mangi, Aliyu na (1972), *Nuniyatul Amdahi*. Zaria: NNPC.

Mangi, Abdulmalik (1954), *Bayan Wuya Sai Dadi! Azbinawa Sun Je Neman Rijiyar Kudi*. Zaria: NORLA.

Martin, B. G. (1967), 'Two poems by Al-hajj Umar of Kete-Krachi', in J. A. Braimah and J. R. Goody (eds), *Salaga: The Struggle for Power*, pp 189–209. London: Longman.

Mashi, Musa Barah (1982), 'Gudunmawar Hajiya Barmani Choge mai Amada ga adabin Hausa', BA final paper, Bayero University.

Mashi, Musa Barah (1986), 'Waƙoƙin baka na siyasa: dalilansu da tasirinsu ga rayuwar Hausawa', MA thesis, Bayero University.

Matazu, S.G.A. (1982), 'Alhaji Dangani da waƙoƙinsa', BA final paper, Ahmadu Bello University.

Mazawaje, Mohammed Isma'el (1985), 'Zambo da habaici a waƙar fada', BA final paper, Ahmadu Bello University.

Modibbo, Abubakar S. (1989), 'Nazari da sharhi kan yabo da zambo na waƙoƙin Musa Dankwairo na fada', BA final paper, University of Sokoto.

Mohammed, Abdullahi (1978), 'A Hausa scholar-trader and his library collection: the case study of Umar Falke of Kano', PhD thesis, Northwestern University.

Mohammed, Aminu B. K. (1986), 'Tashe a matsayin wasan kwaikwayo', BA final paper, Ahmadu Bello University.

Mohammed, Binta Ladi (1987), 'Adabin baka a wasan kwaikwayo: nazarin karin magana a littafin Tabarmar Kunya', BA final paper, Ahmadu Bello University.

Mohammed, Ibrahim (1977), 'Waƙoƙin maza na Dan Anace', BA final paper, Bayero University.

Mohammed, Jamaiuddeen (1989), 'Kwatanta littafin Iliya Dan Maiƙarfi da littafin Ganɗoki', BA final paper, Bayero University.

Mohammed, Mohammed Yunusa (1985), 'Kasancewar tatsuniyar ruwan bagaja tushen littafin Ruwan Bagaja na Dr Abubakar Imam', BA final paper, University of Sokoto.

Mohammed, Murtala (1985), 'Bincike kan Waƙar Zina da Waƙar Tsari na Alhaji Mohammed Giɗaɗo', BA final paper, University of Maiduguri.

Mohammed, Umaru Alhaji (1989), 'Kwatanta jigon rubutaccen wasan kwaikwayo da wanda ba rubutacce ba', BA final paper, Bayero University.

Monfouga-Nicolas, Jacqueline (1972), *Ambivalence et culte de possession: contribution à l'étude du Bori hausa*. Paris: Editions Anthropos.

Mora, Abdurrahman (ed.), (1989), *The Abubakar Imam Memoirs*. Zaria: NNPC.

Mu'awiya, Idris Bala (1990), 'Tarihi da ayyukan Alhaji Sani Mandawari', BA final paper, Bayero University.

Muffett, D. J. M. (1964), *Concerning Brave Captains*. London: Deutsch.

Muhammad, Bello (1974), *Malam Mahamman*. Zaria: NNPC.

Muhammad, Dalhatu (1971), 'Hausa oral poetry', in B. King (ed.), *Introduction to Nigerian Literature,* pp 23–7. Lagos: Evans.

Muhammad, Dalhatu (1973a), 'Sharhin "Hausa mai ban Haushi" ta Alhaji Aƙilu Aliyu', *Harsunan Nijeriya* 3: 47–67.

Muhammad, Dalhatu (1973b), 'A vocabulary of literary terms in Hausa', *Harsunan Nijeriya* 3: 1–11.

Muhammad, Dalhatu (1977), 'Individual talent in the Hausa poetic tradition: a study of Aƙilu Aliyu and his art', PhD thesis, University of London.

Muhammad, Dalhatu (1978a), 'Structural tension in poetry: case notes on enjambement and run-on in Hausa', *Harsunan Nijeriya* 8: 79–90.

Muhammad, Dalhatu (1978b), 'The two facets of rhyme in Hausa poetry: syllabic and tonal', *Harshe* 1: 6–18.

Muhammad, Dalhatu (1979), 'Interaction between the oral and the literate traditions of Hausa poetry', *Harsunan Nijeriya* 9: 85–90.

Muhammad, Dalhatu (1980a), 'Tonal rhyme: a preliminary study of the role of linguistic tone in Hausa verse', *African Language Studies* 17: 89–98.

Muhammad, Dalhatu (1980b), 'Zumunta tsakanin marubutan waƙoƙin Hausa da makaɗa', *Harsunan Nijeriya* 10: 85–102.

Muhammad, Dalhatu (1981), 'Bakandamiya: towards the characterization of the poetic masterpiece in Hausa', in U. N. Abalogu, G. Ashiwaju and R. Amadi-

Tshiwala (eds), *Oral Poetry in Nigeria*, pp 57–70. Lagos: Nigeria Magazine.

Muhammad, Dalhatu (1982), 'The Tabuka epic in Hausa; an exercise in narratology', in I. Y. Yahaya, A. Rufa'i and A. Abu-Manga (eds), *Studies in Hausa Language, Literature and Culture: Proceedings of the Second International Hausa Conference, April 1981*, pp 397–416. Kano: Bayero University.

Muhammad, Dalhatu (1984), 'Waka Bahaushiya', in I. Y. Yahaya and A. Rufa'i (eds), *Studies in Hausa Language, Literature and Culture: Proceedings of the First International Hausa Conference, July 1978*, pp 47–62. Kano: Bayero University.

Muhammad, Dalhatu (1985), 'Visual imagery in blind poetry – illustrations from Namangi's Imfiraji and Audu Makaho's Tabuka', *Nigeria Magazine* 53(4): 66–75.

Muhammed, Ibrahim Yaro (1974), *Wakokin Hikimomin Hausa*. Zaria: NNPC.

Muhammed, Ibrahim Yaro (1975), *Duniya Tumbin Giwa Ce*. Kano: private publication, Zaria: Evans Bros, 1975.

Muhammad, Liman (1966), 'Comments on "Kano Hausa poetry"', *Kano Studies* 2: 44–52.

Muhtar, Isa (1984), 'Nahawun waka: yanaye-yanayensa da sigoginsa cikin rubutattun wakokin Hausa', MA thesis, Bayero University.

Muhtar, Isa (1990), 'A stylistic study of Sulaiman Ibrahim Katsina's novels', PhD thesis, Bayero University.

Mukoshy, Sutura S. (1979), 'The contribution of Nana Asma'u bint Al-shaikh Uthman b. Fudi to West African literature from the 18th to the 19th century', BA final paper, Ahmadu Bello University.

Munkaila, Usman (1982), 'Umaru sarkin taushin Katukan Zazzau da wakokinsa', BA final paper, Ahmadu Bello University.

Musa, Ali Alhaji (1985), 'Abubuwan la'akari ga jama'ar Nijeriya cikin kagaggun labarai na Sulaiman Ibrahim Katsina', BA final paper, University of Maiduguri.

Musa, Ibrahim ibn (1982), 'Alhaji Muhammadu Dankurji da wakokinsa', BA final paper, Ahmadu Bello University.

Mustapha, Haruna (1992), 'Kwatanta littafin Gogan Naka da littafin Gandoki', BA final paper, Bayero University.

Nadama, Garba (1977), 'The rise and collapse of a Hausa state: a social and political history of Zamfara', PhD thesis, Ahmadu Bello University.

Nafada, Abdulrazzak, Umar Abubakar Sadauki and Abdullahi Mohammed Kabir (1987), 'Gudunmawar da gidan rediyo Najeriya na Kaduna ke bayarwa wajen bunkasa wasan kwaikwayo, yada al'adun Hausawa da kuma wayarwa da Hausawa kai', BA final paper, University of Sokoto.

Na'inna, Aminu Abdu (1991a), *Kauna Adon Zuciya*. Kano: private publication.

Na'inna, Aminu Abdu (1991b), *So Marurun Zuciya*. Kano: private publication.

Nasr, Ahmad Abd Al-Rahim (1977), 'Maiwurno of the Blue Nile: a study of an oral biography', PhD thesis, University of Wisconsin, Madison.

Nasr, Ahmad Abd Al-Rahim (1982), 'The malam in Hausa oral narratives', in I. Y. Yahaya, A. Rufa'i and A. Abu-Manga (eds), *Studies in Hausa Language, Literature and Culture: Proceedings of the Second International Hausa Conference, April 1981*, pp 473–86. Kano: Bayero University.

Nasr, Ahmad Abd Al-Rahim (1984), 'Shaihu Umar: a re-interpretation', in I.Y. Yahaya and A. Rufa'i (eds), *Studies in Hausa Language, Literature and Culture: Proceedings of the First International Hausa Conference, July 1978*, pp 512–8. Kano: Bayero University.

Ngaski, Haruna M. (1989), 'Alhaji Ahmadu Mailauni da wakokinsa', BA final paper, University of Sokoto.

Ngugi wa Thiongo (1986), *Decolonizing the Mind: The Politics of Language in African Literature*. London: James Currey.

Nicolas, Guy (1975), *Dynamique social et apprehension du monde au sein d'une société hausa*. Paris: Institut d'Ethnologie, Musée Nationale d'Histoire Naturelle.

Nicolas, Jacqueline (1967), *'Les Juments des dieux': rites de possession et condition féminine en pays haoussa*. Etudes Nigériennes, 21. Niamey: IFAN–CNRS.

Nuruddeen, Mohammed (1982), 'Sallar Gani a Daura', BA final paper, Ahmadu Bello University.

Nwosu, T. L. (1981), 'The structure, form and content of Nigerian folktales', *Nigeria* 136: 64–71.

Ogawa, Ryo (1980), 'L'enfant et le lionceau: étude comparative de contes peul et haoussa', *Senri Ethnological Studies* 6: 197–221.

Ogunbiyi, Y. (ed.), (1981), *Drama and Theatre in Nigeria: A Critical Source Book*. Lagos: Nigeria Magazine.

Olofson, Harold A. (1976), 'Funtua: patterns of migration to a new Hausa town', PhD thesis, University of Pittsburg.

Omar, Sa'adiya (1983), 'Style and themes in the poems of Mu'azu Haɗeja', MA thesis, SOAS, University of London.

Ong, Walter (1982), *Orality and Literacy. The Technologizing of the Word*. London and New York: Methuen.

Onwuejeogwu, Michael (1969), 'The cult of bori spirits among the Hausa', in Mary Douglas and Phyllis M. Kaberry (eds), *Man in Africa*, pp 279–305. London: Tavistock Publications.

Oral Documentation Unit, Ahmadu Bello University (1983), *Catalogue of Recordings*. Zaria: Department of Nigerian and African Languages.

Othman, Abdulkadir Jilani (1975), 'Waƙoƙin ƙarni na ashirin da jigoginsu', BA final paper, Bayero University.

Othman, Fatima (1979), 'Waƙe-waƙen matan Hausawa da mahallansu', BA final paper, Ahmadu Bello University.

Othman, Fatima (1981), 'Style in Ganɗoki: a study of the fictional prose of Alhaji Muhammadu Bello Kagara', MA thesis, SOAS, University of London.

Paden, John N. (1965), 'A survey of Kano Hausa poetry', *Kano Studies* 1: 33–9.

Paden, John N. (1973a), 'A note on Hausa religious poetry in ajami script', *Kano Studies* 1(2): 111–5.

Paden, John N. (1973b), *Religion and Political Culture in Kano*. Berkeley: University of California Press.

Paden, John N. (1986), *Ahmadu Bello, Sardauna of Sokoto: Values and Leadership in Nigeria*. London: Hodder and Stoughton.

Paulme, Denise (1976), *La Mère Dévorante: Essai sur la Morphologie des Contes Africaines*. Paris: Gallimard.

Peterson, Barbara (1971), 'Some relationships between music features and language features in seven Hausa popular songs', MA thesis, SOAS, University of London.

Piłaszewicz, Stanislaw (1974), 'The song of poverty and wealth: a Hausa poem on social problems by al-Haji Umaru', *Africana Bulletin* 21: 67–116.

Piłaszewicz, Stanislaw (1975), 'The "Arrival of the Christians": a Hausa poem on the colonial conquest of West Africa', *Africana Bulletin* 22: 55–129.

Piłaszewicz, Stanislaw (1981a), 'Homiletic poetry of al-Haji Umoru', *Africana Bulletin* 30: 73–110.

Piłaszewicz, Stanislaw (1981b), 'Warning against social evils of modern times and ideas about social improvement in the Hausa drama', in F. Gruner (ed.), *Literaturen Asiens und Afrikas*, pp 351–8. Berlin: Akademie Verlag.

Piłaszewicz, Stanislaw (1982), 'Kalmomi Miyagu – a Hausa poem by Alhaji Umaru', in I. Y. Yahaya, A. Rufa'i and A. Abu-Manga (eds), *Studies in Hausa Language*,

Literature and Culture: Proceedings of the Second International Hausa Conference, *April 1981,* pp 449–72. Kano: Bayero University.

Piłaszewicz, Stanislaw (1984), 'The craft of the Hausa oral praise-poets', in S. Biernaczky (ed.), *Folklore in Africa Today,* pp 269–76. Budapest: African Research Project, Department of Folklore.

Piłaszewicz, Stanislaw (1985), 'Literature in the Hausa language', in B. W. Andrzejewski, S. Pilaszewicz and W. Tyloch (eds), *Literatures in African Languages: Theoretical Issues and Sample Surveys,* pp 190–254. Cambridge: Cambridge University Press and Warsaw: Wiedza Powszechua.

Piłaszewicz, Stanislaw (1987), 'Arabic and Hausa: two vehicles of the Hausa literary tradition', *Rocznik Orientalistyczny* 45(2): 67–72.

Piłaszewicz, Stanislaw (1988a), *Historia literatur afrykansckich w jezykach rodzimych: Literatura hausa.* Warsaw: Wydawnictwa Uniwersytetu Warszawskiego.

Piłaszewicz, Stanislaw (1988b), 'Images of the temporal world in Hausa verse', *Africana Bulletin* 35: 67–80.

Piłaszewicz, Stanislaw (1988c), 'In the service of the nation and state: a study of novel writings of the Hausa author Sulaiman Ibrahim Katsina', *Studies on the Developing Countries* 1: 39–56.

Piłaszewicz, Stanislaw (1988d), 'New vocabulary and idioms in modern Hausa literature', in Graham Furniss and Philip J. Jaggar (eds), *Studies in Hausa Language and Linguistics: In Honour of F. W. Parsons,* pp 202–17. London and New York: Kegan Paul International in association with the International African Institute.

Piłaszewicz, Stanislaw (1989a), *Antologia Wspolczesnej Literatury Hausa/Zababbun rubuce-rubucen Hausa na Zamani.* Warsaw: Wydawnictwa Universytetu Warszawskiego.

Piłaszewicz, Stanislaw (1989b), 'From Arabic to Hausa: the case of the Hausa poet Alhaji Umaru', *Rocznik Orientalistyczny* 46(1): 97–104.

Piłaszewicz, Stanislaw (1991/2), 'New trends in recent Hausa novels', *Harsunan Nijeriya* 16: 29–46.

Piłaszewicz, Stanislaw (1992a), 'Hausa poems on the Tijaniyya brotherhood from the OASAR Collection, University of Ghana', in M. Nowaczyk and Z. Stachowski (eds), *Language, Religion and Culture: In Memory of Prof. W. Tyloch,* pp 61–6. Warsaw: Polish Society for the Study of Religions and the International Association for the History of Religions.

Piłaszewicz, Stanislaw (1992b), 'The image of changing society in recent Hausa literature', in F. Plit et al (eds), *Changing Faces of Developing Countries,* pp 95–103. Warsaw: Instytut Krajow Rozwijajacych sie UW.

Piłaszewicz, Stanislaw (1992c), 'In praise of Shaykh Ahmad al-Tijani: a Hausa poem from the IASAR/23 manuscript', in E. Ebermann, E. R. Sommerauer and K. E. Thomanek (eds), *Komparative Afrikanistik: Sprach-, Geschichts- und Literaturwissenschaftliche Aufsätze zu Ehren von Hans G. Mukarovsky,* pp 269–85. Vienna: Institut für Afrikanistik.

Piłaszewicz, Stanislaw (1993), 'An image of the Hausa diaspora of Kumasi in an ajami poem from the IASAR/292 manuscript', *Africana Bulletin* 41: 7–98.

Pittin, Renée (1979), 'Marriage and alternative strategies: career patterns of Hausa women in Katsina city', PhD thesis, University of London.

Pittin, Renée (1983), 'Houses of women: a focus on alternative life-styles in Katsina city', in Christine Oppong (ed.), *Female and Male in West Africa,* pp 291–302. London: George Allen and Unwin.

Powe, Edward L. (1981), 'Kirarin Duniya: a semiological study of selected Hausa epithets', *Harsunan Nijeriya* 11: 42–66.

Powe, Edward L. (1983), *Hausa Studies:A Select Bibliography of B.A., M.A., and Ph. D. Papers available in Northern Nigerian Universities* (revised edn). Madison: African Studies Program, University of Wisconsin, 1986.

Powe, Edward L. (1984), 'Hausa combat literature: an exposition, analysis and interpretation of its form, content and effect', PhD thesis, University of Wisconsin, Madison.

Preminger, Alex and T. V. F. Brogan (eds), (1993), *The New Princeton Encyclopedia of Poetry and Poetics*. Princeton: Princeton University Press.

Prietze, Rudolf (1904), *Haussa-Sprichwörter und Haussa-Lieder*. Kirchhain: Max Schmersow.

Prietze, Rudolf (1924/5), 'Wüstenreise des Haussa-Händlers Mohammed Agigi. In Gesprächen geschildert von Hajj Ahmed aus Kano', *Mitteilungen des Seminars für Orientalische Sprachen* 27(3): 1–36; 28(3): 175–246.

Propp, Vladimir (1968), *The Morphology of the Folktale*. Austin: University of Texas Press.

Pucheu, Jacques (1982), *Contes Haoussa du Niger*. Paris: Karthala and ACCT.

Pucheu, Jacques (n.d.), 'Recueil de contes populaires dans la région de Filingué', *Mu Kaara Sani* 2: 20–33.

Pweddon, Nicholas (1977), 'Thematic conflict and narrative technique in Abubakar Imam's "Ruwan Bagaja" ', PhD thesis, University of Wisconsin, Madison.

Ramat, Hajiya Balaraba (1990a), *Alhaki Kwikwiyo*. Kano: private publication.

Ramat, Hajiya Balaraba (1990b), *Budurwar Zuciya*. Kano: private publication.

Ramat, Hajiya Balaraba (1990c), *Wa Zai Auri Jahila?*. Kano: private publication.

Rattray, R. S. (1913), *Hausa Folklore, Customs, Proverbs, etc.*, (2 vols). Oxford: Clarendon Press.

Rattray, R. S. (1934), 'Hausa poetry', in E. Evans-Pritchard (eds), *Essays Presented to C. G. Seligman*, Oxford: Oxford University Press.

Reichmuth, Stefan (1993), 'Imam Umaru's account of the origins of the Ilorin emirate: a manuscript in the Heinz Sölken collection, Frankfurt', *Sudanic Africa* 4: 155–73.

Richards, Paul (1972), 'A quantitative analysis of the relationship between language tone and melody in a Hausa song', *African Language Studies* 13: 137–61.

Rimaye, Armaya'u Liti (1986), 'Rayuwa da aikace-aikacen Malam Shitu Dan-Abdulra'uf', BA final paper, Bayero University.

Ringim, Ado Shehu (1973a), 'Alhaji Aƙilu Aliyu: rayuwarsa da aiyukansa', BA final paper, Bayero University.

Ringim, Ado Shehu (1973b), 'The significance of proverbs in Hausa society and literature', BA final paper, Bayero University.

Robinson, Charles Henry (1896), *Specimens of Hausa Literature*. Cambridge: Cambridge University Press.

Roukbah, Bashari Farouk (1974), *Matar Mutum Kabarinsa*. Zaria: NNPC.

Rufa'i, Abba (1982), 'Huce haushin talaka kan basarake: misalai daga wasu tatsuniyoyi', *Harsunan Nijeriya* 12: 77–92.

Ruma, Abdu Jika (1983), 'Tahamisi a cikin waƙoƙin Hausa', BA final paper, Ahmadu Bello University.

Ryan, Pauline M. (1976), 'Color symbolism in Hausa literature', *Journal of Anthropological Research* 32(2): 141–60.

Sabir, Ahmed (trans.) (1976), *Mutanen Kogo* ['People of the Cave'], Ibadan: Oxford University Press.

Sada, Mohammed (1968), *Uwar Gulma*. Zaria: NNPC.

Sada, Sani Yusuf (1979), 'The social and prosodic features of oral poetry as exemplified by Hausa court poetry', MA thesis, Bayero University.

Sadiq, Ibrahim Abubakar (1990), 'Nazari akan jigon rubutattun waƙoƙin ilimin zamani', BA final paper, Bayero University.

Sa'id, Abdurra'uf (1985), 'Nazarin yanayi a rubutattun ƙagaggun labaran gasa na Hausa', MA thesis, Ahmadu Bello University.

Sa'id, Bello (1975), 'Salon magana', *Harsunan Nijeriya* 5: 17–27.

Sa'id, Bello (1977), 'Ilmin taurari a waƙoƙin masu Jihadi', *Harsunan Nijeriya* 7: 75–92.

Sa'id, Bello (1978), 'Gudunmawar masu Jihadi kan adabin Hausa', 2 vols, MA thesis, Bayero University.

Sa'id, Bello (1982a), 'Bambancin waƙar Hausa ta baka da rubutacciya', in I.Y. Yahaya, A. Rufa'i and A. Abu-Manga (eds), *Studies in Hausa Language, Literature and Culture: Proceedings of the Second International Hausa Conference, April 1981*, pp 235–60. Kano: Bayero University.

Sa'id, Bello (ed.), (1982b), *Dausayin Soyayya*. Lagos: Nigeria Magazine.

Sa'id, Bello (1983/5), 'Verse structure in Hausa poetry', *Harsunan Nijeriya* 13: 49–78.

Sa'id, Bello (1984), 'Salo da tsarin rubutacciyar waƙar Hausa ta ƙarni na 19', in I.Y. Yahaya and A. Rufa'i (eds), *Studies in Hausa Language, Literature and Culture: Proceedings of the First International Hausa Conference, July 1978*, pp 66–84. Kano: Bayero University.

Sa'id, Sani Mohammed (1981), 'Danƙwairo da waƙoƙinsa', BA final paper, Ahmadu Bello University.

Sa'idu, Abdul Ra'ufu (1981), 'Malam Muhammadu na Birnin Gwari da ayyukansa', BA final paper, Ahmadu Bello University.

Sakkwato, Ahmed Abdullahi (1983), 'Rayuwar marigayi Abubakar Maikataru Alkanci Sakkwato da waƙoƙinsa', BA final paper, University of Sokoto.

Salamone, Frank A. (1975a), 'Becoming Hausa: ethnic identity change and its implications for the study of ethnic pluralism and stratification', *Africa* 45: 410–25.

Salamone, Frank A. (1975b), 'A Hausa bibliography', *Africana Journal* 6(2): 99–163.

Salamone, Frank A. (1976), 'The arrow and the bird: proverbs in the solution of Hausa conjugal conflicts', *Journal of Anthropological Research* 32(4): 358–71.

Salamone, Frank A. and James A. McCain (1983), *The Hausa People: A Bibliography*. New Haven, Conn.: Human Relations Area Files.

Sale, Sanusi (1989), 'Kwatanta littafin Matar Mutum Kabarinsa da na Matsolon Attajiri', BA final paper, Bayero University.

Salihu, Kabiru (1982), 'Sani Husaini da waƙoƙinsa', BA final paper, University of Sokoto.

Sani, Abba Aliyu (1989), 'Neo-colonialism and literature in Nigeria: the case of the Northern Nigerian Publishing Company Limited, Zaria, 1966–1980's', paper presented at the Eighth Ibadan Annual African Literature Conference, Ibadan University, 6–9 March.

Sani, Rabo Mohammed (1984), 'Dangantaka da bambance-bambance tsakanin "The Undesirable Elements" and "Kulɓa na Barna"', BA final paper, Ahmadu Bello University.

Sanka, Attahiru Umar (1983), 'Alhaji Muhammadu Sambo Wali Giɗaɗawa da waƙoƙinsa', BA final paper, University of Sokoto.

Sanusi, Abubakar (1985), 'Umar ɗa Suru da waƙoƙinsa', BA final paper, University of Sokoto.

Sarki, Mohammed Abubakar (1988), 'Garba Likoro da waƙoƙinsa', BA final paper, Ahmadu Bello University.

Saulawa, Umar M. (1986), 'Kalankuwa', BA final paper, Ahmadu Bello University.

Scharfe, D. and Y. Aliyu (1964), 'Hausa poetry', in Ulli Beier (ed.), *Introduction to African Literature; An Anthology of Critical Writing from 'Black Orpheus'*, pp 34–40. London: Longman.

Scharfe, D. and Y. Aliyu (1967), 'Hausa poetry', *Black Orpheus* 21: 31–6.

Schildkrout, Enid (1978), *People of the Zongo: The Transformation of Ethnic Identities in Ghana*. Cambridge: Cambridge University Press.

Schildkrout, Enid (1982), 'Dependence and autonomy: the economic activities of secluded Hausa women in Kano, Nigeria', in Edna Bay (ed.), *Women and Work in West Africa,* pp 55–81. Boulder, Col.: Westview Press.

Schön, James Frederick (1876), *Dictionary of the Hausa Language, with Appendices of Hausa Literature.* London: CMS.

Schön, James Frederick (1885), *Magana Hausa.* London: SPCK.

Schuh, Russell G. (1985), 'The scansion of "Waƙar Damina"', unpublished paper, Department of Linguistics, University of California, Los Angeles.

Schuh, Russell G. (1988), 'Préalable to a theory of Hausa poetic meter', in Graham Furniss and Philip J. Jaggar (eds), *Studies in Hausa Language and Linguistics: In Honour of F. W. Parsons,* pp 218–35. London and New York: Kegan Paul International in association with the International African Institute.

Schuh, Russell G. (1988/9), 'The meter of Imfiraji', *Harsunan Nijeriya* 14: 60–70.

Schuh, Russell G. (1989), 'Toward a metrical analysis of Hausa verse prosody: Mutadaarik', in Isabelle Haïk and Laurice Tuller (eds), *Current Approaches to African Linguistics (Vol. 6),* Dordrecht: Foris.

Schuh, Russell G. (1994), 'A case study of text and performance in Hausa metrics', Paper presented at the 25th Annual Conference on African Linguistics, Rutgers University, March 25–27.

Sharifai, Bashir Ibrahim (1981), 'Yusufu Kantu Isa da waƙoƙinsa', BA final paper, Bayero University.

Shea, Philip J. (1975), 'The development of an export-oriented dyed cloth industry in Kano emirate in the nineteenth century', PhD thesis, University of Wisconsin, Madison.

Shea, Philip J. (1983), 'Approaching the study of production in rural Kano', in Bawuro M. Barkindo (ed.), *Studies in the History of Kano,* pp 93–115. Ibadan: Heinemann.

Shehu, Abdulrasheed (1985), 'Haruna Makaɗa da waƙoƙinsa', BA final paper, Ahmadu Bello University.

Shehu, Ɗahiru (1986), 'Muhammadu Sani Ɗangani da waƙoƙinsa', BA final paper, Bayero University.

Sheshe, Isa Nuhu (1977), 'Arulin Hausa', BA final paper, Bayero University.

Sifawa, Ibrahim Aliyu (1985), 'Tasirin karin magana ga adabin baka na Hausa', BA final paper, University of Sokoto.

Sipikin, Mudi (1971), *Tsofaffin Waƙoƙi da Sababbin Waƙoƙi na Alhaji Mudi Sipikin.* Zaria: NNPC.

Sipikin, Mudi (1984), 'Ma'aunin waƙar Hausa', in I. Y. Yahaya and A. Rufa'i (eds), *Studies in Hausa Language, Literature and Culture: Proceedings of the First International Hausa Conference, July 1978,* pp 63–5. Kano: Bayero University.

Skinner, A. Neil (ed.), (1969), *Hausa Tales and Traditions: An English Translation of 'Tatsuniyoyi Na Hausa',* originally compiled by Frank Edgar. Vol. 1 (1969), London: Frank Cass; Vols 2 and 3 (1977), Madison: University of Wisconsin Press.

Skinner, A. Neil (1970a), 'A Hausa poet in lighter vein', *African Language Review* 8: 163–75.

Skinner, A. Neil (1970b), 'NORLA: an experiment in the production of vernacular literature 1954–1959', *Revue des langues vivantes* 36(2): 166–75.

Skinner, A. Neil (1971a), 'Realism and fantasy in Hausa literature', *Review of National Literatures* 2(2): 167–87.

Skinner, A. Neil (1971b), 'The slattern – a theme of Hausa poetry', in Veronika Six, Norbert Cyffer, Ekkehard Wolff, Ludwig Gerhardt and Hilke Meyer-Bahlburg (eds), *Afrikanische Sprachen und Kulturen – ein Querschnitt,* pp 228–97. Hamburg: Deutsches Institut für Afrika-Forschung.

Skinner, A. Neil (1973), 'From Hausa to English: a study in paraphrase', *Research in African Literatures* 4: 154–64.

Skinner, A. Neil (1975), 'Bibliography of creative writing in Hausa', unpublished manuscript, Department of African Languages and Literatures, University of Wisconsin, Madison.

Skinner, A. Neil (1977), *Alhaji Mahmudu Koki: Kano Hausa Mallam*. Zaria: Ahmadu Bello University Press.

Skinner, A. Neil (1980), *Anthology of Hausa Literature in Translation*. Zaria: NNPC.

Skinner, A. Neil (1984), 'Littafin Hausa inda aka fara ba da labarin Tafiya Mabuɗin Ilimi', in I. Y. Yahaya and A. Rufa'i (eds), *Studies in Hausa Language, Literature and Culture: Proceedings of the First International Hausa Conference, July 1978*, pp 256-62. Kano: Bayero University.

Skinner, A. Neil (1988), 'Lexical incompatibility as a mark of karin magana', in Graham Furniss and Philip J. Jaggar (eds), *Studies in Hausa Language and Linguistics: In Honour of F. W. Parsons*, pp 236–45. London and New York: Kegan Paul International in association with the International African Institute.

Skinner, A. Neil and Kabir Galadanci (1973), 'Waƙar Soja – a Hausa poem on the civil war', in W. L. Ballard (ed.), *Essays on African Literature*, pp 97–125. (Spectrum Monograph Series in the Arts and Sciences 3). Atlanta: Georgia State University.

Skinner, A. Neil, Tom Allen and Charles N. Davis (1974), 'Waƙar Bushiya: a Hausa satirical poem by Isa Hashim', *Research in African Literatures* 5(2): 180–93.

Smith, Abdullahi (1987), *A Little New Light: Selected Historical Writings of Abdullahi Smith*. Zaria: Abdullahi Smith Centre for Historical Research.

Smith, M. G. (1957), 'The social functions and meaning of Hausa praise-singing', *Africa* 27(1): 26–43.

Smith, M. G. (1960), *Government in Zazzau, 1800–1950*. Oxford: Oxford University Press for the International African Institute.

Smith, M. G. (1965), 'The Hausa of Northern Nigeria', in James L. Gibbs (ed.), *Peoples of Africa*, pp 121–55. New York: Holt, Rinehart and Winston.

Smith, M. G. (1969), 'Foreword', in A. Neil Skinner (ed.), *Hausa Tales and Traditions: An English Translation of 'Tatsuniyoyi Na Hausa', originally compiled by Frank Edgar*, Vol. 1, pp vii–xxi. London: Frank Cass.

Smith, M. G. (1978), *The Affairs of Daura: History and Change in a Hausa State 1800–1958*. Berkeley and Los Angeles: University of California Press.

Smith, Mary F. (1954), *Baba of Karo*. London: Faber and Faber.

Sölken, H. (1959), 'Die Geschichte von Kebi nach Imam Umaru', *Mitteilungen des Instituts für Orientforschung* 7(1): 123–62.

Sölken, H. (1970), 'Zur Biographie des Imam Umaru von Kete Kratyi', *Africana Marburgensia* 3(2): 24–9.

Stephens, Connie Lee (1981), 'The relationship of certain social symbols and narrative metaphor: a study of fantasy and disguise in the Hausa tatsuniya of Niger', PHD thesis, University of Wisconsin, Madison.

Stephens, Connie Lee (1984), 'The Hausa tale of Ta-kitse', in I. Y. Yahaya and A. Rufa'i (eds), *Studies in Hausa Language, Literature and Culture: Proceedings of the First International Hausa Conference, July 1978*, pp 497–511. Kano: Bayero University.

Stephens, Connie Lee (1991), 'Marriage in the Hausa tatsuniya tradition: a cultural and cosmic balance', in Catherine M. Coles and Beverly Mack (eds), *Hausa Women in the Twentieth Century*, Madison: University of Wisconsin Press.

Sulaiman, Ibrahim Isa (1983), 'Waƙoƙin ɓarayi', BA final paper, Ahmadu Bello University.

Sule, Kabir (1986), 'Salon biɗa a ƙagaggun rubutattun labaran Hausa na gasa ta farko (1933)', BA final paper, Ahmadu Bello University.

Suru, Umaru Liman (1980), 'A critical study of specimens of Hausa political verse relating to the 1979 general election in Nigeria', MA thesis, SOAS, University of London.

Tafida, John and Rupert East (1934), *Jiki Magayi*. Zaria: Literature Bureau.

Taki, Mohammed (1985), 'Bincike kan siffofin duniya a waƙoƙin Hausa', BA final paper, University of Maiduguri.

Tajo, Ibrahim (1979), *Na Tanko*. Kano: private publication.

Talle, Abdullahi Babangida (1990), 'Baki abin magana: nazari a kan hikimomin Muhammadu Na'almumowa Funtuwa', BA final paper, Ahmadu Bello University.

Tanko, Sabitu (1990), 'Uwaliya Mai Amada da waƙoƙinta', BA final paper, Bayero University.

Thompson, Stith (1955–8), *Motif-Index of Folk Literature*, (6 vols). Bloomington: Indiana University Press.

Tijjani, Abu Umar (1983), 'Jituwar kari a waƙoƙin Hausa', BA final paper, Ahmadu Bello University.

Tijjani, Amina (1990), 'Garba Gashuwa da waƙoƙinsa', BA final paper, Bayero University.

Tremearne, A. J. N. (1913), *Hausa Superstitions and Customs: An Introduction to the Folklore and the Folk*. London: John Bale, Sons and Danielsson.

Trevor, Jean (1975), 'Western education and Muslim Fulani/Hausa women in Sokoto, Northern Nigeria', in Godfrey Brown and Mervyn Hiskett (eds), *Conflict and Harmony in Education in Tropical Africa*, pp 247–70. London: George Allen and Unwin.

Tsiga, Hafsatu Ibrahim (1987), 'Tasirin addinin musulunci a ƙagaggun rubutattun littafan zube na gasar farko (1933/34)', BA final paper, Ahmadu Bello University.

Tukur, A. K. (1982), 'Waƙoƙi na musamman', BA final paper, Ahmadu Bello University.

Tukur, Tijjani (1984), 'Mawaƙi da matsayinsa a al'umma', in I. Y. Yahaya and A. Rufa'i (eds), *Studies in Hausa Language, Literature and Culture: Proceedings of the First International Hausa Conference, July 1978*, pp 85–93. Kano: Bayero University.

Tunau, Abubakar (1949), *Wasan Marafa*. Zaria: Gaskiya Corporation.

Turawa, Hassan Muhammad (1982), 'Alhaji Usman Sa'adu Zuru da waƙoƙinsa', BA final paper, University of Sokoto.

Uba, Salihu Iya Abbas (1982), 'Hausa literary genres in Ganɗoki', BA final paper, University of Maiduguri.

Ubah, Mohammed Tsoho (1989), 'Kwatanta littafin Jiki Magayi da littafin So Aljannar Duniya', BA final paper, Bayero University.

Udu, Abubakar (1972), 'Comparison of Narambaɗa and Aliyu Dandawo', BA final paper, Bayero University.

Umar, Auwalu (1984), 'Littafin Kalila wa Dimna: Labaru daga Larabci zuwa Hausa', BA final paper, Ahmadu Bello University.

Umar, Ahmed Mohammed (1982), 'Dangantaka da bambanci tsakanin wasan kwaikwayo da ƙagaggen labari', in I. Y. Yahaya, A. Rufa'i and A. Abu-Manga (eds), *Studies in Hausa Language, Literature and Culture: Proceedings of the Second International Hausa Conference, April 1981*, pp 179–84. Kano: Bayero University.

Umar, Faruk (1984), 'Hikimomin Ahmadu Danmatawalle – sharhi akan waƙar tsuntsaye', in I. Y. Yahaya and A. Rufa'i (eds), *Studies in Hausa Language, Literature and Culture: Proceedings of the First International Hausa Conference, July 1978*, pp 225–36. Kano: Bayero University.

Umar, Garba (1986), 'Mamman Yaro Hore da waƙoƙinsa', BA final paper, University of Sokoto.

Umar, H. D. (1982), 'Kirarin sarautu da sana'o'i da unguwannin Zazzau', BA final paper, Ahmadu Bello University.

Umar, Muhammad Balarabe (1978), 'Dangantakar adabin baka da al'adun gargajiya a Hausa', BA final paper, Bayero University.

Umar, Muhammed Balarabe (1981), *Wasannin Tashe*. Zaria: NNPC.

Umar, Muhammad Balarabe (1982), 'Salon waskiya a adabin Hausa', in I. Y. Yahaya, A. Rufa'i and A. Abu-Manga (eds), *Studies in Hausa Language, Literature and Culture: Proceedings of the Second International Hausa Conference, April 1981*, pp 185–90. Kano: Bayero University.

Umar, Muhammad Balarabe (1984), 'Symbolism in oral poetry: a study of symbolical indices of social status in Hausa court songs', MA thesis, Ahmadu Bello University.

Umar, Muhammad Balarabe (1985), *Dan Maraya Jos*. Ibadan: University Press.

Usman, Suleiman Sheik (1990), 'Ibrahim Dangulbi da waƙoƙinsa', BA final paper, Bayero University.

Usman, Yusufu Bala (1981), *The Transformation of Katsina, 1400–1883*. Zaria: Ahmadu Bello University Press.

Verger, Pierre (1976), *Trade Relations Between the Bight of Benin and Bahia From the 17th to the 19th Century*. Ibadan: Ibadan University Press.

Waƙoƙin Hausa (1957), [anthology: *Gargadi don Falkawa, Damina, Hana Zalunci, Mu Sha Falala, Uwar Mugu, Munafunci da Annamimanci, Sha'anonin Duniya, Tabbat Halkika*]. Zaria: Gaskiya Corporation.

Wali, Zahra Nuhu (1976), 'Nazari a kan Magana Jari Ce', BA final paper, Bayero University.

Wall, L. Lewis (1988), *Hausa Medicine: Illness and Well-being in a West African Culture*. Durham and London: Duke University Press.

Watts, Michael (1983), *Silent Violence: Food, Famine and the Peasantry in Northern Nigeria*. Berkeley: University of California Press.

Watts, Michael (1987), *State, Oil, and Agriculture in Nigeria*. Berkeley: University of California Press.

Waya, Tijjani Musa (1990), 'Habaici, zambo da karin magana: matsayinsu da tasirinsu a cikin al'adar Hausawa', BA final paper, Bayero University.

Westley, David (1981), 'Two Hausa narratives: Malam Maidara. Gizo and the Snake', *Ba Shiru* 12(1): 95–104.

Westley, David (1986a), 'The oral tradition and the beginnings of Hausa fiction', PHD thesis, University of Wisconsin, Madison.

Westley, David (1986b), 'Tradition and creativity in Hausa storytelling', paper read at the 29th Annual Meeting of the African Studies Association, Madison, Wisconsin.

Westley, David (1986c), 'Two Hausa narratives: Balulu and Daskin Daridi', *Ba Shiru* 12(2): 73–9.

Westley, David (1991), *Hausa Oral Traditions: An Annotated Bibliography* (Working Papers in African Studies, 154). Boston, Mass.: African Studies Center.

Westley, David (n.d.), 'Abubakar Imam and the Hausa oral tradition', unpublished paper, Department of African Languages and Literatures, University of Wisconsin, Madison.

Whitting, Charles (1940), *Hausa and Fulani Proverbs*. Lagos: Government Printer.

Whitting, Charles and Muhammadu Hadeja (1931), *Labaru Na Da Da Na Yanzu*. Zaria: Translation Bureau.

Wilks, I. (1963), 'The growth of Islamic learning in Ghana', *Journal of the Historical Society of Nigeria* 2(4): 409–17.

Wilks, I. and J. Goody (1968), 'Writing in Gonja', in J. Goody (ed.), *Literacy in Traditional Societies*, pp 241–6. Cambridge: Cambridge University Press.

Williams, Gavin (ed.), (1976), *Nigeria: Economy and Society*. London: Rex Collings.

Works, John A. (1976), *Pilgrims in a Strange Land*. New York: Columbia University Press.

Wright, W. (1967), *A Grammar of the Arabic Language*. Cambridge: Cambridge University Press.

Yahaya, Dahiru Haruna (1991), 'Alhaji Musa Dankwairo: makaɗin fada ko na jama'a', BA final paper, Bayero University.

Yahaya, Ibrahim Yaro (trans.) (1971), *Daren Sha Biyu* ['Twelfth Night']. Zaria: NNPC.

Yahaya, Ibrahim Yaro (1971/2), *Tatsuniyoyi da Wasanni*, 6 vols. Ibadan: Oxford University Press.

Yahaya, Ibrahim Yaro (1972), 'Style and content of a Hausa tale', *Harsunan Nijeriya* 2: 23–41.

Yahaya, Ibrahim Yaro (ed.), (1973), *Wakokin Hikima*. Ibadan: Oxford University Press.

Yahaya, Ibrahim Yaro (1979a), 'Hausa folklore as an educational tool', *Harsunan Nijeriya* 9: 91–8.

Yahaya, Ibrahim Yaro (1979b), 'Oral art and socialization process: a socio-folkloric perspective of initiation from childhood to adult Hausa community life', PhD thesis, Ahmadu Bello University.

Yahaya, Ibrahim Yaro (1980), *Takaitaccen Tarihin Rubuce-Rubuce cikin Hausa*. Kano: CSNL.

Yahaya, Ibrahim Yaro (1981), 'The Hausa poet', in U. N. Abalogu, G. Ashiwaju and R. Amadi-Tshiwala (eds), *Oral Poetry in Nigeria*, pp 139–56. Lagos: Nigeria Magazine.

Yahaya, Ibrahim Yaro (1983/5), 'Tsarin kayan kiɗan Hausa da muhallan kaɗa su', *Harsunan Nijeriya* 13: 79–90.

Yahaya, Ibrahim Yaro (1984a), 'Nazari kan yanayin wasan kwaikwayon Hausa', in I. Y. Yahaya and A. Rufa'i (eds), *Studies in Hausa Language, Literature and Culture: Proceedings of the First International Hausa Conference, July 1978*, pp 244–55. Kano: Bayero University.

Yahaya, Ibrahim Yaro (1984b), 'Trends in the development of creative writing in Hausa', paper presented to the Conference on New Writing in Africa, Commonwealth Institute/Africa Centre, 1–3 November.

Yahaya, Ibrahim Yaro (1988a), *Hausa a Rubuce: Tarihin Rubuce-Rubuce Cikin Hausa*. Zaria: NNPC.

Yahaya, Ibrahim Yaro (1988b), 'The language of Hausa riddles', in Graham Furniss and Philip J. Jaggar (eds), *Studies in Hausa Language and Linguistics: In Honour of F. W. Parsons*, pp 246–52. London and New York: Kegan Paul International in association with the International African Institute.

Yahaya, Ibrahim Yaro (1988/9), 'The literary works of Alhaji Abubakar Imam in perspective', *Harsunan Nijeriya* 14: 71–98.

Yahaya, Ibrahim Yaro (1991), 'Trends in the development of Hausa drama', paper presented to Studia Chadica et Hamito-Semitica, Frankfurt am Main.

Yahaya, Ibrahim Yaro and Abba Rufa'i (eds), (1984), *Studies in Hausa Language, Literature and Culture: Proceedings of the First International Hausa Conference, July 1978*. Kano: Bayero University.

Yahaya, Ibrahim Yaro, Abba Rufa'i and A. Abu-Manga (eds), (1982), *Studies in Hausa Language, Literature and Culture: Proceedings of the Second International Hausa Conference, April 1981*. Kano: Bayero University.

Yahaya, Ibrahim Yaro, Mu'azu Sani Zariya, Sa'idu Muhammadu Gusau and Tanimu Musa 'Yar'aduwa (1992), *Darussan Hausa Don Manyan Makarantun Sakandare*. 3 vols. Ibadan: University Press.

Yahaya, Magaji Wando (1985), 'Wasan kwaikwayo a gidan rediyo Nijeriya na Kaduna', BA final paper, Ahmadu Bello University.

Yahaya, Musa (1991), 'Matsayin sarautar wawan sarki a fadar sarkin Zazzau', BA final paper, University of Sokoto.

Yahya, A. B. (1990), 'The significance of the 19th century Hausa poetry teachings', in Ahmad Mohammed Kani and Kabir Ahmed Gandi (eds), State and Society in the Sokoto Caliphate, pp 280–90. Sokoto: Usmanu Danfodiyo University.

Yahya, Abdullahi Bayero (1983), 'A critical anthology of the verse of Alhaji Bello Gidaɗawa', MA thesis, Bayero University.

Yahya, Abdullahi Bayero (1987), 'The verse category of madahu, with special reference to theme, style and the background of Islamic sources and belief', PhD thesis, University of Sokoto.

Yakasai, Bashir Lawal (1984), 'Rayuwar Alhaji Na'ibi Sulaiman Wali da waƙoƙinsa', BA final paper, University of Sokoto.

Yakawada, Magaji Tsoho (1983), 'Waƙeƙeniya', BA final paper, Ahmadu Bello University.

Yakawada, Magaji Tsoho (1987), 'Tarkakken matanin waƙar Kanzil Azim ta Aliyu Namangi', MA thesis, Ahmadu Bello University.

Yakubu, Buniya (1972), 'The phenomena of kirari in Hausa', BA final paper, Bayero University.

Yakubu, Sanusi Mohammed (1981), 'Kiɗan goge a ƙasar Hausa', BA final paper, Bayero University.

Yar'adua, Turai Umar (1983), 'Binta Zabaya da waƙoƙinta', BA final paper, Ahmadu Bello University.

Yunusa, Yusufu (1977), Hausa a Dunkule. Zaria: NNPC.

Yunusa, Yusufu (1982), 'Tsari da ma'ana a karin maganar Hausa', in I. Y. Yahaya, A. Rufa'i and A. Abu-Manga (eds), Studies in Hausa Language, Literature and Culture: Proceedings of the Second International Hausa Conference, April 1981, pp 141–62. Kano: Bayero University.

Yusuf, Abdulƙadir (1972), 'Kwatanta "Arewa Jumhuriya ko Mulukiya" da "Tutocin Waninsu"', BA final paper, Bayero University.

Yusuf, Ahmad Babangida (1986), 'Wasannin maguzawan ƙasar Katsina', BA final paper, University of Sokoto.

Yusuf, Hauwa (1988), 'Waƙoƙin 'yanmata a dandali', BA final paper, Ahmadu Bello University.

Yusuf, Hafiz (1992), 'Gudummawar malaman zaure wajen haɓaka adabin Hausa a Kano', BA final paper, University of Sokoto.

Yusuf, Harun al-Rashid (1979), Hamza Caji da Waƙoƙinsa. Kano: private publication through Shonuga Commercial Press.

Yusufu, Yunusa (1972), 'Gambara: the art of the Hausa comedians', BA final paper, Bayero University.

Zagga, Nana Muhammed (1985), 'Salo da jigo da tsarin al'adun Hausawa a wasan Idon Matambayi na gidan talabijin Sakkwato', BA final paper, University of Sokoto.

Zagga, Umaru (1980), 'Jankiɗi da waƙoƙinsa', BA final paper, Bayero University.

Zango, Abubakar Jumare (1983), 'Waƙoƙin 'yan tauri', BA final paper, Ahmadu Bello University.

Zango, Tanko (1952), Da'u Fataken Dare. Zaria: NORLA.

Zaria, Ahmadu Bello (1973), 'Kamil and Rajaz in Hausa poetry', BA final paper, Bayero University.

Zaria, Mu'azu Sani (1978), 'Karin "Mujtath" a waken Hausa', Harsunan Nijeriya 8: 99–107.

Zarruƙ, Rabi'u Mohammed and Habib Alhasan (1982), *Kirarin Duniya*. Zaria: Ganuwa Publishers.

Zukogi, Abdullahi A (1982), 'Sharhi akan waƙoƙin Alhaji Musa Danƙwairo', BA final paper, University of Maiduguri.

Zungur, Sa'adu (1955), *Waƙoƙin Sa'adu Zungur*. Zaria: Gaskiya Corporation.

Zurmi, Idi (1981), 'Form and style in Hausa oral praise songs', in U. N. Abalogu, G. Ashiwaju and R. Amadi-Tshiwala (eds), *Oral Poetry in Nigeria*, pp 96–117. Lagos: Nigeria Magazine.

Zurmi, Muhammad Ambaya (1986), 'Rayuwar Alhaji Kassu Zurmi da waƙoƙinsa', BA final paper, University of Sokoto.

INDEX

The Hausa letters ɓ, ɗ and ƙ are indexed after English b, d and k. Hausa titles and terms are shown in italic: where given in the text English translations are cross referenced.